In the name of God, the Com

Sayyid Quṭb

❧

IN THE SHADE OF
THE QUR'ĀN

Fī Ẓilāl al-Qur'ān

VOLUME II
❧
SŪRAH 3

Āl 'Imrān

❧

Translated and Edited by
Adil Salahi & Ashur Shamis

❧

THE ISLAMIC FOUNDATION

Published by

The Islamic Foundation, Markfield Conference Centre,
Ratby Lane, Markfield, Leicester LE67 9SY, United Kingdom
Tel: (01530) 244944, Fax: (01530) 244946
E-mail: i.foundation@islamic-foundation.org.uk
Web site: http://www.islamic-foundation.org.uk

Quran House, PO Box 30611, Nairobi, Kenya

PMB 3193, Kano, Nigeria

ISBN 0 86037 365 7 (HB)
ISBN 0 86037 370 3 (PB)

Contents

Part I
Basic Concepts of Faith

Part II
The Battle of Uḥud

Part III
Main Issues Re-emphasised

Transliteration Table

Consonants. Arabic

initial: unexpressed medial and final:

ء	ʿ	د	d	ض	ḍ	ك	k
ب	b	ذ	dh	ط	ṭ	ل	l
ت	t	ر	r	ظ	ẓ	م	m
ث	th	ز	z	ع	ʿ	ن	n
ج	j	س	s	غ	gh	هـ	h
ح	ḥ	ش	sh	ف	f	و	w
خ	kh	ص	ṣ	ق	q	ي	y

Vowels, diphthongs, etc.

Short: ´ a;   — i;   ´ u.

long: اـَ ـَا ā;   ـُو ū;   ـِي ī;   ىّ īy

diphthongs: ـَوْ aw;

ـَىْ ay

Preface

The influence of the Qur'ān in shaping the paradigm and ethos of Muslim culture and civilisation has been overpowering. It is because of the Qur'ān that the Muslim *ummah* rose to power and prominence in different periods of history and it is because of their neglect of this Divine Scripture that they have suffered humiliation and ignominy. The rise and fall of the Muslim individual and community is therefore intrinsically linked with the principles and values given by the Qur'ān. It is not without significance that God describes the Qur'ān as a "light" which enables people to find their way in the darkness of ignorance and prejudice, a "healing" for the ailments of the soul, a "criterion" to distinguish between right and wrong and, above all, a "book of guidance" to lead humanity to its destiny along a path which is characterised as "straight".

Islam looks at life as a composite whole, therefore it is appropriate that God provides all the necessary guidance through the Qur'ān and its interpreter, the Prophet Muḥammad (God's peace and blessings be upon him) and does not leave any aspect of life unguided whether it is private or public, individual or collective, spiritual or mundane, national or international, this-worldly or that-worldly. It is no surprise that Muslim scholars and students of the Qur'ān spend their life with great devotion in understanding and interpreting the Qur'ān to derive guidance in the comprehensive sense of the term. The effort to study and understand the meaning and teachings of the Qur'ān has given rise to the specialised discipline of *tafsīr* (exegesis) and over the period of fourteen centuries a large number of commentaries, or *tafsīr*, in Arabic alone and a similar, if not greater, number in other world languages have been produced. The effort to appreciate the message of the Qur'ān and derive guidance on contemporary and civilisational issues continues as does the proliferation of *tafsīr* literature in Arabic and other world languages.

Sayyid Quṭb's *tafsīr*, *Fī-Zilāl al-Qur'ān*, has been acclaimed as one of the best contemporary exegesis of the Qur'ān in any language and one that has passed through several editions and reprints and been translated in several languages including Urdu, Bengali, Persian, Indonesian and Turkish. Sayyid Quṭb's *tafsīr*, in fact, is not a *tafsīr* in the traditional sense of the term. It is more than that. It is an effort to reflect on the dynamic and revolutionary message of the Qur'ān in its comprehensive sense and invite not only Muslims but all of humanity to come and enjoy the shade and blessings of the Qur'ān. The title *Fī-Ẓilāl al-Qur'ān* or "In the Shade of the Qur'ān" is, therefore, not without significance. The author acknowledges this fact and regards it a "privilege" and "a great blessing" to be able to live in the shade of the Qur'ān and gain "the uplifting experience" and appreciate the power of the Qur'ān in transforming human perception, experience and history. One cannot but sympathise with him when, commenting on the contemporary world situation he asks with a sense of anxiety, "how has life been allowed to degenerate into such darkness and despair, while this rich treasure of guidance and enlightenment is readily available?" He therefore takes upon himself the task of explaining the meaning and message of the Qur'ān to the people at large, suggesting that it can only be enjoyed and its concomitant spiritual contentment achieved if one is prepared to live in the shade of the Qur'ān, internalising its message to the best of one's ability.

The process of writing a commentary on the Qur'ān is so involved and engaging that the author often feels the need to revise, edit, improve and add to what he has written. This is particularly true in the case of Sayyid Quṭb and his life experience, especially his long periods in prison under extremely harsh conditions, for no crime other than his writings. That gave him a profound insight into the nature of injustice and the central aim of Islam to liberate mankind from all forms of injustice.

Sayyid Quṭb, in fact, started writing this *tafsīr* for the monthly journal *al-Muslimūn* towards the end of 1951 when it was serialised up to verse 103 of *sūrah* al-Baqarah. Within a few months he realised that although serialisation of *tafsīr* in a monthly journal is an effective method of disseminating the message of the Qur'ān to a selective audience, it is rather a slow process and perhaps it does not reach the wider audience it is meant for. He therefore decided to publish his commentary separately in book form with the result that in October 1952 he was able to bring out its first volume and within a short period of one year and four months (October 1952–January 1954) he published additional volumes containing commentary of some fourteen out of thirty parts (*ajzā*) of the Qur'ān. Like his illustrious contemporary *mufassir* of the Indo-Pak subcontinent, Mawlānā Mawdūdī (1903–79) he, too, completed and revised the major part of his *tafsīr* while in prison (1954–64). The commentary on *sūrahs* 1–32 was written before the author's first imprisonment in 1954. While in prison (1954–64), the author adopted a more penetrating, expansive and trenchant approach, evident in his commentary on *sūrahs* 33–114. He then embarked on re-writing the commentary on *sūrahs* 1–32 using the new approach but, having been denied all writing facilities, he was only able to do so up to *sūrah* 15, leaving the commentary on the remaining *sūrahs* (16–32) in the original succinct style.

Like Mawdūdī, Sayyid Quṭb has provided a very useful introduction to most of the *sūrahs* of the Qur'ān, summarising the main message of the *sūrah* in such a profound and masterly way that it opens the "gate of understanding" even for the uninitiated reader. Moreover, for the better understanding of the message of the Qur'ān he divides the chapters into lessons or topical units and also makes his work distinguishable from others by highlighting the link of the beginning of a *sūrah* with its conclusion and thereby showing the harmonised structure or interlinking of the message with the verses and the *sūrahs*. Some other distinguishing features of this monumental *tafsīr* are that it avoids relying on Biblical material, known as *Isrā'iliyyāt* and does not delve too much into *fiqhī* or jurisprudential discussion, unless it is essential to clarify the point under discussion. Similarly, on matters where the Qur'ān does not provide more than basic information and the Prophet has also not provided any clear indication or details, unlike some *mufassirīn*, he scrupulously avoids speculation, and refrains from putting forward any subjective judgements or opinions. Not only does he carefully avoid unnecessary legal polemics, he also refuses to engage in speculative *tafsīr* arguing for or against various schools of philosophical thought, his main concern being to present the clear message of the Qur'ān as expounded by the Prophet, his Companions, and scholars of the earlier generations. Using a lively and refined literary style, he presents the commentary on the Qur'ān in such a "modern" and forceful way that the reader feels captivated and eventually motivated to devote his life to the active struggle to make Islam a living reality in the world and share its blessings with those who have not been fortunate enough to benefit from its "shade".

First and foremost we would like to record our special gratitude to Professor Muḥammad Quṭb and the members of the Quṭb family for granting the Islamic Foundation the permission and the honour of publishing this work. We are likewise grateful to Mr. Adil Salahi and Mr. Ashur Shamis, for undertaking the difficult task of translating and editing the work from Arabic to English and offering all possible help to the Foundation for the publication of this monumental work, planned to be completed in some fifteen volumes. The English-speaking world had its first taste of this remarkable exegesis when the translation of the 30th part was serialised in the FOSIS's monthly journal *The Muslim* and later published in book form by the Muslim Welfare House, London in 1979. It was our great privilege to bring out, in 1999, Volume I, containing *sūrahs* 1 and 2, which was very well received. We hope and pray to Allah, *subḥānahū wa taʿālā*, to enable us to publish the complete work within the next few years, a target not impossible to achieve. We request our readers to have patience and forbearance and pray that we accomplish this rewarding task as planned and earn the blessings of Allah in this world and in the hereafter.

I will be failing in my duty if I do not mention and thank my many colleagues who have worked tirelessly to make this publication possible. My special thanks go Br. Naiem Qaddoura, who deserves special thanks and appreciation for his hard work and computer skills in the design and page layout, and Dr. A.R. Kidwai, for his help and assistance provided in various ways. I am also grateful to Dr. Susanne Thackray for editing this manuscript and giving a number of valuable suggestions.

Rabīʿ al-Thānī, 1421 AH
July 2000

M. Manazir Ahsan
Director General

Foreword

It is with humble and sincere gratitude to God that we present this second volume[1] of Sayyid Quṭb's priceless work, *In the Shade of the Qur'ān*, which was the culmination of his life work for Islam. The author himself speaks at length of his experience and his feelings as he "lived" in this cool shade, protected from the searing heat of materialism that has bedevilled human life in this century. This is the theme of his introduction published in Volume I. As translators working with his text, we feel that we have been able to share a little of his experience, and to taste to the full the blessings of life as it is moulded and fashioned by God's final message to mankind, the Qur'ān. As we present this second volume to readers of English, Muslims and non-Muslims alike, we hope that we contribute to a better understanding of the Qur'ān, the book which God wants to be mankind's guide to happiness in this life and in the life to come.

The author, may God bless his soul, was a stalwart of Arabic literature long before he started his Islamic writings. His book *Literary Criticism: Its Principles and Methodology*, published in the late 1930s or early 1940s, remains one of the best Arabic works in this field. The author also wrote poetry of high quality, but his Islamic writings overshadowed his poetic talent, as he felt it his duty to help develop a proper understanding of the Qur'ān. In this, he did not rely on a literary study of the Qur'ān, or on explaining words and terms, phrases and sentences. Such studies are available in plenty.

Sayyid Quṭb approached the Qur'ānic text as a whole unit, looking at the theme of each passage and each *sūrah*. He always reminds his reader

---

1. This is the second volume in the new edition of the book. Another volume, bearing the number 30 was published more than 20 years ago by the same translators. That volume, corresponding to the 30th part of the Qur'ān, covers *sūrahs* 78–114. The book was published by MWH (London) Publishers. It is hoped that a new edition of this volume will appear in this series in due course.

that, first and foremost, the Qur'ān is a book that sets the faith in clear terms and calls on mankind to adopt it. What he aimed to achieve is that Muslims should understand the Qur'ān in the same way as the Prophet's Companions understood it: a code of living which they must apply in practice. To that end, his book scores remarkable success.

It is evident that *In the Shade of the Qur'ān* was written for Muslims to help them understand God's revelations and implement them in life. However, we feel that it is very helpful to anyone who wishes to study the Qur'ān, or learn about the Islamic faith. There is no better way to know about a faith than to study its original texts. Sayyid Quṭb provides that study in modern, simple and powerful language. What is more is that he steers away from all questions that raise controversy. When scholars differ in their interpretation of a certain verse, he disregards all their differences that do not rely on clear evidence, and confines himself to the understanding of the text itself. In this way, he provides a succinct understanding, uncoloured by preconceptions or narrow views.

Readers will have realised that we are following a division of the volumes of this book which is different from that of the Arabic original. The author divided his book into 30 volumes, following the well-known "parts" of the Qur'ān. That division was made by scholars on the basis of length. Thus, the Qur'ān is divided into 30 equal parts which run in 20 pages each. If a person reads one part every day, he or she will complete the Qur'ān once a month. That is a perfectly valid division for that particular purpose. For Arabic readers, these parts have become well known and are followed for purposes of worship by Qur'ānic recitation. But the basis adopted for this division, i.e. length, means that a "part" often finishes in the middle of a *sūrah*, which is the basic unit of the Qur'ān, as revealed by God. The only division of the Qur'ān which retains completeness of a theme and keeps its units together is that based on the Qur'ānic *sūrahs*.

The Qur'ān comprises 114 *sūrahs*, some of which are very long, while others run in a few lines only. The name, "*sūrah*", is not used in Arabic for any sort of division in any book or work other than the Qur'ān. The word is derived from the noun *sūr*, which means a fence or wall. Thus, each *sūrah* is a separate and complete whole. Hence it should be treated in its totality. The nearest English word to *sūrah* is "chapter", but we cannot say that the Qur'ān is divided into chapters because this suggests that each *sūrah* speaks of a different topic and that all of them complete a whole book. The fact is that all *sūrahs* of the Qur'ān speak about the same topic, faith, but tackle different aspects of it. Hence, the Arabic word is retained. Moreover, the English edition of this work will be divided on the basis of the proper Qur'ānic division, i.e. its *sūrahs*. The first volume covered *sūrahs* 1 and 2. The first is short, composed of 7 short verses. The second is the longest in the Qur'ān, running into 48 pages, and 286 verses. This second volume covers *sūrah* 3, *Āl 'Imrān*, which is the third longest, running into 27 pages and 200 verses. As the next few *sūrahs* are, more or less, of equal length, it is proposed that each of them will appear in a separate volume. Thereafter we will take 2, 3 or 4 *sūrahs* in each volume, to keep the English edition in approximately equal volumes. Later, with shorter *sūrahs*, we will have more *sūrahs* in one volume. It is estimated that the complete English edition will run into 15 or 16 volumes.

In the longer *sūrahs*, the author divides the Qur'ānic text into passages on the basis of the theme or its treatment in each passage. When we produced the first volume, this division was felt unnecessary in the English translation. We, therefore, did not follow that division, allowing the *sūrah* to run its course without separation. We published the Arabic text of each Qur'ānic verse, or group of verses, at the head of the page in which they first appeared. However, on reflection and on the basis of feedback, it has been decided to revert to the author's division. This is what we have followed in dividing this volume into 3 parts and 12 passages. However, passages 6–10 appear in the Arabic text in one long passage dealing with the Battle of Uḥud. We felt it is more helpful to the English reader to divide this passage further, according to the points of treatment of the events of the Battle in this *sūrah*. As for the three parts, the Arabic text only refers to them, without making them separate divisions. We hope to follow this pattern in future volumes and return the first volume to this arrangement in future editions.

In rendering the Qur'ānic text, the translators felt that adopting a single translation of the many existing ones may not be suitable. They have consulted several such translations, taking whatever rendering they felt was closer to the original and fitted better with the author's understanding and explanation of the meaning. They relied mainly on the translations of Muhammad Asad, Yusuf Ali and N.J. Dawood. Other translations, particularly those by Pickthall and Irving were also consulted. At times, they felt a different rendering is needed and they provided that. They express their gratitude to all those translators and others. They hope that they were thus able to give the meaning of the text a readable and suitable rendering, realising that no human attempt to express the meaning of the Qur'ān will ever be successful. How can a human being express the meaning of God, given in the highest form of literary excellence?

The translators wish to reiterate what they wrote in their Preface to volume 30, that despite working to the best of their ability, this English edition is nowhere near the Arabic original for excellence of style and perfection of expression. Whatever shortcomings this edition suffers from, the translators acknowledge as their own. The author is in no way responsible for them. But those who have had some experience in translation, and in the translation of Islamic texts in particular, recognise the difficulty of the task we have undertaken and will acknowledge that, humble as it may be, the result, in some measure, serves the purpose.

The translators wish to record their gratitude to the Islamic Foundation for undertaking to publish their work, putting into its production all its excellent resources. They also wish to thank those who have rendered support to this effort, preferring to remain anonymous as they seek no reward other than what God, in His generosity, may confer on them, praying to Him to reward them according to their sincere intentions.

London
Rabī' al-Thānī, 1421 H
July 2000

Adil Salahi
Ashur Shamis

SŪRAH 3

Āl 'Imrān

(The House of 'Imrān)

Prologue

The Qur'ān is the Book of Islam. It is the soul and *raison d'être* of the Islamic mission. It is the backbone and edifice of its existence. It is its guardian and protector; its expression and manifestation; its constitution and way of life. Once all is said and done, the Qur'ān is the fountain, and the reference point, from which Islam and Muslims draw the ways and means of their actions, their systems and approach, and the provisions for their journey in this life.

However, a vast chasm will continue to separate us from the Qur'ān unless we understand deep down in our consciousness that the Qur'ān was addressed to a living community that existed in real life. It dealt with genuine situations in the life of that community and interacted with human life in its true manifestation on this earth. It was the main factor in a tremendous battle within the human soul that took place on a specific part of our planet; a battle that teemed with changes, passions and responses.

This divide between our hearts and the Qur'ān will continue to exist as long as we recite or listen to it as though it were a collection of fanciful religious hymns, totally disassociated from the realities of daily life facing this being we call man, and this community we call Muslims. These verses were revealed to address living souls, actual realities and events, with real meaning. They did indeed guide those souls, realities and events in an effective and vigorous manner, bringing forth a particular tangible situation with particular characteristics in man's life, in general, and in the life of the Muslim community, in particular.

1

The Qur'ān's distinctive miracle lies in the fact that it was revealed to deal with the actual experience of a particular human community, at a specific and finite time in history. It led that community in a momentous battle that was to change the whole history of mankind. That notwithstanding, the Qur'ān continues to provide us with the competence and the capability to live life today, as though it were being revealed at this very moment to organise the affairs of the Muslim community, and its ongoing struggle against pervasive universal ignorance. It continues to lead Muslims in their struggle with their own souls and conscience and with the same vigour and down-to-earth spirit it displayed so long ago.

In order for us, today, to capture the Qur'ān's penetrating power, appreciate its latent vitality and receive the guidance it conveys to Muslims in every generation, we need to visualise the true nature of the earliest Muslim generation who received the Qur'ān for the first time. We need to perceive the Muslims of that generation as they went about their daily lives, facing up to events and developments in Madinah and the rest of Arabia, dealing with their enemies as well as their allies, and struggling against their own passions and desires. The Qur'ān was being revealed to deal with all that and to follow the progress of the Muslim community in their greatest battle – with their own souls, with those enemies poised to strike in Madinah, Makkah and the surrounding lands, and even beyond.

Indeed, we have to live with that pioneering community of Muslims and picture them in their downright humanity, their actual life and in their human predicaments. We ought to reflect on how the Qur'ān guided that community directly in their daily affairs as well as in their greater global aspirations. We have to see how the Qur'ān led those Muslims by the hand, step by step, as they stumbled and rose, deviated and returned to the true path, weakened and resisted, as they suffered and endured, as they climbed upwards slowly and painfully, striving and persevering, showing all their human characteristics, their weaknesses and capabilities.

In this way, we can feel that we are being addressed by the Qur'ān in exactly the same manner as that earlier Muslim community. We can realise that the humanity whose attributes we see and know and feel within ourselves is also capable of responding to the Qur'ān and benefiting from its guidance along the same true path.

Thus, we will find the Qur'ān actively working in the life of that Muslim community, but also working in our own lives as well. We will feel that as the Qur'ān is here with us today, so will it be with us tomorrow. It is not merely hymns or hollow rituals, far-removed from our changing reality; nor is it some historic record that has passed and been forgotten, having lost its efficacy and dynamic ability to interact with human life.

The Qur'ān is a reality with a perpetual existence akin to that of the cosmos itself; the cosmos being God's visual "book" while the Qur'ān is God's recited "book". Each book is a testimony and a witness to the Creator, and a force in the world. The universe continues to move and fulfil the functions ordained for it by its Creator: the sun moves in its orbit and performs its role, as do the moon, the earth and all the stars and planets, unhindered by the passing of time or the changes affecting their role in the universe. Similarly, the Qur'ān has fulfilled its role towards humanity, and continues to exist in its original form. Likewise, as far as his true character and original nature are concerned, man has not changed. The Qur'ān is God's message to man. It is immutable because, despite the changes that may have taken place around him and despite the mutual effect between him and those changes, man has not changed or become a different being. The Qur'ān addresses man's basic being and his original nature which have remained the same. It is capable of guiding human life today and in the future because it is destined so to do. That is because it is God's last and final message and because human nature, like that of the physical universe, is constant and dynamic but never changing.

Would it not be laughable if the sun, for instance, were described as old or "reactionary" and hence it should be replaced by a new and more "progressive" star? Similarly, is it not also laughable for man to be considered antiquated and "reactionary" and his replacement by some other more "enlightened" being to rule the world be argued for?

It would also be ludicrous to say the same with regard to the Qur'ān, God's last and final message to mankind.

The *surah* under examination here covers a lively period in the history of the Muslims in Madinah, extending from the end of the famous Battle of Badr, in the second year of *Hijrah* (622 CE), to the aftermath of the Battle of Uḥud, a year later. It describes the

3

circumstances and the atmosphere surrounding the events of that period, the impact of the Qur'ān on the life of that community, and how it interacted with the prevailing conditions, across all walks of life.

The force and vitality of the Qur'ānic text brings into sharp focus the images of that period, the life of the community, and the interactions and circumstances in which that life was engulfed. It penetrates deep into the Muslims' consciences, exploring their innermost thoughts, feelings and sensibilities; so much so that the reader feels those events in the same way that members of that community experienced them. If one closes one's eyes, one may begin to see – as I have seen – those Muslims going about their daily lives, hither and thither, with their smiling faces and serenity, but with enemies lurking all around. Those enemies were conspiring, spreading lies and suspicion, harbouring grudges, and rallying their forces for combat with the Muslims, for them to be defeated initially at Uḥud, but later to re-group and inflict heavy losses upon the Muslims. One can picture every movement and every action that took place on the battlefield, and every inner or outward emotion and reaction that accompanied it. One can see the Qur'ān being revealed to counteract the conspiracy and the intrigue, to refute the lies and the allegations, to strengthen Muslim morale and bolster the Muslim position, to direct Muslim spirit and thoughts, to comment on events and actions and draw appropriate lessons, to establish and clarify concepts, to alert the Muslims to the treachery and deceit of their scheming enemies, and to provide them with an enlightened and judicious lead through the thorns, nettles and traps laid in their path.

Beyond that, the directives and exhortations contained in this surah remain eternal and universal, not restricted by time, place, or circumstance. The surah addresses the human soul and the Muslim community – today and in the future – and the whole of mankind, as though it is being revealed at this very moment. It deals with contemporary issues and current situations, because it deals with emotional and spiritual issues, events and feelings as though these were already taken into account within the context of the surah. Indeed, they would have been taken into account in the overall scheme of God, the omniscient, who has full knowledge of everything.

Thus, it becomes clear that the Qur'ān is the guiding light of Islam everywhere and at all times. It is the life code for every generation of Muslims whoever they may be, and their beacon along the way, century after century. For, it is God's last and final message to mankind in all ages.

The Early Years in Madinah

At the time of the revelation of this *sūrah*, the Muslim community began to settle in their new homeland, Madinah, the city of the Prophet Muḥammad (peace be upon him) and had gone some way into the state of affairs already described in our Introduction to *sūrah 2, al-Baqarah,* or The Cow (Vol. I, pp 9–19).

The Battle of Badr had already taken place, and the Muslims had been blessed with victory over the Quraysh. The circumstances concomitant with achieving that victory suggested a "miracle". This forced notable figures such as 'Abdullāh ibn Ubayy ibn Salūl, a grand personality of the Khazraj tribe of Madinah, to suppress his pride, put aside his hatred for Islam, and contain his spite and envy towards the Prophet Muḥammad in order to assimilate into the Muslim community, albeit hypocritically. His only comment was: "This, Islam, is here to stay." He had come to accept that Islam was firmly established and its progress unstoppable.

This was how the seeds of the phenomenon known as hypocrisy were planted in Madinah, and which began to grow and spread. Before Badr, some people whose relatives had converted to Islam were obliged to pretend not to mind; some of the more prominent of these even pretended to have accepted Islam and joined the Muslim community while, at the same time, they continued to harbour a grudge and animosity. They were ready to scheme against the Muslims and to seek the weaker points in the structure of the new community in order to undermine Muslim ranks and strength, satisfy their own prejudices and await the appropriate moment to strike their final blow, if possible.

The hypocrites found natural allies among the Jews of Madinah who had a similar or even stronger grudge and prejudices of their own towards Islam and the Prophet. Islam had posed a real and formidable threat to the status of the Jews among the Arabs of Madinah. It deprived them of the one reason they had to cause rancour and division between the two main Arab tribes of Madinah: the Aws and the Khazraj. Under Islam, people of the two tribes became "brothers and sisters", belonging to the same united side.

The Jews of Madinah were stifled and choked at the Muslim victory at Badr. From then on, they would use all their powers of intrigue, deceit and scheming to break Muslim ranks and throw doubt and confusion into Muslim hearts and minds; spreading rumours and allegations against Islam and against the Muslims personally.

Then came that episode with the Jewish tribe of Qaynuqāʿ bringing all that animosity into the open. This they did, despite the agreements and covenants the Prophet Muḥammad had made with the Jews of Madinah following his arrival there in 622 CE.

On the other hand, in the wake of their defeat at Badr, the non-Muslim Arabs were growing increasingly bitter. They could no longer afford to ignore Muḥammad's achievements or those of the Madinah camp; nor could they underestimate the threat posed to their trade, their status and their very existence in Arabia. They were, therefore, keen to eliminate that imminent threat before it was beyond their capacity to do so.

As the hatred and power of the enemies of Islam were reaching their peak, the Muslim camp in Madinah was still in its infancy. It was hardly a homogeneous community; there were the élites of the earlier Muslims of Makkah (the *Muhājirūn*) and Madinah (the *Anṣār*) as well as individuals who were yet to mature. The community as a whole lacked any practical experience to be able to smooth away the rough edges in its composition and to present a clear image of Islam and the phase it was going through, or to express the sum and substance of its approach and obligations.

The hypocrites, headed by ʿAbdullāh ibn Ubayy, commanded a strong position in society. They maintained strong family and tribal ties. The Muslims, on the other hand, were yet to develop the understanding that Islam alone represented their family and tribal relationships and the only bond that united them. A certain amount of dislocation could still be found within Muslim ranks due to the existence of hypocrite and dishonest elements and their influence on the destiny and future of the whole community, as we will see clearly when we come to review the verses in this *sūrah* relating to the Battle of Uḥud.

The Jews also enjoyed a strong position in Madinah as well as maintaining their economic ties and covenant alliances with its inhabitants. Their hostility was yet to become open, while the Muslims had yet to develop the feeling that their faith was the only covenant binding upon them, the sole symbol of their nationhood, and the basis of their behavioural and contractual dealings. They were yet to appreciate that ties and bonds, which clashed with their faith, would have no efficacy or validity. In this atmosphere, the Jews found openings for meddling, and for sowing doubts and confusion. There were Muslims who would listen to their talk and be influenced by it. There were Muslims even prepared to intervene with the Prophet on their behalf so as to spare them any possible penalty or punishment and to mitigate the harm they might cause the Muslim community. A stark example is that of ʿAbdullāh ibn Ubayy who spoke harshly to the Prophet in his plea on behalf of the Qaynuqāʿ Jews.

The total and decisive victory of the Muslims at Badr, however, was achieved with minimum effort and cost. The small band of Muslims who joined that expedition were scantily equipped for armed conflict. Although they confronted a much larger and well-prepared Quraysh battalion, the latter were overcome swiftly and convincingly.

That victory, coming in the very first confrontation between the army of God and that of the infidels, was part of God's scheme of things, and we may be able to discern some of its underlying purpose today. Perhaps it was designed to reinforce and strengthen the fledgling religion of Islam, or to demonstrate its efficacy in the battlefield so that it could proceed and progress thereafter.

The Muslims, themselves, might have taken their victory for granted and considered that they would prevail at every stage of their ascent. After all, were they not believing Muslims and their enemies unbelievers? Was it not the case, then, that whenever the two camps met in battle, the Muslims would be certain of triumph.

The Divine principles governing victory and defeat are not so simplistic or naïve. There are prerequisites pertaining to mental preparation, organisational readiness, equipment and provisions, discipline and control, as well as mental and physical alertness. This is what God meant to teach them through the setback they suffered at Uḥud, as this *sūrah* portrays in vivid, breathtaking and meaningful terms. It identifies the behaviour of some Muslims as the reason for their defeat and delivers constructive lessons for both individuals and the community as a whole.

As we review the Battle of Uḥud, we can see that its lessons cost the Muslims enormous pain and sacrifice. They lost some of their dearest and most important members, including Ḥamzah ibn 'Abd al-Muṭṭalib, the Prophet Muḥammad's uncle. More serious and shocking than that, they saw God's Messenger sustain wounds to his forehead, break one of his teeth, fall into a ditch, and have the rings of his armour embedded in his cheek. Nothing could have been more horrific and distressing for the Muslims to witness.

The events of the Battle of Uḥud are preceded in the *sūrah* by a lengthy section completely devoted to a series of directives and exhortations aimed at an elaborate and crystal-clear statement of Islamic belief. It presents the principle of the oneness of God, or *tawḥīd*, in precise and unambiguous terms; it refutes the lies and suspicions propagated by Jews and Christians in Arabia, whether those emanated from their own deviation and false beliefs or those they aimed to sow in Muslim ranks so as to undermine their faith and break their unity and solidarity.

Several accounts identify verses 1–83 as being revealed in connection with a visit, during the ninth year of the Muslim calendar, to Madinah by a Christian delegation from Najran in southern Arabia. However, I doubt if these verses were revealed in that year because their context and content indicate that they were received over the earlier part of the Madinah era, during the Muslim community's formative years. It was during that period that the Muslims were exposed to the largest part of Jewish and other intrigues, which affected both the development of their community as well as their individual behaviour.

However, whether we accept those reports or not, it is clear that the verses address Christian claims and allegations, especially those relating to Jesus (peace be upon him) and focus on the principle of oneness of God. The verses clear the Christian faith of the confusion and distortions that had crept into it, and call upon Christians to believe in the one true God identified in their own scriptures which the Qur'ān had come to confirm and endorse.

The section also contains references and reprimands addressed to the Jews. Specifically, it warns the Muslims against intrigues by their non-Muslim neighbours, especially the Jews of Madinah.

This section, delineated in this work as Part I, which represents about half of the *surah*, covers aspects of the confrontation between Islam and other religious beliefs existing in the Arabian peninsula at the time. This conflict was not merely theological, but rather represented the theoretical aspects of the wider confrontation between the developing Muslim community and its many antagonists who connived and schemed against it, and who strenuously sought to undermine the Islamic faith itself. The essence of that confrontation between the Muslim nation and its opponents remains fundamentally the same today: secularism, international Zionism and modern-day Crusaders.

It is also clear from the text of the *surah* that the means and the ends of the confrontation remain the same. This confirms that the Qur'ān is the Book of Islam and the guidebook for the Muslim nation, now and in the future, as it was its reference during its formative years so long ago. In today's struggle, only those who are mentally unsound would reject the means that would bring certain victory and refuse to consult the Qur'ān or follow its guidance. Through weak-mindedness, carelessness or malice, those would be deceiving themselves and the Muslim nation, and rendering its enemies a great service.

The discourses and the accounts given in this part of the *surah* also expose the attitude of the Jews and Christians, peoples who have deviated from their own true Scriptures, towards the Muslim community and the new faith of Islam. (See, for instance, verses 7, 23, 65, 69–72, 75, 78, 98–9, and 119–20.)

It is clear from the numerous and pointed references that the instruments of war used against the Muslim community were not limited to swords and spears. First and foremost, Islam's enemies targeted the Muslim faith. They deployed deception and intrigue, spread false allegations, plotted and conspired. They aimed to dislodge Islam, the essence that had brought the Muslim community into being. They sought to undermine and destroy the Islamic faith, because they knew, as their counterparts know today, it was the mainstay of the community; the community is only defeated when its spirit of faith is defeated. Their enemies could do the Muslims no harm so long as the Muslims themselves held fast to their faith, depended on it, lived according to its principles, championed its banner, represented its true supporters, and proudly identified with it alone.

From this it is clear that the most evil of enemies are those who divert Muslims away from their faith and belief, and who lead them away from God's path or deceive them regarding the true identity of their enemies and their long-term objectives.

The struggle between the Muslim community and its enemies is, first and foremost, a struggle of faith and belief. Even when the struggle is over land or resources or economic gain or raw materials, winning the war of beliefs and ideas comes first. Long experience has taught Islam's enemies that they cannot prevail over the Muslim community as long as the latter adhere to their faith and religion and commit themselves to its system, remaining constantly vigilant. This is why Islam's enemies and their lackeys expend colossal energy and resources in order to deceive the Muslims and camouflage the real nature of the conflict. In this way they seek to get what they want, to dominate and exploit the Muslims, safe in the knowledge that no faith or belief can motivate them.

Although its enemies today adopt more sophisticated means of intrigue against the Muslim community and use more advanced methods to sow doubts among its people and weaken their bonds, their fundamental objective remains unchanged: to lead the Muslims astray, away from their faith and their religion.

The Qur'ān, therefore, concentrated first of all on frustrating these noxious efforts. It would strengthen the Muslim community's belief in the truth it advocated; it would refute the lies and suspicions that the Jews and Christians spread about Islam; it would expound unequivocally, the grand concepts it promoted, impressing upon the Muslims the need to see the essence and value of their existence on this earth, and to appreciate their role and the role of the faith they uphold in shaping the history of mankind.

The Qur'ān warned the Muslims against their opponents' intrigue, exposed their clandestine schemes, dirty tricks and sinister aims. It identified this hatred towards Islam and Muslims as the result of the favour conferred by God for the great honour of conveying the message of Islam to the world.

The Qur'ān guides the Muslims by affirming the realities and criteria of power in this world, stressing the inherent weakness of their enemies and their disgrace in the eyes of God. It cites their infidelity and deviation from God's revealed messages and their slaying of their own prophets and messengers. It reassures them that God is on their side; He is One, the unmatched Supreme Ruler of everything, and He alone bestows power or takes it away. He will severely punish the faithless (who, in this context, are the Jews). He will humiliate them, just as He did the polytheist Arabs. (See verses 1–5, 10–13, 19, 26, 28, 68, 83, 85, 100–3, 110–12, and 118–20.)

A number of facts arise from the concerted and diverse campaign depicted in these verses: Firstly; the extent to which the Jews of Madinah were prepared to go to subvert Islam and undermine the Muslim community, the depth of their hatred and the wide variety of means and methods they were willing to deploy. Secondly; the great impact the campaign had on individual Muslims, thereby calling for such extensive and detailed Qur'ānic coverage. Thirdly; that, after all these centuries, we still find the same antagonists perpetrating a similar campaign of vilification and demonisation against Islam and the Muslims all over the world. They continue to pose the main threat, and so God Almighty, in His infinite wisdom, has preserved the Qur'ān as a guiding beacon for subsequent Muslim generations to be able to identify their traditional enemies clearly and accurately.

The Battle of Uḥud

The second part of the *sūrah* deals exclusively with the Uḥud campaign, but also carries affirmations relating to the principles of Islam and its outlook, together with commands and exhortations on how to build the Muslim community on those principles. It reviews the facts and events of the campaign, and the feelings and thoughts generated by it, in vivid detail. It describes most accurately the state of the Muslim community at the time and its various constituents, as outlined at the beginning of this Prologue.

The link between this section and the preceding one is quite clear. It also attends to the articulation of the Islamic outlook – immediately and decisively in the heat of battle. It guides and counsels the Muslim community how to uphold their faith and to take on their obligations and responsibilities. It instructs the Muslims in the Divine rules and criteria regarding victory and defeat, complementing the lessons they had learned from their practical experience.

It is hardly possible, in this general Prologue, to do justice to this section of the *sūrah*, but we shall return to it at the appropriate point in the commentary.

The final section of the *sūrah* provides a summary of its main themes. It begins with a revealing reference to the physical world, God's observed book, and its inspiring effect on believing hearts. It continues with a serene and flowing invocation on behalf of those faithful hearts, recited with God's 'observed book' as a fitting backdrop. It says: *"In the creation of the heavens and the earth, and in the succession of night and day, there are indeed signs for men endowed with insight, who remember God when they stand, sit and lie down, and reflect on the creation of the heavens and the earth: 'Our Lord, You have not created all this in vain. Limitless are You in Your glory. Guard us, then, against the torment of the fire. Our Lord, him whom You shall commit to the fire, You will have condemned to disgrace. The evildoers shall have none to help them. Our Lord, we have heard the voice of one who calls to faith, [saying], "Believe in your Lord," and we have believed. Our Lord, forgive us then our sins and efface our bad deeds and let us die with the truly virtuous. Our Lord, grant us what You have promised us through Your Messengers and do not disgrace us on the Day of Resurrection. Surely, You never fail to fulfil Your promise.'"* (Verses 190–4)

God's response comes next, citing the displacement, struggle and persecution suffered by the believers for the cause of God Almighty:

> *Their Lord answers them: "I will not suffer the work of any worker among you, male or female, to be lost. Each of you is an issue of the other. Therefore, those who emigrate and are driven out of their homes and suffer persecution in My cause, and fight and are slain [for it] – I shall indeed efface their bad deeds and admit them to gardens through which running waters flow, as a reward from God. With God is the best of rewards."* (Verse 195)

It is clear that these verses directly relate to the events and the aftermath of the Battle of Uḥud.

The *sūrah* then refers to those people who received earlier revelations, and to whom it devotes the whole of its first part. It reassures the Muslims that the revelation they received has not been rejected by all of those earlier communities, as some of them believe its teachings and attest to its veracity. It says: *"There are indeed among the people of earlier revelations some who believe in God and what has been bestowed from on high upon you and in what has been bestowed upon them, humbling themselves before God. They do not barter away God's revelations for a trifling price."* (Verse 199)

The *sūrah* closes with an appeal to believing Muslims to persevere, to forebear, and to hold fast to their faith and to fear God, a call that fits perfectly with the whole ambience of the *sūrah* and its many themes.

No introduction to the *sūrah* would be complete without understanding three broad themes whose constituent elements are dotted throughout it.

Firstly, the clear and precise statements made on the meaning of "religion" and "Islam". Religious faith, as defined and affirmed by God Almighty, is not a haphazard or irrational belief in the existence of God. There is only one form of belief in God and that is an absolute, definite and certain affirmation of the oneness of God, *tawḥīd*. He is a God to whom mankind submit, as do all other creatures in this world. He is the power that controls and oversees the affairs of mankind and of everything in existence. Nothing can exist or function without God Almighty, and none but Him has absolute power and authority over creation. Accordingly, the religion that God would approve of is Islam, which in this context means total and absolute submission to the Divine Being. Islam is to acknowledge God as the only source of guidance in all walks of life, to recognise His revealed Book, the Qur'ān, as the final arbiter and reference and to follow the Messenger to whom it was revealed. The Book, in its essence, is one and the same, and the religion, in its essence, is one and the same. It is Islam, in its realistic and practical meaning as perceived in the human mind and conscience and in man's daily affairs. By adopting this one religion, all believing followers of God's appointed Messengers, in their respective generations, fall into line as long as they believe in the oneness of God and in His absolute authority and submit to Him in all aspects of their life, without exception.

The *sūrah* highlights this theme, expanding upon it, in clear and emphatic terms, on more than thirty occasions. (See, for example, verses 2, 18–20, 23, 31–2, 52, 64, 67, 83, and 85.)

Secondly, the *sūrah* deals with the relationship between Muslims and God. It emphasises their full submission to Him and their total acceptance of, compliance with, and acquiescence in all that He had revealed. References to this theme will be dealt with in full in their respective places in this *sūrah*. (See verses 7–8, 16–17, 52–3, 110, 113–14, 146–7, 172–3, 191–4, and 199.)

Thirdly, the Muslims are warned against seeking alliances with the unbelievers whose position and strength are shown to be of little consequence. It emphasises that alliances with the unbelievers, who do not adhere to God's Book or comply with the way of life He ordains, negate any presumed belief in God or ties with Him. Reference has already been made to this aspect, but since it is such a prominent feature of the *sūrah*, further amplification is given here. Some quotations which deal with this theme include verses 28–9, 69, 100–3, 111–12, 118, 149–51, and 196.

These three broad themes complement one another perfectly in presenting the Islamic outlook and the true concept of the oneness of God, *tawḥīd*. The prerequisites of this concept in human life and in man's consciousness of God Almighty are clearly delineated as also the effect all this has on the Muslims' attitude towards the enemies of God.

When read in their proper place and context in this *sūrah*, these verses provide greater vigour and deeper meaning. They were revealed in the thick of battle; the battle for faith and belief. During both the internal battle raging within Muslim hearts and minds, and the battle taking place in their daily lives. Hence the *sūrah* has come to contain such extraordinary accounts of movement, inspiration and impact.

Part I

Basic Concepts of Faith

I

Concepts Outlined

Āl-ʿImrān (The House of ʿImrān)

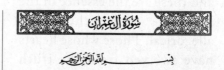

In the name of God, the Compassionate, the Merciful

Alif. Lām. Mīm. (1)

God: there is no deity save Him, the Ever-living, the Eternal Master of all. (2)

He has revealed to you this Book with the truth, confirming what was revealed before it; and He has already revealed the Torah and the Gospel (3)

before this as guidance for people. And He has revealed the Criterion (to distinguish the true from the false). Those who disbelieve in God's revelations shall endure grievous suffering. God is Mighty, able to requite. (4)

Nothing on earth or in the heavens is hidden from God. (5)

It is He Who shapes you in the wombs as He pleases. There is no deity save Him, the Almighty, the Wise. (6)

هُوَ ٱلَّذِى يُصَوِّرُكُمْ فِى ٱلْأَرْحَامِ كَيْفَ يَشَآءُ لَآ إِلَٰهَ إِلَّا هُوَ ٱلْعَزِيزُ ٱلْحَكِيمُ ٦

He it is Who has sent down to you the Book, containing verses which are clear and precise – and these are the essence of the Book – and others are allegorical. Those whose hearts have swerved from the truth pursue that part of it which is allegorical, seeking to create dissension and trying to give it an arbitrary meaning. None save God knows its final meaning. Those who are firmly grounded in knowledge say: "We believe in it; it is all from our Lord." But only those who are endowed with insight take heed. (7)

هُوَ ٱلَّذِىٓ أَنزَلَ عَلَيْكَ ٱلْكِتَٰبَ مِنْهُ ءَايَٰتٌ مُّحْكَمَٰتٌ هُنَّ أُمُّ ٱلْكِتَٰبِ وَأُخَرُ مُتَشَٰبِهَٰتٌ فَأَمَّا ٱلَّذِينَ فِى قُلُوبِهِمْ زَيْغٌ فَيَتَّبِعُونَ مَا تَشَٰبَهَ مِنْهُ ٱبْتِغَآءَ ٱلْفِتْنَةِ وَٱبْتِغَآءَ تَأْوِيلِهِۦ وَمَا يَعْلَمُ تَأْوِيلَهُۥٓ إِلَّا ٱللَّهُ وَٱلرَّٰسِخُونَ فِى ٱلْعِلْمِ يَقُولُونَ ءَامَنَّا بِهِۦ كُلٌّ مِّنْ عِندِ رَبِّنَا وَمَا يَذَّكَّرُ إِلَّآ أُوْلُواْ ٱلْأَلْبَٰبِ ٧

"Our Lord, let not our hearts swerve from the truth after You have guided us; and bestow on us mercy from Yourself. You are indeed the great Giver. (8)

رَبَّنَا لَا تُزِغْ قُلُوبَنَا بَعْدَ إِذْ هَدَيْتَنَا وَهَبْ لَنَا مِن لَّدُنكَ رَحْمَةً إِنَّكَ أَنتَ ٱلْوَهَّابُ ٨

"Our Lord, You will indeed gather mankind together to witness the Day of which there is no doubt. Surely, God never fails to keep His promise." (9)

رَبَّنَآ إِنَّكَ جَامِعُ ٱلنَّاسِ لِيَوْمٍ لَّا رَيْبَ فِيهِ إِنَّ ٱللَّهَ لَا يُخْلِفُ ٱلْمِيعَادَ ٩

18

As for those who disbelieve, neither their riches nor their offspring will in the least avail them against God; it is they who shall be the fuel of the fire. (10)

إِنَّ ٱلَّذِينَ كَفَرُوا لَن تُغْنِيَ عَنْهُمْ أَمْوَٰلُهُمْ وَلَآ أَوْلَٰدُهُم مِّنَ ٱللَّهِ شَيْئًا وَأُوْلَٰٓئِكَ هُمْ وَقُودُ ٱلنَّارِ ۝

Just like the cases of the people of Pharaoh and those before them: they disbelieved Our revelations; therefore, God took them to task for their sins. God's retribution is severe indeed. (11)

كَدَأْبِ ءَالِ فِرْعَوْنَ وَٱلَّذِينَ مِن قَبْلِهِمْ كَذَّبُوا بِـَٔايَٰتِنَا فَأَخَذَهُمُ ٱللَّهُ بِذُنُوبِهِمْ وَٱللَّهُ شَدِيدُ ٱلْعِقَابِ ۝

Say to those who disbelieve: "You shall be overcome and gathered unto hell, an evil resting place. (12)

قُل لِّلَّذِينَ كَفَرُوا سَتُغْلَبُونَ وَتُحْشَرُونَ إِلَىٰ جَهَنَّمَ وَبِئْسَ ٱلْمِهَادُ ۝

"You have had a sign in the two armies which met in battle. One was fighting for God's cause, the other an army of unbelievers. They saw with their very eyes that the others were twice their own number. But God strengthens with His succour whom He wills. In this there is surely a lesson for all who have eyes to see." (13)

قَدْ كَانَ لَكُمْ ءَايَةٌ فِى فِئَتَيْنِ ٱلْتَقَتَا فِئَةٌ تُقَٰتِلُ فِى سَبِيلِ ٱللَّهِ وَأُخْرَىٰ كَافِرَةٌ يَرَوْنَهُم مِّثْلَيْهِمْ رَأْىَ ٱلْعَيْنِ وَٱللَّهُ يُؤَيِّدُ بِنَصْرِهِۦ مَن يَشَآءُ إِنَّ فِى ذَٰلِكَ لَعِبْرَةً لِّأُوْلِى ٱلْأَبْصَٰرِ ۝

Alluring to man is the enjoyment of worldly desires through women and offspring, heaped-up treasures of gold and silver, horses of high mark,

زُيِّنَ لِلنَّاسِ حُبُّ ٱلشَّهَوَٰتِ مِنَ ٱلنِّسَآءِ وَٱلْبَنِينَ وَٱلْقَنَٰطِيرِ ٱلْمُقَنطَرَةِ مِنَ ٱلذَّهَبِ وَٱلْفِضَّةِ وَٱلْخَيْلِ ٱلْمُسَوَّمَةِ

cattle and plantations.
These are the comforts of
this life. With God is the best
of all goals. (14)

وَالْأَنْعَامِ وَالْحَرْثِ ذَٰلِكَ مَتَاعُ الْحَيَاةِ الدُّنْيَا وَاللَّهُ عِنْدَهُ حُسْنُ الْمَآبِ ۝

Say: Shall I tell you of better
things than these? For the God-
fearing there are, with their Lord,
gardens through which running
waters flow where they shall
dwell forever, and wives of
perfect chastity, and God's good
pleasure. God is mindful of His
servants, (15)

۞ قُلْ أَؤُنَبِّئُكُم بِخَيْرٍ مِّن ذَٰلِكُمْ لِلَّذِينَ اتَّقَوْا عِندَ رَبِّهِمْ جَنَّاتٌ تَجْرِي مِن تَحْتِهَا الْأَنْهَارُ خَالِدِينَ فِيهَا وَأَزْوَاجٌ مُّطَهَّرَةٌ وَرِضْوَانٌ مِّنَ اللَّهِ وَاللَّهُ بَصِيرٌ بِالْعِبَادِ ۝

those who say: "Our Lord, we
have indeed accepted the faith.
Forgive us our sins and keep us
safe from the torments of the
fire." (16)

الَّذِينَ يَقُولُونَ رَبَّنَا إِنَّنَا آمَنَّا فَاغْفِرْ لَنَا ذُنُوبَنَا وَقِنَا عَذَابَ النَّارِ ۝

They are the patient in
adversity, the true to their
word, the devoted who spend
in the cause of God, and those
who pray for forgiveness at the
time of dawn. (17)

الصَّابِرِينَ وَالصَّادِقِينَ وَالْقَانِتِينَ وَالْمُنفِقِينَ وَالْمُسْتَغْفِرِينَ بِالْأَسْحَارِ ۝

Overview

Based on the reports that verses 1–83 were revealed in relation to
the visit by a Christian delegation from Najran in Yemen to Madinah
and their debates with the Prophet Muḥammad about the Prophet
Jesus, one would expect these opening verses to form part of those

debates. However, the reports give the date of that visit as being the ninth year of the Muslim calendar which dates from the migration, *Hijrah*, in 622 CE, of the Prophet Muḥammad from Makkah to Madinah. The ninth year of *Hijrah* is also known as "the Year of Delegations" during which a succession of delegations from various parts of Arabia, having seen the power and influence of Islam spread throughout Arabia and beyond, arrived in Madinah to pay homage to the Prophet Muḥammad or to conclude agreements with him or find out more about his mission.

As already pointed out, I feel that the subject matter of these verses and their approach to the subject favour the opinion that they were revealed much earlier in the Madinian period. Accordingly, I am more inclined to conclude that the debates with the people of earlier revelations (i.e. the Jews and Christians), the refutation of their distorted beliefs, the doubts they deliberately spread about the Prophet Muḥammad and the faith of Islam, as well as the subsequent warnings and reassurances addressed to the Muslims, were not directly connected with the Najran delegation in the ninth year of *Hijrah*. Other and earlier occasions must have inspired the revelation of these verses.

We now continue to take a general look at these verses as Qur'ānic arguments addressed to the people of earlier revelations but not directly linked with that event which came at a much later date[1].

These verses, as has already been pointed out, present the on-going and fundamental struggle between the Muslim community and its belief, on the one hand, and the people of earlier revelations and their beliefs, on the other. It is a struggle that has never ceased since the advent of Islam, and specifically since its emergence and the

---

1. In his commendable book, *The Life of the Prophet: a version based on the Qur'ānic text*, Muḥammad 'Izzat Darwāzah says: "The reports suggest that the (Najran) delegation arrived in Madinah during the first quarter of the Madinian period (i.e. the first two and a half years)." I am not sure, however, what reports he uses to arrive at this date. All the accounts I have seen give the ninth year as the date and mention the delegation of Najran as only one of several other delegations (who, as is well-established, arrived during the ninth year of *Hijrah*, known as "the Year of Delegations"). Indeed, Ibn Kathīr in his commentary, does mention the possibility that the Najran delegation could have arrived before the campaign of Ḥudaybīyah (in 6 AH, 628 CE) but he does not give his sources or evidence for such a suggestion. The suggestion that the verses were revealed in connection with the Najran delegation is, at any rate, concomitant with the likelihood that the delegation arrived before Ḥudaybīyah; in other words, if one is true, then so is the other. But if we take the numerous reports that give the date of the delegation as the ninth year of *Hijrah*, we have no alternative but to distinguish between the verses and the occasion on which the reports claim they were revealed.

establishment of its state in Madinah. The Qur'ān documents this encounter, in which the unbelievers and the Jews of Madinah emerged as close allies, in a brilliant and succinct style.

It would hardly be surprising that certain Christian priests from distant parts in Arabia should, in one way or another, participate in that controversy. Nor is it implausible that some of them, whether in groups or as individuals, would have gone to Madinah to take part in debates on the controversial aspects of the difference between their distorted beliefs and the beliefs of the new faith, based on the concept of God's absolute oneness, especially the identity and nature of the Prophet Jesus (pbuh).

The opening verses of the *sūrah* emphasise the parting of the ways between the principle of God's absolute oneness and that of falsehood and distortion. It delivers a warning to those who reject the Qur'ān and God's revelations it contains. All such people are branded as unbelievers, even though they may profess to be Christian or Jewish. It describes the Muslims' attitude towards their Lord and their reactions to His revelations in a manner that makes the situation crystal clear. This it does by defining in no uncertain terms the true meanings of belief, or *īmān*, and disbelief, or *kufr*. (Verses 2–7, and 18–19)

The passage also carries a warning which contains a clear reference to the Jews, when it says: *"Those who deny God's revelations, and slay the prophets against all right, and slay the people who enjoin equity among people: promise them a painful suffering."* (Verse 21) The Israelites would immediately spring to mind at the mere mention of a prophet being slain.

The same reprimand is repeated in the instruction: *"Let not the believers take unbelievers for their allies in preference to the believers..."* (Verse 28) Most likely this is a reference to the Jews, although it could possibly include the idolaters as well. For, until that time many Muslims maintained various alliances with their non-Muslim blood relatives as well as with Jews in Madinah. The Qur'ān ordered them to desist from such associations, warning them in the severest terms. Regardless of whether those allies were Jews or non-Muslim Arabs, they were all identified as "unbelievers".

It is also obvious that the references in verse 12 are to the Badr campaign and that they are addressed to the Jews of Madinah. Ibn 'Abbās reported that having triumphed over the Quraysh at Badr, the Prophet Muḥammad on his return to Madinah called the Jews together

and urged them to convert to Islam before they met a similar fate to
that of the Quraysh. Their reply was: "Look here, Muḥammad. Do
not let yourself be deceived by the fact that you have done away with
a few men from the Quraysh, inexperienced in the skills of battle.
Were you to fight us, you would realise that we are the true men, and
you would never fight a more courageous people." Ibn 'Abbās adds
that it was on that occasion that verses 12 and 13 were revealed. (Related
by Abū Dāwūd.)

It is also evident that although the instructions addressed to the
Prophet Muḥammad in verse 20 are inspired by concurrent events,
they are meant to be general and universal, relevant to confrontation
with all adversaries who oppose his faith.

God's assertion that: *If they turn away, then your only duty is to
convey your message. God is watching over His servants*" (20), indicates
clearly that, up to that point, Muḥammad was not ordered to use
force against the people of earlier revelations or to impose taxes on
them. All this reinforces what has been stated previously that these
verses were revealed at an earlier stage in Madinah.

The overall purport of the passage, as we can see, indicates that they
represent a general argument that is not restricted to a particular occasion
such as the Najran delegation's visit to Madinah. Indeed, this could
well be one of the events the verses were revealed to cover, but there
are frequent other occasions throughout the struggle between Islam
and its many adversaries in Arabia, especially the Jews of Madinah.

This opening passage also includes robust expositions of the
principles of the Muslim religious outlook, complemented by a
powerful elucidation of the nature of Islam and its influences on daily
life. Islam is a religion based on belief in the oneness of God, and it
therefore demands submission to God and no one else besides Him.
Islam means submission and obedience to, and compliance with, the
commands and laws of God and the teachings and leadership of His
messenger. He that neither submits, obeys nor complies is not a Muslim,
and his religious belief will be rejected by God. God accepts no other
religion except that of Islam, in the sense of total submission, obedience
and compliance. This *sūrah* expresses astonishment at those people of
earlier revelations who are called to the Book of God to judge between
them, "... *some of them turn away and pay no heed*" (23). Such obstinacy
and intransigence towards God's Book are a sign of rejection and
infidelity that negates any claims of belief or submission to God.

The second aspect of this part of the *sūrah* revolves entirely around this fundamental truth. Let us now turn to a closer examination of the text.

The Cornerstone of the Islamic Faith

> *Alif. Lām. Mīm. God: there is no deity save Him, the Ever-living, the Eternal Master of all. He has revealed to you this Book with the truth, confirming what was revealed before it; and He has already revealed the Torah and the Gospel before this as guidance for people.* (Verses 1–4)

We choose as the most probable explanation of the three individual letters of the Arabic alphabet, which open the *sūrah*, namely, *Alif; Lām; Mīm*, the same explanation given in our commentary on the opening passage of the preceding *sūrah al-Baqarah*. These letters are mentioned here in order to draw people's attention to the fact that this book, the Qur'ān, is composed of the same type of letters as those available to the Arabs addressed by it. It remains at the same time a miraculous book which they cannot imitate despite the fact that their language is composed of the same letters. This most probable of explanations helps us understand, without difficulty, the need for such references to the nature of the Qur'ān in many *sūrahs* that open with individual letters. In the preceding *sūrah al-Baqarah*, this reference points to the challenge thrown down subsequently in the *sūrah* in these terms: *"If you are in doubt as to what We have revealed to Our servant, then produce one sūrah comparable to it and call upon all your witnesses, other than God, if you were truthful."* (2: 23)

In this *sūrah* a different occasion necessitates this reference to the letters of which the Qur'ān is composed. The *sūrah* stresses that this Book is revealed by God, the One and only deity. It is yet composed of letters and words in the same way as earlier revelations acknowledged by their followers, who are primarily addressed by this *sūrah*. There is nothing new in the fact that God has chosen to reveal this Book to His Messenger in this way.

The *sūrah* begins with confronting the People of the Book, a Qur'ānic term used to denote people of earlier Divine revelation, especially the Jews and Christians, who deny the Prophet's message, even though their knowledge of earlier Prophets, messages, and revelations should have made them the first to accept and believe in the new message. That should have been the case if the matter was simply one of evidence and conviction.

The first passage of the *sūrah* confronts these people in clear terms, dismissing all doubts they entertain or deliberately try to raise in people's minds. It points out how these doubts press on the minds of people. It defines the attitude of true believers towards God's message and defines the attitude of doubters and those who go astray. It vividly portrays the believers' attitude towards their Lord and how they seek refuge with Him and appeal to Him. They know all His attributes.

"God: there is no deity save Him, the Ever-living, the Eternal Master of all." This emphatic opening stresses the absolute oneness of God. It identifies itself as the very basic difference between the faith of Muslims and all other religions and ideologies, whether atheist and polytheist creeds or the religions of those people of the Book, Jews and Christians alike, who have gone astray. It distinguishes the faith of Islam from all other faiths, creeds and ideologies. It is also the basic difference between the way of life of Muslims and that of the followers of all other religions. It is the faith which determines the direction and the system of life in an elaborate and perfect manner.

"God: there is no deity save Him." He has no partner in His most essential attribute of Divinity. *"The Ever-living,"* Who has true, self-sustaining life with absolutely no restrictions. Hence, nothing is similar to Him in this attribute. *"The Eternal Master of all,"* Who gives every life and sustains every existence. No life can exist in this universe without His permission.

This is the central point at issue between the Islamic faith and all other ideologies; between ascribing Divinity only to God and all the multitude of erring beliefs, including idolatry, concepts which were rife at the time in the Arabian Peninsula, as well as Jewish and Christian concepts. The Qur'ān tells us that the Jews used to say that Ezra was the son of God. Something to this effect is included in the fallacies recorded in what the Jews claim to be the Holy Book (Genesis, chapter 6). As for erroneous Christian concepts, the Qur'ān speaks of the Christian belief in the Trinity and their claim that Jesus, son of Mary, was God Himself. They also attribute Divinity to Jesus and his mother, considering them gods. They also consider their priests and monks to have Divine authority. In his book, *The Preaching of Islam*, Thomas Arnold refers to some of these deviant concepts.

A hundred years before, Justinian had succeeded in giving some show of unity to the Roman Empire, but after his death it rapidly fell asunder, and at this time there was an entire want of common national feeling between the provinces and the seat of government. Heraclius had made some partially successful efforts to attach Syria again to the central government, but unfortunately the general methods of reconciliation which he adopted had served only to increase dissension instead of allaying it. Religious Passions were the only existing substitute for national feeling, and he tried, by propounding an exposition of faith, that was intended to serve as an eirenicon, to stop all further dispute between the contending factions and unite the heretics to the Orthodox Church and to the central government. The Council of Chalcedon (451) had maintained that Christ was "to be acknowledged in two natures, without confusion, change, diversion or separation; the difference of the natures being in nowise taken away by reason of their union, but rather the properties of each nature being preserved, and concurring into one person and one substance, not as it were divided or separated into two persons, but one and the same Son and only begotten, God the Word." The council was rejected by the Monophysites, who only allowed one nature in the person of Christ, who was said to be a composite person, having all attributes divine and human, but the substance bearing these attributes was no longer a duality, but a composite unity. The controversy between the orthodox party and the Monophysites, who flourished particularly in Egypt and Syria and in countries outside the Byzantine empire, had been hotly contested for nearly two centuries, when Heraclius sought to effect a reconciliation by means of the doctrine of Monotheism: while conceding the duality of the natures, it secured unity of the person in the actual life of Christ, by the rejection of two series of activities in this one person; the one Christ and Son of God effectuates that which is human and that which is divine by one divine human agency, *i.e.*, there is only one will in the Incarnate Word.[2]

---

2. T.W. Arnold, *The Preaching of Islam* (Lahore, Sh. Muhammad Ashraf, 1968), p.53.

As for deviation in the beliefs of idolaters, the Qur'ān speaks of their worship of the *jinn*, the angels, the sun, the moon and idols. The least deviant in all their beliefs being the assertion by some of them that they only worshipped these idols in order that they would act as intermediaries endearing them to God.

It confronting such a great heap of erring beliefs and deviant concepts, Islam declares in the clearest and strongest of terms: *"God: there is no deity save Him, the Ever-living, the Eternal Master of all."* As we have said, this declaration identifies the central point at issue in matters of faith. Moreover, it is the departing point for different ways of life and codes of behaviour. When belief in the existence of God, the only God Who is Ever-living, and Who is the Eternal Master from Whom every life and every existence are derived and Who controls every living thing, is firmly established in someone's mind, his way of life must, by necessity, be totally different from that of a person who holds to any of the confused and erring concepts. The latter cannot feel the influence on his life of the Divine Being, the One, who is actually in control of his life. With the concept of the absolute oneness of God, submission to anyone other than Him is inadmissible. There can be no room for deriving any laws or systems, moral values, economic or social systems except from God. He is the only One to Whom we turn for guidance in every matter which concerns this life or in what follows this life. With all other confused beliefs and concepts there is no one to whom we may turn. There are no boundaries distinguishing right from wrong, what is forbidden from what is lawful. All these can be determined only when the source from which they are derived is determined. For it is that source to which we turn for guidance and to which we submit ourselves in total obedience.

Hence, it was necessary to put the issue very clearly right at the outset: *"God: there is no deity save Him, the Ever-living, the Eternal Master of all."* This is, indeed, what gives Islamic life its unique character, one which is not confined to the realm of beliefs only. All aspects of Islamic life are derived from this basic Islamic concept of the total and absolute oneness of God. This concept cannot be truly established in our minds unless its practical influence is felt in our lives, starting with deriving our laws which relate to all fields of life from God alone, and turning to Him for guidance in every sphere of life.

When the central issue is thus resolved by the declaration of the absolute oneness of God and outlining His unique attributes, which no one shares with Him, are outlined, the *sūrah* moves on to speak of the unity of the source from which all religions, Scriptures and Divine messages are revealed. That is to say the source of the revealed code implemented throughout all generations of human life.

The Qur'ān and Earlier Revelations

... And He has revealed the Criterion (to distinguish the true from the false). Those who disbelieve in God's revelations shall endure grievous suffering. God is Mighty, able to requite. Nothing on earth or in the heavens is hidden from God. It is He Who shapes you in the wombs as He pleases. There is no deity save Him, the Almighty, the Wise. (Verses 4–6)

These initial verses provide an affirmation of several essential principles in formulating the correct ideological concept, i.e. Islam, and for silencing the people of earlier revelations and others who denied the Prophet's message and its Divine source. It states first the unity of the source which reveals Divine messages to Prophets and Messengers. It is God the only deity, the Ever-living, the Eternal Master of all Who has revealed this Qur'ān as He has indeed revealed the Torah to Moses and the Gospel to Jesus (pbu them). There can, therefore, be no confusion between the position of the Divine Being and that of His servants. There is only One God Who reveals messages to His chosen servants. For their part, they are servants who submit themselves to God, despite the fact that they are Prophets sent with messages from Him.

The verses also state the unity of Divine faith, as well as the fact that the Truth included in the Scriptures revealed by God is also one. This Book which has been sent down to Muḥammad has been revealed, *"with the truth, confirming what was revealed before it,"* i.e. the Torah and the Gospel. All these Scriptures have been sent down for a single purpose, that is, to serve *"as guidance for people."* This newly revealed Book is a *"Criterion"* distinguishing the Truth embodied in the revealed Scriptures from all sorts of deviation and confused ideas which have found their way into the Scriptures whether by way of personal prejudices, intellectual trends or political considerations.

These verses also include an implicit insertion that there can be no valid reason for the denial of the new message by the people of earlier revelations. In this way, it follows the same line of earlier messages. It is a book sent down with the truth in the same way as all revealed books and Scriptures are. It too has been revealed to a human messenger. Furthermore, it confirms all Divine Scriptures revealed before it. It clearly sets out the "Truth" which they have stated earlier. Moreover, it has been sent down by the One Who is able to send down His revelations and Who has the right to lay down a code of living for mankind which sets for them their concepts of faith, law, and morality.

Verse 4 also delivers a stern threat to those who deny God's revelations. It reminds them of God's might, His grievous punishment, and His ability to enforce justice. Those who deny God's messages are those who reject this one faith in its absolute nature. The people of earlier revelations who have deviated from the Divine revelations and who deny this new book, a clear criterion distinguishing right from wrong, are the first to be described here as non-believers. They are foremost amongst those to whom God's threat of severe punishment and grievous suffering is directed.

Within the context of this threat an emphatic assertion is given that God knows everything. Nothing at all can be hidden from Him: *"Nothing on earth or in the heavens is hidden from God."* This assertion of God's absolute knowledge fits well with the statement of the absolute oneness of the Divine Being Who is the Eternal Master of all. This attribute of God is stated right at the outset, in verse 5. It also fits well with the stern threat delivered in the preceding verse. Since nothing on earth or in the heavens may be withheld from God's knowledge and no secrets can be kept from Him, then all intentions and all schemes are known to Him. Hence, nothing can escape His fair judgement and His just punishment.

Having stated this fact of God's absolute knowledge of everything in the universe, the *sūrah* gently but effectively touches upon human nature with a reference to man's origin. It is an origin well hidden from man in the darkness of mothers' wombs and in the realm to which man's knowledge cannot aspire: *"It is He Who shapes you in the wombs as He pleases. There is no deity save Him, the Almighty, the Wise."*

It is He Who gives you whatever shape He pleases. He also gives you your distinctive characteristics. This He does alone, according to His absolute will, *"as He pleases."* For He is the only deity in the universe, and He is *"the Almighty"* Who has the power and the ability to shape and fashion His creation, *"the Wise"* Who determines everything according to His wisdom. He has no partner or associate to influence what He creates and fashions.

This statement dispels all the confusion created by the Christians concerning Jesus's birth and origin. It is God Who shaped Jesus (pbuh) as He pleased. There is no truth whatsoever in the claims that Jesus (pbuh) was the Lord, or was God, or the son of God, or a being with a dual nature: Divine and human. All deviant and confused concepts which are at variance with the Truth of the absolute oneness of God are false and without substance.

Two Types of Revelation

In this brief passage, the *sūrah* uncovers the reality of those who swerve from the truth. These people turn their back on the facts stated with absolute clarity in the Qur'ān, pursuing other Qur'ānic statements which admit more than one explanation in order to use the same as a basis for their fabrications. It also shows the distinctive characteristics of those who truly believe in God and submit to Him, accepting everything they receive from Him without any doubt or argument.

One report suggests that the Christian delegation from Najran said to the Prophet: "Do you not state that Jesus Christ was the word of God and His spirit?" They wanted to utilise this statement to support their own doctrines that Jesus was not a human being, but the spirit of God. At the same time they paid no heed to those unequivocal verses which emphatically state the absolute oneness of God, categorically rejecting all claims of His having any partner or son. The report says that verse 7 was revealed by way of reply, showing the reality of their attempt to make use of such allegorical statements, while at the same time abandoning other clear and precise statements.

This verse does, however, have more general significance than its relevance to that particular historical case. It shows the attitudes of different people towards this Book which God has revealed to the Prophet, stating the essentials of the correct concept of faith and the basics of the Islamic way of life. It also includes other statements which relate to matters kept beyond the realm of human perception. The human mind cannot fathom these matters beyond what the relevant Qur'ānic statements point out.

As for the basics of faith and Islamic law, these are definitively stated, clearly understood and have well-defined aims. These are the essence of this Qur'ān. Those matters which are stated allegorically, including the origin and birth of Jesus (pbuh) are so given in order that we accept them at face value. We believe in them because they come to us from the source which speaks the truth: their sense and form are difficult to comprehend because, by nature, they are beyond our human, finite means of comprehension.

People's reception of both types of revelation differs according to whether their nature has remained straightforward or has swerved from the truth. Those whose hearts have deviated and erred deliberately overlook the clear and precise essentials which make up the foundation of the faith, the law and the practical way of life. Instead, they pursue those allegorical verses which can only be accepted on the basis of believing in their source and acknowledging that He is the One Who knows all the truth, while human perception is limited. Acceptance of both types of revelation also depends on human nature remaining pure and straightforward, believing as a matter of course that this whole book is a book of truth, and that it has been sent down with the truth and that no deviation or error can creep into it. Deviants, however, create trouble and dissension by attributing interpretations to those allegorical statements which shake the foundation of the faith, and which bring about confusion as a result of forcing the human mind into a realm which lies way beyond it. *"None save God knows its final meaning."*

"Those who are firmly grounded in knowledge" and who have recognised the nature of human thinking and the area within which the human mind can operate say with confidence and reassurance: *"We believe in it; it is all from our Lord."* Such scholars are reassured because they know that it is all from their Lord; hence it must tell the truth, simply because whatever originates with God is the truth. It is not part of the function or ability of the human mind to look for reasons and arguments to support it. Nor is it within its ability to fathom its nature or the nature of the causes which give rise to it. True knowledge presupposes that the human mind need not try to penetrate what is kept beyond it nor what man has not been given the means to discover or understand.

This is a true description of those firmly grounded in knowledge. Only those who are deluded by the scanty knowledge they have acquired make boastful statements that they have acquired omnipotent knowledge and only they deny the very existence of what they cannot understand. Furthermore, they sometimes impose their own understanding on universal facts, allowing them to exist only in the manner they understand them. Hence, they try to measure God's Word, which is absolute, by their own rational dictates formulated by their own finite minds. Those who are truly learned, however, are much more humble in their attitude, and they readily accept that the human mind cannot fathom the great many facts beyond its capability. They are more faithful to human nature, recognising the truth and accepting it: *"… only those who are endowed with insight take heed."*

It seems that those who have insight need only reflect and take heed in order to recognise the truth and to have it well established in their minds. When this is achieved they repeat their prayers in total devotion, asking God to enable them to hold on to that truth, to not let their hearts swerve from it, and to give them of His abundant grace. They also remember the undoubted day when all mankind will be gathered together, and they remember the promise which will never fail: *"Our Lord, … bestow on us mercy from Yourself. You are indeed the great Giver. Our Lord, You will indeed gather mankind together to witness the Day of which there is no doubt. Surely, God never fails to keep His promise."*

This is the sort of attitude those who are firmly grounded in knowledge adopt, and it is the attitude which suits the believers. It emanates from the reassurance that what God says is the truth and that His promise will be fulfilled. It is an attitude influenced by knowledge of God's mercy and His grace, and by fear of what His will may determine. It is an attitude shaped by fear of God and the great sensitivity faith implants in the hearts of believers so that they never forget or overlook these facts at any moment of day or night.

A believer's heart appreciates the value of having guidance after being misguided, the value of clarity after impaired vision, the value of following a straight road after confusion, the value of reassurance after being at a loss, the value of liberation from subjugation to other people, through submission to God alone, the value of having high concerns after being preoccupied with pettiness. It appreciates that God has given him all that through faith. Hence, the believer fears to return to error as much as a person who follows a bright, clear way fears to return to a dark, endless labyrinth, or a person who has enjoyed the cool shade fears to return to the burning sun of the desert. Only a person who has experienced the bitter misery of unbelief can appreciate the sweetness and happiness of faith, and only a person who has tasted the bitterness of deviation and error can enjoy the reassurance of faith.

Hence, the believers address their Lord with this prayer which reflects their sincere devotion: *"Our Lord, let not our hearts swerve from the truth after You have guided us."* They pray for more of God's mercy which has saved them from error, provided them with guidance, and given them what they could not have from any other source: *"... and bestow on us mercy from Yourself. You are indeed the great Giver."*

Their faith tells them that they cannot attain anything except through God's mercy and grace. They do not even have control over their own hearts; for they are in God's hand. Hence, they pray for God's help. 'Ā'ishah, the Prophet's wife reports: "God's messenger (peace be on him) often repeated this prayer: Lord, You are the One Who turns hearts over. Let my heart stick firmly to your faith. I said: Messenger of God, you often repeat this prayer. He said: Every single heart is held in between two of the Merciful's fingers; He will keep it on the right path if He wills, and He will let it swerve from the truth if He wills."

When the believer appreciates that God's will is accomplished in this way, he realises that his only choice is to hold tight to God's guidance, and to pray to God to bestow His mercy on him so that he may keep the great treasure which God has given him.

A Lesson for the Discerning

As for those who disbelieve, neither their riches nor their offspring will in the least avail them against God; it is they who shall be the fuel of the fire. Just like the cases of the people of Pharaoh and those before them: they disbelieved Our revelations; therefore, God took them to task for their sins. God's retribution is severe indeed. Say to those who disbelieve: "You shall be overcome and gathered unto hell, an evil resting place. You have had a sign in the two armies which met in battle. One was fighting for God's cause, the other an army of unbelievers. They saw with their very eyes that the others were twice their own number. But God strengthens with His succour whom He wills. In this there is surely a lesson for all who have eyes to see." (Verses 10–13)

This passage follows the opening verses of the *sūrah* which outline the attitude of the believers towards God's revelations, whether of the clear and precise type or of the type expressed in allegory. Here we have an explanation of the end which awaits the unbelievers, and the Divine Law which never fails to inflict punishment on them for their sins. A warning is also included to the unbelievers among the people of earlier revelations who stand in opposition to Islam. The Prophet is instructed to warn them, and to remind them of what they saw with their own eyes at the Battle of Badr when such a small group of believers achieved a great victory over a much larger force of unbelievers.

The context of this passage is an address to the Israelites warning them of a similar fate to that of the unbelievers who lived before them and who may live after them. It also reminds the Israelites of the doom which befell Pharaoh and his soldiers when God saved the Israelites themselves. That, however, does not give the Israelites any right to special treatment should they revert to disbelief and denial of the truth. There is nothing to prevent them from being branded as unbelievers should they err, and there is nothing to save them from doom either in this life or in the life to come, in the same way as doom befell Pharaoh and his army.

They are also reminded of the fate of the Quraysh army of unbelievers at the Battle of Badr. This drives it home to them that God's law will never fail. Nothing will protect them from being overwhelmed by the same fate as the Quraysh. The cause of that fate was the Quraysh's rejection of the faith. In essence they are being told that no one has a special position with God and no one will have any immunity except through true faith.

"As for those who disbelieve, neither their riches nor their offspring will in the least avail them against God; it is they who shall be the fuel of the fire." (Verse 10) Wealth and children are normally thought of as two sources of protection. Neither, however, will be of any avail on that Day, about the arrival of which there is no doubt, because God never fails to keep His promise. On that Day, they will be *"the fuel of the fire."* This metaphor deprives them of all the characteristics which distinguish man. They are grouped together with logs, wood and all manner of fuel.

Indeed, wealth and children cannot be of any avail in this life, even when they are coupled with power and authority: *"Just like the cases of the people of Pharaoh and those before them: they disbelieved Our revelations; therefore, God took them to task for their sins. God's retribution is severe indeed."* (Verse 11) This case has had frequent parallels throughout history. God relates it in detail in this book. It is a case which outlines God's law, which applies to those who reject His revelations as lies. He implements this law as He wills. Hence, no one who rejects God's revelations can have any immunity or safeguard.

This means that those who rejected the faith and dismissed Muḥammad's call and the message contained in the book God has revealed to him with the truth, lay themselves open to the same fate in both this life and the life to come. The Prophet is instructed to warn them against the same fate in both lives. He is further instructed to give them the recent example of what happened to them in Badr, for they may have forgotten the example of Pharaoh and the unbelievers before him and how they were overwhelmed by God's stern retribution. *"Say to those who disbelieve: 'You shall be overcome and gathered unto hell, an evil resting place. You have had a sign in the two armies which met in battle. One was fighting for God's cause, the other an army of unbelievers. They saw with their very eyes that the others were twice their own number. But God strengthens with His succour whom He wills. In this there is surely a lesson for all who have eyes to see.'"* (Verses 12–13)

The statement, *"they saw with their very eyes that the others were twice their own number,"* admits of two possible interpretations. The pronoun "they", preceding the verb "saw" may be taken to refer to the unbelievers, whilst "the others," in this case, refers to the Muslims. This means that despite their numerical superiority, the unbelievers imagined the much smaller group of Muslims to be "twice their own number". This was by God's own design. He led the unbelievers to perceive the Muslims as a very large force when they were indeed few in number, and this put fear into their hearts.

The same statement could be interpreted in the opposite fashion, which suggests that the Muslims saw the unbelievers as "twice their own number" when in actual fact they were three times as many. Nevertheless, the Muslims were steadfast and achieved victory.

The most important factor here is the attribution of victory to God's aid and His planning. This, in itself, serves as a warning to the unbelievers and has a demoralising effect on them. At the same time, it strengthens the believers and decries their enemies, so much so that the believers have no fear. The particulars of the situation pertaining at Badr required both elements. In other words, the Qur'ān was working on both aspects.

God's promise to defeat those unbelievers who swerve from the truth and who reject God's constitution is valid for all time. Similarly, God's promise to grant victory to the believers, even though they may be few in number, is also valid for all time. That victory depends, in the last resort, on God's help, which He grants to whomever He wills. This fact also remains true for the present as for the future.

The believers need only to be certain that this is the truth and to be confident that God's promise will be fulfilled. They must do all in their power and then be patient until God's will is done. They must not precipitate events, nor should they despair if victory seems long coming. Everything is done in God's own good time, according to His wisdom which determines the most suitable time for every event.

"In this there is surely a lesson for all who have eyes to see." There must be eyes to see and hearts to understand and minds to reflect, so that the lesson is fully understood. Otherwise, lessons are given at every moment of the day and night, but few pay heed.

False and True Comforts

The next few verses in the *sūrah* fall within that part of the Qur'ān which is mainly concerned with educating the Muslim community. The first of these verses identifies those subtle, natural incentives which cause people to deviate from the right path, unless they are properly checked. In order to control them, one must always be on the alert, yearn for more sublime horizons and aspire to those comforts which remain with God, for these are indeed far superior to worldly comforts.

Pursuing worldly pleasures and giving priority to personal desires and pleasures will no doubt distract a person's mind and prevent him from reflecting on what fruits one is bound to reap or what lessons one can learn from the facts of life. People are thus drowned in easy, physical pleasures, unable to see what lies beyond of better and superior comforts. They are thus deprived of the enjoyment of looking beyond cheap, physical pleasure, or being preoccupied with the nobler concerns which fit with the great role of man, the creature God has placed in charge of this great dominion, the earth.

Those physical pleasures and worldly comforts and incentives are, nevertheless, naturally infused in man by the Creator to fulfil the essential role of preserving the continuity of life. Hence, Islam does not approve of their suppression. It advocates that they should be regulated, moderated and brought under control. Islam wants man to be able to control these desires, not to be controlled by them. Islam promotes the feeling of the sublime in man and helps him look to what is higher and superior.

Hence, that Qur'ānic statement, which is concerned with the education of the Muslim community, mentions all these comforts and pleasures, but portrays alongside them a variety of physical and spiritual pleasures which are provided in the life to come for those who control their natural desires in this life. These are, in part, the reward awaiting those who maintain their noble human standard, and who do not allow themselves to be overwhelmed by the cheap, physical enjoyments of this world.

In a single verse the *surah* groups together the most enjoyable pleasures of this life: women, children, endless wealth, splendid horses, fertile land and cattle. These represent the total sum of worldly pleasures, either by themselves, or because of what they can provide for their owners by way of other pleasures. The verse which follows, however, identifies the pleasures of the hereafter: gardens through which running waters flow, spouses renowned for their chastity, and what is much more: God's good pleasure. These are in store for anyone who looks beyond the pleasures of this world and maintains good relations with God.

Alluring to man is the enjoyment of worldly desires through women and offspring, heaped-up treasures of gold and silver, horses of high mark, cattle and plantations. These are the comforts of this life. With God is the best of all goals. Say: Shall I tell you of better things than these? For the God-fearing there are, with their Lord, gardens through which running waters flow where they shall dwell forever, and wives of perfect chastity, and God's good pleasure. God is mindful of His servants, those who say: "Our Lord, we have indeed accepted the faith. Forgive us our sins and keep us safe from the torments of the fire." They are the patient in adversity, the true to their word, the devoted who spend in the cause of God, and those who pray for forgiveness at the time of dawn. (Verses 14–17)

"Alluring to man is the enjoyment of worldly desires." In the original Arabic text, the verb in this sentence is expressed in the passive voice which indicates that this love is part of man's nature. Hence, this is a statement of fact. Man certainly loves to enjoy these pleasures. There is no need, then, either to deny that love or to denounce and condemn it. It is essential for human life so that it may continue and progress. But there is certainly another side which is also infused in human nature and that is to balance that love and to guard man against total consumption by it to the extent that he loses the great effects of the spiritual element in his constitution. That aspect provides man with the ability to look up to the sublime and to control his desires and fulfil them in a befitting and appropriate measure. He can thus achieve his fulfilment here but, at the same time, elevate human life spiritually and look forward to the life to come where he can enjoy God's good pleasure. This ability can hold worldly desires in check, purify them and keep them within safe limits so that physical pleasures do not overwhelm the human soul and its aspirations. To turn to God and to fear Him is the way to the achievement of those aspirations.

The verse speaks of those worldly desires as being made alluring to man. There is no suggestion, implicit or explicit, that they are contemptible, or that they should be treated as such. We are only called upon to understand their nature in order to place them in their appropriate place in our lives and not allow them to suppress what is superior to and nobler than them. We are, indeed, called upon to aspire to higher horizons after we have taken what is sufficient and necessary for us of those pleasures.

Islam is distinguished by its realistic approach to human nature and its constant effort to elevate rather than suppress it. Those who talk nowadays of the harmful effects of the "suppression" of natural desires, or about psychological complexes which result from such suppression, agree that the main reason for such problems is the suppression of natural desires, not their control. Suppression stems from the condemnation of natural desires, or looking down on them with contempt. This places the individual under two kinds of pressure which pull in opposite directions. There is first the emotional pressure from within, the result of social traditions or religion, that physical desires are contemptible and should not have existed in the first place. They are portrayed as sinful and evil. There is, on the other hand, the pressure of these desires themselves which cannot be overcome because they are deeply rooted in human nature, having an essential role to play in human life. Indeed, they have not been made part of human nature in vain. As this conflict rages within man, it gives rise to psychological complexes. This is the opinion held by scientists specialised in psychology. Assuming that their theory is correct, we still find that Islam has kept man safe from this conflict between the two parts of his human soul, the temptation to indulge in wanton satisfaction of desire and seek every type of easy pleasure and the aspirations to a nobler existence. It caters for the fulfilment of both, combining continuity with moderation.

It goes without saying that women and children are among the most important and strongest desires of man. Coupled with these in the text listing the desires of this world are *"heaped-up treasures of gold and silver"*. The phrase *"heaped-up treasures"* implies a consuming greed for wealth. If it was merely a love of wealth that is meant here, the Qur'ān would simply have used the term "money", or "gold and silver". *"Heaped-up treasures,"* however, adds a further connotation, that is treasure for its own sake. The implication here being the greed to amass gold and silver, because the mere amassing of wealth is a human desire, regardless of what that wealth may be used for, especially in satisfying other desires.

The Qur'ānic verse then adds, *"horses of high mark."* Even in the material world of machines in which we live, horses remain among those pleasures loved and desired by all people. A stallion combines beauty with vigour, strength, intelligence and a close relationship with his owner. Even those who do not ride horses warm to the sight of a lively horse as it runs. Cattle and plantations are then mentioned. The two are closely linked together in our minds and in real life. People love the scene of plants growing out of the earth, of life blossoming. When the desire of ownership is coupled with this, then cattle and plantations are certainly craved.

All the desires mentioned in this verse are mere examples of what people strive to have. The ones so identified were particularly appealing to the community which the Qur'ān addressed for the first time, but many of them appeal to all people in all ages. The Qur'ān mentions them before stating their real value so that they are given their proper place in the list of priorities of any believer: *"These are the comforts of this life."* (Verse 14)

Better Than All Comforts

All these cherished desires, and all similar ones, are the comforts of this life. Perhaps we should add here that in the Arabic text, the term "this life", or *"dunyā"*, connotes "the lower life". Hence, they are not part of the sublime life or of the higher horizon. They are indeed the easy comforts of the life of this world. What is better than all this, because it is essentially nobler and it helps protect the human soul against being consumed by worldly desires, is that which remains with God. This is available to anyone who wants it, and it more than compensates for the pleasures of this world: *"Say: Shall I tell you of better things than these? For the God-fearing there are, with their Lord, gardens through which running waters flow where they shall dwell forever, and wives of perfect chastity, and God's good pleasure. God is mindful of His servants."* (Verse 15)

The Prophet is commanded to give the happy news of these comforts of the hereafter to those who are described as "the God-fearing". We note that these comforts are, generally speaking, physical. There is, however, an essential difference between them and the comforts of this world. These are provided only to the God-fearing, who are always conscious of God. This consciousness has a definite moderating influence on both the spirit and the body. It prevents man from being totally consumed by his desires, striving like an animal to fulfil them in any way he can. Hence, when the God-fearing look forward to these physical comforts which they are promised, they do so with a sublimity which remains free of the uncontrolled vigour of animal desire. Even in this life, long before they arrive in their promised abode, close to God, they are elevated by looking forward to these heavenly comforts.

They find in them more than a mere compensation of the worldly desires and pleasures they miss in this world. If the pleasures of this life included fertile plantations, they have in the hereafter gardens through which running waters flow. Moreover, both they and their gardens live forever, unlike the plantations of this world which people enjoy only for a limited period of time. In contrast to the pleasures of women and children in this life, there are in the hereafter wives of perfect chastity. Their purity makes them far superior to what people desire of women in this life. As for the horses of high mark and the cattle, and the heaped-up treasures of gold and silver, all these are viewed in this life as means to achieve more and greater comforts. In the hereafter, all comforts are freely available to everyone. No special means are required to achieve any ends.

There remains what is far superior to all comforts, namely, *"God's good pleasure."* His pleasure is, to a believer, more precious than this life and the life to come combined. The Arabic term which is used to express this pleasure has endless connotations of love, tenderness, care and compassion.

"God is mindful of His servants." He knows their nature and the motivations and incentives which form part of it. He also knows what suits human nature in the way of directives and instructions. He knows how to deal with it in this life and the life to come.

The passage then describes the relationship of the God-fearing with their Lord, which earns them this blessing of God's good pleasure: *"Those who say: 'Our Lord, we have indeed accepted the faith. Forgive us our sins and keep us safe from the torment of the fire.' They are the patient in adversity, the true to their word, the devoted who spend in the cause of God, and those who pray for forgiveness at the time of dawn."* (Verses 16–17)

Their prayer is indicative of the fact that they are God-fearing. They state first that they are believers, before they appeal to God on the strength of that faith to forgive them their sins and to keep them safe from the Fire.

Every one of their qualities is of great value in human life and in the life of the Muslim community. Their patience in adversity suggests that they endure pain without complaint. They remain steadfast, happy to fulfil the duties of their faith, submitting themselves to God and accepting whatever happens to them as part of God's will and design. Being truthful shows that they hold the truth, which is the mainstay of human life, dear to their hearts. They find lying contemptible, for lying is indicative of a state of weakness which prevents one from telling the truth, in order to realise some benefit or to avoid some harm.

Their devotion is a fulfilment of the duty of the servant towards his Lord. Moreover, it elevates man because he addresses his devotion to the only God in the universe, not to anyone else. Spending in the cause of God liberates man from the captivity of the material world, and from the greed for wealth. It also places the reality of human brotherhood above the desire for personal comfort. It achieves social security on a mutual basis which is worthy of human life.

To pray at dawn for forgiveness adds to all this connotations of purity and compassion. Indeed, the mere mentioning of dawn reminds us of the lovely feelings of this particular part of the night, shortly before the break of day. At that time, everything is beautiful, pure and still. Man's thoughts are at their purest. The inner motives of uncorrupted human nature are at work. When we add to all this the condition of praying to God for forgiveness, then the atmosphere is one of total purity in both the inner soul of man and the inner soul of the universe. Both are truly submissive to God, the Creator of both man and the universe.

The God-fearing, who are characterised by these essential qualities, will have *"God's good pleasure."* They deserve it, and with it all that is associated with God's compassion and grace. It is certainly superior to any worldly comfort and to any of man's desires.

We note how the Qur'ān deals with the human soul. Its approach begins with man on earth. Gradually but steadily it elevates the human soul to higher horizons until it brings it into the highest society with ease and compassion. It never forgets man's weakness, nor his motives and nature. However, it directs man's abilities and aspirations gently, without the suppression of any motive and without the use of force. It is also mindful that human life should continue and progress. This is the nature of God's method: *"God is mindful of His servants."*

2

Concepts Clarified

God Himself bears witness, and so do the angels and men of knowledge, that there is no deity save Him, the Executor of Justice. There is no deity save Him, the Almighty, the Wise. (18)

The only true faith acceptable to God is [man's] self-surrender to Him. Disagreements spread, through mutual aggression, among those who were given revelations only after knowledge had been granted to them. He who denies God's revelations will find that God is indeed swift in reckoning. (19)

If they argue with you, say: "I have surrendered my whole being to God, and so have all who follow me." Say to those who were given revelations and to unlettered people, "Will you also surrender yourselves (to God)?" If they surrender, they are on the right path. But if they turn away, then your only duty is to convey your message. God is watching over His servants. (20)

شَهِدَ ٱللَّهُ أَنَّهُۥ لَآ إِلَٰهَ إِلَّا هُوَ وَٱلْمَلَٰٓئِكَةُ وَأُوْلُواْ ٱلْعِلْمِ قَآئِمَۢا بِٱلْقِسْطِ لَآ إِلَٰهَ إِلَّا هُوَ ٱلْعَزِيزُ ٱلْحَكِيمُ ۝

إِنَّ ٱلدِّينَ عِندَ ٱللَّهِ ٱلْإِسْلَٰمُ وَمَا ٱخْتَلَفَ ٱلَّذِينَ أُوتُواْ ٱلْكِتَٰبَ إِلَّا مِنۢ بَعْدِ مَا جَآءَهُمُ ٱلْعِلْمُ بَغْيَۢا بَيْنَهُمْ وَمَن يَكْفُرْ بِـَٔايَٰتِ ٱللَّهِ فَإِنَّ ٱللَّهَ سَرِيعُ ٱلْحِسَابِ ۝

فَإِنْ حَآجُّوكَ فَقُلْ أَسْلَمْتُ وَجْهِيَ لِلَّهِ وَمَنِ ٱتَّبَعَنِ وَقُل لِّلَّذِينَ أُوتُواْ ٱلْكِتَٰبَ وَٱلْأُمِّيِّۦنَ ءَأَسْلَمْتُمْ فَإِنْ أَسْلَمُواْ فَقَدِ ٱهْتَدَواْ وَّإِن تَوَلَّوْاْ فَإِنَّمَا عَلَيْكَ ٱلْبَلَٰغُ وَٱللَّهُ بَصِيرٌۢ بِٱلْعِبَادِ ۝

Those who deny God's revelations, and slay the Prophets against all right and slay people who enjoin equity among all people: promise them a painful suffering. (21)

إِنَّ ٱلَّذِينَ يَكْفُرُونَ بِـَٔايَٰتِ ٱللَّهِ وَيَقْتُلُونَ ٱلنَّبِيِّـۧنَ بِغَيْرِ حَقٍّ وَيَقْتُلُونَ ٱلَّذِينَ يَأْمُرُونَ بِٱلْقِسْطِ مِنَ ٱلنَّاسِ فَبَشِّرْهُم بِعَذَابٍ أَلِيمٍ ۞

It is they whose works shall come to nothing in this world and in the life to come; and they shall have none to help them. (22)

أُوْلَٰٓئِكَ ٱلَّذِينَ حَبِطَتْ أَعْمَٰلُهُمْ فِى ٱلدُّنْيَا وَٱلْـَٔاخِرَةِ وَمَا لَهُم مِّن نَّٰصِرِينَ ۞

Have you considered the case of those who have received a share of revelation? When they are called upon to accept the judgement of God's book in their affairs, some of them turn away and pay no heed. (23)

أَلَمْ تَرَ إِلَى ٱلَّذِينَ أُوتُواْ نَصِيبًا مِّنَ ٱلْكِتَٰبِ يُدْعَوْنَ إِلَىٰ كِتَٰبِ ٱللَّهِ لِيَحْكُمَ بَيْنَهُمْ ثُمَّ يَتَوَلَّىٰ فَرِيقٌ مِّنْهُمْ وَهُم مُّعْرِضُونَ ۞

For they claim: "The fire will most certainly not touch us save for a limited number of days." They are deceived in their own faith by the false beliefs they used to invent. (24)

ذَٰلِكَ بِأَنَّهُمْ قَالُواْ لَن تَمَسَّنَا ٱلنَّارُ إِلَّآ أَيَّامًا مَّعْدُودَٰتٍ وَغَرَّهُمْ فِى دِينِهِم مَّا كَانُواْ يَفْتَرُونَ ۞

How, then, will it be with them when We shall gather them all together to witness the Day about which there is no doubt, when every soul will be paid in full what it has earned, and they shall not be wronged? (25)

فَكَيْفَ إِذَا جَمَعْنَٰهُمْ لِيَوْمٍ لَّا رَيْبَ فِيهِ وَوُفِّيَتْ كُلُّ نَفْسٍ مَّا كَسَبَتْ وَهُمْ لَا يُظْلَمُونَ ۞

Say: "Lord, Sovereign of all dominion, You grant dominion to whom You will and take dominion away from whom You will. You exalt whom You will and abase whom You will. In Your hand is all that is good. You are able to do all things. (26)

قُلِ ٱللَّهُمَّ مَٰلِكَ ٱلْمُلْكِ تُؤْتِي ٱلْمُلْكَ مَن تَشَآءُ وَتَنزِعُ ٱلْمُلْكَ مِمَّن تَشَآءُ وَتُعِزُّ مَن تَشَآءُ وَتُذِلُّ مَن تَشَآءُ بِيَدِكَ ٱلْخَيْرُ إِنَّكَ عَلَىٰ كُلِّ شَيْءٍ قَدِيرٌ ٢٦

"You cause the night to pass into the day, and You cause the day to pass into the night. You bring forth the living from the dead, and You bring forth the dead from that which is alive. You grant sustenance to whom You will, beyond all reckoning." (27)

تُولِجُ ٱلَّيْلَ فِي ٱلنَّهَارِ وَتُولِجُ ٱلنَّهَارَ فِي ٱلَّيْلِ وَتُخْرِجُ ٱلْحَيَّ مِنَ ٱلْمَيِّتِ وَتُخْرِجُ ٱلْمَيِّتَ مِنَ ٱلْحَيِّ وَتَرْزُقُ مَن تَشَآءُ بِغَيْرِ حِسَابٍ ٢٧

Let not the believers take unbelievers for their allies in preference to the believers. He who does this has cut himself off from God, unless it be that you protect yourselves against them in this way. God warns you to beware of Him: for to God you shall all return. (28)

لَّا يَتَّخِذِ ٱلْمُؤْمِنُونَ ٱلْكَٰفِرِينَ أَوْلِيَآءَ مِن دُونِ ٱلْمُؤْمِنِينَ وَمَن يَفْعَلْ ذَٰلِكَ فَلَيْسَ مِنَ ٱللَّهِ فِي شَيْءٍ إِلَّا أَن تَتَّقُوا۟ مِنْهُمْ تُقَىٰةً وَيُحَذِّرُكُمُ ٱللَّهُ نَفْسَهُ وَإِلَى ٱللَّهِ ٱلْمَصِيرُ ٢٨

Say: "Whether you conceal what is in your hearts or bring it into the open, it is known to God. He knows all that is in the heavens and all that is on earth; and God has the power to accomplish anything. (29)

قُلْ إِن تُخْفُوا۟ مَا فِي صُدُورِكُمْ أَوْ تُبْدُوهُ يَعْلَمْهُ ٱللَّهُ وَيَعْلَمُ مَا فِي ٱلسَّمَٰوَٰتِ وَمَا فِي ٱلْأَرْضِ وَٱللَّهُ عَلَىٰ كُلِّ شَيْءٍ قَدِيرٌ ٢٩

"On the day when every soul will find itself confronted with whatever good it has done and whatever evil it has done, they will wish that there were a long span of time between them and that Day. God warns you to beware of Him; and God is Most Compassionate towards His servants." (30)

يَوْمَ تَجِدُ كُلُّ نَفْسٍ مَّا عَمِلَتْ مِنْ خَيْرٍ مُّحْضَرًا وَمَا عَمِلَتْ مِن سُوٓءٍ تَوَدُّ لَوْ أَنَّ بَيْنَهَا وَبَيْنَهُۥٓ أَمَدَۢا بَعِيدًا وَيُحَذِّرُكُمُ ٱللَّهُ نَفْسَهُۥ وَٱللَّهُ رَءُوفٌۢ بِٱلْعِبَادِ ﴿٣٠﴾

Say: "If you love God, follow me; God will love you and forgive you your sins. God is Much-Forgiving, Merciful." (31)

قُلْ إِن كُنتُمْ تُحِبُّونَ ٱللَّهَ فَٱتَّبِعُونِي يُحْبِبْكُمُ ٱللَّهُ وَيَغْفِرْ لَكُمْ ذُنُوبَكُمْ وَٱللَّهُ غَفُورٌ رَّحِيمٌ ﴿٣١﴾

Say: "Obey God and the messenger." If they turn their backs, God does not love the unbelievers. (32)

قُلْ أَطِيعُوا۟ ٱللَّهَ وَٱلرَّسُولَ فَإِن تَوَلَّوْا۟ فَإِنَّ ٱللَّهَ لَا يُحِبُّ ٱلْكَٰفِرِينَ ﴿٣٢﴾

Overview

God Himself bears witness, and so do the angels and men of knowledge, that there is no deity save Him, the Executor of Justice. There is no deity save Him, the Almighty, the Wise. (Verse 18)

So far the *sūrah* has concentrated mainly on establishing the basic fact of the oneness of God, the Lord and sustainer of the whole universe, Who controls all its affairs. It has also emphasised the unity of the Divine revelation and message. It has described the attitudes of the true believers, and those whose hearts have swerved from the truth, towards God's revelations and His book. It has also threatened the deviants with a doom similar to that which befell those who denied the truth both in the past and in the present. It has further pointed out the natural motives which prevent people from learning these lessons, showing at the same time how the God-fearing turn to their Lord and seek His refuge.

Beginning with verse 18 and continuing up to verse 32, the *sūrah* now speaks of another fact which logically results from the preceding one. The fact that God is One and has no partners requires practical confirmation in human life and this is clearly stated in this passage of the *sūrah*.

The passage begins with a reiteration of the fact stated in the opening verses of the *sūrah* in order to outline its essential consequences. We have here a testimony from God, as well as a testimony from the angels and the people of knowledge that *"there is no deity save Him."* Added to this is the Divine attribute which results from the fact that He is the Sustainer of the universe, that is, He maintains justice among people and in the universe at large.

We are required to accept this basic fact of God being the only Lord and Sustainer of the whole universe. Our acceptance is manifested primarily by our submitting ourselves to God alone and referring to Him in all matters. It is further manifested by obeying God, our Eternal Master, and following His messenger and implementing His revelations in our lives.

This is the purport of the Divine Statement: *"The only true faith acceptable to God is [man's] self-surrender to Him."* (Verse 19) He does not accept any other religion or creed from anyone. Islam means willing submission, obedience and conscious following of the Prophet. This means that the religion which God accepts from people is not merely a concept formulated in their minds, nor is it the mere acceptance of a fact. It is, indeed, the practical translation of this acceptance and that concept. It takes the form of implementing the Divine method in all our affairs, total obedience to all God's laws, and following the guidance of His messenger in His implementation of the Divine Faith.

The passage then moves on to publicise the attitude of the people of earlier revelations, wondering at them. Despite their claim that they follow God's religion, some of them turn away when they are invited to put their disputes forward to be adjudged according to God's revelations. Their whole claim is thus rendered baseless. God accepts no religion other than Islam, and Islam means true submission to God, obedience to His Prophet and the implementation of His revelations in all spheres of life.

We are then told of the real reason for their turning away, which actually means that they do not believe in the Divine religion. That is, they do not take seriously the concept of reckoning and reward on the Day of Judgement: *"For they claim: 'The fire will most certainly not touch us except for a limited number of days.'"* (Verse 24) In this, they rely on their belief that they are followers of a Divine book: *"They are deceived in their own faith by the false beliefs they used to invent."* (Verse 24) Their whole notion is a false delusion. They are neither followers of a Divine book nor are they believers. They have nothing whatsoever to do with the Divine faith, since they are being invited to put their disputes to the judgement of Divine revelations, but they continue to turn away. In such absolute clarity, God states in the Qur'ān the meaning of religion and the true nature of being religious. He accepts from His servants only one clear view: namely, the true religion is Islam, which means self-surrender. In practice, Islam means to consider God's book as the final arbiter and to accept its judgement. Anyone who does not do this in practice cannot be considered a Muslim, even though he may claim to be so or may claim to follow God's religion. It is God who defines and explains His own religion. His definition and explanation does not take into account the desires or personal concepts of human beings.

Indeed, the one who takes the unbelievers, i.e. those who do not accept the judgement of God's book and revelations, as patrons, *"He who does this has cut himself off from God."* (Verse 28) There is absolutely no relationship between him and God. This applies to those who patronise and support or seek the patronage or support of the unbelievers who reject the judgement of Divine revelations, even though they may claim to follow God's religion.

The warning against such patronage which destroys faith altogether is further elaborated upon. The Muslim community is also made aware of the true nature of the forces which operate in the universe. God has absolute control over it; He owns it all, and gives kingship to whom He wills and deprives of it whom He wills. It is He Who gives honour to, or causes to sink in contempt, whom He wills. This is only part of the fact that He controls the whole universe and runs it as He wishes. It is He Who causes the night to overwhelm the day and then causes the day to overpower the night. It is He Who makes life come from death and causes death to end life. He thus maintains justice in human life and in the universe at large. There is no need, then, for the patronage of anyone else, no matter how powerful or wealthy they are.

These repeated, emphatic warnings give us an insight into what was actually taking place within the Muslim community at that time and about which matters needed further clarification. Some Muslims still maintained their family, national and economic relations with the unbelievers in Makkah or with the Jews in Madinah. Hence, the need for this explanation and warning. The repeated warnings also suggest that human nature is normally influenced by the physical power of human beings. Hence, people need to be reminded of the true nature of human power and real power. This needs to be added to the clear explanation of the correct concept of faith and its practical effects in life.

The passage concludes with a decisive statement that Islam means true obedience to God and His Messenger. The way to win God's pleasure is simply to follow His Messenger. God's love cannot be earned by the mere mental acceptance of His existence, nor simply by any verbal acknowledgement of that: *"Say: 'If you love God, follow me. God will love you and forgive you your sins. God is Much-Forgiving, Merciful.' Say: 'Obey God and the messenger.' If they turn their backs, God does not love the unbelievers."* (Verses 31–2) The issues then are very clear: either obedience and conscious following of the Prophet, which is what God likes, or rejection of the faith, which is what God dislikes. There can be no meeting point between the two.

Let us now look in more detail at the significance of this passage starting with verse 18.

The Ultimate Witness

God Himself bears witness, and so do the angels and men of knowledge, that there is no deity save Him, the Executor of Justice. There is no deity save Him, the Almighty, the Wise. (Verse 18)

We have here a statement of the most essential facet of Islamic ideology, namely the fact of the oneness of God and that He is the Eternal Master of the universe Who maintains and executes justice. It is the same principle with which this *sūrah* opens: *"God: there is no deity save Him, the Ever-living, the Eternal Master of all."* The ultimate objective of this *sūrah* is to establish in absolute clarity the true nature of the Islamic faith, and to dispel all doubts about it raised by people of earlier revelations. It seeks to dispel such doubts both from the minds of those unbelievers as also from the minds of those Muslims who may fall under their influence.

A testimony from God that there is no deity other than Him is sufficient for anyone who believes in God. Indeed, such a testimony may be thought sufficient only for a believer in God, for he is not in need of it as such. However, this is not absolutely true. People of earlier revelations believe in God, but at the same time they maintain that He has a son and a partner. The idolaters themselves used to profess that they believed in God. Their deviation and error took the form of ascribing partners and equals and children to God. When both groups of people are told that God Himself bears witness to the fact that there is no deity save Him, then this statement has a marked effect in correcting their beliefs.

The matter, however, is much finer and more profound. God's testimony that there is no deity except Him is given here as a prelude to outlining what it entails. Since He Himself stresses His oneness, He, therefore, does not accept from His servants anything other than pure devotion to Him, which takes the form of Islam or submission to Him. Such submission is not confined to the realm of beliefs and feelings; it must be translated into total obedience to God and a conscious implementation of His law outlined in His revelations. If we view the matter from this angle, we will find many people in all ages claiming to believe in God but at the same time ascribing Divinity to others. This they do when they implement a law which is in conflict with His law, and obey those who do not follow His messenger or His book, and when they derive their values, standards and morals from sources other than Him. All such actions run contrary to their claim that they believe in God. They conflict with God's own testimony that He is the only God in the universe.

The testimony of the angels and the people of knowledge takes the form of their total obedience to God's orders and looking to Him alone for guidance, accepting everything which comes to them from Him without doubt or argument, once they are certain that it has come from Him. This *sūrah* has already referred to the attitude of such people of knowledge: *"Those who are firmly grounded in knowledge say: 'We believe in it; it is all from our Lord.'"* This is, then, the testimony of the people of knowledge and the angels: total acceptance, obedience and submission.

The testimony of God, the angels and the men of knowledge to the oneness of God is coupled with their testimony to the fact that He establishes and maintains justice, since justice is an essential quality of Godhead. The Arabic text is phrased in such a way as to leave no doubt that justice, at all times and in all situations, is an attribute of God. This also explains the meaning of God being the Eternal Master of the universe which is stated at the beginning of this *sūrah*: *"God: there is no deity save Him, the Ever-living, the Eternal Master of all."* He maintains His authority with justice.

God's control of the universe and His conduct of its affairs and of people's lives is always characterised by justice. Indeed, justice cannot be established in human life, which, in turn, cannot be set on its proper course as the rest of the universe where every single creature fulfils its function in perfect harmony with the rest of creation except through the implementation of the method and the way of life God has chosen for people, as outlined in His revelation. Otherwise, justice cannot be established, harmony cannot be achieved and there can be no interrelation between man and the universe. What takes place, then, is injustice, conflict and total ruin.

Throughout history, justice was established only during those periods when God's method was adhered to. These were the times when human life was set on a perfect and straight course like everything else in the universe. However, human nature being what it is means that human beings tend to waver between obedience and disobedience to God. They move nearer to obedience to God whenever His method is established and His law is implemented. Wherever man-made laws are established, ignorance and shortcomings abound. A direct consequence of this is injustice in one form or another: an individual may do injustice to the community, or the community may be unjust to the individual, or one class tyrannises another, or one nation subjugates another, or one generation treats another with injustice. It is only Divine justice which remains free of any favouritism towards any of these. He is the Lord of all creation Who does not overlook anything on earth or in the heavens.

"There is no deity save Him, the Almighty, the Wise." The same truism of the Oneness of God is repeated again in the same verse, but this time it is coupled with the two attributes of God's might and wisdom. Both power and wisdom are essential for the purpose of maintaining justice. Justice can only be maintained when matters are set in their

proper places and with the ability to so set them. God's attributes suggest positive activity. Nothing in the Islamic concept associates God with any negative attribute. This is the proper and true concept of the Divine Being, because it is His own description of Himself. When we believe in God, in the light of His positive attributes, our thoughts remain concentrated on His will and His power. Our faith, then, becomes much more than an academic concept; it provides us with a dynamic motive to act and do what is required of us.

> *The only true faith acceptable to God is [man's] self-surrender to Him. Disagreements spread, through mutual aggression, among those who were given revelations only after knowledge had been granted to them. He who denies God's revelations will find that God is indeed swift in reckoning. If they argue with you, say: "I have surrendered my whole being to God, and so have all who follow me." Say to those who were given revelations and to unlettered people, "Will you also surrender yourselves (to God)?" If they surrender, they are on the right path. But if they turn away, then your only duty is to convey your message. God is watching over His servants. (Verses 19–20)*

The *sūrah* now moves on to establish the logical result that since there is only one God, then all worship must be addressed to that one God: *"The only true faith acceptable to God is [man's] self-surrender to Him."*

The oneness of the Divine Being requires that all submission must be to Him. There is nothing in people's minds or in their lives which is not subject to God's authority. The oneness of God means that there is only One Being who has the right to set values and standards for people, to require them to submit to Him, obey Him, implement the legislation He has enacted for them in all the affairs of their lives. There is only one faith, namely, pure submission to God alone, which is acceptable to Him.

When we state that the only true faith acceptable to God is self-surrender to Him, we mean true Islam. This is not merely a claim to be stated, a flag to be raised or a detached academic concept to be discussed which does not stir hearts or minds, or even a set of acts of worship such as Prayer, fasting and pilgrimage. This is not the sort of Islam which God describes as the only faith acceptable to Him. True Islam means complete obedience, total submission to God and the implementation of His revelations in human life, as will be stated presently in the same Qurʾānic text.

Islam also means the oneness of the Divine Being who is the Eternal Master of all. People of earlier revelations used to confuse the person of God and the person of Jesus Christ. They also confused God's will and that of Christ's. They disagreed among themselves so violently that they fought and killed one another on numerous occasions. God, therefore, makes the reasons for these disputes clear for both the people of earlier revelations and for the Muslim community: *"Disagreements spread, through mutual aggression, among those who were given revelations only after knowledge had been granted to them."*

Their disputes did not arise out of ignorance of the truth. They had been given certain knowledge of God's oneness and the fact that He is the only Lord in the universe. They were also given the knowledge they needed about human nature and true submission to God. They simply disagreed *"through mutual aggression"* when they abandoned the course of justice embodied in the faith and the law God revealed to them.

Christian historians have shown that political considerations were behind these doctrinal disputes. The same has frequently happened in both Jewish and Christian histories. It was the hatred felt by Egypt, Syria and other regions towards the rulers of Rome which resulted in the rejection of the official Roman doctrine and the adoption of a different one. On certain occasions, the keenness of a Byzantine Emperor to maintain his rule over certain parts of his empire was the reason behind the invention of compromise doctrines which sought to achieve the required results. Faith to them was a ball game serving political goals. As such, it represented one of the worst forms of injustice. Worse still, it was done knowingly and deliberately.

A timely and appropriately stern warning is then given: *"He who denies God's revelations will find that God is indeed swift in reckoning."* Disagreement over the truism of the oneness of God is thus considered a denial and rejection of God's revelations. The rejecters are here threatened with swift reckoning in order that people do not persist with their disbelief, denials and disputes.

God then instructs the Prophet to make his attitude towards the people of earlier revelations and the idolaters well known. The real issue is stated in absolute clarity. Their fate is left to God. The Prophet, however, proceeds along his absolutely clear path: *"But if they argue with you, say: 'I have surrendered my whole being to God, and so have all who follow me.' Say to those who were given revelations and to unlettered people, 'Will you also surrender yourselves (to God)? If they surrender, they are on the right path. But if they turn away, then your only duty is to convey your message. God is watching over His servants.'*

Thereafter, there can be no further clarification. Either God's oneness and authority over the universe is acknowledged with its practical correlative which is pure submission to Him, or futile arguments and excuses are pursued.

God teaches His Messenger a single word which explains his faith and way of life: *"If they argue with you,"* in matters of faith and the oneness of God, *"say: 'I have surrendered my whole being to God.'"* This applies to me and also to *"all who follow me."* The usage here of the word *"follow"* is very significant. What is required is not a mere acceptance of the Prophet's message, but also its following in practice. Similarly, the phrase *"surrendered my whole being to God"* is highly significant. It is not sufficient for one to just state verbally or accept in one's mind the fact of the oneness of God. One must also surrender one's whole being to God. Practically this means obeying God and following His Messenger. Literally translated, the Arabic phrase says: "I have submitted my face to God." Since one's face is the noblest part of a human being, then its submission indicates willing acceptance and implementation of God's laws.

Such is, then, the faith of Muḥammad, God's Messenger, and such is his way of life. Muslims follow him in their faith and code of living. Let the people of earlier revelations and unlettered people, which is a reference to the idolaters, answer the question which is aimed at identifying each group in such a way as leaves no room for confusion about their stance: *"Say to those who were given revelations and to unlettered people, 'Will you also surrender yourselves (to God)?'"* Both the idolaters and the people of earlier revelations are placed on the same level since they are all called upon to accept Islam in the sense we have just explained. They are called upon to acknowledge the oneness of God and that He is the only Master of the whole universe. They are also required, when they have made this acknowledgement, to make it a practical reality through the implementation of God's revelations in human life.

"If they surrender, they are on the right path." Right guidance has only one form, namely, Islam in its fullest meaning. There is simply

no other form, concept, situation, or code which reflects right guidance. Anything which is in conflict with Islam represents error, ignorance, confusion and rejection of the truth.

"But if they turn away, then your only duty is to convey your message." The Prophet's task is simply to convey his message. When he has done this, his mission is over. This applied before God commanded the Prophet to fight those who rejected Islam until they either accepted its faith and submitted to it, or until they pledged their obedience to its political authority by paying a loyalty tax. No one is compelled to accept the faith.

"God is watching over His servants." He conducts all their affairs as He wishes and according to His knowledge. The ultimate decision is with Him. However, they are made fully aware of the fate that awaits them and all transgressors who, like them, reject the true faith.

When Prophets Are Killed

Those who deny God's revelations, and slay the Prophets against all right and slay people who enjoin equity among all people: promise them a painful suffering. It is they whose works shall come to nothing in this world and in the life to come; and they shall have none to help them. Have you considered the case of those who have received a share of revelation? When they are called upon to accept the judgement of God's book in their affairs, some of them turn away and pay no heed. For they claim: "The fire will most certainly not touch us save for a limited number of days." They are deceived in their own faith by the false beliefs they used to invent. How, then, will it be with them when We shall gather them all together to witness the Day about which there is no doubt, when every soul will be paid in full what it has earned, and they shall not be wronged? (Verses 21–5)

The first verse in the above passage, verse 21, warns against a painful suffering. Its timing is not specified. Hence, it is to be expected either in this life or in the life to come. It is coupled with an assurance that all their works shall come to nothing in either life. This is given in a highly vivid mode of expression which draws upon a well-known image of an animal grazing in a poisoned area. It swells up before it dies. Similarly, the actions of such people may appear to gather momentum and to yield great results. This is no more than the swelling up of a poisoned animal prior to its death. All their actions are thus aborted and they will have no one to help or defend them.

We note that the denial and rejection of God's revelation is coupled in the Qur'ānic statement with the totally unjust killing of the Prophets – for there can be no right respected when a Prophet is killed. Furthermore, the killing of those who enjoin equity in human life, which is a reference to those who advocate the implementation of the code God has laid down for human life, which is based on justice and which alone can maintain absolute justice, suggests that the warning is directed at the Jews, for such are their distinctive qualities in history. This does not mean that the warning is not also directed to Christians who in the past killed many thousands of followers of doctrines which were at variance with that adopted by the Roman Empire, including those who declared that God was One and that Jesus Christ was a human being. This latter group are included among those *"who enjoin equity among all people."* It is also a permanent warning to anyone who may perpetrate such ghastly crimes, and these may live in any and every age.

It is worth remembering that when the expression *"those who deny God's revelations"* is mentioned in the Qur'ān, it does not simply refer to those who may declare themselves to be unbelievers. Instead, anyone who does not acknowledge the oneness of God and that He alone is worthy of worship is included in this group. Such a recognition entails that the authority to legislate and to set values and standards for human life belongs only to God. Anyone who claims or attributes any measure of that authority to anyone other than God is either an idolater or an unbeliever, even though he may claim a thousand times that he believes in God. The verses which follow confirm this view.

"Have you considered the case of those who have received a share of revelation? When they are called upon to accept the judgement of God's book in their affairs, some of them turn away and pay no heed." This is clearly a rhetorical question, one so delivered as to emphasise the contradiction in the attitudes of those who have received a share of revelation. The reference here is to the Torah in respect of the Jews and the Bible in respect of the Christians. Each one is simply *"a share"* of God's Divine revelation, a portion of all the revelations God has vouchsafed to His messengers, which emphasises the unity of Godhead, and the fact that God alone conducts the affairs of the universe. All

such revelations are in essence a single book; part of it was given to the Jews, and another part was given to the Christians while the Muslims received the whole book. This is because the Qur'ān embodies all the bases of faith and confirms all messages God revealed in the past. It is certainly something to wonder at, when those who *"have received a share of revelation"* are called upon to accept the judgement of God's book in their disputes and in all the affairs of their lives, but they nevertheless do not respond positively. Some of them are left behind. They turn their backs on God's legislation, an action that is in flagrant contradiction to their stated belief in any portion of His book. In other words, it belies their claim that they follow God's revelations: *"Have you considered the case of those who have received a share of revelation? When they are called upon to accept the judgement of God's book in their affairs, some of them turn away and pay no heed."* (Verse 23)

God invites us to wonder at the people of earlier revelations when some of them, not all, refuse to allow God's book to judge in their affairs of both faith and life. What, then, should our attitude be towards those who claim to be Muslims, but who nevertheless banish God's law from their lives, while they continue to claim to be Muslim? This is, indeed, an example given by God so that Muslims should know the true nature of faith, generally, and Islam, in particular. They must be careful lest they themselves become subject to God's condemnation for their attitude. If God Himself so denounces the attitude of the people of earlier revelations who did not claim to be Muslims simply because they refused to accept the judgement of God's book in their affairs, what degree of denunciation or condemnation would be suitable for Muslims who adopt a similar attitude? There is no doubt that they would incur God's anger, be totally rejected by God and live in utter misery, deprived of Divine Mercy in any form.

The cause of their contradictory, erroneous attitude is then given: *"For they claim: 'The fire will most certainly not touch us save for a limited number of days.' They are deceived in their own faith by the false beliefs they used to invent."*

This, then, is the reason for people turning their backs on the judgement of God's book. It places them in total contradiction with their claim to be believers or followers of Divine revelation. They simply do not take seriously the notion of reckoning on the Day of Judgement. Nor do they consider as serious the administration of

Divine justice. The import of their claim is that they will not suffer the fire except for a limited number of days. How is this possible when they deviate from the most fundamental principle of faith which imposes on them the duty to accept the judgement of the Divine book in all matters? How can they make such a claim if they truly believe in God's justice, or even if they feel that they will definitely be raised to God on the Day of Judgement? What they state is simply an invention which they themselves perpetrate, and by which they are then deceived: *"They are deceived in their own faith by the false beliefs they used to invent."*

It is indeed a fact that believing seriously in meeting God cannot be combined with such a futile notion in respect to His justice and reward. No man can combine fear of God and punishment on the Day of Judgement with turning his back on God's rulings outlined in His book or the implementation of His law in human life.

These people of earlier revelations stand in the same position as those whom we meet today who claim to be Muslims but who turn their backs when they are called upon to implement God's laws in their lives. Some of them even go further than this and impudently claim that human life has nothing to do with religion. They say that there is no need to impose religion on the practical side of human life, or on economic, social, and indeed family relations. They, nevertheless, continue their claim to be Muslims. Some of them are so naïve that they believe that God's punishment will be limited to purifying them of their sins only and that thereafter they will be admitted into heaven. They ask in absolute naïvety: "Are we not Muslims?" It is the same false belief which was maintained by such people of earlier revelations. They show the same conceit and they deceive themselves with the same false beliefs which have no foundation in the religion God has revealed. Both groups are the same in their rejection of the very basics of faith and in their isolation from its fundamental practical expression, namely, submission to God and total obedience to His commands in all affairs of life, which they receive through His messengers.

> *How, then, will it be with them when We shall gather them all together to witness the Day about which there is no doubt, when every soul will be paid in full what it has earned, and they shall not be wronged?* (Verse 25)

How? This is a very stern warning which every believer shudders to face since he knows that that Day will inevitably come and that God's justice is certain to be done. That belief is in no way weakened by any false hopes or invented beliefs. This warning applies to all: idolaters and atheists, those who claim to follow earlier revelations and those who claim to be Muslims. They are all alike in the essential fact that they do not submit to God in their lives.

"How, then, will it be with them when We shall gather them all together to witness the Day about which there is no doubt," and when God's justice is done? *"Every soul will be paid in full what it has earned,"* without any injustice or favouritism. *"They shall not be wronged,"* nor shall they receive any favours.

It is a question which remains without answer. Man's heart shakes when it imagines what will happen.

What God's Sovereignty Entails

Say: "Lord, Sovereign of all dominion, You grant dominion to whom You will and take dominion away from whom You will. You exalt whom You will and abase whom You will. In Your hand is all that is good. You are able to do all things. You cause the night to pass into the day, and You cause the day to pass into the night. You bring forth the living from the dead, and You bring forth the dead from that which is alive. You grant sustenance to whom You will, beyond all reckoning." (Verses 26–7)

These verses take the form of a direct instruction from God to His Messenger and every believer to turn to God, stating the absolute truth of the oneness of God and that He is the only One Who controls human life and the universe at large. This latter quality is simply a demonstration of God's Lordship of the whole universe in which He has no equals or partners.

When we carry out this instruction we note that it takes the form of an address made with all humility. The rhythm of a prayer is very clear in its construction, and its total effect is that of a heartfelt appeal. Its references to the universe as an open book touch gently on our feelings. It groups together God's conduct of human life and His full control of the universe, thus stressing the absolute truth of a single Godhead sustaining all. It also stresses the fact that human life is but one ingredient in the life of the universe. Submission to God alone is acknowledged by the universe, as it is indeed the proper attitude expected of man. Any deviation is a folly which leads to perversion.

"Say: 'Lord, Sovereign of all dominion, You grant dominion to whom You will and take dominion away from whom You will. You exalt whom you will and abase whom You will.'" This expresses the natural result of the oneness of God. Since there is only a single deity, He is then the only Master, *"the Sovereign of all dominion"* Who has no partners. He gives whatever portion He wishes of His dominion to whomever He wants of His servants. What is given becomes simply like a borrowed article. Its owner retains his absolute right of taking it back whenever he wants. No one, then, has any claim of original dominion giving him the right of absolute power. It is simply a received dominion, subject to the terms and conditions stipulated by the original Sovereign. If the recipient behaves in any way which constitutes a violation of these conditions, his action is invalid. Believers have a duty to stop him from that violation in this life. In the life to come, he will have to account for his violation of the terms stipulated by the original Sovereign.

He is also the One Who exalts whom He wills and abases whom He wills. He needs no one to ratify His judgement. No one grants protection against the will of God, and no one has the power to prevent His will taking its full course. His power is absolute and His control is total.

The authority of God ensures the realisation of all goodness. He exercises it with justice. When He gives dominion to anyone or takes it away from him, He does so with justice. Similarly, it is with justice that He exalts or abases any of His servants. This ensures real goodness, in all situations. It is sufficient that He should will something for it to be realised: *"In Your hand is all that is good. You are able to do all things."*

God's supervision of the affairs of human beings with all that is good resulting from it is simply an aspect of His control and supervision of life in general and of the universe at large: *"You cause the night to pass into the day, and You cause the day to pass into the night. You bring forth the living from the dead, and You bring forth the dead from that which is alive. You grant sustenance to whom You will, beyond all reckoning."* In this way verse 27 refers to great universal phenomena and paints them in a manner which overwhelms man's whole being: his heart, feelings and senses. It paints a subtle interwoven movement whereby each of the day and night enter into the other, and whereby the living are brought out of the dead and the dead out of the living. When man gives his full attention to the observation of this movement and listens to the voice of uncorrupted human nature identifying its origin, he is bound to conclude, with all certainty, that it is God Who controls it and makes it possible.

Some commentators explain that what is meant by the night and day passing into each other is that each of them takes part of the other when one of the four seasons succeeds another. Others believe that it refers to each of them creeping into the other with the first shades of darkness every evening and the first rays of light every morning. Whichever explanation we prefer, our hearts can almost visualise God's hand as it works in the universe wrapping one ball in darkness and opening another to daylight, reversing one position into another. We can see the dark lines gradually creeping into the light of day, and we can see the dawn slowly beginning to breathe, with the darkness all around. The night stretches little by little as it gains more and more of the hours of day at the beginning of winter, and the day stretches little by little, gaining on the night, as summer approaches. No man ever claims to control either movement with its fine subtleties. No rational person can ever claim that either movement happens by chance.

The same applies to the cycle of life and death: each creeps into the other very slowly and gradually. Every single minute death creeps into every living thing so as to be side by side with life. Death works into a living being and life builds up. Living cells die and disappear, while new living cells come into existence and begin their work. Those cells which have died come back to life in a different cycle, and what comes into life dies again in yet another cycle. All this happens within every single living thing. The circle, however, becomes wider and the living thing dies. Its cells, however, become minute particles which are incorporated in another formula, then enter the body of another living being and come back to life. It is an ever continuing cycle which goes on throughout the day and night. No man claims to control or do any part of this whole process. No rational person can claim that it comes about by chance.

It is a complete cycle which goes on within the whole universe and within every living thing. It is a fine, subtle and, at the same time, great cycle brought about before our own eyes and minds by this brief Qur'ānic statement. It is a strong pointer to the One Who is able to create, plan and control. How can human beings, then, try to isolate themselves and their affairs from the Creator Who controls and plans everything? How can they devise for themselves systems which satisfy their own whims when they are only a sector of this universe, regulated by the Wise Who knows all?

How can some of them enslave others? How can some look at others as gods when all of them look to God for their own sustenance: *"You grant sustenance to whom You will, beyond all reckoning."*

This final touch puts our human hearts face to face with the greatest truism of the oneness of God: there is only one deity Who controls, sustains, plans, owns and grants sustenance to all. People must submit only to the Eternal Master of all, the Sovereign of all dominion, Who exalts and abases, gives life and causes death, Who gives His grace to whom He wills and withdraws it from whom He wills. In every situation He ensures justice and brings about what is good.

An Unwelcome Confrontation

Let not the believers take unbelievers for their allies in preference to the believers. He who does this has cut himself off from God, unless it be that you protect yourselves against them in this way. God warns you to beware of Him: for to God you shall all return. Say: "Whether you conceal what is in your hearts or bring it into the open, it is known to God. He knows all that is in the heavens and all that is on earth; and God has the power to accomplish anything. On the day when every soul will find itself confronted with whatever good it has done and whatever evil it has done, they will wish that there were a long span of time between them and that day. God warns you to beware of Him; and God is Most Compassionate towards His servants." Say: "If you love God, follow me; God will love you and forgive you your sins. God is Much-Forgiving, Merciful." Say: "Obey God and the messenger." If they turn their backs, God does not love the unbelievers. (Verses 28–32)

In these verses, we have first a statement confirming the denunciation made in the preceding verses of the attitude of those who have been given a share of God's revelations, but who have nevertheless turned their backs and refused to submit their disputes for arbitration according to God's book which lays down God's code for human life. They have rejected the Divine code which regulates the life of the universe as well as human life. The preceding verses were also a prelude to the stern warning included in the current passage against the believers forging an alliance with the unbelievers. Since the unbelievers have no power to control the universe, and since all power belongs to God, He alone is the guardian of the believers and their allies.

In the preceding passage, the *surah* placed much emphasis on the fact that all power belongs to God, Who is in absolute control of the universe and Who alone provides sustenance to all His creation. How, then, can a believer be justified in forming an alliance with the enemies of God? True faith in God cannot be combined with an alliance with, or patronage of the enemies of God, who are themselves called upon to implement God's revelations, but who instead turn their backs in contempt.

Hence, we have this very stern warning in verse 28, making it absolutely clear that a Muslim disowns Islam if he forges a relationship of alliance or patronage with someone who refuses to acknowledge God's revelation as the arbiter in life: *"Let not the believers take unbelievers for their allies in preference to the believers. He who does this has cut himself off from God."* What a decisive statement! He has cut himself off from God. He has no relationship whatsoever with Him: no faith, no tie, no support. He never comes near to God nor has any contact with Him whatsoever.

Concessions are only granted to those who find themselves in a state of fear. Such people may try to protect themselves by pretending to support the unbelievers, but this must be understood to be only a verbal support given for a specific purpose. It cannot be an expression of any firmly established alliance or deeply rooted love. Ibn 'Abbās says: "The concession here must not be understood as to seek protection through acting in support of unbelievers; it must be limited only to verbal statements." There is no concession whatsoever for a relationship of love between a believer and an unbeliever. It is implied here and explicitly stated elsewhere in this *surah* that an unbeliever is a person who does not accept that God's revelation be implemented in all aspects of life. Nor does this concession permit a believer to aid an unbeliever, in any form or way, pretending that he only seeks to protect himself. God cannot be so deceived.

Since the case here is one of conscience and the control is exercised only through the fear of God, Who knows everything, the warning to the believer against God's punishment is given in a most unfamiliar mode of expression: *"God warns you to beware of Him: for to God you shall all return."*

A further warning is also driven home to man whereby he should be aware that God watches him and knows his every action and intention: *"Say: 'Whether you conceal what is in your hearts or bring it into the open, it is known to God. He knows all that is in the heavens and all that is on earth; and God has the power to accomplish anything.'"* (Verse 29) A real threat is implied here, one which arouses man's fear and makes him conscious that he must not make himself liable to God's punishment which is inflicted on the basis of His knowledge and ability, and hence, cannot be avoided or repelled.

The warning and threat are further amplified with an image of the Day of Judgement brought before our eyes. It is indeed a fearful day, when nothing escapes attention. Everyone will find a full and detailed account of all his actions and intentions: *"On the day when every soul will find itself confronted with whatever good it has done and whatever evil it has done, they will wish that there were a long span of time between them and that Day."* (Verse 30) This is a confrontation which leaves the human heart and mind totally overwhelmed. Every human being is cornered by both his good and evil actions. There is no escape. Hence, he inevitably entertains the wish that the confrontation could be long delayed. The confrontation is, however, actually taking place and this leaves any person totally helpless. It is important to point out that the original Arabic text admits two different interpretations regarding that wish; it may be taken to mean that every soul wishes that the day itself be far removed, and alternatively that everyone wishes that the evil they have done be placed far away from them.

The general warning to people to guard against incurring God's anger is repeated again, but this is coupled with a reminder of God's compassion and mercy. There is still a chance to take heed before it is too late: *"God warns you to beware of Him; and God is Most Compassionate towards His servants."* (Verse 30) These very warnings and reminders are indicative of His compassion and that He wants only what is good for His servants.

These verses are nothing short of a sustained campaign made in a variety of hues and expressions. It suggests that there was at the time a real danger facing the Muslim community in Madinah and involving relations between individuals in the Muslim camp and their relatives, friends, or clients who belonged to the idolaters in Makkah or the Jews in Madinah. Islam sought to lay down the foundations of the Muslim community on the basis of its supreme tie, i.e. faith. The way of life derived from that faith must be the only one to implement. No hesitation or second thoughts could be tolerated in this regard.

These verses also suggest that man will need to exert sustained efforts in order to rid himself of these pressures and shackles, in order to associate himself only with God, and to be committed only to the Divine way of life.

Islam does not restrain any of its followers from being kind to any non-Muslim who does not stand in opposition to Islam. The forging of alliances, however, is different from kind treatment. An alliance means a commitment of mutual support and loyalty. This cannot be given by any true believer except to believers who share with him his faith in God, adopt the Divine way of life and willingly accept the rulings embodied in His revelations in all their disputes.

The whole passage ends on a high note stating in absolute clarity the final verdict on the whole issue which is central to the *sūrah*. In just a few words, the essence of faith and submission are stated in such a way which admits of no confusion whatsoever between faith and unfaith: *"Say: 'If you love God, follow me; God will love you and forgive you your sins. God is Much-Forgiving, Merciful.' Say: 'Obey God and the messenger.' If they turn their backs, God does not love the unbelievers."* (Verses 31–2)

True love of God is not a mere verbal claim or a spiritual passion. The claim and the passion must be confirmed with a conscious following of God's Messenger and implementation of the Divine way of life. To be a true believer is not to repeat certain words or to experience certain feelings or to observe certain rituals. True faith is total obedience to God and His Messenger and a conscious implementation of the constitution conveyed to us through God's Messenger.

Imām Ibn Kathīr comments on the verse which states: *"Say: 'If you love God, follow me; God will love you and forgive you your sins. God is Much-Forgiving, Merciful.'"* He says: "This verse gives a verdict in the case of anyone who claims to love God but does not follow the way of life laid down by Prophet Muḥammad. His very claim is an absolute lie unless he follows the Muḥammadan legislation in all his actions and statements. This is endorsed by the authentic tradition of the Prophet (peace be upon him) which states: 'Anyone who does something which is not in conformity with this matter of ours will have it rejected.'"

In his commentary on the final verse, *"Say: 'Obey God and the messenger.' If they turn their backs, God does not love the unbelievers,"* Imām Ibn Kathīr says this verse indicates that to disobey God's Messenger is to reject the faith. God does not love anyone who may be described as an unbeliever, even though he may claim to love God.

In his well-known biography of the Prophet Muḥammad, Imām Ibn al-Qayyim writes: "There are well documented reports of many a person from among the people who follow other religions or idolaters who have admitted that the Prophet was a messenger from God and that whatever he said was the truth, but they nevertheless did not become Muslims by that mere admission. When we consider this fact we are bound to conclude that to be a Muslim is much more than the mere knowledge or even the admission of the truthfulness of the Prophet's message; that knowledge and admission must be combined with conscious obedience of the Prophet and the implementation of his religion in every aspect of life."

This faith of Islam has a distinctive component which is essential for its very existence, namely, obedience to God's law and following His Messenger and referring all disputes to God's book for arbitration. It is a fact which is derived from the faith in the Oneness of God as preached by Islam. It is the faith based on the oneness of the deity who alone has the right to impose his authority on people and provide them with the legislation to implement and set for them the values and standards to observe. Overall authority in human life and all its aspects belong to God alone in the same way as He alone has the absolute authority in the whole universe. After all, man represents only a small element of the great universe.

As we have seen, in these two opening passages of the *sūrah*, and indeed in its very first verse, this fact is stated in absolutely clear terms: *"God: there is no deity save Him, the Ever-living, the Eternal Master of all."* Anyone who wants to be a Muslim must recognise this fact and accept it. This is the only form of Islam acceptable to God, Who accepts no other faith.

3

The Birth and Prophethood
of Jesus (pbuh)

God raised Adam and Noah, and the House of Abraham and the House of 'Imrān above all mankind. (33)

۞ إِنَّ ٱللَّهَ ٱصْطَفَىٰٓ ءَادَمَ وَنُوحًا وَءَالَ إِبْرَٰهِيمَ وَءَالَ عِمْرَٰنَ عَلَى ٱلْعَٰلَمِينَ ﴿٣٣﴾

They were the offspring of one another. God hears all and knows all. (34)

ذُرِّيَّةَ بَعْضُهَا مِنۢ بَعْضٍ وَٱللَّهُ سَمِيعٌ عَلِيمٌ ﴿٣٤﴾

'Imrān's wife said: "My Lord, I vow to You that which is in my womb, to be devoted to Your service. Accept it from me. You alone are the One Who hears all and knows all." (35)

إِذْ قَالَتِ ٱمْرَأَتُ عِمْرَٰنَ رَبِّ إِنِّي نَذَرْتُ لَكَ مَا فِي بَطْنِي مُحَرَّرًا فَتَقَبَّلْ مِنِّيٓ إِنَّكَ أَنتَ ٱلسَّمِيعُ ٱلْعَلِيمُ ﴿٣٥﴾

When she had given birth she said: "My Lord, I have given birth to a female." – God well knew to what she would give birth. – "The male is not like the female. I have named her Mary and I seek Your protection for her and her offspring against Satan, the accursed." (36)

فَلَمَّا وَضَعَتْهَا قَالَتْ رَبِّ إِنِّي وَضَعْتُهَآ أُنثَىٰ وَٱللَّهُ أَعْلَمُ بِمَا وَضَعَتْ وَلَيْسَ ٱلذَّكَرُ كَٱلْأُنثَىٰ وَإِنِّي سَمَّيْتُهَا مَرْيَمَ وَإِنِّيٓ أُعِيذُهَا بِكَ وَذُرِّيَّتَهَا مِنَ ٱلشَّيْطَٰنِ ٱلرَّجِيمِ ﴿٣٦﴾

Her Lord graciously accepted her. He made her grow up a goodly child, and placed her in the care of Zachariah. Whenever Zachariah visited her in the sanctuary he found her provided with food. He would say: "Mary, where has this come to you from?" She would answer: "It is from God. God gives sustenance to whom He wills, beyond all reckoning." (37)

فَتَقَبَّلَهَا رَبُّهَا بِقَبُولٍ حَسَنٍ وَأَنبَتَهَا نَبَاتًا حَسَنًا وَكَفَّلَهَا زَكَرِيَّا كُلَّمَا دَخَلَ عَلَيْهَا زَكَرِيَّا ٱلْمِحْرَابَ وَجَدَ عِندَهَا رِزْقًا قَالَ يَٰمَرْيَمُ أَنَّىٰ لَكِ هَٰذَا قَالَتْ هُوَ مِنْ عِندِ ٱللَّهِ إِنَّ ٱللَّهَ يَرْزُقُ مَن يَشَآءُ بِغَيْرِ حِسَابٍ ۝

At that point, Zachariah prayed to his Lord, saying: "Lord, bestow on me, out of Your grace, goodly offspring. Indeed, You hear all prayers." (38)

هُنَالِكَ دَعَا زَكَرِيَّا رَبَّهُۥ قَالَ رَبِّ هَبْ لِى مِن لَّدُنكَ ذُرِّيَّةً طَيِّبَةً إِنَّكَ سَمِيعُ ٱلدُّعَآءِ ۝

Thereupon, the angels called out to him as he stood praying in the sanctuary: "God gives you the happy news of [the birth of] John, who shall confirm the truth of a word from God. He shall be noble, utterly chaste and a Prophet from among the righteous." (39)

فَنَادَتْهُ ٱلْمَلَٰٓئِكَةُ وَهُوَ قَآئِمٌ يُصَلِّى فِى ٱلْمِحْرَابِ أَنَّ ٱللَّهَ يُبَشِّرُكَ بِيَحْيَىٰ مُصَدِّقًۢا بِكَلِمَةٍ مِّنَ ٱللَّهِ وَسَيِّدًا وَحَصُورًا وَنَبِيًّا مِّنَ ٱلصَّٰلِحِينَ ۝

[Zachariah] said: "Lord, how can I have a son when old age has already overtaken me and my wife is barren?" He answered: "Thus it is. God does what He wills." (40)

قَالَ رَبِّ أَنَّىٰ يَكُونُ لِى غُلَٰمٌ وَقَدْ بَلَغَنِىَ ٱلْكِبَرُ وَٱمْرَأَتِى عَاقِرٌ قَالَ كَذَٰلِكَ ٱللَّهُ يَفْعَلُ مَا يَشَآءُ ۝

[Zachariah] said: "Lord, grant me a sign." He replied: "Your sign shall be that for three days you will not speak to people except by gestures. Remember your Lord unceasingly and glorify Him in the early hours of night and day." (41)

قَالَ رَبِّ ٱجْعَل لِّيٓ ءَايَةً قَالَ ءَايَتُكَ أَلَّا تُكَلِّمَ ٱلنَّاسَ ثَلَٰثَةَ أَيَّامٍ إِلَّا رَمْزًا وَٱذْكُر رَّبَّكَ كَثِيرًا وَسَبِّحْ بِٱلْعَشِيِّ وَٱلْإِبْكَٰرِ ﴿٤١﴾

The angels said: "Mary, God has chosen you and made you pure, and raised you above all the women of the world. (42)

وَإِذْ قَالَتِ ٱلْمَلَٰٓئِكَةُ يَٰمَرْيَمُ إِنَّ ٱللَّهَ ٱصْطَفَىٰكِ وَطَهَّرَكِ وَٱصْطَفَىٰكِ عَلَىٰ نِسَآءِ ٱلْعَٰلَمِينَ ﴿٤٢﴾

"Mary, remain truly devout to your Lord, prostrate yourself (to Him) and bow down with those who bow down in worship." (43)

يَٰمَرْيَمُ ٱقْنُتِي لِرَبِّكِ وَٱسْجُدِي وَٱرْكَعِي مَعَ ٱلرَّٰكِعِينَ ﴿٤٣﴾

This is an account of something which remained beyond the reach of your perception We now reveal to you. You were not present with them when they cast lots as to which of them should have charge of Mary; nor were you present when they contended about it with one another. (44)

ذَٰلِكَ مِنْ أَنۢبَآءِ ٱلْغَيْبِ نُوحِيهِ إِلَيْكَ وَمَا كُنتَ لَدَيْهِمْ إِذْ يُلْقُونَ أَقْلَٰمَهُمْ أَيُّهُمْ يَكْفُلُ مَرْيَمَ وَمَا كُنتَ لَدَيْهِمْ إِذْ يَخْتَصِمُونَ ﴿٤٤﴾

The angels said: "Mary, God sends you the happy news, through a word from Him, [of a son] whose name is the Christ, Jesus, son of Mary, honoured in this world and in the life to come, and shall be among those who are favoured by God. (45)

إِذْ قَالَتِ ٱلْمَلَٰٓئِكَةُ يَٰمَرْيَمُ إِنَّ ٱللَّهَ يُبَشِّرُكِ بِكَلِمَةٍ مِّنْهُ ٱسْمُهُ ٱلْمَسِيحُ عِيسَى ٱبْنُ مَرْيَمَ وَجِيهًا فِي ٱلدُّنْيَا وَٱلْءَاخِرَةِ وَمِنَ ٱلْمُقَرَّبِينَ ﴿٤٥﴾

He shall speak to people in his cradle, and as a grown man, and shall be of the righteous." (46)

وَيُكَلِّمُ ٱلنَّاسَ فِى ٱلۡمَهۡدِ وَكَهۡلٗا وَمِنَ ٱلصَّـٰلِحِينَ ﴿٤٦﴾

Said she: "My Lord! How can I have a son when no man has ever touched me?" [The angel] answered: "Thus it is. God creates what He wills. When He wills a thing to be, He only says to it 'Be', and it is. (47)

قَالَتۡ رَبِّ أَنَّىٰ يَكُونُ لِى وَلَدٞ وَلَمۡ يَمۡسَسۡنِى بَشَرٞۖ قَالَ كَذَٰلِكِ ٱللَّهُ يَخۡلُقُ مَا يَشَآءُۚ إِذَا قَضَىٰٓ أَمۡرٗا فَإِنَّمَا يَقُولُ لَهُۥ كُن فَيَكُونُ ﴿٤٧﴾

"He will teach him the book and wisdom, and the Torah and the Gospel, (48)

وَيُعَلِّمُهُ ٱلۡكِتَٰبَ وَٱلۡحِكۡمَةَ وَٱلتَّوۡرَىٰةَ وَٱلۡإِنجِيلَ ﴿٤٨﴾

and will make him a messenger to the Israelites: 'I have brought you a sign from your Lord. I will fashion for you out of clay the likeness of a bird. I shall breathe into it and, by God's leave, it shall become a living bird. I will heal the blind and the leper, and bring the dead back to life by God's leave. I will announce to you what you eat and what you store up in your houses. Surely, in all this there is a sign for you, if you are truly believers. (49)

وَرَسُولًا إِلَىٰ بَنِىٓ إِسۡرَٰٓءِيلَ أَنِّى قَدۡ جِئۡتُكُم بِـَٔايَةٖ مِّن رَّبِّكُمۡ أَنِّىٓ أَخۡلُقُ لَكُم مِّنَ ٱلطِّينِ كَهَيۡـَٔةِ ٱلطَّيۡرِ فَأَنفُخُ فِيهِ فَيَكُونُ طَيۡرَۢا بِإِذۡنِ ٱللَّهِۖ وَأُبۡرِئُ ٱلۡأَكۡمَهَ وَٱلۡأَبۡرَصَ وَأُحۡيِ ٱلۡمَوۡتَىٰ بِإِذۡنِ ٱللَّهِۖ وَأُنَبِّئُكُم بِمَا تَأۡكُلُونَ وَمَا تَدَّخِرُونَ فِى بُيُوتِكُمۡۚ إِنَّ فِى ذَٰلِكَ لَأٓيَةٗ لَّكُمۡ إِن كُنتُم مُّؤۡمِنِينَ ﴿٤٩﴾

'And [I have come] to confirm that which has already been sent down of the Torah and to make lawful to you some of the things which were forbidden you. I have come to you with a sign from your Lord; so remain conscious of God and obey me. (50)

وَمُصَدِّقٗا لِّمَا بَيۡنَ يَدَىَّ مِنَ ٱلتَّوۡرَىٰةِ وَلِأُحِلَّ لَكُم بَعۡضَ ٱلَّذِى حُرِّمَ عَلَيۡكُمۡۚ وَجِئۡتُكُم بِـَٔايَةٖ مِّن رَّبِّكُمۡ فَٱتَّقُوا۟ ٱللَّهَ وَأَطِيعُونِ ﴿٥٠﴾

'God is indeed my Lord and your Lord, so worship Him alone. That is the straight path.'" (51)

إِنَّ ٱللَّهَ رَبِّى وَرَبُّكُمْ فَٱعْبُدُوهُ هَٰذَا صِرَاطٌ مُّسْتَقِيمٌ ۝

When Jesus became conscious of their rejection of the faith, he asked: "Who will be my helpers in the cause of God?" The disciples replied: "We are [your] helpers in God's cause. We believe in God. Bear you witness that we have surrendered ourselves to Him. (52)

۞ فَلَمَّآ أَحَسَّ عِيسَىٰ مِنْهُمُ ٱلْكُفْرَ قَالَ مَنْ أَنصَارِىٓ إِلَى ٱللَّهِ قَالَ ٱلْحَوَارِيُّونَ نَحْنُ أَنصَارُ ٱللَّهِ ءَامَنَّا بِٱللَّهِ وَٱشْهَدْ بِأَنَّا مُسْلِمُونَ ۝

"Our Lord, we believe in what You have bestowed from on high, and we follow the messenger, so write us down among those who bear witness [to the truth]." (53)

رَبَّنَآ ءَامَنَّا بِمَآ أَنزَلْتَ وَٱتَّبَعْنَا ٱلرَّسُولَ فَٱكْتُبْنَا مَعَ ٱلشَّٰهِدِينَ ۝

They schemed, and God also schemed. God is the best of schemers. (54)

وَمَكَرُوا۟ وَمَكَرَ ٱللَّهُ وَٱللَّهُ خَيْرُ ٱلْمَٰكِرِينَ ۝

God said: "Jesus, I shall gather you and cause you to ascend to Me, and I shall cleanse you of those who disbelieve, and I shall place those who follow you above those who disbelieve until the Day of Resurrection. Then to Me you shall all return, and I shall judge between you with regard to everything on which you used to differ. (55)

إِذْ قَالَ ٱللَّهُ يَٰعِيسَىٰٓ إِنِّى مُتَوَفِّيكَ وَرَافِعُكَ إِلَىَّ وَمُطَهِّرُكَ مِنَ ٱلَّذِينَ كَفَرُوا۟ وَجَاعِلُ ٱلَّذِينَ ٱتَّبَعُوكَ فَوْقَ ٱلَّذِينَ كَفَرُوٓا۟ إِلَىٰ يَوْمِ ٱلْقِيَٰمَةِ ثُمَّ إِلَىَّ مَرْجِعُكُمْ فَأَحْكُمُ بَيْنَكُمْ فِيمَا كُنتُمْ فِيهِ تَخْتَلِفُونَ ۝

"As for those who disbelieve, I shall inflict on them severe suffering in this world and in the life to come; and they shall have none to help them. (56)

فَأَمَّا ٱلَّذِينَ كَفَرُوا۟ فَأُعَذِّبُهُمْ عَذَابًا شَدِيدًا فِى ٱلدُّنْيَا وَٱلْأَخِرَةِ وَمَا لَهُم مِّن نَّٰصِرِينَ ﴿٥٦﴾

But to those who believe and do good works, He will grant their reward in full. God does not love the wrongdoers. (57)

وَأَمَّا ٱلَّذِينَ ءَامَنُوا۟ وَعَمِلُوا۟ ٱلصَّٰلِحَٰتِ فَيُوَفِّيهِمْ أُجُورَهُمْ وَٱللَّهُ لَا يُحِبُّ ٱلظَّٰلِمِينَ ﴿٥٧﴾

"This which We recite to you is a revelation and a wise reminder." (58)

ذَٰلِكَ نَتْلُوهُ عَلَيْكَ مِنَ ٱلْءَايَٰتِ وَٱلذِّكْرِ ٱلْحَكِيمِ ﴿٥٨﴾

The case of Jesus in the sight of God is the same as the case of Adam. He created him of dust and then said to him: "Be", and he was. (59)

إِنَّ مَثَلَ عِيسَىٰ عِندَ ٱللَّهِ كَمَثَلِ ءَادَمَ خَلَقَهُۥ مِن تُرَابٍ ثُمَّ قَالَ لَهُۥ كُن فَيَكُونُ ﴿٥٩﴾

This is the truth from your Lord: be not, then, among the doubters. (60)

ٱلْحَقُّ مِن رَّبِّكَ فَلَا تَكُن مِّنَ ٱلْمُمْتَرِينَ ﴿٦٠﴾

If anyone should dispute with you about this [truth] after all the knowledge you have received, say: "Come. Let us summon our sons and your sons, our women and your women, and ourselves and yourselves; then let us pray humbly and solemnly and invoke God's curse upon the ones who are telling a lie." (61)

فَمَنْ حَآجَّكَ فِيهِ مِنۢ بَعْدِ مَا جَآءَكَ مِنَ ٱلْعِلْمِ فَقُلْ تَعَالَوْا۟ نَدْعُ أَبْنَآءَنَا وَأَبْنَآءَكُمْ وَنِسَآءَنَا وَنِسَآءَكُمْ وَأَنفُسَنَا وَأَنفُسَكُمْ ثُمَّ نَبْتَهِلْ فَنَجْعَل لَّعْنَتَ ٱللَّهِ عَلَى ٱلْكَٰذِبِينَ ﴿٦١﴾

This is indeed the truth of the matter. There is no deity save God. Indeed, it is God Who is the Mighty, the Wise. (62)

إِنَّ هَٰذَا لَهُوَ ٱلْقَصَصُ ٱلْحَقُّ وَمَا مِنْ إِلَٰهٍ إِلَّا ٱللَّهُ وَإِنَّ ٱللَّهَ لَهُوَ ٱلْعَزِيزُ ٱلْحَكِيمُ ﴿٦٢﴾

And if they turn away, God has full knowledge of those who spread corruption. (63)

فَإِن تَوَلَّوْاْ فَإِنَّ ٱللَّهَ عَلِيمٌ بِٱلْمُفْسِدِينَ ﴿٦٣﴾

Say: "People of earlier revelations. Let us come to an agreement which is equitable between you and us: that we shall worship none but God, that we shall associate no partners with Him, and that we shall not take one another for lords beside God." And if they turn away, then say: "Bear witness that we have surrendered ourselves to God." (64)

قُلْ يَٰٓأَهْلَ ٱلْكِتَٰبِ تَعَالَوْاْ إِلَىٰ كَلِمَةٍ سَوَآءٍ بَيْنَنَا وَبَيْنَكُمْ أَلَّا نَعْبُدَ إِلَّا ٱللَّهَ وَلَا نُشْرِكَ بِهِۦ شَيْئًا وَلَا يَتَّخِذَ بَعْضُنَا بَعْضًا أَرْبَابًا مِّن دُونِ ٱللَّهِ فَإِن تَوَلَّوْاْ فَقُولُواْ ٱشْهَدُواْ بِأَنَّا مُسْلِمُونَ ﴿٦٤﴾

Overview

Reports of the encounter between the Yemeni Najran delegation and the Prophet Muḥammad indicate that the accounts relating to the family of 'Imrān, the birth of Jesus, his mother Mary, and John, son of Zachariah, which appear in this *sūrah,* form part of the argument put forward by the Qur'ān to counter the delegation's allegations. This argument is based on the Qur'ānic view that Jesus was God's "word" given to Mary and created from His "spirit". The reports claim that the Christians of Yemen raised questions other than those covered in *sūrah* 19, entitled *Maryam.*

This may well be the case, but the accounts fall into the general Qur'ānic pattern of citing historic events and episodes in order to establish certain facts and truths, which are almost always the central theme of the *sūrah* in which they appear. The amount of detail and the approach are often determined by how much the stories are used to emphasise, highlight or evoke those facts and truths. Undeniably, narrative, as a literary tool, is a special way of presenting and conveying facts in graphic and lively terms and has a strong and lasting impact. It depicts ideas and concepts in a tangible and moving manner as they translate into real life situations, and leaves aside the merely abstract presentation of those ideas.

In this instance, we find that the narratives cover the same subjects, facts and concepts that the *sūrah* deals with. In this way, it loses its parochial and limited context and emerges as a fundamental element of the whole discussion, in its own right, conveying essential and eternal aspects of Islamic concepts and beliefs.

The central theme of the *sūrah*, as already pointed out, revolves around the issue of the oneness of God, i.e. *tawḥīd*. The story of Jesus and the other accounts related to it reinforce this concept as they refute and completely exclude the idea of offspring or partners as far as God is concerned. The *sūrah* rejects these notions as false and naïve, and presents the birth and life of Maryam and Jesus in such a manner that leaves no room for doubting his full humanity or that he was one of God's messengers; whatever applies to them applies to him. It explains the supernatural phenomena that accompanied the birth and life of Jesus in simple, clear and reassuring terms. The whole issue is presented as a natural and normal one that should raise no confusion or suspicion. It simply says: *"The case of Jesus in the sight of God is the same as the case of Adam. He created him of dust and then said to him, 'Be', and he was."* (Verse 59) Believing hearts find certainty and peace in these words, and wonder how this evident concept could ever have been shrouded in doubt and confusion.

The other issue which is reiterated throughout this *sūrah* is that the true religion is Islam, or total submission and obedience to God Almighty. This issue also emerges from the narratives quite clearly. We find it in Jesus's response to the Israelites when he says: *"... I have come to confirm that which has already been sent down of the Torah and to make lawful to you some of the things which were forbidden you. ...."* (Verse 50) This is an affirmation of the nature of God's message and its purpose as being to establish a way of life and implement a system defining what is permissible and what is not, to be adopted and adhered to by believers. This concept of submission and compliance is asserted by the disciples of Jesus where we read: *"And when Jesus become conscious of their rejection of the faith, he asked: 'Who will be my helpers in the cause of God?' The disciples replied, 'We are [your] helpers in God's cause. We believe in God. Bear you witness that we have surrendered ourselves to Him. Our Lord, we believe in what You have bestowed from on high, and we follow the messenger, so write us down among those who bear witness.'"* (Verses 52–3)

Another theme which is quite evident in this passage is a description of the believers' relationship with their Lord. It presents a host of laudable examples in the person of that select group of God's prophets and messengers in successive generations. This noble example is manifested in the earnest plea by ʿImrān's wife to God Almighty regarding the new-born baby girl, in Mary's conversation with Zachariah, in the latter's appeal to his Lord, and in the response of the disciples to God's Messenger, Jesus, and their invocations to God.

Once the narrative is completed, the *sūrah* gives a brief commentary and summary of the facts, referring back to the accounts already cited. It expounds the true nature of Jesus, and the nature of creation, Divine will and pure monotheism, or *tawḥīd*. It recalls how people of earlier revelations were called to believe in the oneness of God and how they were challenged to accept it. The passage, verses 33–64, closes with a comprehensive statement which the Prophet Muḥammad could use to address Jews and Christians everywhere, those who attended the debates as well as those who did not, until the end of time. It says: *"Say, 'People of earlier revelations. Let us come to an agreement which is equitable between you and us: that we shall worship none but God, that we shall associate no partners with Him, and that we shall not take one another for lords beside God.' And if they turn away, then say: 'Bear witness that we have surrendered ourselves to God.'"* (Verse 64)

There the debate ends and the purpose of Islam and what order of human life it is proposing become very clear. The meaning of religion and submission to God are defined, and all distorted or falsified versions of religion or submission are rejected. This is the ultimate objective of this section and of the *sūrah* as a whole expressed through some of the most charming, interesting and meaningful of narratives. This is the function of historic accounts and narration in the Qur'ān and these are the premises that govern its style and presentation.

The story of Jesus is covered in *sūrah* 19, *Maryam*, as well as in the present *sūrah*. When we compare the two accounts, we find certain additional, albeit brief details in this *sūrah*. In *sūrah Maryam*, we are given a lengthy account of the birth of Jesus, but not of his mother, while here that part is condensed but more details are given of the message of Jesus and about his disciples. The Qur'ānic commentary here is longer because the issue under debate, that of God's oneness, religion and revelation, is more significant and comprehensive.

God's Chosen Servants

God raised Adam and Noah, and the House of Abraham and the House of 'Imrān above all mankind. They were the offspring of one another. God hears all and knows all. 'Imrān's wife said: "My Lord, I vow to You that which is in my womb, to be devoted to Your service. Accept it from me. You alone are the One Who hears all and knows all." When she had given birth she said: "My Lord, I have given birth to a female." – God well knew to what she would give birth. – "The male is not like the female. I have named her Mary and I seek Your protection for her and her offspring against Satan, the accursed." Her Lord graciously accepted her. He made her grow up a goodly child, and placed her in the care of Zachariah. Whenever Zachariah visited her in the sanctuary he found her provided with food. He would say: "Mary, where has this come to you from?" She would answer: "It is from God. God gives sustenance to whom He wills, beyond all reckoning." (Verses 33–7)

The narration begins with mentioning God's chosen servants whom He has selected for the task of conveying the one message of the single faith preached from the beginning of creation. They are the leaders of the procession of believers in all its phases and throughout history. We are told that these people form a continuous chain or a lineage. However, this does not necessarily mean a family lineage, even though they have all descended from Adam and Noah. Rather the tie which groups them together is that they have been chosen by God and that they belong to the same faith: *"God raised Adam and Noah, and the House of Abraham and the House of 'Imrān above all mankind."* (Verse 33)

This verse mentions two individuals, Adam and Noah, and two families, the House of Abraham and the House of 'Imrān. It is, thus, made clear that Adam and Noah have been exalted as individuals, while Abraham and 'Imrān were favoured along with their descendants, on that basis which was firmly established in the preceding *sūrah al-Baqarah*, with regard to Abraham's seed. This confirms that the inheritance of prophethood and blessings is not determined by the relationship of blood, but by that of faith: *"When his Lord tested Abraham with certain commandments and he fulfilled them, He said: 'I have appointed you a leader of mankind.' Abraham asked: 'And what of my descendants?' God said: 'My covenant does not apply to the wrong doers.'"* (2: 124)

Some reports suggest that 'Imrān belonged to the House of Abraham. He is, then, mentioned here by name for a particular purpose which pertains to the stories of Mary and Jesus. We also note that this *sūrah* makes no mention of Moses or Jacob, who also belonged to the House of Abraham because the occasion does not require such a reference to answer the arguments raised about Jesus, son of Mary, or about Abraham.

A Child Dedicated to Divine Service

The opening verse in this section is a declaration: *"God raised Adam and Noah, and the House of Abraham and the House of 'Imrān above all mankind."* This serves as a preparatory announcement and an introduction to the story which immediately follows, giving information about the House of 'Imrān. Its events begin to unfold with the birth of Mary.

The vow made by 'Imrān's wife reveals to us the fact that she is a woman with a heart full of faith. She looks up to her Lord making an offering of the dearest thing to her, namely, the child she is bearing. She dedicates the child to her Lord, free of all conditions and all partnerships, free of all claims which may be made by anyone other than God. The Arabic term used here to denote that the offering is made absolutely purely to God is derived from the root meaning "freedom" or "liberation". This in itself is very significant. No one is truly free unless he devotes himself totally to God, liberating himself from servitude to anyone, anything, or any value.

When submission to God alone is total, it indicates total freedom. Any other situation is a form of slavery although it may appear in the guise of freedom.

This shows that to believe in God as the only Lord is perfect freedom. No human being is truly free if he recognises any degree of authority which belongs to anyone other than God. When Islam preaches the Oneness of God, it preaches the only true form of human freedom.

The devoted prayer 'Imrān's wife addresses to her Lord to accept her offering is an indication of her total submission to God. She appears to us free from all shackles. Her only motivation is to seek God's pleasure and acceptance: *"My Lord, I vow to You that which is in my womb, to be devoted to Your service. Accept it from me. You alone are the One Who hears all and knows all."* (Verse 35)

She is, however, delivered of a daughter, not a son: *"When she had given birth she said: 'My Lord, I have given birth to a female.' – God well knew to what she would give birth. – 'The male is not like the female, I have named her Mary and I seek Your protection for her and her offspring against Satan, the accursed.'"* (Verse 36) She was hoping for a male child, because only male children were devoted for service in temples, so that they may free themselves from any preoccupation with anything other than worship and prayer. When she discovered that she had given birth to a daughter, she addressed her Lord in a sorrowful tone: *"'My Lord, I have given birth to a female.'"* She realises that God is fully aware of the fact. She, however, makes the offering with what she has, and appears to apologize for not having a male child who might have been better able to fulfil the mission for which the baby was devoted: *"The male is not like the female."* In this particular consideration, a female cannot fulfil the tasks for which the male is better suited. *"I have named her Mary."*

This address sounds close, familiar, made by one who feels to be having a private conversation with her Lord, explaining what is on her mind and making her offering gently and directly. This is the type of relationship which God's chosen people have with their Lord: it is a relationship of friendship, closeness and simple address, free of all complications. They feel they are speaking with the One Who is near, loving and certain to respond.

"I seek Your protection for her and her offspring against Satan, the accursed." These are the final words spoken by the mother as she gives up her offering to her Lord, entrusting her baby to His care and seeking His protection for her and her offspring against Satan. They are words which express the desire of a devoted heart. No mother could wish for her new-born baby anything better than protection by God from Satan.

"Her Lord graciously accepted her. He made her grow up a goodly child." (Verse 37) This acceptance is given in return for the dedication which fills the mother's heart and motivates her to make such a dedicated vow. God's gracious acceptance of Mary also serves as a preparation for her to receive the breathing of God's spirit and His word so that she will be able to give birth to Jesus in a way which is totally unfamiliar to human beings.

God *"placed her in the care of Zachariah."* (Verse 37) He made Zachariah, the chief of the Jewish temple, the custody of which was entrusted to Aaron's priestly descendants, Mary's guardian.

Mary was a blessed child, enjoying a state of abundance. God ensured that she would always have an abundance of everything: *"Whenever Zachariah visited her in the sanctuary he found her provided with food. He would say: 'Mary, where has this come to you from?' She would answer: 'It is from God. God gives sustenance to whom He wills, beyond all reckoning.'"* (Verse 37)

We do not wish to indulge in any discussion of the nature of the provisions made available to Mary as others have done. It is sufficient for us to know that she was a blessed child whose blessings benefited others around her. She had more than she needed of everything which may be termed as "provisions". Her guardian, himself a Prophet, wondered at this abundance and asked her how and where she got it from. A humble servant of God as she was, she would acknowledge God's grace, saying no more than: *"It is from God. God gives sustenance to whom He wills, beyond all reckoning."*

Her answer is indicative of the relationship between a believer and her Lord. She keeps to herself the secret which exists between Him and her, referring to it with modesty, and without any trace of boastfulness.

This unfamiliar aspect which makes Zachariah wonder serves as a prelude to the forthcoming wonders associated with the birth of John and with the birth of Jesus.

A Very Strange Birth

> *At that point, Zachariah prayed to his Lord, saying: "Lord, bestow on me, out of Your grace, goodly offspring. Indeed, You hear all prayers." Thereupon, the angels called out to him as he stood praying in the sanctuary: "God gives you the happy news of [the birth of] John, who shall confirm the truth of a word from God. He shall be noble, utterly chaste and a Prophet from among the righteous." [Zachariah] said: "Lord, how can I have a son when old age has already overtaken me and my wife is barren?" He answered: "Thus it is. God does what He wills." [Zachariah] said: "Lord, grant me a sign." He replied: "Your sign shall be that for three days you will not speak to people except by gestures. Remember your Lord unceasingly and glorify Him in the early hours of night and day."* (Verses 38–41)

Zachariah, an old man without progeny, experienced a renewal of that yearning to have a child of his own. This is a natural desire which cannot be suppressed even by those who dedicate themselves to Divine Service and preoccupy themselves with worship. God has made this desire a part of human nature so that life can continue and progress.

Here we witness an event which demonstrates that God's will is absolute, not confined to what is familiar to men. Human beings tend to think that what they know of natural laws are final, inviolable, absolute. Hence, they raise doubts about any event which does not seem to fall within the confines of these laws. If they cannot deny the event altogether because they know it to be an accomplished fact, they start to fabricate legends around it.

Here we find Zachariah, a man overtaken by old age, and his barren wife who had not had children even in her youth. As Zachariah brings up Mary, a goodly child provided with abundance from God, his deep, natural desire to have offspring of his own begins to stir inside him. He turns to his Lord with a passionate prayer to give him out of His grace goodly offspring: *"At that point, Zachariah prayed to his Lord, saying: 'Lord, bestow on me, out of Your Grace' goodly offspring. Indeed, You hear all prayers.'"* (Verse 38) And what does this passionate prayer achieve? God answers his prayer in a way which is not restricted to age or what is familiar to people. It is an answer determined by God's absolute will: *"Thereupon, the angels called out to him as he stood praying*

in the sanctuary: 'God gives you the happy news of [the birth of] John,
who shall confirm the truth of a word from God. He shall be noble,
utterly chaste and a Prophet from among the righteous.'" (Verse 39)

This is the sincere prayer of a man of pure heart who has placed his
hopes in the One Who hears all prayers and Who is able to answer
them when He chooses. The angels bid Zachariah rejoice at the news
of the birth of a son whose name, John, is known even before he is
born. His qualities are also well known: he is to be a man of nobility
and distinction, utterly chaste, able to control his desires and a firm
believer who will confirm the word of God. Moreover, he will be a
Prophet and a righteous man.

God has answered Zachariah's prayer in such a way that the natural
phenomena familiar to man are put aside. People may think these
phenomena to be a law which restricts even the will of God. Whatever
is familiar to man and thought by him to be an inviolable law is no
more than a relative law. It is neither final nor absolute. Since man is
confined by the limitations of his age and knowledge, and since our
minds can only work within our natural limitations, we cannot
appreciate any final law or comprehend any fact which is absolute.
Hence, it is more suitable for man not to exceed the boundaries of
propriety when he thinks of God. It is far better for man to confine
himself to the limitations of his own world when he speaks of what is
possible and what is impossible. He must not, in any way, try to set a
framework by virtue of his own experience and scanty knowledge in
which to restrict God's absolute will.

The way his prayer was answered surprised even Zachariah. After
all, Zachariah was a man like us. He wanted to know from his Lord
how this could happen when it was something "supernatural" by the
standards of human beings. He said: *"Lord, how can I have a son when*
old age has already overtaken me and my wife is barren?" He was given
an easy, simple answer which puts matters in the right perspective and
which need not be surprising to anyone: *"Thus it is. God does what He*
wills." (Verse 40)

"Thus it is." The whole thing is familiar and it happens all the time
when we take it within the context of God's absolute will and His
actions which are always accomplished. But people do not think of
this nor do they remember this fact.

"Thus it is," absolutely easy, unrestricted. God does what He wills.
What is so strange about Him giving Zachariah a son when Zachariah

has been overtaken by old age and his wife is barren? These restrictions apply to men because they are familiar to men. As for God, there is nothing familiar or unfamiliar. Everything happens according to God's will. His will is subject to no restrictions whatsoever.

Zachariah, nevertheless, was so overwhelmed by the news that he prayed to his Lord to give him a sign which would reassure him. He said: *"Lord, grant me a sign."* God directs him at this point to that which gives him the perfect reassurance. He gives him a totally unfamiliar experience. The sign was that Zachariah's tongue was to be tied for three days when he tried to address people, but would remain untied when he addressed his Lord and glorified Him: *"He replied: 'Your sign shall be that for three days you will not speak to people except by gestures. Remember your Lord unceasingly and glorify Him in the early hours of night and day.'"* (Verse 41)

The Qur'ānic account stops here. We know that this is what actually took place. Zachariah had an experience which was unfamiliar in his own life and in the lives of other beings. His tongue was unable to utter a word of ordinary speech while it uttered the praises and glorification of God. What law controls such a phenomenon? It is the law of God's absolute will. There can be no other explanation of this strange event. Similarly, there is no other explanation of the birth of John when his father had been overtaken by old age and his mother was barren.

Preparation for a Special Event

The angels said: "Mary, God has chosen you and made you pure, and raised you above all the women of the world. Mary, Remain truly devout to your Lord, prostrate yourself [to Him] and bow down with those who bow down in worship. This is an account of something which remained beyond the reach of your perception We now reveal to you. You were not present with them when they cast lots as to which of them should have charge of Mary; nor were you present when they contended about it with one another. (Verses 42–4)

Within the context of this *sūrah*, the miraculous nature of the of birth of John, born to Zachariah and his wife despite their respective old age and barrenness, comes as a prelude to the account of another event around which legends have been woven, even though it is no more than one in a series of events which prove that God's will is free of all restrictions. At this point, the *sūrah* begins the story of Christ with the preparation of Mary with purification and worship to receive the spiritual light.

"The angels said: 'Mary, God has chosen you and made you pure, and raised you above all the women of the world. Mary, remain truly devout to your Lord, prostrate yourself [to Him] and bow down with those who bow down in worship." (Verses 42–3) What a great honour to be bestowed upon her. She is chosen to receive the Divine spirit directly in the same way as Adam, the first human being to be created, received it. She is to be the means through which this miraculous event is shown to humanity. It is an event which has not been repeated in the entire history of mankind. Hence, it is undoubtedly a great moment. She, however, had no knowledge whatsoever of the event up to that point.

The reference here to Mary's purification is highly significant because the Jews did not hesitate to raise suspicions about Mary's purity in connection with the birth of her son. Making use of the fact that such a birth is without parallel in humanity, they claimed that there must be something dishonourable behind it. Confound them.

Here we see in full light a remarkable aspect of the greatness of this religion of Islam, one which illustrates its great origin. Muḥammad, who conveyed the message of Islam, faced determined opposition by the people of earlier revelations, including the Christians, which manifested itself in various forms of denunciation, argument and doubt. Nevertheless, Muḥammad announced what God revealed to him of the great truth of Mary and her exaltation above all the women of the world. He did not mince words about her great honour, even though he was involved in a debate with people who honoured Mary and considered her honour sufficient justification for their refusal to believe in Muḥammad and his message. Can there be any greater honesty and truthfulness? This account shows beyond doubt the source from which this religion of Islam has come and confirms the absolute honesty and integrity of the messenger who conveyed it. He received "the truth" from his Lord about Mary and Jesus and he did not hesitate to declare that truth in that debate. Had he not been a messenger from God who describes Himself as "the truth", he would not have made that declaration at that particular time.

"Mary, remain truly devout to your Lord, prostrate yourself [to Him] and bow down with those who bow down in worship." Total obedience

and constant worship. It is a life totally devoted to God which serves as preparation for the forthcoming event.

At this point in the story and before relating the details of these great events, the *sūrah* briefly refers to one of the purposes behind relating such historical accounts. It proves the fact of revelation which informs the Prophet of events which he did not attend and could not have known from any source other than God: *"This is an account of something which remained beyond the reach of your perception We now reveal to you. You were not present with them when they cast lots as to which of them should have charge of Mary; nor were you present when they contended about it with one another."* (Verse 44)

This statement refers to the competition among the custodians of the temple to take guardianship of Mary when her mother brought her as a baby to the temple in fulfilment of her vow to her Lord. This verse, in fact, refers to an event which is not related either in the Old or the New Testaments, although it must have been known to the priests and rabbis. The custodians of the temple had to cast their lots in order to determine who would have charge of Mary. The Qur'ānic verse does not provide many details, perhaps because the matter was well known to those to whom the verse was recited, or because it does not add anything to the fact which is meant to be told to future generations. We understand, however, that those custodians agreed on a formula among themselves, through casting lots, to determine Mary's future guardian, just as we do nowadays when we toss up for one thing or another. Some reports suggest that they cast their pens in the river Jordan. The river swept all the pens away, except that of Zachariah which remained in its place. That could equally have been the agreed formula among them, but no matter what it was, they acknowledged his claim to be Mary's guardian.

All this was of the secrets unknown to the Prophet. He did not attend those events. Moreover, it may have been one of the secrets of the temple not told to anyone. The Qur'ānic account uses it in the debate with the learned authorities of the people of earlier revelations as a proof of God's revelation to His honest and trustworthy messenger. We have no reports of any reply they might have given to this argument. Had it been debatable, they would have argued it, considering that that was their primary purpose.

A Miraculous Birth

The angels said: "Mary, God sends you the happy news, through a word from Him, [of a son] whose name is the Christ, Jesus, son of Mary, honoured in this world and in the life to come, and shall be among those who are favoured by God. He shall speak to people in his cradle, and as a grown man, and shall be of the righteous." Said she: "My Lord! How can I have a son when no man has ever touched me?" [The angel] answered: "Thus it is. God creates what He wills. When He wills a thing to be, He only says to it 'Be', and it is. He will teach him the book and wisdom, and the Torah and the Gospel, and will make him a messenger to the Israelites."

"I have brought you a sign from your Lord. I will fashion for you out of clay the likeness of a bird. I shall breathe into it and, by God's leave, it shall become a living bird. I will heal the blind and the leper, and bring the dead back to life by God's leave. I will announce to you what you eat and what you store up in your houses. Surely, in all this there is a sign for you, if you are truly believers." (Verses 45–9)

To the human mind, Jesus's birth remains the greatest of all miracles. According to God's will, which is free of all restrictions, it is nothing out of the ordinary.

We are told that Mary qualified, through purification, devotion and sincere worship, to receive this honour and to be chosen for this great event. Here she is receiving the news for the first time through the angels: *"The angels said: 'Mary, God sends you the happy news, through a word from Him, [of a son] whose name is the Christ, Jesus, son of Mary, honoured in this world and in the life to come, and shall be among those who are favoured by God.'"* (Verse 45) It is a complete piece of news which tells of the whole affair. She receives the news in a word from God, namely the Christ, Jesus, son of Mary. In the construction of the sentence, the name "the Christ" is a substitute for the term "a word". Yet, he is indeed the "Word". What does this expression actually mean?

This and similar statements are of those matters which lie beyond our human perception. There is no way to determine what they precisely mean. They may be part of what God referred to in His earlier statement in the *sūrah*: *"He it is Who has sent down to you the Book, containing verses which are clear and precise – and these are the essence of the Book – and others are allegorical. Those whose hearts have swerved from the truth pursue that part of it which is allegorical, seeking to create dissension and trying to give it an arbitrary meaning."* (Verse 7) The matter, however, appears to be much simpler if our purpose is to understand this fact in such a way which keeps our hearts in direct contact with God and His perfect creation, His limitless ability and unrestricted will. It was God's will that human life should start with the creation of Adam from clay. Whether He has made Adam directly from clay or He made from clay an earlier species which continued to develop until the humankind came into existence has no bearing whatsoever on the nature of the secret which remains known only to God. That is, the secret of life which was given to the first living creature, or given to Adam if he was created directly out of lifeless clay. Both are the same in relation to God's work. Neither should be considered preferable to the other in explaining existence.

Where has this life come from, and how? It is certainly something different from dust and different from all the lifeless materials available in the earth. It is something extra, something different. It is something which brings about certain aspects which can never be found in the dust, clay or in any lifeless material whatsoever. How has this secret come about? The fact that we do not know does not justify our denial of its existence or our indulging in petty arguments as those who believe only in matter do.

They pursue their arguments with a narrow-mindedness which cannot be respected by any man of reason, let alone any scientist. The fact remains that we do not know. All the attempts which we, human beings, have made with our limited means to determine the origin of life, or to initiate life from something which is lifeless, have achieved nothing.

We do not know, but God, Who has given life, knows. He tells us that life is a breathing of His spirit into something. He further tells us that giving it is achieved by a word from Him: *"Be, and it is."* What is this spiritual breathing? How is spirit blown into something lifeless so as to bring it into existence? This is a secret which remains incomprehensible to human reason. We cannot achieve that understanding because it is not part of our business. To know these answers does not benefit man in the discharge of his mission for which God has created him, namely, to be in charge of the earth. He will never need to create life from death. Hence, what is the value to him of knowing the nature of life, or the nature of the breathing of the Divine spirit, or how it has been given to Adam or to the first creature in the chain of living beings?

God tells us that the breathing of His spirit in Adam is what gave Adam his honourable place and distinction, even above the angels. It must be, then, something different from that mere "life" given to worms and germs. This leads us to consider man as a kind of creation with a separate existence. He has a special place in the general order of the universe which is not shared by any other creature. This, however, is not our immediate subject. We have only made this brief reference to it in order to warn the reader against any doubts which may arise as a result of arguments surrounding the advent of man.

What is important here is that God is telling us about the initiation of life. It does not matter that we remain unable to comprehend the nature of this secret or understand how life is breathed into something lifeless.

It was God's will, after Adam came into existence in that direct way, to establish a certain procedure for the regeneration of human life. This procedure requires that a male and a female come together and that the female egg be fertilised by a male sperm for conception to take place. Neither the egg nor the sperm is lifeless.

People were familiar with this process for countless generations until God chose to make an exception to it in the case of an individual human being. He made his birth similar to the very first beginning, although not exactly the same. In this case, a female on her own receives the Divine spirit which initiates life, and the process is completed.

Was this breathing of the spirit what is described as the word? Or, was the word the line God's will has taken? Or, does the word mean the command "be", which may be taken as it is or may express that God's will has chosen something in particular? Was the word Jesus, or is his existence derived from it? The pursuit of all such questions can only result in creating doubts. The only true conclusion is that God willed to initiate life in a manner which had no parallel. His unrestricted will accomplished such an initiation of life through a breathing of His spirit, the nature of which remains unknown to us while we understand its effects. There is no reason for us to understand its nature because such an understanding does not add to our ability to discharge our mission on earth, since to initiate life is not part of our appointed task. Viewed in this manner, the whole question becomes easy to understand and raises no doubts in our minds.

Jesus: A Testimony to God's Free Will

The angels gave Mary the happy news of a word from God whose name was the Christ, Jesus, son of Mary. That piece of news included his sex, name and lineage which revealed that he descended from his mother. It also included his qualities as well as his position with his Lord: *"Honoured in this world and in the life to come, and shall be among those who are favoured by God."* As given by the angels, that piece of news refers to a miraculous aspect associated with his birth, *"He shall speak to people in his cradle,"* a glimpse of his future, *"and as a grown man,"* his character and the type of people to whom he belongs: *"and shall be of the righteous."*

Mary, the pure virgin, whose experience is limited to what is familiar in human life receives that piece of news as any girl would receive it. She appeals to her Lord trying to understand this highly perplexing secret: *"Said she: 'My Lord! How can I have a son when no man has ever touched me?'"*

The answer she is given reminds her of the simple fact which is often overlooked by human beings, whose experience and knowledge is limited to that with which they are familiar of causes and effects: *"[The angel] answered: 'Thus it is. God creates what He wills. When He wills a thing to be, He only says to it "Be", and it is.' "* When the whole question is thus referred to this basic fact, all wonder disappears. Man is reassured and even wonders at himself for overlooking this simple and clear fact of God's unrestricted will.

The angel goes on to give Mary more information about the child to whom God has chosen her to give birth in a unique way, and what his position shall be among the Israelites. At this point the news given to Mary is interwoven with Jesus's future as if both were taking place now, in front of our eyes, in the inimitable style of the Qur'ān: *"He will teach him the book and wisdom, and the Torah and the Gospel."*

The term *"the book"*, as used in the Arabic original, may be understood to mean "to write", or to mean the Torah and the Gospel. If it is the latter, then the fact that they are mentioned immediately afterwards is perfectly acceptable usage in Arabic which provides the details of something already mentioned in general terms. *"Wisdom"* is a certain condition which enables a person to look at things in their right perspective, understand what is right and follow it. To be granted wisdom is to be granted much grace by God. The Torah is the book of Jesus in the same way as the Gospel, for it represents the basis of the religion he preached. The Gospel is a complement renovating the spirit of the Torah and reviving the essence of faith which had been smothered by the Israelites. Many of those who speak about Christianity make the mistake of neglecting the Torah when it is the basis of the religion preached by Jesus and contains the law which should be implemented in a Christian society. The Gospel contains only a few amendments to the Torah. Otherwise, it is a message reviving what has already been established by the Torah. It has a refining effect on human conscience enabling man to be in direct contact with God through the revealed text. It is for this revival and refinement that Jesus strove, and because of them his enemies schemed against him, as will be shown later in this *sūrah*.

> *And will make him a messenger to the Israelites. "I have brought you a sign from your Lord. I will fashion for you out of clay the likeness of a bird. I shall breathe into it and, by God's leave, it shall become a living bird. I will heal the blind and the leper, and bring the dead back to life by God's leave. I will announce to you what you eat and what you store up in your houses. Surely, in all this there is a sign for you, if you are truly believers."* (Verse 49)

This verse makes it clear that Jesus was given a message to deliver to the Israelites. He was one of their Prophets. Consequently, the Torah revealed to Moses, containing the law to be implemented in the life of the Israelite community and laying down legislation for various aspects of human life, continued to be upheld by Jesus, although it was complemented by the Gospel which places much emphasis on the spiritual aspect of life and the role of human conscience.

The sign which he was to be granted and of which God informed his mother, Mary, and with which he actually confronted the Israelites was the miracle of breathing into the dead to give it life. He was to bring the dead back to life, to heal the one who was born blind, to heal the leper and to inform people of what they eat or store up of food in their houses, although he could not see it or know of it by his own means.

We also note that the Qur'ānic text emphasises, both at the time when the angel gives that happy news to Mary and when these matters came to take place later on, that each of these miracles shown by Jesus to his people was given to him by God. The Qur'ān quotes him as saying that and mentions the phrase *"by God's leave"* after every single one of them in order to emphasise that fact most strongly. That phrase could have been left to the end of the statement, but it was used repeatedly in order to leave absolutely no room for confusion.

These miracles in general relate to either the initiation or restoration of life, or to the restoration of sound health which is a branch of life, or to the knowledge of something which lies beyond ordinary human perception.

In essence, they are all particularly relevant to the birth of Jesus and the bringing of him into existence in a fashion which is unparalleled, except in the case of Adam. When people realise that God can enable one of His own creatures to accomplish such miracles, they will be able to understand that He Himself is able to create that creature in a totally unfamiliar fashion. There is, therefore, no need for any of the great legends and unfounded reports which have been woven around the birth of Jesus. It is sufficient for man to remember that God's will remains free of all restrictions. When man does not try to impose what is familiar to him on the work of God, he will have no problem understanding how Jesus was born.

Jesus Endorsing a Message

> And [I have come] to confirm that which has already been sent down of the Torah and to make lawful to you some of the things which were forbidden you. I have come to you with a sign from your Lord; so remain conscious of God and obey me. God is indeed my Lord and your Lord, so worship Him alone. That is the straight path. (Verses 50–1)

This is the final part of the address made by Jesus to the Israelites. Here, certain basic facts are revealed which concern the nature of Divine religion as outlined in the messages preached by all prophets and messengers. These facts acquire an even greater importance when stated by Jesus himself, considering all the mistaken notions which have been formulated about his birth and his nature. All such mistaken notions are the result of deviation from the basic truth of Divine faith which remains the same with all messengers.

When Jesus says: *"And I have come to confirm that which has already been sent down of the Torah and to make lawful to you some of the things which were forbidden you,"* he highlights the nature of true Christianity.

The Torah, which was revealed to Moses, and which contained the legislation to be implemented in the life of the community, according to the needs of that particular time and the special circumstances of the life of the Israelites, is here endorsed by Jesus. Indeed, his message was a confirmation of the Torah with some modifications, making lawful to the Israelites certain things which had previously been forbidden them. The prohibition of these things was originally a punishment inflicted by God for certain acts of disobedience and deviation they had committed. It was now God's will to grant them His mercy through Jesus and to make lawful to them again what they were forbidden for a time.

This shows that it is in the nature of any religion to include legislation to organise the life of the community, and not to be confined to providing moral standards, or restricted to the realms of feelings and conscience or worship and rituals. Religion is the way of life God lays down for people to implement and a social order which ensures that implementation.

The elements of faith and belief cannot be isolated from worship, morality or general law in any religion which aims at organising human life according to God's constitution. All these elements constitute a complete whole and any dichotomy between them is bound to nullify the effect of religion on the life of people and is contrary to the concept and nature of faith as God defines it.

This is what has happened to Christianity. Owing to certain historical circumstances on the one hand, and to the fact that although it was intended for a certain period, until the last message was revealed, it continued to be upheld after its time, and a split occurred between its legislative aspect on the one hand and its spiritual and moral ones on the other. The deeply rooted and mutual hostility between the Jews and the followers of Jesus caused a separation between the Torah, which contained the legal code, and the Gospel, which placed its strong emphasis on spiritual revival and moral refinement. Moreover, that legal code was intended for a limited period and a particular group of people. It was the will of God that the permanent and comprehensive legal code for all humanity would be revealed later, at its appointed time.

Whatever the reasons, the net result was that Christianity was reduced to a creed which lacked a legal code. As such, it was unable to regulate the social life of the nations which embraced it. Such a regulation of social life requires an ideological concept with a clear interpretation of the existence of the universe and of human life, as well as the position of man in the universe. It also requires a system of worship, a moral code and, inevitably, a set of legislative rules derived from all these to put the life of the community on a sound basis. This is the proper structure of religion which ensures the establishment of a social system with a clear and sound basis and effective safeguards. When Christianity suffered the dichotomy delineated above, it was no longer able to provide a comprehensive system for human life. Hence, its followers were forced to divorce their moral and spiritual values from their practical values in all aspects of their lives, including their social system. This led to the establishment of social systems in the Christian world on bases other than their only natural one. Hence, they were lame systems.

This was not a simple incident or a trifling matter in human history. It was a far reaching catastrophe, generating all the misery, confusion, perversion and immorality which haunt the present material civilisation in all the countries which still profess to be Christian. The case is practically the same in countries which have discarded Christianity even though they have not introduced great changes in their practical lifestyle.

As preached by Jesus Christ himself, Christianity, like every religion worthy of the name, is the legal code which regulates human life on the basis of a clear ideological concept of faith in God and sound moral values derived from that concept. Without such a wholesome structure there can be no Christianity, and indeed no faith. Without such a structure there can be no social system which satisfies the needs of man, whether spiritual or practical, and which elevates human life so that it comes into direct contact with God.

This essential fact is one of the concepts which we can deduce from Jesus's statement: *"And [I have come] to confirm that which has already been sent down of the Torah and to make lawful to you some of the things which were forbidden you."* (Verse 50)

When he so addresses people, he relies on the paramount fact of the oneness of God which is stated in the clearest of terms: *"I have come to you with a sign from your Lord; so remain conscious of God and obey me. God is indeed my Lord and your Lord, so worship Him alone. That is the straight path."* (Verses 50–1)

He thus declares the essence of the ideological concept which is basic to the Divine religion in all its forms. The miracles he performed were not of his own doing. As a human being, he had no power to accomplish them. He was given them by God. His message is based, first and foremost, on the need to fear God and to remain conscious of Him and to obey His Messenger. He also stresses that God is his Lord and the Lord of all people. Jesus himself was not the Lord; he was the Lord's servant. Those who follow him must, therefore, address their worship to the Lord, for He alone is worthy of worship. He concludes with a comprehensive statement of fact: to believe in God alone and worship God alone, and to obey His Messenger and implement the system He laid down – all this is "the straight path". Everything else is deviation and cannot be part of the true faith.

An Appeal for Help

When Jesus became conscious of their rejection of the faith, he asked: "Who will be my helpers in the cause of God?" The disciples replied: "We are [your] helpers in God's cause. We believe in God. Bear you witness that we have surrendered ourselves to Him. Our Lord, we believe in what You have bestowed from on high, and we follow the messenger, so write us down among those who bear witness [to the truth]." (Verses 52–3)

Here the *sūrah* moves on directly to a point in time when Jesus became conscious that the Israelites were bent on denying his message and rejecting the faith altogether. He then appeals for helpers to convey God's message and explain the faith acceptable to Him.

There is, then, a wide gap in the line of the story the *sūrah* is telling. There is no mention that Jesus was actually born, and that his mother confronted her people acknowledging that he was her own son, and that he spoke to them straightway, when he was still a new-born baby. There is no mention either that he began to call on his people to abide by the teachings of the Divine faith when he was in his prime.

Nothing is mentioned either of the miracles to which reference was made in the happy news of his birth given to his mother, as mentioned in *sūrah* 19, entitled "*Maryam*". Such gaps do occur in the stories related in the Qur'ān for the dual purpose of avoiding unnecessary repetition, and for highlighting those episodes which are directly relevant to the subject matter of the *sūrah* in hand.

Jesus was conscious that the Israelites had hardened their attitude against the faith and its implementation despite all the miracles he had shown them. Such miracles could not be accomplished by any human being. They provided concrete evidence that they were the work of God, accomplished by His will as a confirmation of the truth told by the messenger who demonstrated them. Furthermore, although Jesus was also sent to remove some of the restrictions and reduce some of the obligations which were imposed on the Israelites, they were hardened against his message. At this point, he made his appeal: *"Who will be my helpers in the cause of God?"* Who will help me convey God's message and explain it to people? Who will help me to establish God's method and implement His law?

Every man with a message or ideology must have helpers who support him, believe in his message, defend it and convey it to others and make sure that it remains in its original form when he has passed away. *"The disciples replied: 'We are [your] helpers in God's cause. We believe in God. Bear you witness that we have surrendered ourselves to Him.'"* (Verse 52)

We note here that the term they use to describe themselves is "Muslim", which is a reference to Islam in its broad sense, i.e. surrender to God, which is the essence of true faith. They ask Jesus to bear witness to their surrender and their pledging themselves to be God's helpers, which means to help His Messenger and His religion and way of life.

They then turn to God, their Lord, addressing Him directly in this very essential matter: *"Our Lord, we believe in what You have bestowed from on high, and we follow the messenger, so write us down among those who bear witness [to the truth]."* The fact that they address their pledges specifically to God is very significant. A believer makes his covenant directly with his Lord. When the messenger conveys God's message, the messenger has discharged his task in as far as faith is concerned. The pledge is made between the believer and God and it remains binding on the believer after the messenger has passed away. The disciples' statement also includes a pledge to God to obey His

Messenger. This is again significant because it shows that the matter is not simply a question of simple beliefs to be accepted. It is also a commitment to a certain way of life which is received through the messenger. This is a basic factor of this *sūrah* which is repeatedly emphasised in different moods and styles.

The disciples' statement also includes another point which merits special consideration: *"Write us down among those who bear witness."* What testimony? And what witnesses?

A person who surrenders himself to God and believes in the Divine faith is required to make a testimony in favour of this faith which stresses its right to be the religion to follow. It also points out very clearly the countless benefits this religion gives to mankind. No one can make such a testimony unless he makes of himself a practical example of this religion in his lifestyle, manners and morality. People will find, in such a practical example, something superior to everything else, something which confirms the right of this religion to continue to exist and which endorses its superiority to all other systems, regimes and methods known to man.

Again, no one can make such a testimony unless he makes this religion the basis of his life, and the foundation of his society and the law both he and his community follow. Thus, a new social order is brought about which conducts all its affairs according to this straightforward Divine way of life. When a believer struggles to make such a society a reality and to establish this method as the way of life followed by that society, and when he prefers to die rather than live under any system which does not implement a Divine constitution, he in effect gives his testimony that this religion is more important than life itself, the most valuable possession of the living. It is for this reason that he is called "a witness".

Those disciples prayed to God to write them down among those who bear witness to His religion. That is, they pray that God will guide and help them make of themselves a practical example of this religion. That He will direct them to struggle for the cause of implementing it in human life and in a society which mirrors its way of life, even if they will have to sacrifice their lives in order to be chosen as "witnesses" for this religion.

It is a prayer worthy of careful study by everyone who claims to surrender himself to God. This is indeed the meaning of Islam as understood by the disciples and as understood by true Muslims, who actually surrender themselves to God. Anyone who suppresses his testimony and is reluctant to give it in favour of his religion is a sinner at heart. If he claims to be a Muslim but chooses a lifestyle other than that of Islam, or tries to live according to Islam within his own private life but not in the generality of this social life, or does not strive to establish a Divine method in the life of his society either to evade hardship or to spare his own life at the cost of his faith, then he is one who does not give full testimony to this religion, or, indeed, he gives a testimony against it. In so doing, he makes a testimony which deters others from accepting this faith. Can we contemplate the fate of a person who deters others from accepting the Divine faith through his own claim that he is a believer when actually he is not?

Full Heavenly Reward

They schemed, and God also schemed. God is the best of schemers. God said: "Jesus, I shall gather you and cause you to ascend to Me, and I shall cleanse you of those who disbelieve, and I shall place those who follow you above those who disbelieve until the Day of Resurrection. Then to Me you shall all return, and I shall judge between you with regard to everything on which you used to differ. As for those who disbelieve, I shall inflict on them severe suffering in this world and in the life to come; and they shall have none to help them. But to those who believe and do good works, He will grant their reward in full. God does not love the wrongdoers." (Verses 54–7)

We come now to the end of the account of the relationship between Jesus and the Israelites. This begins with the verse: *"They schemed, and God also schemed. God is the best of schemers."* The Jews who did not believe in Jesus, the messenger God sent to them, schemed against him in the most terrible, wicked and relentless of manners. They made all sorts of accusations against him and against his mother, the pure, and her fiancé, Joseph the carpenter, who, according to the Gospels, had not actually married her. They also accused Jesus of lying and taking advantage of people. They reported him to Pontius Pilate, the Roman Governor, describing him as an agitator who stirred up the masses and encouraged rioting and rebellion. They further accused him of being an impostor who tried to corrupt the faith of the masses.

They continued with this line of false accusations until Pilate granted them their request of punishing him themselves as they saw fit. Pilate, a pagan ruler, dared not take upon himself the responsibility of punishing a man whom he could not condemn on the basis of any real evidence. These are only a few examples of the endless scheming by the Jews.

"They schemed, and God also schemed. God is the best of schemers." We note here that the Qur'ān uses the same term to describe what the Jews plotted against Jesus and what God plans for them. This, in effect, ridicules their scheming, since it will have to be set against what God schemes. How can their scheming be compared to what God plans? Indeed, how can their power be compared to God's might?

They wanted to crucify and kill Jesus. God, on the other hand, willed to gather him and cause him to ascend to Himself. He further willed to purify and cleanse him from mixing with the unbelievers and remaining with them. Such a purification is necessary since all unbelievers are impure. It was also the will of God to elevate the followers of Jesus above the unbelievers until the Day of Resurrection. What God willed came true, and the scheming of the Jews was of no consequence whatsoever: *"God said: 'Jesus, I shall gather you and cause you to ascend to Me, and I shall cleanse you of those who disbelieve, and I shall place those who follow you above those who disbelieve until the Day of Resurrection.'"* (Verse 55) How Jesus was gathered and how he ascended to God are matters which lie beyond our human perception. They are unknown except to God. To try to pursue these matters is of no use whatsoever in respect of faith or its implementation. Those who pursue them will inevitably end up more confused, struggling with complicated and endless arguments, gaining no certainty or satisfaction whatsoever. For the whole matter is part of God's own knowledge.

It is not difficult, on the other hand, to explain God's statement that He has placed those who follow Jesus above the unbelievers, and that this elevation continues until the Day of Resurrection. Those who follow Jesus are the ones who believe in God's true religion, Islam, or surrender to God. Every Prophet is fully aware of the true nature of this religion. Every messenger preached the same religion and everyone who truly believes in the Divine faith believes in it. These believers are indeed far superior to the unbelievers, according to God's measure, and they will continue to be so until the Day of Judgement. Moreover, they prove their superiority in our practical life every time they confront the forces of un-faith with the true nature of faith and the reality of following God's messengers. The Divine faith is one, preached by Jesus, son of Mary, as preached by every messenger sent before him and by the messenger sent after him. Those who follow Muḥammad at the same time follow all the messengers sent by God, starting with Adam until the last messenger.

This comprehensive outlook conforms with the theme of the *surah* and its presentation. It is also in conformity with the essence of faith.

The destiny of both the believers and the unbelievers is stated in the form of information given by God to Jesus: *"Then to Me you shall all return, and I shall judge between you with regard to everything on which you used to differ. As for those who disbelieve, I shall inflict on them severe suffering in this world and in the life to come; and they shall have none to help them. But to those who believe and do good works, He will grant their reward in full. God does not love the wrongdoers."* (Verses 55–7)

This statement proves the seriousness of reward and punishment, the Divine justice which is absolute and which cannot be influenced by people's wishes or fabrications. The return to God, then, is inevitable. His judgement on all matters of dispute is irrevocable. The punishment He inflicts on the unbelievers in this world and in the life to come shall overwhelm them and they can have none to help them against it. The believers who do good works, on the other hand, will have their reward in full, without favouritism, but with great generosity. *"God does not love the wrongdoers."* Far be it from Him, then, to do anyone any wrong when He Himself does not love the wrongdoers.

All that people of other religions claim in variance with this, particularly when they say that their stay in hell will last only for a few days, and all their deceptive, wishful thinking of God's reward and their flimsy concept of Divine justice are incorrect and without foundation.

A Challenge to Stop All Argument

"This which We recite to you is a revelation and a wise reminder." *The case of Jesus in the sight of God is the same as the case of Adam. He created him of dust and then said to him: "Be", and he was. This is the truth from your Lord: be not, then, among the doubters. If anyone should dispute with you about this [truth] after*

*all the knowledge you have received, say: "Come. Let us summon
our sons and your sons, our women and your women, and ourselves
and yourselves; then let us pray humbly and solemnly and invoke
God's curse upon the ones who are telling a lie."* (Verses 58–61)

At this point in the story of Jesus, which has been beset by
controversy, the *sūrah* adds certain comments establishing the basic
facts which are deduced from such a narration. The Prophet is
instructed on how to answer the people of earlier revelations with
a decisiveness which ends all controversy and makes the facts, as
stated by Islam, absolutely clear to all. These conclusions begin in
this *sūrah* with a statement about the truthfulness of the revelations
received by Muḥammad: *"This which We recite to you is a revelation
and a wise reminder."* (Verse 58)

These stories and all the Qur'ānic instructions are revelations
from God. God recites His revelations to His Messenger. This
expresses the honour and compassion God bestows on His
Messenger. What honour could be greater than that God Himself
recites to His Prophet His own revelation and wise reminder? That
it is a wise reminder needs no assertion because it states the great
and basic facts which concern man and life in a method and a style
that address human nature directly and gently, appealing to it in a
friendly way, unknown in any other address.

This is followed by a final comment on Jesus's true nature and
on the phenomenon of creation in relation to God's will, which
creates everything as it has created Jesus: *"The case of Jesus in the
sight of God is the same as the case of Adam. He created him of dust
and then said to him: 'Be,' and he was."* (Verse 59) The birth of
Jesus is indeed amazing when compared to what is familiar to man.
It is, however, far from amazing when it is compared with the
creation of Adam, the father of the human race. The people of
earlier revelations who debated and argued about Jesus's nature,
because of his miraculous birth, and wove around him all sorts of
legends and fantasies because he had no father, believed that Adam
was created of dust, and that it was the breathing of God's spirit
into him which made of him a human being. They did not, however,
weave any similar legends around Adam as they did around Jesus.
They did not claim that Adam had any Divine nature. Yet, the very
element which made Adam a human being is the same one which

caused Jesus to be born without a father: God's spirit was breathed into both Adam and Jesus. There was also the Divine command, *"Be"*, to initiate whatever God wanted to initiate and cause to come into existence.

We can, then, appreciate the simplicity of the creation of Jesus, Adam and all creatures. We find ourselves accepting it with ease and clarity. We indeed wonder why the birth of Jesus should lead to all these disputes and arguments when it took place according to God's law which applies to all creation.

We can also appreciate the method of the Qur'ān, the wise reminder, in addressing human nature with simple, realistic and natural logic which makes even the most complicated of matters appear to be so simple.

When we have had this clear statement of the facts, a direct address is made to the Prophet reassuring him of the truth which he has received and which is recited to him. That truth is impressed on the mind of the Prophet as also the minds of his Companions who were exposed to the doubts raised by the people of earlier revelations and their baseless arguments: *"This is the truth from your Lord: be not, then, among the doubters."* (Verse 60)

The Prophet did not entertain even the slightest of doubts as to the truth of what was revealed to him from his Lord at any moment in his life. The fact that this reassurance is needed, however, gives us an idea of how effective the schemes of the enemies of the Muslim community had been at the time. It also indicates that the Muslim community will always be subject to such schemes, and will always need reassurance of the truth it holds in the face of all deceivers. For these renew their scheming and adopt new methods of deception in every generation.

Now that the whole affair is stated absolutely clearly and the truth has appeared to all, God instructs His noble Messenger to end all arguments and debates about this straightforward affair and invite those who continue to argue to join him in a mutual prayer to God to judge between them, in the form which is explained in the next verse: *"If anyone should dispute with you about this [truth] after all the knowledge you have received, say: 'Come. Let us summon our sons and your sons, our women and your women, and ourselves and yourselves; then let us pray humbly and solemnly and invoke God's curse upon the ones who are telling a lie.'"*

The Prophet did actually call on those who disputed what he said on this matter to present themselves at a meeting to be attended by all people. All those who attended would pray humbly and solemnly to God to curse the party which lied. His opponents, however, feared the results of such a prayer and refused the offer. The truth was then clear for everyone to see. The reports which we have of that particular affair tell us that those deceivers had not accepted Islam because they were keen to maintain their position among their people. The clergy at the time enjoyed a great many privileges, much power, and a luxurious lifestyle. We have to remember that those who try to turn people away from this religion, do not need any proof to accept it. They simply follow their own interests and try to safeguard their own ambitions. Such an attitude is bound to make people turn away from the clear truth which is apparent to all.

When There Is Nothing More to Say

This is indeed the truth of the matter. There is no deity save God. Indeed, it is God Who is the Mighty, the Wise. And if they turn away, God has full knowledge of those who spread corruption. Say: "People of earlier revelations Let us come to an agreement which is equitable between you and us: that we shall worship none but God, that we shall associate no partners with Him, and that we shall not take one another for lords beside God." And if they turn away, then say: "Bear witness that we have surrendered ourselves to God." (Verses 62–4)

In this short passage, which concludes the story of Jesus as related in this *sūrah*, we have a statement explaining the true nature of revelation and Qur'ānic stories, and the Oneness of God which is the subject matter of all this revelation. There is also a stern warning for those who turn away from this truth in order to spread corruption in the world: *"This is indeed the truth of the matter. There is no deity save God. Indeed, it is God Who is the Mighty, the Wise. And if they turn away, God has full knowledge of those who spread corruption."* (Verses 62–3) Having been stated earlier, these facts are repeated here, after those who disputed the true nature of Jesus with the Prophet have rejected his invitation to them to join him in a humble prayer to God invoking His curse upon those who lie. The only new element in this verse is the description of those who turn away from the truth as people who spread corruption, and the warning that God has full knowledge of what they do.

The corruption which is spread by those who reject the truth of the oneness of God is surely great. Indeed, corruption does not appear on earth except as a result of refusing to acknowledge this most important fact. I do not mean verbal acknowledgement; for such an acknowledgement is of little value. Nor do I mean a negative mental acknowledgement which leaves no practical effects on people's lives. What is meant is a refusal to acknowledge this fact with its far-reaching effects on human life. The first of these stresses that the Lord of all the universe is One, which means in effect that all worship should be addressed to Him alone. He is the One to be obeyed and He is the only source of legislation from whom we receive our values, standards and morality as well as everything that relates to human life. If such an acknowledgement of the oneness of God is refused, then the person concerned is either an idolater or a non-believer, no matter how strong his verbal claim to believe in God is and no matter how strong his assurances are that at heart he is a believer.

This universe, as a whole entity, is not set on its right course unless it is run by one God who determines all its affairs: *"Had there been in them [i.e. the heavens and the earth] any deities other than God, they would surely have been overwhelmed by corruption."* (al-Anbiyā' 21: 22) The most essential characteristics of Godhead, according to man, are: that He be worshipped, and that He lays down legislation and sets standards for people to apply in their lives. He who claims any of these for himself, claims in effect to be a deity alongside God.

Corruption does not spread on earth unless Divinity is thus ascribed to beings other than God. It is only when a human being enslaves others, claiming that he himself must be obeyed, or that he has the power to legislate and to set values and standards for human society that corruption becomes rife. Such an assertion is a claim of Godhead, even though the claimant may not state it in as many words as Pharaoh did when he cried: *"I am your lord, most high."* (al-Nāzi'āt 79: 24) To acknowledge such an assertion by anyone is to be an idolater or to disbelieve in God. It is indeed the worst type of corruption.

Hence, the warning in this *sūrah* is followed by an address to the people of earlier revelations to come to an equitable agreement stipulating that worship is to be addressed to God alone and that no partners may be associated with Him, and that people do not take one another for lords beside God. If they reject this offer, then there can be no agreement or argument with them: *"Say: 'People of earlier revelations. Let us come to an agreement which is equitable between you and us: that we shall worship none but God, that we shall associate no partners with Him, and that we shall not take one another for lords beside God.' And if they turn away, then say: 'Bear witness that we have surrendered ourselves to God.'"* (Verse 64)

It is indeed an equitable agreement proposed by the Prophet. It does not seek to win any favours for the Prophet himself or for the Muslim community. It only aims to establish a clear agreement which applies to all at the same level, so that none is elevated above another, and none enslaves another. It is the fairest of offers which cannot be rejected except by those corrupters who have determined not to abide by the truth. According to this agreement, all will submit to God as His servants. None is His partner. He has chosen them to convey His message to mankind, not to share with Him His Divinity and Lordship.

"If they turn away, then say: 'Bear witness that we have surrendered ourselves to God.'" If they decline to worship God alone without partners and to submit themselves to Him alone, when worship and submission are the two clear aspects which determine people's attitudes towards God, then the Muslims have to declare their own attitude of surrendering themselves to God. The contrast shown here is between the Muslims and those who take one another for lords beside God, and it demonstrates decisively who the true Muslims are.

They are indeed those who worship God alone, submit to Him and do not enslave one another. These are the characteristics which distinguish them from the followers of all other religions. These characteristics single out the Islamic way of life as unique among all the alternatives known to man. When these characteristics apply to a certain community, it is a Muslim community. When these characteristics do not exist in a community it cannot be described as Muslim, even though people may emphatically profess that they are Muslims. Islam is the total liberation of man from enslavement by others. The Islamic system is the only one which makes that liberation a reality.

In all man-made systems, people enslave one another, and take one another for lords beside God. This happens in the most advanced democracies as well as in the worst types of dictatorship. Under all human systems, the authority to legislate and set values and standards is claimed by a group of people, in one form or another, who have the final authority. This group, which requires others to submit to its legislation, are the lords. They are acknowledged by the others as such since they allow them to claim for themselves the essential characteristics of Godhead. When people do acknowledge this authority for such a group, they are in effect worshipping them although they may not bow or prostrate before them.

It is only under Islam that man is free from such subjugation. He is free because he receives his values, standards, morality, systems, laws and legislation from God alone like everyone else who does the same. All people under the Islamic system stand at one level, looking up to one Lord Who is the Master of them all. None claims lordship over others. Submission to God, in this sense, is the Divine faith preached by every messenger God sent to man. When God sent His messengers to preach this faith, their task was to help people free themselves from subjugation to others, so that worship of God alone could be established. They were to help liberate people from the injustice inflicted by human beings so that they could enjoy God's absolute justice. Those who reject the message of the Prophets are not Muslims, no matter how deceptively and persuasively they may try to describe themselves as such. For, *"In the sight of God, the true faith is [man's] self-surrender to Him."* That is indeed the meaning of Islam.

4

The Heirs of Abraham's Faith

People of earlier revelations! Why do you argue about Abraham when both the Torah and the Gospel were not revealed till after him? Have you no sense? (65)

You have indeed argued about that of which you have some knowledge; why then do you argue about that of which you have no knowledge at all? God knows, whereas you do not know. (66)

Abraham was neither a Jew nor a Christian; but he was wholly devoted to God, having surrendered himself to Him. He was not of those who associate partners with God. (67)

The people who have the best claim to Abraham are those who followed him, and this Prophet and those who are true believers. God is the Guardian of the believers. (68)

يَٰٓأَهْلَ ٱلْكِتَٰبِ لِمَ تُحَآجُّونَ فِىٓ إِبْرَٰهِيمَ وَمَآ أُنزِلَتِ ٱلتَّوْرَىٰةُ وَٱلْإِنجِيلُ إِلَّا مِنۢ بَعْدِهِۦٓ أَفَلَا تَعْقِلُونَ ۝

هَٰٓأَنتُمْ هَٰٓؤُلَآءِ حَٰجَجْتُمْ فِيمَا لَكُم بِهِۦ عِلْمٌ فَلِمَ تُحَآجُّونَ فِيمَا لَيْسَ لَكُم بِهِۦ عِلْمٌ وَٱللَّهُ يَعْلَمُ وَأَنتُمْ لَا تَعْلَمُونَ ۝

مَا كَانَ إِبْرَٰهِيمُ يَهُودِيًّا وَلَا نَصْرَانِيًّا وَلَٰكِن كَانَ حَنِيفًا مُّسْلِمًا وَمَا كَانَ مِنَ ٱلْمُشْرِكِينَ ۝

إِنَّ أَوْلَى ٱلنَّاسِ بِإِبْرَٰهِيمَ لَلَّذِينَ ٱتَّبَعُوهُ وَهَٰذَا ٱلنَّبِىُّ وَٱلَّذِينَ ءَامَنُوا۟ وَٱللَّهُ وَلِىُّ ٱلْمُؤْمِنِينَ ۝

A party of the people of earlier revelations would love to lead you astray; but they lead astray none but themselves, although they may not perceive it. (69)

يَوَدَّت طَّآئِفَةٌ مِّنْ أَهْلِ ٱلْكِتَٰبِ لَوْ يُضِلُّونَكُمْ وَمَا يُضِلُّونَ إِلَّآ أَنفُسَهُمْ وَمَا يَشْعُرُونَ ۝

People of earlier revelations! Why do you disbelieve in God's revelations when you yourselves bear witness [to their truth]? (70)

يَٰٓأَهْلَ ٱلْكِتَٰبِ لِمَ تَكْفُرُونَ بِـَٔايَٰتِ ٱللَّهِ وَأَنتُمْ تَشْهَدُونَ ۝

People of earlier revelations! Why do you cloak the truth with falsehood, and knowingly conceal the truth? (71)

يَٰٓأَهْلَ ٱلْكِتَٰبِ لِمَ تَلْبِسُونَ ٱلْحَقَّ بِٱلْبَٰطِلِ وَتَكْتُمُونَ ٱلْحَقَّ وَأَنتُمْ تَعْلَمُونَ ۝

A party of the people of earlier revelations say [to one another]: "Declare at the beginning of the day, that you believe in what has been revealed to the believers, and then deny it at the end of the day, so that they may go back on their faith. (72)

وَقَالَت طَّآئِفَةٌ مِّنْ أَهْلِ ٱلْكِتَٰبِ ءَامِنُوا۟ بِٱلَّذِىٓ أُنزِلَ عَلَى ٱلَّذِينَ ءَامَنُوا۟ وَجْهَ ٱلنَّهَارِ وَٱكْفُرُوٓا۟ ءَاخِرَهُۥ لَعَلَّهُمْ يَرْجِعُونَ ۝

"But do not really trust anyone except those who follow your own faith" – Say: "All true guidance is God's guidance – That anyone may be given the like of what you have been given. Or that they should contend against you before your Lord." Say: "Grace is in God's hand: He bestows it on whom He wills. God is Munificent and All-Knowing." (73)

وَلَا تُؤْمِنُوٓا۟ إِلَّا لِمَن تَبِعَ دِينَكُمْ قُلْ إِنَّ ٱلْهُدَىٰ هُدَى ٱللَّهِ أَن يُؤْتَىٰٓ أَحَدٌ مِّثْلَ مَآ أُوتِيتُمْ أَوْ يُحَآجُّوكُمْ عِندَ رَبِّكُمْ قُلْ إِنَّ ٱلْفَضْلَ بِيَدِ ٱللَّهِ يُؤْتِيهِ مَن يَشَآءُ وَٱللَّهُ وَٰسِعٌ عَلِيمٌ ۝

He singles out for His mercy whom He wills. And God's grace is great indeed. (74)

يَخْتَصُّ بِرَحْمَتِهِۦ مَن يَشَآءُ وَٱللَّهُ ذُو ٱلْفَضْلِ ٱلْعَظِيمِ ۝

Among the people of earlier revelations there is many a one who, if you trust him with a treasure, will return it to you intact; and there is among them many a one who, if you trust him with a small gold coin, will not return it to you, unless you keep standing over him. For they say: "We have no obligation to keep faith with Gentiles." Thus they deliberately say of God what they know to be a lie. (75)

۞ وَمِنْ أَهْلِ ٱلْكِتَٰبِ مَنْ إِن تَأْمَنْهُ بِقِنطَارٍ يُؤَدِّهِۦٓ إِلَيْكَ وَمِنْهُم مَّنْ إِن تَأْمَنْهُ بِدِينَارٍ لَّا يُؤَدِّهِۦٓ إِلَيْكَ إِلَّا مَا دُمْتَ عَلَيْهِ قَآئِمًا ذَٰلِكَ بِأَنَّهُمْ قَالُوا۟ لَيْسَ عَلَيْنَا فِى ٱلْأُمِّيِّنَ سَبِيلٌ وَيَقُولُونَ عَلَى ٱللَّهِ ٱلْكَذِبَ وَهُمْ يَعْلَمُونَ ۝

Indeed those who fulfil their pledges and guard themselves against evil [enjoy God's love]; for God loves the righteous. (76)

بَلَىٰ مَنْ أَوْفَىٰ بِعَهْدِهِۦ وَٱتَّقَىٰ فَإِنَّ ٱللَّهَ يُحِبُّ ٱلْمُتَّقِينَ ۝

Those who barter away their covenant with God and their oaths for a trifling gain will have no share in the life to come. God will neither speak to them, nor cast a look on them on the Day of Resurrection, nor will He cleanse them of their sins. Theirs will be a grievous suffering. (77)

إِنَّ ٱلَّذِينَ يَشْتَرُونَ بِعَهْدِ ٱللَّهِ وَأَيْمَٰنِهِمْ ثَمَنًا قَلِيلًا أُو۟لَٰٓئِكَ لَا خَلَٰقَ لَهُمْ فِى ٱلْأَخِرَةِ وَلَا يُكَلِّمُهُمُ ٱللَّهُ وَلَا يَنظُرُ إِلَيْهِمْ يَوْمَ ٱلْقِيَٰمَةِ وَلَا يُزَكِّيهِمْ وَلَهُمْ عَذَابٌ أَلِيمٌ ۝

There are some among them who twist their tongues when quoting the Scriptures, so that you may think that [what they say] is from the Scriptures, when it is not from the Scriptures. They say: "It is from God", when it is not from God. Thus, they deliberately say of God what they know to be a lie. (78)

وَإِنَّ مِنْهُمْ لَفَرِيقًا يَلْوُونَ أَلْسِنَتَهُم بِٱلْكِتَٰبِ لِتَحْسَبُوهُ مِنَ ٱلْكِتَٰبِ وَمَا هُوَ مِنَ ٱلْكِتَٰبِ وَيَقُولُونَ هُوَ مِنْ عِندِ ٱللَّهِ وَمَا هُوَ مِنْ عِندِ ٱللَّهِ وَيَقُولُونَ عَلَى ٱللَّهِ ٱلْكَذِبَ وَهُمْ يَعْلَمُونَ ۞

It is not conceivable that any human being to whom God had given revelation and wisdom and prophethood would subsequently say to people: "Worship me instead of God." But rather: "Be devoted servants of God, by virtue of spreading the knowledge of the Scriptures and your constant study of them." (79)

مَا كَانَ لِبَشَرٍ أَن يُؤْتِيَهُ ٱللَّهُ ٱلْكِتَٰبَ وَٱلْحُكْمَ وَٱلنُّبُوَّةَ ثُمَّ يَقُولَ لِلنَّاسِ كُونُوا۟ عِبَادًا لِّي مِن دُونِ ٱللَّهِ وَلَٰكِن كُونُوا۟ رَبَّٰنِيِّينَ بِمَا كُنتُمْ تُعَلِّمُونَ ٱلْكِتَٰبَ وَبِمَا كُنتُمْ تَدْرُسُونَ ۞

Nor would he bid you to take the angels and the Prophets as your gods. Would he bid you to be unbelievers after you have surrendered yourselves to God? (80)

وَلَا يَأْمُرَكُمْ أَن تَتَّخِذُوا۟ ٱلْمَلَٰٓئِكَةَ وَٱلنَّبِيِّۦنَ أَرْبَابًا أَيَأْمُرُكُم بِٱلْكُفْرِ بَعْدَ إِذْ أَنتُم مُّسْلِمُونَ ۞

God made a covenant with the Prophets: "If, after what I have vouchsafed to you of the Scriptures and wisdom, there comes to you a messenger confirming the truth of what you have in your possession, you shall believe in him and you shall help him. Do you," said He, "affirm this and accept the obligation I lay upon you in these terms?" They answered: "We do affirm it." Said He: "Then bear witness, and I am also a witness with you." (81)

Then those who turn away afterwards are indeed transgressors. (82)

Do they seek a religion other than God's, when every soul in the heavens and the earth has submitted to Him, willingly or by compulsion, and to Him they shall all return? (83)

Say: "We believe in God and in that which has been bestowed from on high upon us, and that which has been bestowed on Abraham, Ishmael, Isaac, Jacob and their descendants, and that which has been vouchsafed by their Lord to Moses and Jesus and all the prophets. We make no distinction between them. To Him do we surrender ourselves." (84)

وَإِذْ أَخَذَ ٱللَّهُ مِيثَٰقَ ٱلنَّبِيِّـۧنَ لَمَآ ءَاتَيْتُكُم مِّن كِتَٰبٍ وَحِكْمَةٍ ثُمَّ جَآءَكُمْ رَسُولٌ مُّصَدِّقٌ لِّمَا مَعَكُمْ لَتُؤْمِنُنَّ بِهِۦ وَلَتَنصُرُنَّهُۥ قَالَ ءَأَقْرَرْتُمْ وَأَخَذْتُمْ عَلَىٰ ذَٰلِكُمْ إِصْرِى قَالُوٓا۟ أَقْرَرْنَا قَالَ فَٱشْهَدُوا۟ وَأَنَا۠ مَعَكُم مِّنَ ٱلشَّٰهِدِينَ ﴿٨١﴾

فَمَن تَوَلَّىٰ بَعْدَ ذَٰلِكَ فَأُو۟لَٰٓئِكَ هُمُ ٱلْفَٰسِقُونَ ﴿٨٢﴾

أَفَغَيْرَ دِينِ ٱللَّهِ يَبْغُونَ وَلَهُۥٓ أَسْلَمَ مَن فِى ٱلسَّمَٰوَٰتِ وَٱلْأَرْضِ طَوْعًا وَكَرْهًا وَإِلَيْهِ يُرْجَعُونَ ﴿٨٣﴾

قُلْ ءَامَنَّا بِٱللَّهِ وَمَآ أُنزِلَ عَلَيْنَا وَمَآ أُنزِلَ عَلَىٰٓ إِبْرَٰهِيمَ وَإِسْمَٰعِيلَ وَإِسْحَٰقَ وَيَعْقُوبَ وَٱلْأَسْبَاطِ وَمَآ أُوتِىَ مُوسَىٰ وَعِيسَىٰ وَٱلنَّبِيُّونَ مِن رَّبِّهِمْ لَا نُفَرِّقُ بَيْنَ أَحَدٍ مِّنْهُمْ وَنَحْنُ لَهُۥ مُسْلِمُونَ ﴿٨٤﴾

He who seeks a religion other than self-surrender to God, it will not be accepted from him, and in the life to come he will be among the lost. (85)

وَمَن يَبْتَغِ غَيْرَ ٱلْإِسْلَٰمِ دِينًا فَلَن يُقْبَلَ مِنْهُ وَهُوَ فِي ٱلْآخِرَةِ مِنَ ٱلْخَٰسِرِينَ ۝

How shall God guide people who have lapsed into disbelief after having accepted the faith and having borne witness that this messenger is true, and after having received clear evidence of the truth? God does not guide the wrongdoers. (86)

كَيْفَ يَهْدِى ٱللَّهُ قَوْمًا كَفَرُوا۟ بَعْدَ إِيمَٰنِهِمْ وَشَهِدُوٓا۟ أَنَّ ٱلرَّسُولَ حَقٌّ وَجَآءَهُمُ ٱلْبَيِّنَٰتُ وَٱللَّهُ لَا يَهْدِى ٱلْقَوْمَ ٱلظَّٰلِمِينَ ۝

Of such people the punishment shall be the curse of God, the angels and all men. (87)

أُو۟لَٰٓئِكَ جَزَآؤُهُمْ أَنَّ عَلَيْهِمْ لَعْنَةَ ٱللَّهِ وَٱلْمَلَٰٓئِكَةِ وَٱلنَّاسِ أَجْمَعِينَ ۝

Under it they shall abide. Neither their suffering shall be lightened, nor shall they be granted respite. (88)

خَٰلِدِينَ فِيهَا لَا يُخَفَّفُ عَنْهُمُ ٱلْعَذَابُ وَلَا هُمْ يُنظَرُونَ ۝

Excepted shall be those who afterwards repent and mend their ways; for God is Much-Forgiving, Merciful. (89)

إِلَّا ٱلَّذِينَ تَابُوا۟ مِنۢ بَعْدِ ذَٰلِكَ وَأَصْلَحُوا۟ فَإِنَّ ٱللَّهَ غَفُورٌ رَّحِيمٌ ۝

But those who return to disbelief after having accepted the faith and then grow more stubborn in their rejection of the faith, their repentance will not be accepted. For they are those who have truly gone astray. (90)

إِنَّ ٱلَّذِينَ كَفَرُوا۟ بَعْدَ إِيمَٰنِهِمْ ثُمَّ ٱزْدَادُوا۟ كُفْرًا لَّن تُقْبَلَ تَوْبَتُهُمْ وَأُو۟لَٰٓئِكَ هُمُ ٱلضَّآلُّونَ ۝

As for those who disbelieve and die unbelievers, not even the earth full of gold shall be accepted from any one of them, were he to offer it in ransom. They shall have grievous suffering and they shall have none to help them. (91)

إِنَّ ٱلَّذِينَ كَفَرُوا۟ وَمَاتُوا۟ وَهُمْ كُفَّارٌ فَلَن يُقْبَلَ مِنْ أَحَدِهِم مِّلْءُ ٱلْأَرْضِ ذَهَبًا وَلَوِ ٱفْتَدَىٰ بِهِۦٓ أُو۟لَٰٓئِكَ لَهُمْ عَذَابٌ أَلِيمٌ وَمَا لَهُم مِّن نَّٰصِرِينَ ﴿٩١﴾

You will never attain to true piety unless you spend on others out of what you dearly cherish. God has full knowledge of what you spend. (92)

لَن تَنَالُوا۟ ٱلْبِرَّ حَتَّىٰ تُنفِقُوا۟ مِمَّا تُحِبُّونَ وَمَا تُنفِقُوا۟ مِن شَىْءٍ فَإِنَّ ٱللَّهَ بِهِۦ عَلِيمٌ ﴿٩٢﴾

Overview

This part of the *sūrah*, from verse 65 to verse 92, takes up the same general theme of the controversy surrounding religious beliefs between the people of earlier revelations, i.e. the Jews and Christians, and the Muslims. It explores the relentless and devious efforts lined up against Islam; the scheming, smears, slandering, vilification, lies and devilish intrigues of its opponents. It presents the Qur'ān's argument on behalf of the Muslims and reassures them of the truth of their cause and exposes the deviation and hopelessness of their detractors. It openly and closely probes the habits, ethics, intentions and activities of those enemies in order to make the Muslims fully aware of the threat they pose and to take away the mantle of knowledge and wisdom those enemies had assumed. It moves to dissipate any trust some gullible Muslims may have placed in them. It discourages following their example, and eliminates the dangers of their intrigue by exposing it so that no one may be deceived or misled by it.

This section begins with castigating Jewish and Christian claims of affinity to the Prophet Abraham, who pre-dated both the Torah and the Gospel. Each had professed him to be a follower of their respective religious beliefs. Their arguments are dismissed as totally baseless. Abraham, the *sūrah* asserts, was a devotee to God's true religion based on submission to God, i.e. Islam, and his natural patrons are those

111

who adhere to that same religion. God shall be the Guardian of all true believers. Thus, the assertions of both Jews and Christians are refuted and a continuous line emerges linking all prophets and messengers of God throughout the ages. The *sūrah* states: *"The people who have the best claim to Abraham are those who followed him, and this Prophet, and those who are true believers. God is the Guardian of the believers."* (Verse 68)

The *sūrah* then goes on to expose the real, undeclared objective of the controversies stirred up by the Jews and Christians regarding Abraham as also other issues. Their aim had always been to mislead and distract the Muslims, and to sow doubts in their hearts about Islam. Here the Qur'ān lashes out against such detractors: *"People of earlier revelations! Why do you disbelieve in God's revelations when you yourselves bear witness [to their truth]? People of earlier revelations! Why do you cloak the truth with falsehood, and knowingly conceal the truth?"* (Verses 70–1)

The *sūrah* then reveals aspects and manifestations of that evil intrigue. The culprits declare adherence to Islam in the morning but reject it before the day is out in order to feed uncertainty and suspicion in the hearts of weaker Muslims who are found among all communities. Surely, there must be a valid reason why Jewish and Christian individuals, whose people had a much longer association with, and experience of, prophets and Divine revelations, rejected Islam. The *sūrah* says: *"A party of the people of earlier revelations say [to one another]: 'Declare at the beginning of the day, that you believe in what has been revealed to the believers, and then deny it at the end of the day, so that they may go back on their faith.'"* (Verse 72) How vile and malicious their actions are.

The nature of some Jews and Christians is then further examined, together with their ethical standards and their commitment to agreements and covenants. There is no doubting the honesty and integrity of many of them, but some are not to be trusted or relied on to honour an agreement or respect a pledge. These find religious justification for their greed and deceit, but their religions are not to be blamed for such behaviour. The *sūrah* says: *"Among the people of earlier revelations there is many a one who, if you trust him with a treasure, will return it to you intact; and there is among them many a one who, if you trust him with a small gold coin, will not return it to you, unless you keep standing over him. For they say: 'We have no obligation to keep faith with Gentiles.' Thus, they deliberately say of God what they know to be a lie."* (Verse 75)

At this point the *surah* outlines an aspect of Islam's ethical outlook, its basis and direct link to fear of God Almighty, saying: *"Indeed those who fulfil their pledges and guard themselves against evil [enjoy God's love]; for God loves the righteous. Those who barter away their covenant with God and their oaths for a trifling gain will have no share in the life to come. God will neither speak to them, nor cast a look on them on the Day of Resurrection, nor will He cleanse them of their sins. Theirs will be a grievous suffering."* (Verses 76–7)

The *surah* then gives another instance whereby some Jews and Christians resort to devious behaviour and lies about Islam in order to score short-term gains. It says: *"There are some among them who twist their tongues when quoting the Scriptures, so that you may think that [what they say] is from the Scriptures, when it is not from the Scriptures. They say: 'It is from God', when it is not from God. Thus, they deliberately say of God what they know to be a lie."* (Verse 78)

This is a reference to Christian attempts to show that the Qur'ān supported their belief in the Divinity of Jesus and the Holy Spirit. However, God denounces such notions and refutes the claims that Jesus ever made such assertions. It says: *"It is not conceivable that any human being to whom God has given revelation and wisdom and prophethood would subsequently say to people: 'Worship me instead of God.' But rather: 'Be devoted servants of God, by virtue of spreading the knowledge of the Scriptures and your constant study of them.' Nor would he bid you to take the angels and the Prophets as your gods. Would he bid you to be unbelievers after you have surrendered yourselves to God?"* (Verses 79–80)

It then turns to mention the essence of God's covenant with successive messengers whereby they endorse and support one another. It says: *"God made a covenant with the Prophets: 'If, after what I have vouchsafed to you of the Scriptures and wisdom, there comes to you a messenger confirming the truth of what you have in your possession, you shall believe in him and you shall help him. Do you,' said He, 'affirm this and accept the obligation I lay upon you in these terms?' They answered: 'We do affirm it.' said He: 'Then bear witness, and I am also a witness with you.'"* (Verse 81) Hence the obligation upon the people of earlier revelations to believe in the last and final Prophet and to champion his cause. Alas, they did not respect God's covenant or the covenants they made with their own prophets.

With that on-going covenant in the background, the *surah* asserts that anyone seeking a religion other than Islam, or complete surrender to God, would be breaking away from the whole grand and universal order God has ordained for all creation. It says: *"Do they seek a religion other than God's, when every soul in the heavens and the earth has submitted to Him, willingly or by compulsion, and to Him they shall all return?"* (Verse 83) Those who choose not to surrender totally to God or humbly and freely comply with His order of life, appear abnormal and out of place in this majestic world design.

At this point, the *sūrah* turns to direct the Prophet Muḥammad and the Muslims to declare their unshakeable faith in the One God, as set out in what was revealed to all prophets, as the only religious belief sanctioned by God Almighty. It says: *"He who seeks a religion other than self-surrender to God, it will not be accepted from him, and in the life to come he will be among the lost."* (Verse 85)

Those who reject God's religion, however, have no prospect of either being guided by God or being spared His punishment unless they heed and repent. As for those who leave this world without believing in God, nothing they may have done will save them, even if they were to give the earth's weight in gold.

The *sūrah* goes on to urge the Muslims to give those possessions closest to their hearts to good causes, as an investment with God to be collected in the hereafter. It says: *"You will never attain to true piety unless you spend on others out of what you dearly cherish. God has full knowledge of what you spend."* (Verse 92)

Thus, in one relatively short passage, this *sūrah* packs an impressive and important host of issues, facts and directives. It covers a mere round in the wider confrontation which the *sūrah* as a whole addresses. It is the confrontation between the Muslim community and its opponents, which has been going on for centuries and which continues to rage on today. It bears the same ends and objectives, despite the different forms it takes and the variety of means or methods it employs today. It is the same endless controversy.

We now turn to look at the text more closely.

A Dispute Over Abraham's Faith

People of earlier revelations! Why do you argue about Abraham when both the Torah and the Gospel were not revealed till after him? Have you no sense? You have indeed argued about that of which you have some knowledge; why then do you argue about that of which you have no knowledge at all? God knows, whereas you do not know. Abraham was neither a Jew nor a Christian; but he was wholly devoted to God, having surrendered himself to Him. He was not of those who associate partners with God. The people who have the best claim to Abraham are those who followed him, and this Prophet and those who are true believers. God is the Guardian of the believers. (Verses 65–8)

Muḥammad ibn Isḥāq relates a report attributed to Ibn 'Abbās, the Prophet's cousin, which says: "A number of Christians from Najran and a number of Jewish rabbis met at the Prophet's place and disputed among themselves. The rabbis claimed that Abraham was nothing but a Jew, while the Christians maintained that Abraham was a Christian. God then revealed this verse starting with: *"People of earlier revelations! Why do you argue about Abraham ... "*

Whether it was true or not that that particular occasion was the time when this verse was revealed, it is apparent that this verse is meant to be an answer to the claims of people who professed to believe in earlier revelations. There seem to have been arguments either with the Prophet (peace be upon him) or arguments among themselves in the presence of the Prophet. The ultimate aim of these claims was to monopolise God's covenant with Abraham which meant that prophethood would remain in Abraham's seed, and to monopolise honour and Divine guidance. More importantly, they sought through these claims to reject the Prophet's statement that he followed the faith of Abraham and that the Muslims were the rightful heirs of the original pure faith. The disputants also hoped to raise doubts concerning this fact in the minds of at least some Muslims.

It is for this reason that God condemns their attitude here so strongly and shows clearly that their arguments are without basis. Abraham lived long before the revelation of the Torah or the Gospel; how could he, then, be a Jew or a Christian? It is a totally illogical claim which collapses at the first glance at history: *"People of earlier revelations! Why do you argue about Abraham when both the Torah and the Gospel were not revealed till after him? Have you no sense?"* (Verse 65)

They are further condemned in the verse that follows. All their arguments are shown to be without foundation. They appear to indulge in an endless dispute without providing supporting evidence, consistency or logic: *"You have indeed argued about that of which you have some knowledge; why then do you argue about that of which you have no knowledge at all? God knows, whereas you do not know."*

They argued about Jesus, and they argued about certain Divine legislation when they were called upon to submit to the rulings included in God's Book. Instead, they turned their backs on it. In these matters, they had some knowledge. They could not, however, claim any basis, even technical, for their arguments about things which took place before the revelation of their Scriptures and the preaching of their religions. They argue, then, for argument's sake. It is a worthless argument which is advanced for vested interests and which follows no logical method. A person who advances such an argument cannot be trusted at all. He is, indeed, not worth listening to.

When the *sūrah* has shown the worthlessness of their argument, it states the truth known to God. He alone knows the truth of that distant period in history and the true nature of the faith He revealed to His servant, Abraham. When God states something, His word is final. No one can say anything which differs with God's statement, unless he wishes to make a worthless, futile argument. *"Abraham was neither a Jew nor a Christian; but he was wholly devoted to God, having surrendered himself to Him. He was not of those who associate partners with God."* (Verse 67) Here, we have a clear statement of what has already been implied, that Abraham was neither a Jew nor a Christian, since both the Torah and the Gospel were revealed after his time. It is further stated that Abraham had no interest whatsoever in any creed or doctrine other than complete devotion to God. He was a Muslim in the broad sense of Islam, meaning total surrender to God.

"He was not of those who associate partners with God." This is again implied in the preceding statement that Abraham *"was wholly devoted to God, having surrendered himself to Him."* That it is re-emphasised here is significant because it indicates first that both the Jews and the Christians, who had over the years come to accept deviant beliefs, were in effect associating partners with God. Hence, Abraham could neither be a Jew nor a Christian, but an upright man who surrendered himself to God. It further indicates that Islam and polytheism are two diametrically opposed doctrines. Islam means the absolute oneness of God with everything that this oneness entails. Hence, it can have no common ground with any form of polytheism. Moreover, it shows that the claim of the Quraysh idolaters that they followed Abraham's religion since they were the custodians of the Ka'bah, the House he

built for worship in Makkah, is also false. Abraham believed in God alone and surrendered himself to Him, while those people of the Quraysh were idolaters: *"He was not of those who associate partners with God."*

In view of the truth stated in the Qur'ān about Abraham, neither the Jews, nor the Christians, nor indeed the idolaters could lay any claim to his heritage or to his religion since they had all moved far away from his faith. It is faith which is, indeed, the paramount relation which groups people together, according to Islam. If that relationship which unites the people of faith is lacking, no other tie of blood, lineage, race or land is of any value. In the Islamic view, man achieves his humanity through his spirit, the blow which has made out of him a man. Hence, faith, which is the most essential quality of his spirit, forms the basis which unites human beings together. It is only animals that are grouped together on the basis of land, species, food, pasture, boundaries and fences. Patronage between individuals, communities and generations can only be based on faith. It is faith which unites one believer with another, one Muslim community with another, and one generation of believers who surrender themselves to God and all other generations, bypassing the limitations of time and place, blood and lineage, race and nationality. They are all united by their belief in God Who is the Guardian of all the believers: *"The people who have the best claim to Abraham are those who followed him, and this Prophet and those who are true believers. God is the Guardian of the believers."* (Verse 68)

Those who followed Abraham when he was alive and implemented his method and abided by his teachings had the best claim to him. The same applies to this Prophet who shared with Abraham the quality of surrendering himself to God, according to the testimony of God Himself, the best of all witnesses. Then come those who believe in this Prophet and, thereby, follow Abraham's method and practice.

"God is the Guardian of the believers." They are His party, sheltered by His cover, devoting their loyalty totally to Him, to the exclusion of everyone else. They are one family and one nation, the unity of which transcends all barriers of time, place, country, nationality, race and lineage.

This is the noblest form of social unity which alone is worthy of man. Moreover, it is the only method to establish a community free of all artificial restrictions. The only bond which brings people together in this form is a voluntary one. Every individual can release himself of it by his own choice. That bond is a faith which he personally chooses.

On the other hand, a person cannot change his race if his society is based on race. Neither can he change his community or colour, nor can he easily change his language or caste if any of these is the basis upon which his society is set up. Such barriers will always be divisive, keeping people apart, unless they take up the bond of ideology and faith as their uniting bond. Such a bond relies on personal conviction. Every individual can consciously choose it and join the community on its basis without having to change his race, colour, language or caste. This is, indeed, an honour given to man because it makes its uniting bond based on the noblest of his qualities.

The choice before humanity is either to live as Islam wishes: human beings united by what nourishes their spirits and refines their feelings, or to live like cattle, confined within the boundaries of race, colour and place. We have to remember here that all these are similar to the distinctive marks given to cattle so that they remain identifiable.

A Deliberate Attempt to Conceal the Truth

> *A party of the people of earlier revelations would love to lead you astray; but they lead astray none but themselves, although they may not perceive it. People of earlier revelations! Why do you disbelieve in God's revelations when you yourselves bear witness [to their truth]? People of earlier revelations! Why do you cloak the truth with falsehood, and knowingly conceal the truth? A party of the people of earlier revelations say [to one another]: "Declare at the beginning of the day, that you believe in what has been revealed to the believers, and then deny it at the end of the day, so that they may go back on their faith. But do not really trust anyone except those who follow your own faith" – Say: "All true guidance is God's guidance – That anyone may be given the like of what you have been given. Or that they should contend against you before your Lord" Say: "Grace is in God's hand: He bestows it on whom He wills. God is Munificent and All-Knowing." He singles out for His mercy whom He wills. And God's grace is great indeed.* (Verses 69–74)

In this passage, the Muslim community is told of the intentions of the people of earlier revelations behind every argument they may raise. The Qur'ān confronts those people with what they actually plot and scheme in close proximity to the Muslim community. Their masks are torn from them and their reality is made apparent to all.

The grudge which the people of earlier revelations bear to the Muslim community relates to the faith of that community. They hate that the Muslims should have Divine guidance. They hate to see them holding to their own faith with firmness and reassurance. They, therefore, mobilise all their efforts to cause the Muslims to go astray: *"A party of the people of earlier revelations would love to lead you astray."* It is, then, an inner desire which lies behind all their plotting, scheming, arguments and concealment of the truth. There is no doubt that such a desire, motivated by prejudice and grudge, is deviant. An evil desire cannot be based on any right guidance. Hence, the moment they entertain a desire to turn the Muslims away from their faith, they cause themselves to go astray. It is only a person who finds himself lost in a labyrinth of deviation that loves to lead astray those who are following a straight path: *"But they lead astray none but themselves, although they may not perceive it."* (Verse 69)

The Muslims will come to no harm from what their enemies may scheme against them as long as they maintain and implement their faith. God guarantees them that the scheming and plotting of their enemies will be counter-productive as long as the Muslims hold on to their faith.

The people of earlier revelations are then made to face the reality of their untenable situation: *"People of earlier revelations! Why do you disbelieve in God's revelations when you yourselves bear witness [to their truth]? People of earlier revelations! Why do you cloak the truth with falsehood, and knowingly conceal the truth?"* (Verses 70–1)

Those people who had received earlier revelations were at that time, and still are, able to recognise the truth clearly embodied in this religion. This applies to those who know the references contained in their own Scriptures about this religion. Some of them were candid about what they read, so much so that a number of them embraced Islam on this basis. It also applies to those who are not so aware of these references but who are nonetheless able to recognise the clear truth of Islam which is sufficient to persuade them to accept it. Both groups, however, continue to reject the truth of Islam, not because of any lack of evidence and proof, but because of personal prejudices and vested interests. The Qur'ān addresses them as "people of earlier revelations", because it is this very quality which should have prompted them to hearken to God's new revelations and follow His new Book.

They are addressed again in order to unmask their efforts at confounding truth with falsehood, deliberately and knowingly. This is an action which merits uncompromising censure.

This attitude of the people of earlier revelations so condemned by God is the one which they have adopted since the time of the Prophet until the present day. The Jews began by adopting it at the very first moment, and they were followed later by the Christian Crusaders.

Over the centuries, they have unfortunately been able to plant in Islamic heritage that which has nothing to do with this religion of Islam and which cannot be discovered without Herculean efforts. They have managed to confound truth with falsehood in much of our heritage, with the exception, however, of this Book which God has undertaken to preserve intact for the rest of time. Praise be to God for His limitless grace.

They have distorted much of Islamic history and its events as well as the images of its best men of action. They have also put their alien plants in the field of the *ḥadīth* until God has enabled the great scholars of *ḥadīth* to verify and sift out the true from the false, as much as is humanly possible. Their distortions have also crept into commentaries on the Qur'ān to the extent that it has become very difficult for a student of the Qur'ān to find his clear way to a correct understanding. They have also implanted their own men, hundreds if not thousands, to distort our Islamic heritage. Some of these are with us even today in the shape of Orientalists and their disciples who occupy positions of intellectual leadership in the countries whose peoples claim to be Muslim. They have also implanted in our societies scores of people who are given the status of heroes when they have actually been carefully brought up by Zionism and Christian fanaticism in order to serve the enemies of Islam in a way which cannot be achieved by any open enemy.

Such evil schemes continue to be pursued with no sign of weakening. The only way to guard against them and to be spared their damaging effects is to hold tight to God's Book which He Himself has undertaken to preserve, and to refer to it for guidance and for plotting our strategy in this ever-continuing battle. A reference is then made to some of the attempts undertaken by a party of the people of earlier revelations to cause internal confusion within the Muslim community and to turn them away from Divine guidance: *"A party of the people of earlier revelations say [to one another]: 'Declare, at the beginning of the day, that you believe in what has been revealed to the believers, and then deny it at the end of the day, so that they may go back on their faith.'"* (Verse 72)

As we have said, this is an act of wicked deception. When such people pretend to accept Islam, then reject it, their action is bound to perplex those who do not have strong faith, and those who have not fully appreciated the truth of Islam and its nature. This was true in an even greater measure in the case of the illiterate Arabs, at the time of the Prophet, who took it for granted that the people of earlier revelations were more aware than themselves of the nature of religions and revelation. When they saw such people accepting Islam one day and rejecting it the next day, they thought that their subsequent action was the result of their coming to realise that there was something wrong with that religion. This caused them considerable consternation and they were uncertain what attitude to adopt.

This trick continues to be employed even today, in a variety of ways suitable to each particular situation and adapted to the mentality of people in every generation.

A Dirty Tricks Campaign to Confuse Believers

The enemies of Islam have realised that to employ this trick in a simple form is no longer possible. They, therefore, resort to a wide range of methods of concealment which are no more than variations on the old theme.

These forces rely today on a large army of disciples all over the Muslim world. Among these are professors, lecturers, thinkers and scholars, as well as writers, poets, artists and journalists who all have Muslim names because they come from Muslim families. Some of them indeed are included in the ranks of Islamic "scholars".

This army of disciples is mobilised for the achievement of the ultimate goal of shaking the foundations of faith within the Muslim community. It employs all methods of scientific research, literary works, art and information. All these complement one another in the onslaught on Islamic faith and Islamic law. They belittle the role of Islamic faith, interpret it in their own way, and overburden it with what is alien to it. They never tire of branding Islam as "reactionary" and calling on people to break away from it. They try hard to keep Islam away from human life either because they fear the effect of human life on Islam or because they fear the effect of Islam on human life. They work hard to invent concepts, ideals, values and standards which are in direct conflict with those of the Islamic faith, painting the former in the most appealing of pictures while distorting the latter so that they appear in the most grotesque of forms. Moreover, they try to facilitate the breaking loose of carnal desires, seeking to erode the moral basis upon which clean faith is founded. What is more, they distort history in the same way as they distort Scriptures.

To compound their evil, they claim to be Muslims. They, after all, have Muslim names. With these names they declare to be believers at the beginning of the day. With their evil designs they deny the faith at the end of the day. In both their actions, they play the same role as the people of earlier revelations. All that has changed is the framework.

The people of earlier revelations used to encourage one another to pretend to be Muslims one day and to reject Islam the next, so that the Muslims would go back on their faith. They also counselled each other to keep this secret between themselves, not to reveal it to anyone except the followers of their own religion: *"But do not really trust anyone except those who follow your own faith."* (Verse 73) Their secret was closely guarded against the Muslims. The same applies today to the servants of Zionism and Christian fanaticism. They are all working together for a definite objective, that is, the total destruction of the Islamic faith. They may not have sat together to sign a contract or to draw up a plot defining their respective roles, but they, nevertheless, have the sort of understanding which normally exists between stooges who work for the same goal defined by their common master. They trust each other and compare notes. They, or some of them at least, subsequently adopt false pretences. Everything around them is placed in their service and those who are aware of the nature of this faith all over the world are suffering persecution and imprisonment. *"But do not really trust anyone except those who follow your own faith."*

At this point, God directs the Prophet to declare that true guidance is that provided by God, and that unless people accept and abide by it they will never find real guidance by any other method or way of life: *"Say: 'All true guidance is God's guidance.'"* This statement is given in answer to their encouragement to one another to *"declare at the beginning of the day, that you believe in what has been revealed to the believers, and then deny it at the end of the day, so that they may go back on their faith."* This serves as a warning to the Muslims and helps them to foil the evil goal of their enemies. Since there is no true guidance except that provided by God, then those schemers only want the believers to sink back into deviation and total disbelief. It should be mentioned here that this instruction to the Prophet to declare that true guidance is that provided by God, is given even before the statements of people of earlier revelations are quoted in full. The *sūrah* then goes on quoting them: *"That anyone may be given the like of what you have been given. Or that they should contend against you before your Lord"* (Verse 73) These are the reasons they give for stating earlier: *"Do not really trust anyone except those who follow your own faith."* This betrays their grudge, envy and hatred of the idea that God should give prophethood and revelation to anyone other than them. It also betrays their fear that should the Muslims come to know the truth they themselves know, despite their denials, they will take it as an argument against them before God. They say this as if God does not take against them anything other than verbal statements. The fact is that such thoughts cannot be entertained by anyone who has a sound concept of God and His attributes, or who has a correct knowledge of the true nature of Divine messages and prophethood, or the duties required by faith.

God directs His Messenger to teach them and the Muslim community the nature of God's grace when He wills to favour any nation with a messenger and a message: *"Say: 'Grace is in God's hand: He bestows it on whom He wills. God is Munificent and All-Knowing.' He singles out for His mercy whom He wills. And God's grace is great indeed."* (Verses 73–4)

He has willed to give His message and revelation to a nation other than that which received His earlier revelations. He has chosen to do so after they violated their covenant with Him, breached the pledges of their father, Abraham, knowingly confounded the truth with falsehood, betrayed the trust He has placed in them, abandoned the rulings of their Book and the laws of their religion and showed their unwillingness to refer their disputes to God's revelations for arbitration. What this meant in practice was that human life was no longer following God's constitution and its leadership was no longer in the hands of believers. Hence, He has given the leadership to the Muslim nation in which He placed His trust as an act of infinite honour and grace from Him: *"God is Munificent and All-Knowing. He singles out for His mercy whom He wills."* This He does on the basis of His knowledge of where His mercy should be placed and on the basis that when He bestows His grace, there is no limit to what He gives. *"God's grace is great indeed."* There is no grace greater than His guidance provided to any nation in the shape of a Book, or His limitless bounty given in the shape of a message, or His great mercy bestowed in the form of a messenger.

When the Muslims listen to this they realise what great favour God has given them when He has chosen them to carry His message, and they will hold tight to it, defend it with all the power available to them, and try to foil the schemes of their enemies. We see here an aspect of how the Qur'ān was educating the first Muslim community. It remains the Qur'ānic method of educating the Muslim community in every generation.

A Transaction Ending in Ruin

> *Among the people of earlier revelations there is many a one who, if you trust him with a treasure, will return it to you intact; and there is among them many a one who, if you trust him with a small gold coin, will not return it to you, unless you keep standing over him. For they say: "We have no obligation to keep faith with Gentiles." Thus they deliberately say of God what they know to be a lie. Indeed those who fulfil their pledges and guard themselves against evil [enjoy God's love]; for God loves the righteous. Those who barter away their covenant with God and their oaths for a trifling gain will have no share in the life to come. God will neither speak to them, nor cast a look on them on the Day of Resurrection, nor will He cleanse them of their sins. Theirs will be a grievous suffering. (Verses 75–7)*

In these verses, the Qur'ān describes the people of earlier revelations as they are, identifying the points of weakness in their characters. It also states the correct values of the Islamic faith. It begins by describing two types of people and their behaviour in commercial and social transactions. We note here that the Qur'ān maintains a high standard of fairness, stating the facts and denying no one his due credit, despite the fact that those people of earlier revelations were in conflict with the Muslim community. It seems that the same is true of those people in all generations. Nevertheless, their hostility towards, their plotting and scheming against and their attempts to undermine Islam and the Muslims, are not cause for the Qur'ān to deny the good ones among them their due credit. Here we note the Qur'ānic statement that among the people of earlier revelations, there are trustworthy individuals who will not usurp anyone his right, even under the greatest of temptations: *"Among the people of earlier revelations there is many a one who, if you trust him with a treasure, will return it to you intact."* (Verse 75)

Others among them, however, are too greedy and have no respect for the rights of others. They do not return something which rightfully belongs to another person, no matter how small, unless they are faced with continuous and insistent demands. They try to justify this contemptible habit by knowingly and deliberately telling lies about God: *"And there is among them many a one who, if you trust him with a small gold coin, will not return it to you, unless you keep standing over him. For they say: 'We have no obligation to keep faith with Gentiles.' Thus they deliberately say of God what they know to be a lie."* (Verse 75)

This particular characteristic is typical of the Jews. It is they who make this statement and have, in moral and social dealings, double standards. When there is a transaction between one Jew and another, they are honest and trustworthy. When they deal with non-Jews, cheating, false pretences, deception and swindling become admissible practices which stir no conscience and cause no twinge of remorse. We note here that the Qur'ān quotes them as saying, *"We have no obligation to keep faith with Gentiles."* The Arabic term used in the Qur'ānic text for the word "Gentiles" means "the illiterate or unlettered people". This was a reference to the Arabs, since the Arabs at that time were largely an illiterate nation. In fact, that was the term they employed to denote all non-Jews.

What is worse, they allege that they are instructed to do so by their God and their religion. However, they know this to be false. They know that God does not approve of any falsehood or any evil manner. He does not allow any community of people to usurp the property of others by fraud and deceit, or to betray their trust or indeed to deal with them unfairly. The Jews, however, have made their hatred to the rest of mankind an essential characteristic of theirs, and indeed part of their religion: *"They deliberately say of God what they know to be a lie."*

At this point, the Qur'ān states its universal rule of morality, in essence its universal moral standard. Moreover, it relates this to the basic requirement of being conscious of God and fearing Him: *"Indeed those who fulfil their pledges and guard themselves against evil [enjoy God's love]; for God loves the righteous. Those who barter away their covenant with God and their oaths for a trifling gain will have no share in the life to come. God will neither speak to them, nor cast a look on them on the Day of Resurrection, nor will He cleanse them of their sins. Theirs will be a grievous suffering."* (Verses 76–7)

What we have here is a single rule applicable to all. Anyone who observes this rule by fulfilling his pledges and guarding himself against evil will earn himself God's love and honour. Anyone who takes a paltry price in exchange for his covenant with God and his oaths – needless to say, any worldly gain or, indeed, this whole world is nothing but a paltry price and a trifling gain – will have no share whatsoever in the life to come. He will be rejected by God and he will not be purified by Him. The only wages he gains himself are simply a grievous suffering.

We note here that the fulfilment of one's pledges relates to fear of God. Hence, there can be no double standards, one for friends and another for enemies. Pledges are not viewed from the point of view of self-interest. Their fulfilment is a matter which relates to dealing with God: the identity of the other party to whom a pledge is given is of little significance.

This explains the general Islamic theory of morality which is applicable to the fulfilment of pledges and to other moral considerations. We deal in the first place with God, and we are, therefore, keen to please Him and to avoid His anger. Hence, our moral incentive is not our self-interest. Nor is it the tradition of the community, nor its particular circumstance. A community may go astray and it may have false standards. It is important, therefore, to have a constant standard which is applicable to both the community and the individual. In addition, this standard must derive its strength from a higher source which is universally valued as taking priority over what people may decide for themselves or what their changing circumstances may require of them. In other words, values and standards must be derived from God. We must try to determine what moral practices and values are acceptable to Him and implement these in the hope that we earn His pleasure and remain righteous. It is in this way that Islam nurtures man's aspiration to a more sublime horizon.

Those who betray their trust and do not honour their pledges are indeed people who *"barter away their covenant with God and their oaths for a trifling gain."* In matters of pledges and trust the relationship is between man and God in the first place although the pledges are made to other people. For this reason, people who do not honour their agreements have no share with God in the life to come. The betrayal of their trust and pledges is perpetrated for only a trifling gain, for something which is available in this life. Therefore, as punishment for their disavowal of His covenant, and their pledge to convey His message to other people, God does not care for them.

Here, the Qur'ān employs its familiar method of drawing an image in order to express a certain attitude. God's neglect of such people and the fact that He withdraws His care from them are described in terms of His not speaking to them, looking at them or cleansing them. These are all familiar symptoms of neglect. The Qur'ān chooses to make use of them in order to draw a vivid image of what happens on the Day of Judgement. In this way, the verses have a much more profound effect on man than a mere statement of fact.

When Men of Religion Become Corrupt

There are some among them who twist their tongues when quoting the Scriptures, so that you may think that [what they say] is from the Scriptures, when it is not from the Scriptures. They say: "It is from God", when it is not from God. Thus, they deliberately say of God what they know to be a lie. It is not conceivable that any human being to whom God had given revelation and wisdom and prophethood would subsequently say to people: "Worship me instead of God." But rather: "Be devoted servants of God, by virtue of spreading the knowledge of the Scriptures and your constant study of them." Nor would he bid you to take the angels and the Prophets as your gods. Would he bid you to be unbelievers after you have surrendered yourselves to God? (Verses 78–80)

These verses speak of a certain type of people of earlier revelations, namely, the deceivers who make use of God's revelations in order to lead other people astray. They twist their tongues when they read or quote it, and interpret its statements so that they may be made to agree with certain prejudices. In return for all this, they receive a paltry price, a trifling worldly gain. One example of such distortion and deliberate misinterpretion relates to their invented beliefs about Jesus, son of Mary, in order to make people's beliefs agree with the prejudices of the Church and political rulers.

When religious men are corrupt they allow themselves to be used as a tool for the falsification of facts. In this manner, they take advantage of their guise as men of religion. The example employed by the Qur'ān in relation to the people of earlier revelations is well known to us today. They impose on the verses and statements of their own revelations arbitrary interpretations and conclusions, claiming that these represent the precise meaning intended and that, as such, they constitute God's message. In actual fact, however, their conclusions are in sharp conflict with the very essence of Divine faith. They are able to achieve this contortion because the majority of people cannot differentiate between the true essence of faith and the true meaning of these statements on the one hand, and the fabricated conclusions they arbitrarily impose on these same statements on the other.

We are today well aware of such people who are wrongly described as religious. Indeed, they are religious professionals who look upon religion as a profession and who use it in order to satisfy all sorts of prejudice. They do not hesitate to make use of any religious text when it seems to them that by so doing they serve their own material interests. It does not concern them that their arbitrary interpretations of God's revelations contradict the basic principles of faith. They try hard to detect even the slightest hint of linguistic ambiguity in a Qur'ānic verse so that they can endorse any desire, tendency or prejudice which serves their immediate interests: *"They say: 'It is from God', when it is not from God. Thus, they deliberately say of God what they know to be a lie."* (Verse 78)

This sort of corruption is not exclusive to the people of earlier revelations. It is evident in every nation where religious faith has been greatly devalued as a result of the relentless pursuit of trifling worldly gains. It gains currency in any nation where people are so dishonest that they do not hesitate to deliberately and knowingly tell a lie about God and distort His words in order to win favours and satisfy their own perverted desires. Here God warns the Muslim community against falling into this slippery way; a path on which the Children of Israel fell and which led them to be deprived of what they had been entrusted with, namely the leadership of mankind.

Taken together, these verses suggest that this element of the Children of Israel deliberately misquoted God's revelations which express their intent in a figurative way and instead attributed arbitrary interpretations to them. In so doing, they deluded the masses into believing that the conclusions they stated were taken from the Divine Book. They, who subsequently became the Christians we know today, indeed say that *"It is from God"*, when God has said nothing of the sort. Their aim was to prove the Divine nature of Jesus and to attribute the same to the "Holy Spirit". They alleged that there are three elements, namely, the father, the son and the holy spirit, constituting the trinity which is God. Limitless is God in His glory, far be it for Him to be as they falsely describe.

They also attributed certain statements to Jesus confirming their allegations. God here refutes their false interpretations. He states that it is not possible for a prophet whom God has honoured with prophethood and chosen for such a great task to order people to make him or the angels as gods. *"It is not conceivable that any human being to whom God had given revelations and wisdom and prophethood would subsequently say to people: 'Worship me instead of God.' But rather: 'Be devoted servants of God, by virtue of spreading the knowledge of the Scriptures and your constant study of them.' Nor would he bid you to take the angels and the Prophets as your gods. Would he bid you to be unbelievers after you have surrendered yourselves to God?"* (Verses 79–80)

A prophet knows that he is a servant of God, and that God alone is the only Lord to whom people should address their worship. It is not conceivable for a prophet to claim for himself the quality of Godhead which requires people to surrender themselves to him. Hence, no prophet would ever say to people: *"Worship me instead of God."* What he will always say to them is: *"Be devoted servants of God."* Declare your allegiance to God as servants who surrender themselves to Him. Address your worship to Him alone and adopt only the way of life He has approved for you so that you can be totally devoted to Him. You can achieve this devotion by virtue of your knowledge of the Scriptures and your constant study of what God has revealed. The more you understand your Scriptures, the clearer this task becomes to you.

No prophet would ever instruct people to take the angels or the prophets as lords or gods. For no prophet would ever instruct people to be unbelievers after they have surrendered themselves to God and acknowledged His Divinity. Prophets come to provide guidance for men, not to lead them astray. They set the example for people to be good believers and surrender themselves to God. It is far removed from them to encourage people to be unbelievers.

The impossibility of what these people of earlier revelations attribute to Jesus is thus made apparent. Equally apparent is their deliberate lie when they allege that this is from God. At the same time, all what these people allege in order to create doubts and suspicions within the Muslim community are shown to be baseless once the Qur'ān has revealed the true nature of these lies and the people who spread them.

Today there are still people who purport to be Muslims and who claim to be well read in Islam but who do the same thing as those people of earlier revelations. These Qur'ānic verses, then, are equally applicable to them. For they try to distort Qur'ānic statements and impose arbitrary interpretations on them in order to create all sorts of idols to be worshipped instead of God. They make use of every connivance in order to make their allegations plausible: *"They say: 'It is from God', when it is not from God. Thus, they deliberately say of God what they know to be a lie."*

A Pledge Binding on All Prophets

God made a covenant with the Prophets: "If, after what I have vouchsafed to you of the Scriptures and wisdom, there comes to you a messenger confirming the truth of what you have in your possession, you shall believe in him and you shall help him. Do you," said He, "affirm this and accept the obligation I lay upon you in these terms?" They answered: "We do affirm it." Said He: "Then bear witness, and I am also a witness with you." Then those who turn away afterwards are indeed transgressors. Do they seek a religion other than God's, when every soul in the heavens and the earth has submitted to Him, willingly or by compulsion, and to Him they shall all return? (Verses 81–3)

This passage explains the link between all the messengers and messages. It is based on the covenant made with God which judges as a transgressor anyone who declines to follow the last of the Divine messages. It shows that such a person would be guilty of violating his covenant with God and of disobeying the law which applies to the whole universe. God, limitless He is in His glory, has made a binding and solemn covenant with every prophet He sent. He Himself witnessed this covenant as did His prophets. The covenant states that if a prophet is followed by a messenger who confirms his own message, he is required to declare his belief in this messenger, give him his support and follow his religion, no matter what he himself has been given of Scriptures and wisdom. God has made this binding agreement with every prophet and messenger He has sent.

The Qur'ānic presentation overlooks the time intervals which separated God's messengers, but instead groups them all in one scene with God, in His majesty, addressing them all at the same time. He asks whether they acknowledge this covenant and accept the obligation it places on them: *"Do you affirm this and accept the obligation I lay upon you in these terms?' They answered: 'We do affirm it.'"* (Verse 81) God, the Sublime, witnesses this covenant and asks them to witness it as well: *"He said: 'Then bear witness, and I am also a witness with you.'"* (Verse 81)

As we replay this majestic scene in our minds, we are overawed with the image of all messengers assembled in the presence of God.

United in their submission to the sublime directive, they uphold the single truth, which God has willed should serve as the foundation of human life and remain pure of deviation, contradiction and conflict. God selects one of His servants to establish this truth on earth, before he passes it over to his successor, to whom he pledges his support, as the latter takes over the task of conveying God's message. No prophet has any personal interest in this matter, nor does he seek any personal glory. He is simply a servant of God, chosen by Him to convey His message. It is God Who determines how this message is carried forward from one generation to another, and it is He Who controls the movement of its followers as He pleases.

With this covenant, Divine religion is assured of being free from any narrow prejudice, be it the prejudice of the messenger to himself or to his people, or the prejudice of his followers to their own faith, interests, or to their own people. This single faith remains, in this way, pure, as God wishes it to be.

In light of this fact, how do those among the people of earlier revelations justify their attitude, when their religions call upon them to believe in the last messenger and to help and support him? How do these people who reject the last messenger appear, when their own messengers have made such a solemn and binding covenant with their Lord in a grand, awesome scene? They appear, indeed, to be transgressors. They have moved away from the teachings of their own Prophets, violated God's covenant and rebelled against this system which applies to the whole universe and which surrenders to its Creator. *"Then those who turn away afterwards are indeed transgressors. Do they seek a religion other than God's, when every soul in the heavens and earth has submitted to Him, willingly or by compulsion, and to Him they shall all return?"* (Verses 82–3)

No one refuses to follow the last of the Prophets but a transgressor, and no one rejects God's faith but a deviant who stands alone in rebellion against the whole universe, which submits to God.

God's faith is one. All messengers preached the same faith and pledged their covenants to dedicate themselves to it. The covenant God has made with every messenger is the same. Hence, to believe in the new faith, to follow its messenger, and to help implement it so that it attains supremacy over all other creeds and methods is indeed to honour this covenant. Anyone who rejects Islam, therefore, rejects God's faith as a whole, and violates his covenant with God.

Islam, or submission to God, is the constitution and religion which applies to everything in this universe. It becomes a reality when the way of life God has chosen for mankind is implemented to the exclusion of every other way. This is indeed a universal version of Islam and submission. It has a profound effect on our feelings and conscience. It speaks of an omnipotent rule which subjects all beings to the same constitution and the same destiny.

"To Him they shall all return." There is no way out, for the end is the return to God, the Almighty, Who has created all and controls all.

If man's aim is to be happy, to enjoy peace of mind and to have a good system for his life, then he must inevitably return to God's constitution and implement it in his life both as an individual and in the life of his community. This ensures that man's life is in perfect harmony with the system followed by the universe and devised by the Creator. Only when man achieves harmony between his own system, encompassing his feelings, motives, relations and practices and the system of the universe is he able to work in cooperation, rather than in conflict, with the great powers in the universe. If he finds himself in conflict with these powers, his world is left in tatters and he cannot fulfil the mission assigned to him by God. Conversely, when he achieves harmony with the laws of nature which operate in the universe and to which all living things are subject, he is able to fathom their secrets and to make use of them in a way which ensures his own happiness and peace of mind. He is then spared all worry, fear and conflict. When we say that man can make use of these powers, we mean that in the case of fire, for example, he will not burn himself by it, but will use it for cooking, heating, and lighting.

In its essence, human nature is in harmony with the laws governing the universe. Human nature submits to its Lord like the nature of every living thing. When man forces his own life out of the system laid down by God, he finds himself in conflict not only with the universe, but also with his own nature. This results in misery and worry. He suffers a great deal just as erring humanity now suffers, despite all its scientific achievements and all the facilities provided for man by this materialistic civilisation.

Man suffers a great deal because he finds himself in a terrible void. His soul is devoid of the truth which it desperately needs, the truth of faith. His life is devoid of the Divine method which achieves harmony of movement between man and the universe in which he lives. When man leaves the cool shade provided by God's way of life, he finds himself in the blazing heat of the desert.

Having left the straightforward path, man suffers a worrying type of corruption. This is indeed the reason for all the misery, worry and confusion suffered by humanity, and for all its hunger, thirst and deprivation. Man tries to escape from all this by resorting to drugs and drink, fast cars and aimless adventures, inventing a new craze every day, but to no avail. Material affluence, high levels of productivity, an easy life and a great deal of spare time do not help reduce his misery and worry. Indeed, the more he has of these, the greater his worry and confusion. This emptiness continues to chase man like a fearful ghost. Man tries to run away, but he can only run into an endless void.

The first impression formed by anyone who visits rich countries is that their peoples are trying to escape. They want to escape even from their own souls. The thin veil of affluence and sensuous enjoyment which is carried too far is soon lifted to reveal all sorts of psychiatric complaints, crime, deviation, perversion, worry, madness, alcohol and drug addiction. There is nothing worthy of respect in such a material life.

The people of these countries cannot determine the true purpose of their lives. They grope in the dark for that divine system which alone

133

will ensure harmony of movement between themselves and the universe around them, and between their system and that of the universe. They cannot enjoy peace of mind because they do not know God, to Whom they shall all return.

Since the Muslim nation – and by this we mean the truly Muslim nation, not that which lives in any particular geographical area or in any particular period of history – is the one which is aware of the true nature of the covenant between God and His messengers, it knows fully the truth of the single faith God has given man through the line of noble prophets and messengers. God instructs the Prophet to declare this truth in absolutely clear terms. He orders him to declare that his nation believes in all past messages, respects and honours all past messengers, and is fully aware of the true nature of the Divine faith which is the only faith acceptable to God: *"Say: 'We believe in God and in that which has been bestowed from on high upon us, and that which has been bestowed on Abraham, Ishmael, Isaac, Jacob and their descendants, and that which has been vouchsafed by their Lord to Moses and Jesus and all the prophets. We make no distinction between them. To Him do we surrender ourselves.' He who seeks a religion other than self-surrender to God, it will not be accepted from him, and in the life to come he will be among the lost."* (Verses 84–5)

This is the reality of Islam: it encompasses all past messages, maintains loyalty to all past messengers. It shows that the Divine faith is one, and returns all religions to their common source. It implies believing in all these messages as a whole, as they have all been given by God.

It is important to note here that the first of these two verses states first the belief in God and what has been revealed to the Muslims, i.e. the Qur'ān, and what has been revealed to all previous messengers. Its concluding comment on this encompassing belief is: *"To Him do we surrender ourselves."* This acknowledgement of submission to God is very significant. It comes after it has been explained that Islam means total surrender, submission and obedience as well as the implementation of a certain system and a well-defined law. This is absolutely clear in the preceding verse: *"Do they seek a religion other than God's, when every soul in the heavens and the earth has submitted to Him, willingly or by compulsion, and to Him they shall all return?"* It is clear that, in relation to all beings, "Islam" means surrender and submission, as well as obedience to the law and implementation of the system. It is for this that God deliberately explains the meaning of Islam and its true nature on every occasion, so that no one can mistake it for a word said verbally, or an acceptance made mentally, without it leaving its practical effects on life in the form of submission to God's law and the implementation of that law in real life: *"He who seeks a religion other than Islam, it will not be accepted from him, and in the life to come he will be among the lost."*

Deliberate Rejection of the Truth

How shall God guide people who have lapsed into disbelief after having accepted the faith and having borne witness that this messenger is true, and after having received clear evidence of the truth? God does not guide the wrongdoers. Of such people the punishment shall be the curse of God, the angels and all men. Under it they shall abide. Neither their suffering shall be lightened, nor shall they be granted respite. Excepted shall be those who afterwards repent and mend their ways; for God is Much-Forgiving, Merciful. But those who return to disbelief after having accepted the faith and then grow more stubborn in their rejection of the faith, their repentance will not be accepted. For they are those who have truly gone astray. As for those who disbelieve and die unbelievers, not even the earth full of gold shall be accepted from any one of them, were he to offer it in ransom. They shall have grievous suffering and they shall have none to help them. You will never attain to true piety unless you spend on others out of what you dearly cherish. God has full knowledge of what you spend. (Verses 86–92)

The preceding verses leave no doubt whatsoever about the true meaning of Islam. In the light of these verses, it is impossible to arbitrarily interpret Qur'ānic statements in order to give Islam a definition other than that given by God. Islam, the religion of the whole universe, means submission to the system God has laid down for life.

Islam can never be confined to a verbal declaration of believing in the oneness of God and Muḥammad's message. Such a declaration must be followed by its practical correlative. This means, in the context of bearing witness that there is no deity save God; to actually believe that God alone is the only Lord of the universe to Whom worship should be addressed and Whose pleasure is to be sought. In the case of bearing witness that Muḥammad is God's Messenger, it means to implement in full the way of life he has explained to us as given him by his Lord, and to apply the laws he has given us and to refer all disputes to the Qur'ān, the Book he has conveyed to us.

As we have said, Islam can never be confined to a mere mental acceptance of the truth of divinity and revelation, devoid of its practical effect. Nor can Islam be limited to a set of worship practices, contemplations, or moral and spiritual education, unless these are followed by their practical correlative represented by a way of life derived from God. Worship, contemplation and moral education have no practical value in people's lives unless they are incorporated into a social system which moulds human life in its own clean fashion, in accordance with God's will.

Such is Islam as God wants it. No value can be attached to Islam in the version devised by people's desires, or coloured by the wishes and prejudices of the enemies of Islam and their stooges everywhere.

Those who do not accept Islam in the form God wants it to take, after having learnt its true nature will definitely be the losers in the hereafter. They will receive no guidance from God and will not be exempt from His punishment: *"How shall God guide people who have lapsed into disbelief after having accepted the faith and having borne witness that this messenger is true, and after having received clear evidence of the truth? God does not guide the wrongdoers. Of such people the punishment shall be the curse of God, the angels and all men: under it they shall abide. Neither their suffering shall be lightened, nor shall they be granted respite."* (Verses 86–8)

It is a sustained campaign which strikes terror in every heart with even the smallest measure of faith, and which views the question of the hereafter with the minimum degree of seriousness. The punishment detailed here is fair for anyone who has been given the chance to save himself, but who deliberately and stubbornly turns away from the path of salvation.

Islam, nevertheless, leaves the door open for repentance. Any erring person who wants to turn back to the right way needs only to knock on the door. Indeed, he does not even need to knock.

There is no one and nothing to prevent him entering. He only needs to turn to the way which ensures his security, and to do good in order to show that his repentance is sincere and truthful: *"Excepted shall be those who afterwards repent and mend their ways; for God is Much-Forgiving, Merciful."* (Verse 89)

However, those who do not repent, who refuse to turn back, who insist on remaining unbelievers and continue in their erring ways until the chance given them is withdrawn, until the test is over, and the time for punishment and reward arrives, cannot be saved. No repentance will be accepted from them. It will not be of any benefit to them that they may have spent the whole earth's weight of gold in what they thought to be good causes. Since their spending was not made for God's sake and not dedicated to Him alone, it has no value with Him. Nor will they be able to save themselves from the punishment of the hereafter even if they were to offer the earth's full weight of gold. Their chance is over and the doors are closed: *"But those who return to disbelief after having accepted the faith and then grow more stubborn in their rejection of the faith, their repentance will not be accepted. For they are those who have truly gone astray. As for those who disbelieve and die unbelievers, not even the earth full of gold shall be accepted from any one of them, were he to offer it in ransom. They shall have grievous suffering and they shall have none to help them."* (Verses 90–1) The discussion is thus concluded in a fearful and decisive manner, leaving no doubt in anyone's heart.

Since spending for causes other than that of God is mentioned as well as the offering of a ransom when none may be accepted, God explains the sort of spending which earns His pleasure: *"You will never attain to true piety unless you spend on others out of what you dearly cherish. God has full knowledge of what you spend."* (Verse 92) The Muslims at the time understood this Divine directive perfectly well. They were keen to achieve that standard of true piety, which means the culmination of everything that is good, by offering what they cherished most dearly. They came forward with such offerings in the hope of receiving a much greater reward in the hereafter.

Imām Aḥmad relates on the authority of Anas ibn Mālik: "Abū Ṭalḥah was one of the richest people among the Anṣār in Madinah. His property, which he cherished most dearly, was a plot of land called Ḥā'. It was opposite to the Prophet's mosque. The Prophet used to go there and drink of its fine spring. Anas says that when God revealed the Qur'ānic verse: '*You will never attain to true piety unless you spend on others out of what you dearly cherish,*' Abū Ṭalḥah said: 'Messenger of God, God says: "You will never attain to true piety unless you spend on others out of what you dearly cherish." My property, which I cherish most dearly, is this piece of land. I am offering it as a charity dedicated for God's sake. I do this in the hope that I will be rewarded for it by God. You, Messenger of God, may dispense with it in any way you please.' The Prophet said: 'Good. Good. That is an investment with high return. I have heard what you said. I think the best course is for you to divide it among your relatives.' Abū Ṭalḥah said: 'I will do that, Messenger of God.' He divided it among his relatives and cousins." (Related by Al-Bukhārī and Muslim.)

Al-Bukhārī and Muslim also relate that 'Umar said: "Messenger of God, I have never acquired any property which is more valuable than my share in Khaybar. How do you advise me to dispense with it?" The Prophet said: "Make the land a permanent endowment and its produce free for all."

Many of them have followed this line in fulfilment of God's instruction, Who has outlined for us the way to true piety when He has guided us to Islam. In this way, we attain our freedom from being enslaved by wealth and self-aggrandisement. We can aspire to attain a more sublime level, free of all shackles, undeterred by any impediments.

5

One God, One Faith

All food was lawful to the Children of Israel except what Israel forbade himself, in the days before the Torah was bestowed from on high. Say: "Bring the Torah and recite it, if what you say is true." (93)

۞ كُلُّ ٱلطَّعَامِ كَانَ حِلًّا لِّبَنِىٓ إِسْرَٰٓءِيلَ إِلَّا مَا حَرَّمَ إِسْرَٰٓءِيلُ عَلَىٰ نَفْسِهِۦ مِن قَبْلِ أَن تُنَزَّلَ ٱلتَّوْرَىٰةُ قُلْ فَأْتُواْ بِٱلتَّوْرَىٰةِ فَٱتْلُوهَآ إِن كُنتُمْ صَٰدِقِينَ ۝

Those who fabricate lies about God after this are indeed wrongdoers. (94)

فَمَنِ ٱفْتَرَىٰ عَلَى ٱللَّهِ ٱلْكَذِبَ مِنۢ بَعْدِ ذَٰلِكَ فَأُوْلَٰٓئِكَ هُمُ ٱلظَّٰلِمُونَ ۝

Say: "God speaks the truth. Follow, then, the creed of Abraham, who turned away from all that is false and was not one of those who associate partners with God." (95)

قُلْ صَدَقَ ٱللَّهُ فَٱتَّبِعُواْ مِلَّةَ إِبْرَٰهِيمَ حَنِيفًا وَمَا كَانَ مِنَ ٱلْمُشْرِكِينَ ۝

The first House [of worship] ever set up for mankind was indeed the one at Bakkah: rich in blessing; and a source of guidance to all the worlds, (96)

إِنَّ أَوَّلَ بَيْتٍ وُضِعَ لِلنَّاسِ لَلَّذِى بِبَكَّةَ مُبَارَكًا وَهُدًى لِّلْعَٰلَمِينَ ۝

full of clear messages. It is the place whereon Abraham once stood; and whoever enters it finds inner peace. Pilgrimage to this House is a duty owed to God by all people who are able to undertake it. As for those who disbelieve, God does not stand in need of anything in all the worlds. (97)

فِيهِ ءَايَتُۢ بَيِّنَتٌ مَّقَامُ إِبْرَٰهِيمَ وَمَن دَخَلَهُۥ كَانَ ءَامِنًا وَلِلَّهِ عَلَى ٱلنَّاسِ حِجُّ ٱلْبَيْتِ مَنِ ٱسْتَطَاعَ إِلَيْهِ سَبِيلًا وَمَن كَفَرَ فَإِنَّ ٱللَّهَ غَنِيٌّ عَنِ ٱلْعَٰلَمِينَ ۝

Say: "People of earlier revelations, why do you disbelieve in God's revelations, when God Himself is witness to all that you do?" (98)

قُلْ يَٰٓأَهْلَ ٱلْكِتَٰبِ لِمَ تَكْفُرُونَ بِـَٔايَٰتِ ٱللَّهِ وَٱللَّهُ شَهِيدٌ عَلَىٰ مَا تَعْمَلُونَ ۝

Say: "People of earlier revelations, why do you try to turn those who have come to believe away from the path of God, seeking to make it appear crooked, when you yourselves bear witness [to its being straight]? God is not unaware of what you do." (99)

قُلْ يَٰٓأَهْلَ ٱلْكِتَٰبِ لِمَ تَصُدُّونَ عَن سَبِيلِ ٱللَّهِ مَنْ ءَامَنَ تَبْغُونَهَا عِوَجًا وَأَنتُمْ شُهَدَآءُ وَمَا ٱللَّهُ بِغَٰفِلٍ عَمَّا تَعْمَلُونَ ۝

Believers! If you pay heed to some of those who have been given revelations, they will cause you to renounce the truth after you have accepted the faith. (100)

يَٰٓأَيُّهَا ٱلَّذِينَ ءَامَنُوٓا۟ إِن تُطِيعُوا۟ فَرِيقًا مِّنَ ٱلَّذِينَ أُوتُوا۟ ٱلْكِتَٰبَ يَرُدُّوكُم بَعْدَ إِيمَٰنِكُمْ كَٰفِرِينَ ۝

But how can you sink into disbelief when God's revelations are being recited to you and His messenger is in your midst? He who holds fast to God has already been guided along a straight path. (101)

وَكَيْفَ تَكْفُرُونَ وَأَنتُمْ تُتْلَىٰ عَلَيْكُمْ ءَايَٰتُ ٱللَّهِ وَفِيكُمْ رَسُولُهُۥ وَمَن يَعْتَصِم بِٱللَّهِ فَقَدْ هُدِىَ إِلَىٰ صِرَٰطٍ مُّسْتَقِيمٍ ۝

Believers! Fear God as you rightly should, and do not allow death to overtake you before you have surrendered yourselves truly to Him. (102)

يَٰٓأَيُّهَا ٱلَّذِينَ ءَامَنُواْ ٱتَّقُواْ ٱللَّهَ حَقَّ تُقَاتِهِۦ وَلَا تَمُوتُنَّ إِلَّا وَأَنتُم مُّسۡلِمُونَ ۝

Hold fast, all of you together, to the bond with God and do not be disunited. And remember the blessings God has bestowed on you: how, when you were enemies [to one another] He united your hearts and, by His grace, you have become brothers; and how, when you were on the brink of an abyss of fire, He saved you from it. Thus God makes clear His revelations to you, so that you may be rightly guided. (103)

وَٱعۡتَصِمُواْ بِحَبۡلِ ٱللَّهِ جَمِيعًا وَلَا تَفَرَّقُواْ وَٱذۡكُرُواْ نِعۡمَتَ ٱللَّهِ عَلَيۡكُمۡ إِذۡ كُنتُمۡ أَعۡدَآءً فَأَلَّفَ بَيۡنَ قُلُوبِكُمۡ فَأَصۡبَحۡتُم بِنِعۡمَتِهِۦٓ إِخۡوَٰنًا وَكُنتُمۡ عَلَىٰ شَفَا حُفۡرَةٍ مِّنَ ٱلنَّارِ فَأَنقَذَكُم مِّنۡهَا كَذَٰلِكَ يُبَيِّنُ ٱللَّهُ لَكُمۡ ءَايَٰتِهِۦ لَعَلَّكُمۡ تَهۡتَدُونَ ۝

Let there become of you a nation that invites to all that is good, enjoin the doing of what is right and forbid what is wrong. Such are they who shall prosper. (104)

وَلۡتَكُن مِّنكُمۡ أُمَّةٌ يَدۡعُونَ إِلَى ٱلۡخَيۡرِ وَيَأۡمُرُونَ بِٱلۡمَعۡرُوفِ وَيَنۡهَوۡنَ عَنِ ٱلۡمُنكَرِ وَأُوْلَٰٓئِكَ هُمُ ٱلۡمُفۡلِحُونَ ۝

Do not follow the example of those who became divided and fell into conflict with one another after clear proof had come to them. For these there will be grievous suffering, (105)

وَلَا تَكُونُواْ كَٱلَّذِينَ تَفَرَّقُواْ وَٱخۡتَلَفُواْ مِنۢ بَعۡدِ مَا جَآءَهُمُ ٱلۡبَيِّنَٰتُ وَأُوْلَٰٓئِكَ لَهُمۡ عَذَابٌ عَظِيمٌ ۝

on the day when some faces will shine with happiness and some faces will be blackened. Those whose faces are blackened [shall be told]: "Did you disbelieve after having embraced the faith? Taste, then, this suffering for having sunk into disbelief." (106)

يَوْمَ تَبْيَضُّ وُجُوهٌ وَتَسْوَدُّ وُجُوهٌ فَأَمَّا ٱلَّذِينَ ٱسْوَدَّتْ وُجُوهُهُمْ أَكَفَرْتُم بَعْدَ إِيمَٰنِكُمْ فَذُوقُوا۟ ٱلْعَذَابَ بِمَا كُنتُمْ تَكْفُرُونَ ١٠٦

Those with shining faces shall be in God's grace; they abide there for ever. (107)

وَأَمَّا ٱلَّذِينَ ٱبْيَضَّتْ وُجُوهُهُمْ فَفِى رَحْمَةِ ٱللَّهِ هُمْ فِيهَا خَٰلِدُونَ ١٠٧

These are revelations of God. We recite them to you in truth. God wills no injustice to His creatures. (108)

تِلْكَ ءَايَٰتُ ٱللَّهِ نَتْلُوهَا عَلَيْكَ بِٱلْحَقِّ وَمَا ٱللَّهُ يُرِيدُ ظُلْمًا لِّلْعَٰلَمِينَ ١٠٨

To God belongs all that is in the heavens and all that is on earth; to Him shall all things return. (109)

وَلِلَّهِ مَا فِى ٱلسَّمَٰوَٰتِ وَمَا فِى ٱلْأَرْضِ وَإِلَى ٱللَّهِ تُرْجَعُ ٱلْأُمُورُ ١٠٩

You are the best community that has ever been raised for mankind; you enjoin the doing of what is right and forbid what is wrong, and you believe in God. Had the people of earlier revelations believed, it would have been for their own good. Few of them are believers, while most of them are evildoers. (110)

كُنتُمْ خَيْرَ أُمَّةٍ أُخْرِجَتْ لِلنَّاسِ تَأْمُرُونَ بِٱلْمَعْرُوفِ وَتَنْهَوْنَ عَنِ ٱلْمُنكَرِ وَتُؤْمِنُونَ بِٱللَّهِ وَلَوْ ءَامَنَ أَهْلُ ٱلْكِتَٰبِ لَكَانَ خَيْرًا لَّهُم مِّنْهُمُ ٱلْمُؤْمِنُونَ وَأَكْثَرُهُمُ ٱلْفَٰسِقُونَ ١١٠

They cannot harm you beyond causing you some trifling hurt; and if they fight against you they will turn their backs upon you in flight. Then they will receive no help. (111)

لَن يَضُرُّوكُمْ إِلَّآ أَذًى وَإِن يُقَٰتِلُوكُمْ يُوَلُّوكُمُ ٱلْأَدْبَارَ ثُمَّ لَا يُنصَرُونَ ﴿١١١﴾

Ignominy shall be pitched over them wherever they may be, save when they have a bond with God and a bond with men. They have incurred the wrath of God and humiliation shall overshadow them. That is because they persisted in denying God's revelations and killing the Prophets against all right. That is because they persisted in their disobedience and transgression. (112)

ضُرِبَتْ عَلَيْهِمُ ٱلذِّلَّةُ أَيْنَ مَا ثُقِفُوٓا إِلَّا بِحَبْلٍ مِّنَ ٱللَّهِ وَحَبْلٍ مِّنَ ٱلنَّاسِ وَبَآءُو بِغَضَبٍ مِّنَ ٱللَّهِ وَضُرِبَتْ عَلَيْهِمُ ٱلْمَسْكَنَةُ ذَٰلِكَ بِأَنَّهُمْ كَانُوا يَكْفُرُونَ بِـَٔايَٰتِ ٱللَّهِ وَيَقْتُلُونَ ٱلْأَنۢبِيَآءَ بِغَيْرِ حَقٍّ ذَٰلِكَ بِمَا عَصَوا وَّكَانُوا يَعْتَدُونَ ﴿١١٢﴾

They are not all alike. Of the people of earlier revelations there are some upright people who recite the revelations of God in the depth of the night, and prostrate themselves in worship. (113)

۞ لَيْسُوا سَوَآءً مِّنْ أَهْلِ ٱلْكِتَٰبِ أُمَّةٌ قَآئِمَةٌ يَتْلُونَ ءَايَٰتِ ٱللَّهِ ءَانَآءَ ٱلَّيْلِ وَهُمْ يَسْجُدُونَ ﴿١١٣﴾

They believe in God and the Last Day and enjoin the doing of what is right and forbid what is wrong and vie with one another in doing good works. These belong to the righteous. (114)

يُؤْمِنُونَ بِٱللَّهِ وَٱلْيَوْمِ ٱلْأَخِرِ وَيَأْمُرُونَ بِٱلْمَعْرُوفِ وَيَنْهَوْنَ عَنِ ٱلْمُنكَرِ وَيُسَٰرِعُونَ فِى ٱلْخَيْرَٰتِ وَأُوْلَٰٓئِكَ مِنَ ٱلصَّٰلِحِينَ ﴿١١٤﴾

Whatever good they do, they shall never be denied its reward. God knows those who fear Him. (115)

وَمَا يَفْعَلُوا مِنْ خَيْرٍ فَلَن يُكْفَرُوهُ وَاللَّهُ عَلِيمٌ بِالْمُتَّقِينَ ۝

As for the unbelievers, neither their riches nor their children will avail them in any way against God. It is they who are destined for the fire, where they will abide. (116)

إِنَّ الَّذِينَ كَفَرُوا لَن تُغْنِيَ عَنْهُمْ أَمْوَٰلُهُمْ وَلَا أَوْلَٰدُهُم مِّنَ اللَّهِ شَيْئًا وَأُوْلَٰئِكَ أَصْحَٰبُ النَّارِ هُمْ فِيهَا خَٰلِدُونَ ۝

Whatever they spend in this present life is like a biting, icy wind which smites the tilth of people who have wronged themselves, laying it to waste. It is not God Who does them wrong; they wrong themselves. (117)

مَثَلُ مَا يُنفِقُونَ فِي هَٰذِهِ الْحَيَوٰةِ الدُّنْيَا كَمَثَلِ رِيحٍ فِيهَا صِرٌّ أَصَابَتْ حَرْثَ قَوْمٍ ظَلَمُوا أَنفُسَهُمْ فَأَهْلَكَتْهُ وَمَا ظَلَمَهُمُ اللَّهُ وَلَٰكِنْ أَنفُسَهُمْ يَظْلِمُونَ ۝

Believers, do not take for your intimate friends men other than your own folk. They will spare no effort to corrupt you. They love to see you in distress. Their hatred has already become apparent by [what they say with] their mouths, but what their hearts conceal is even much worse. We have made revelations plain to you, if you will only use your reason. (118)

يَٰٓأَيُّهَا الَّذِينَ ءَامَنُوا لَا تَتَّخِذُوا بِطَانَةً مِّن دُونِكُمْ لَا يَأْلُونَكُمْ خَبَالًا وَدُّوا مَا عَنِتُّمْ قَدْ بَدَتِ الْبَغْضَآءُ مِنْ أَفْوَٰهِهِمْ وَمَا تُخْفِي صُدُورُهُمْ أَكْبَرُ قَدْ بَيَّنَّا لَكُمُ الْآيَٰتِ إِن كُنتُمْ تَعْقِلُونَ ۝

See for yourselves how it is you who love them and they do not love you. You believe in all revelations. When they meet you they say: "We, too, are believers." But when they find themselves alone, they bite their fingertips with rage against you. Say: "Perish in your rage. God is fully aware of what is in the hearts [of people]." (119)

هَـٰٓأَنتُمۡ أُوْلَآءِ تُحِبُّونَهُمۡ وَلَا يُحِبُّونَكُمۡ وَتُؤۡمِنُونَ بِٱلۡكِتَٰبِ كُلِّهِۦ وَإِذَا لَقُوكُمۡ قَالُوٓاْ ءَامَنَّا وَإِذَا خَلَوۡاْ عَضُّواْ عَلَيۡكُمُ ٱلۡأَنَامِلَ مِنَ ٱلۡغَيۡظِ قُلۡ مُوتُواْ بِغَيۡظِكُمۡ إِنَّ ٱللَّهَ عَلِيمٌۢ بِذَاتِ ٱلصُّدُورِ ۝

When good fortune comes your way, it grieves them; and if evil befalls you, they rejoice. If you persevere and fear God, their machinations cannot harm you in any way. God encompasses all that they do. (120)

إِن تَمۡسَسۡكُمۡ حَسَنَةٌ تَسُؤۡهُمۡ وَإِن تُصِبۡكُمۡ سَيِّئَةٌ يَفۡرَحُواْ بِهَا وَإِن تَصۡبِرُواْ وَتَتَّقُواْ لَا يَضُرُّكُمۡ كَيۡدُهُمۡ شَيۡـًٔا إِنَّ ٱللَّهَ بِمَا يَعۡمَلُونَ مُحِيطٌ ۝

Overview

In this passage, verses 93 to 120, we witness the culmination of the debate with the people of earlier revelations. Although the concepts outlined here do not form part of the debate with the Najran Christian delegation, they share a common theme and, thereby, complement and resonate with that debate. The passage addresses the Jews in particular, countering their intrigues and scheming against the Muslims of Madinah, and leads to a complete and total break between the two camps. Further on, it directs its attention fully to the Muslim community, pointing out their true identity, their way of life and their obligations, in a similar manner adopted by the Qur'ān in the previous *surah, al-Baqarah*, or The Cow. (Volume 1, pp. 118 ff)

This section opens by the affirmation that the Israelites were permitted to eat all types of food with the exception of what Israel

(Jacob) had chosen to forbid himself and his people from eating before the Torah was revealed to Moses. This statement appears to come in reply to objections raised by the Israelites against the Qur'ān for making permissible certain foods that have been forbidden to them. The reality is, of course, that these were forbidden only to the Israelites as punishment for their transgressions.

It responds to their objection to the change of the direction faced by Muslims during prayer, the *qiblah* – a subject fully covered in *sūrah al-Baqarah* – pointing out that the Ka'bah is the House built by Abraham as the first place of worship ever established for mankind on earth. Since they claim to be descendants of Abraham, their attitude seems all the more objectionable!

It goes on to condemn the people of earlier revelations for their denial of God's revelations, for turning people away from God's path, their refusal to comply with His commands, and for their propensity to deviation as a dominant feature of life when they are well aware of the truth.

It turns to address the people of earlier revelations as a whole, as it warns the Muslims not to comply with their false beliefs. That was all the more urgent as the Qur'ān was being revealed to them and God's Messenger, Muḥammad, was teaching them and calling upon them to fear God and hold fast to Islam until they die and meet their Lord. It reminds them of God's grace which had kept their hearts close together and united them under the singular banner of Islam when they were beseiged with schisms and strife. Islam took them back from the brink and prepared them to be the nation that would uphold all that is good and prevent all that is indecent and harmful, as part of their obligation to establish God's order on earth. They are warned not to succumb to the machinations of the people of earlier revelations or to allow themselves to be divided as those people were. That would only bring them frustration and destruction both in this life and in the life to come. Some reports indicate that this warning refers to certain hostilities instigated by the Jews between the two Arab tribes of Madinah, the Aws and the Khazraj.

Then God Almighty informs the Muslims regarding their rightful place in this world and the reality of their role in human society. He says: *"You are the best community that has ever been raised for mankind; you enjoin the doing of what is right and forbid what is wrong, and you believe in God.* " (Verse 110) He draws the attention of the Muslims to the profundity and uniqueness of their role and the true nature of their society.

This is further reinforced by demeaning their detractors who will never undermine their beliefs or completely prevail over them. Having to face such foes is part of the trials and tribulations of their mission. Victory shall be theirs so long as they hold fast to their way of life. Their enemies are condemned to disgrace and subjugation, and have earned God's wrath for their sins and transgressions, and for slaying their prophets without justification. The *sūrah* makes a certain exception concerning those particular Jews and Christians who acknowledge the truth and profess true faith. They adopt the same way of life as the Muslims, advocating what is right and opposing evil and working for all that is proper and decent. As for those who reject Islam, the *sūrah* asserts that they shall receive the just rewards of their infidelity, and neither their wealth nor their offspring shall spare them a miserable end.

The passage closes with a warning to the Muslims not to take allies from among those who wish them evil and who are full of hatred towards them. It points out that the loathing they conceal within their hearts is far more intense. They rejoice when misfortune strikes the Muslims, but are offended when they are blessed with a happy prospect. God, the Omniscient, promises to afford the believers protection against the intrigue of their opponents, as long as they show patience in adversity and fear God.

This extended and rich exhortation reflects the trials and tribulations the Muslims of Madinah suffered as a result of the betrayal and duplicity of their Jewish neighbours. It is an indication of the insidious confusion and disruption they caused inside the Muslim camp. It also confirms the Muslims' need for strong and firm instruction in order to be able to distinguish themselves, to set themselves apart and take a firm and resolute stand, severing all the ties that bound them to the dark days of Ignorance.

These profound instructions endure the test of time and continue to be valid for all Muslim generations who are required to be aware of Islam's traditional age-old enemies. Their methods and practices may change, but they remain ever the same.

The Beginning of a Long Debate

All food was lawful to the Children of Israel except what Israel forbade himself, in the days before the Torah was bestowed from on high. Say: "Bring the Torah and recite it, if what you say is true." Those who fabricate lies about God after this are indeed wrongdoers. (Verses 93–4)

The Jews used every trick and argument to try to raise suspicion concerning the truthfulness of the Prophet and his message. Their only chance to stop the tide of Islam was to create doubts in the minds of the Muslims and to spread confusion within the Muslim community. When the Qur'ān stated that it endorsed what was in the Torah, the Jews seized the opportunity to proceed with their campaign. They asked: "How is it possible in this case that the Qur'ān makes lawful certain types of food which have been forbidden to the Children of Israel?" Reports suggest that they specifically mentioned camel flesh and milk which were forbidden to the Jews. There are, however, other types of food forbidden in Judaism which God has made lawful to the Muslims.

The Qur'ān refers the Jews back to the historical fact which they chose to overlook because that served their purpose in creating doubts about the Qur'ān. The fact is that all types of food were lawful to the Children of Israel, with the exception of what Israel forbade himself long before the revelation of the Torah. Reports suggest that during a serious illness, Israel, or Jacob, pledged to God that if He were to restore his health for him, he would voluntarily abstain from eating camel flesh and drinking camel milk, his favourite food and drink. God accepted his pledge. It became a tradition with the Children of Israel to follow in their father's footsteps and to forbid themselves what he had forbidden himself. Moreover, God forbade the Israelites certain types of food in punishment for certain sins they had committed. God refers to these types of forbidden food in verse 146 of *sūrah* 6, *Al-An'ām*, or Cattle: *"And to those who followed the Jewish faith did We forbid all beasts that have claws; and we forbade them the fat of both oxen and sheep, excepting that which is in their backs or entrails or that which is within the bone. Thus did We punish them for their evil doing; for, We are indeed true to Our word."* Prior to this prohibition, all these types of food were lawful to the Israelites.

God refers them to this historical fact in order to explain that these types of food were originally lawful. They were forbidden them because of certain special circumstances relevant to them alone. If these types of food are made lawful to the Muslims, this only represents a return to the original status. Hence, it should raise no objection from anyone. Nor can it be used to raise doubts about the Qurʾān and the final Divine law it lays down.

The Qurʾān poses a challenge to the Jews to refer back to the Torah, to bring it forward and read it. They were certain to find in it an explanation that the prohibition was imposed on them alone. It is not a prohibition common to all people: *"Say: 'Bring the Torah and recite it, if what you say is true.'"* (Verse 93)

This is followed by a threat to anyone who fabricates lies about God. Such a person is a wrongdoer who is unfair both to himself and to other people. He is, indeed, unfair to truth itself. The punishment of a wrongdoer is well known. It is sufficient, therefore, that they are described as wrongdoers to determine the type of punishment which awaits them. They certainly fabricate lies about God, and they certainly will return to Him.

The Jews also sought constantly to exploit the question of changing the direction of Muslim prayer which meant that the Muslims faced the Kaʿbah in prayer instead of turning towards Jerusalem. The Prophet and his Companions faced Jerusalem in their prayer for 16 or 17 months after the Prophet's emigration to Madinah. This topic has been discussed at length in the preceding *sūrah*. That discussion explained that to choose the Kaʿbah as the *qiblah* (or direction in prayer) is to opt for the most natural and preferable alternative. When Jerusalem was chosen for a certain period, this was done for a specific reason explained by God. The Jews, nevertheless, continued to exploit this issue, trying to raise doubts and confusion and covering truth with falsehood, in the same way as the enemies of Islam do today. God, however, foils their schemes with a new explanation: *"Say: 'God speaks the truth. Follow, then, the creed of Abraham, who turned away from all that is false and was not one of those who associate partners with God.' The first House [of worship] ever set up for mankind was indeed the one at Bakkah: rich in blessing; and a source of guidance to all the worlds, full of clear messages. It is the place whereon Abraham once stood; and whoever enters it finds inner peace. Pilgrimage to this House is a duty owed to God by all people who are able to undertake it. As for those who disbelieve, God does not stand in need of anything in all the worlds."* (Verses 95–7)

The first sentence here, *"Say: 'God speaks the truth,'"* refers to what has been stated previously. The Kaʿbah was built by Abraham and

Ishmael so that it may be a place of refuge and security for all people
and to serve as a *qiblah* or focal point and a praying place for all those
who believe in Abraham's faith. Hence, the command to follow
Abraham's creed which is based on the belief in the absolute oneness
of God, associating no partners with Him in any form or shape:
*"'Follow, then, the creed of Abraham, who turned away from all that is
false and was not one of those who associate partners with God.'"* The
Jews claimed that they were the descendants of Abraham. Here, the
Qur'ān tells them the true nature of Abraham's faith, namely, the belief
in the absolute Oneness of God. This is emphasised twice in succession:
the first states that Abraham turned away from all that is false, and the
second asserts that he was not one of those who associate partners with
God. How can they, then, go as far as to ascribe partners to God?

The First House for Human Worship

*Say: "God speaks the truth. Follow, then, the creed of Abraham,
who turned away from all that is false and was not one of those
who associate partners with God." The first House [of worship]
ever set up for mankind was indeed the one at Bakkah: rich in
blessing, and a source of guidance to all the worlds, full of clear
messages.* (Verses 95–6)

This verse explains that to face the Ka'bah is the proper choice. The
Ka'bah is the first House ever set up for the exclusive purpose of worship.
God commanded Abraham to build it and to consecrate it for worshippers
who either walk round it, spend periods of time worshipping in it and
who bow and prostrate themselves there in total submission to God.
God has blessed this House and made it like a beacon for mankind
where they find guidance showing them the true faith acceptable to
God, which is indeed the creed of Abraham himself. There are indeed
clear signs in the Ka'bah which show that it is the place where Abraham
stood in his worship. Some scholars suggest that the Arabic term, Maqām
Ibrāhīm, which is used in this verse and rendered in our translation as
"the spot where Abraham stood", refers to the ancient stone on which
Abraham stood when he built the Ka'bah. It used to be stuck to the wall
of the Ka'bah, but the second Caliph, 'Umar, moved it back so that
people doing the *ṭawāf* (i.e. walking round the Ka'bah) did not disturb
those who prayed behind it. We are commanded by God to make that

spot a place where we pray: *"Establish the spot where Abraham stood as a place of worship."* (al-Baqarah 2: 125)

One of the virtues of this House is highlighted here, namely, the sense of security it imparts to anyone who goes there. It is a refuge for anyone who is overtaken by fear, where he can find peace and security. In this particular aspect, this place is absolutely unique. It shares this quality with no other place on earth. It has remained so ever since it was built by Abraham and his son Ishmael. Even in the dark ages of Ignorance in Arabia, when the Arabs deviated far away from Abraham's faith and no longer believed in the oneness of God, the sanctity of this House continued to be observed. Al-Ḥasan al-Baṣrī and other renowned scholars explain that in that period of Ignorance, a man might commit a murder and go into the sanctuary of the House, having put a piece of wool around his neck. He might be met there by the son of the man he murdered but he would not be disturbed there until he had left the House.

This is part of the honour and blessings God has given to this House of His, even when people around it lived in total ignorance. He reminds the Arabs of this great favour He has done them: *"Are they not aware that We have set up a secure sanctuary while people are snatched away all around them?"* (al-'Ankabūt 29: 67) Its sanctity is even extended to animals. Hunting is forbidden in its vicinity and no animals are scared out of their abodes in order to be captured. It is also forbidden to cut down the trees in its vicinity. An authentic *ḥadīth*, related by Al-Bukhārī and Muslim on the authority of Ibn 'Abbās, mentions that the Prophet (peace be upon him), said on the day when Makkah was liberated by the Muslims: "God has made this city a sacred one ever since the day He created the heavens and the earth. It remains, therefore, inviolable by virtue of the sanctity imparted to it by God till the Day of Resurrection. Fighting in this city was never made lawful to anyone before me. It has only been made lawful to me for an hour of one day. It continues to be sanctified by God's order till the Day of Resurrection. Its plants may not be cut, its game may not be scared. No one may pick up something dropped by other people unless he recognizes its owner, etc."

This is, then, the House God has chosen to be the *qiblah*, or direction of Prayer, for Muslims. It is God's House which He has made so rich in blessings. It is the first House ever set up for men to worship in. Moreover, it is the House of Abraham, containing clear signs that it was Abraham himself who built it. Islam, or submission to God, is the creed of Abraham. Hence, the House he built is the one which deserves to serve as the direction of Prayer for Muslims. Moreover, it represents security and peace on earth. Since it is the focal point of Islam, it represents guidance for mankind.

The *sūrah* moves on to state that God has imposed a duty on mankind to make pilgrimage to this House once they are able to do so. Otherwise, they let themselves fall into disbelief which causes God no harm: *"Pilgrimage to this House is a duty owed to God by all people who are able to undertake it. As for those who disbelieve, God does not stand in need of anything in all the worlds."*

One thing which attracts our attention when we read this verse is the fact that the duty of pilgrimage is made in absolutely general terms: *"… a duty owed to God by all people."* This suggests, first of all, that the duty of pilgrimage is also required of the Jews who disputed the validity of the Muslims turning to the Ka'bah in their Prayer. Their argument fails completely when it is realised that they themselves are required to make the pilgrimage to this House, since it is the House built by their father, Abraham, and the first one ever to be set up for worship by mankind. In this light, the Jews appear to be the deviant and disobedient ones. We may also infer from the way this verse is phrased that all mankind are required to accept this faith, fulfil its duties, offer its worship, and make the journey of pilgrimage to the House to which the believers in God turn. Unless they do this, their stand is one of disbelief, no matter how strongly they may profess to be believers. God stands in no need of anything or anyone. He does not need people's belief in Him, nor does He benefit by their pilgrimage. The benefit and prosperity are theirs when they accept the faith and offer the worship.

Pilgrimage is a personal obligation on every individual once in a lifetime, and it becomes due when the conditions of ability are fulfilled, including physical health, ability to travel and safe passage. There is, however, a difference of opinion among scholars with regard to the time when this duty was imposed. Relying on the report that the present passage was revealed in the ninth year of the Prophet's settlement in Madinah, which is generally known in history books as "the year of delegations", some scholars believe that pilgrimage was made an obligatory duty in that same year. They support their argument with the fact that the Prophet himself went on his pilgrimage after that date. When we discussed the question of changing the direction of the *qiblah*, in our commentary on the preceding *sūrah*, we made the point that the timing of the Prophet's pilgrimage could not be taken as an argument in support of the view that the pilgrimage was made obligatory at a late stage in the Prophet's life. Several considerations might have contributed to that delay. One of these may have been the fact that the idolaters used to do the walking round the Ka'bah (*ṭawāf*) completely in the nude, and they continued to do so after the liberation of Makkah. The Prophet did not like to join them in their *ṭawāf*. The *sūrah* entitled "Repentance", or "*Al-Tawbah*", was revealed in the ninth year of the Islamic calendar, and idolaters were banned from *ṭawāf* in the Ka'bah altogether. The Prophet offered his pilgrimage in the following year. Hence, the duty of offering the pilgrimage may have been legislated earlier, and this verse may have been revealed in the early part of the Prophet's settlement in Madinah, probably around the time of the Battle of Uḥud which took place in the third year of the Islamic calendar.

Nonetheless, this statement imposes the obligation of pilgrimage, in the terms of a right which God demands from all people who are able to make the journey.

Pilgrimage is the Muslims' annual general assembly which is held at the House from which their message was given to them for the first time, and which witnessed the birth of the pure faith of Abraham, their first father, and which was the first House God has set up on earth for His own worship. Pilgrimage is, therefore, an assembly of great significance. Its historical associations centre round the noble concept of faith, which highlights the link between man and his Creator. Faith means man's spiritual response to God, a fact of great significance considering that only by the breathing of God's spirit has man acquired his humanity. It is a worthy concept to form the basis for human unity. Hence, it is appropriate that people should assemble every year at the Sacred Place which witnessed the birth of this call to mankind to unite on pure faith.

An Appeal in the Interest of Truth

Having provided this clarification, the *sūrah* instructs the Prophet to address the people of earlier revelations denouncing their attitude towards the truth of the Islamic message. They know this truth full well, yet they try to turn people away from it. They disbelieve in God's revelations although they bear witness to them and they are certain that these revelations are true: *"Say: 'People of earlier revelations, why do you disbelieve in God's revelations, when God Himself is witness to all that you do?' Say: 'People of earlier revelations, why do you try to turn those who have come to believe away from the path of God, seeking to make it appear crooked, when you yourselves bear witness [to its being straight]? God is not unaware of what you do.'"* (Verses 98–9)

Similar denunciations are made in this *sūrah* as in many others. It is a highly effective denunciation because it does not mince words about the matter in question. The attitude of the people of earlier revelations is truthfully described, and they are shown in their true colours, even though they try to appear as people who have faith when they are in reality unbelievers. They disbelieve in the Qur'ān, which is revealed by God. Anyone who disbelieves in any part of God's book disbelieves in the whole of that book. Were they true believers in the part of God's book which has been revealed to them, they would have believed in every messenger sent by God after their own messenger. The essence of Divine faith is the same. Anyone who knows it knows for certain that whatever is preached by subsequent messengers is also true. He is bound to accept the prophets' call to surrender himself to God in the way they teach. This fact should shake those people and make them fear the consequences of insisting on their erring ways.

Those in the Muslim community who are deceived by the fact that those people adhere to a Divine book can no longer be so deceived. As they listen to God's words declaring the truth about those people, branding them as total unbelievers, all their doubts are bound to disappear. God issues them with warnings which strike fear in their hearts: *"God Himself is witness to all that you do ... God is not unaware of what you do."* It is a fearful warning because it makes man feel that God watches him and sees exactly what he does, which is, in reality, nothing but disbelief, deception and corruption. Moreover, God makes it clear that they are aware of the truth which they deny and away from which they try to turn people: *"... You yourselves bear witness [to its being straight]."* It is absolutely clear, then, that they were aware of the truth which they rejected. They knowingly tried to turn people away from what they realised to be a straight path. What wickedness! Anyone who adopts such a practice is not worthy of trust, but rather of contempt and denunciation.

We need to reflect on God's description of those people in the following terms: *"... Why do you try to turn those who have come to believe away from the path of God, seeking to make it appear crooked?"*

(Verse 99) This is a statement of great significance. God's path is straight, and every other way is crooked. When people are turned away from God's path and believers are forcibly barred from following God's constitution, nothing remains straight. Our standards become faulty and nothing remains on earth except crookedness which can never be set straight.

Corruption, thus, gains the upper hand. Human nature becomes corrupt as it deviates from the straight path, and life becomes corrupt as it follows a crooked line. All this corruption is the result of turning people away from the path of God. Such corruption manifests itself in different ways: erroneous concepts, deviant conscience, crooked morality, wicked behaviour, unfair transactions and injustice in all relations within human society. Either people follow the path of God which is straight and which leads to everything that is good, or they deviate from it in any direction, and this inevitably leads to crookedness, evil and corruption. In man's life, there is no third alternative.

A Warning Against Obeying Non-Muslims

> *Believers! If you pay heed to some of those who have been given revelations, they will cause you to renounce the truth after you have accepted the faith. But how can you sink into disbelief when God's revelations are being recited to you and His messenger is in your midst? He who holds fast to God has already been guided along a straight path.* (Verses 100–1)

Having answered all the arguments advanced by Christians and Jews against the message of Islam, the *sūrah* now makes this direct address to the Muslim community, which begins with a stern warning against paying heed to false claims made by followers of other religions, and outlines the essential characteristics of the Muslim community, its methods, beliefs and way of life.

The Muslim community implements a Divine system which makes it unique among all nations of the world. It owes its very existence to this system which, in turn, assigns to it a role which cannot be played by any other community. It has to establish this Divine system in practice so that it appears to all eyes as real and practical. Statements and clauses are thus translated into actions. They define moral standards, generate certain feelings and establish certain relations.

The Muslim community, however, cannot go along its proper way, realise the purpose of its existence and make the theory a reality unless it receives its instruction from God alone. Only through this can the Muslim community assume the leadership of mankind. This precludes them any possibility of following or paying heed to any human being. The choice before the Muslim community is either to follow this course dictated by its faith, or to sink into utter disbelief.

The Qur'ān emphasises this fact on several occasions. It tries to mould the feelings, thoughts and morality of the Muslim community on the basis of this principle at every possible opportunity. On this particular occasion, by answering the arguments of the people of earlier revelations and forestalling their schemes against the Muslim community in Madinah, this principle is re-emphasised. The fact that it is stated again here, within the context of a particular set of circumstances, does not detract from its permanent validity. It applies to all generations of the Muslim community because it is the basis of its very existence.

If the Muslim community is brought into existence in order to assume the leadership of mankind, how is it possible for that community to receive instructions from the very ignorance which it aims to eradicate? If the Muslim community is to abandon its role of leadership, what purpose has its existence? Its leadership is to provide correct concepts and beliefs for human life, generating perfect moral standards and a perfect social set-up. In such a healthy situation, the human intellect makes its constructive contribution as it tries to learn the secrets of the universe and manipulate its potentials. The leadership which permits and controls all that potential, using it for the benefit of mankind, not to threaten human life with destruction, nor to devote it to satisfy carnal desires, belongs to faith only. It is given to the Muslim community which seeks God's guidance and does not allow itself to be dictated to by anyone of God's servants.

These verses include a warning to the Muslim community against following other people. These are followed later by an explanation of how the Muslim community can create and maintain a proper set-up. The first warning is against following people of earlier revelations, the Christians and Jews, for they will inevitably lead the Muslim community back into disbelief: *"Believers! If you pay heed to some of those who have been given revelations, they will cause you to renounce the truth after you have accepted the faith."* (Verse 100) In the first place, to follow the people of earlier revelations and to copy their methods and systems indicate an inner defeat and suggest that the Muslim community has abandoned its leadership role. It also suggests the existence of doubts in the minds of the Muslims about the adequacy of the Divine system to organise and elevate human life. These very doubts are the beginnings of creeping disbelief, even though in these earlier stages one may not sense the approaching danger.

The people of earlier revelations, on the other hand, are keen to turn the Muslim community away from its faith, which represents both its line of defence and its driving force. The enemies of Islam are well aware of this, as they have always been. Hence, they spare no effort and resort to all manner of schemes and designs so as to divert the Muslim community from its proper way. When they realise that they cannot win an open war against the faith of Islam, they resort to evil. When they feel they cannot launch a war against it by themselves, they recruit hypocrites who pretend to be Muslims so that they work against Islam from within, advocating different systems and pledging their loyalty to different leaderships.

Were the people of earlier revelations to find some Muslims responsive to their arguments, they would lose no time in channelling that responsiveness to their paramount goal of leading those Muslims, and the Muslim community as a whole, to total disbelief and renunciation of the truth. Hence, the sternness of the Divine warning: "Believers! If you pay heed to some of those who have been given revelations, they will cause you to renounce the truth after you have accepted the faith." (Verse 100)

At the time of the Prophet, no prospect was more daunting to any Muslim than to find himself sinking into disbelief after he had accepted the faith. That meant throwing himself back into the fire of hell after he had saved himself and opened his way to heaven. This applies to every true Muslim across generations. Hence, a warning in such terms is sufficient to alert his conscience and keep it wide awake. The *sūrah*, therefore, continues the warning with a reminder to the Muslim community of God's grace. How fearful is that prospect, of finding those who have accepted the faith allowing themselves to be led back into disbelief, when God's revelations continue to be recited to them, and God's Messenger remains in their midst. All the incentives to accept the faith are there, and the call to God continues to be made, and the parting of the ways of belief and disbelief is made absolutely clear: "But how can you sink into disbelief when God's revelations are being *recited to you and His messenger is in your midst?"* (Verse 101)

It is indeed a great calamity that a believer should sink into disbelief in circumstances which are conducive to strengthen his faith. If God's Messenger has completed his term in this life, God's revelations remain with us, and the guidance of His Messenger continues to show us the way. Today, we are addressed by the Qur'ān as the first generation of Muslims were addressed by it. The way to follow that guidance is clear and the banner of the truth continues to fly high: *"He who holds fast to God has already been guided along a straight path."* (Verse 101) The only guarantee against slipping into renunciation of the truth is to hold fast to God. He is the eternal Master of all. He never dies.

Making Sure One's Way Is Right

The Prophet used to adopt a very strict attitude with his Companions in matters of faith and with regard to their way of life. At the same time, he allowed them to use their discretion in practical matters which rely on experience and knowledge. Examples of these include military strategy, agriculture and all purely scientific matters which belong to a domain that has no bearing on faith, social system or the relationships which regulate man's life. The way of life adopted by an individual or a certain society has nothing to do with pure or applied science.

The religion of Islam, which has been revealed to conduct human life according to a certain Divine method, makes its directive clear to man to seek knowledge and to benefit by every material discovery or scientific advance, provided that this is made within the context of implementing Islam's own method of life.

Imām Aḥmad relates, on the authority of 'Abdullāh ibn Thābit, that 'Umar came to the Prophet one day and said: "Messenger of God! I have asked a Jewish friend of mine from the tribe of Quraiẓah to write me the basic teachings of the Torah. Shall I read them to you? The Prophet's face changed colour when 'Umar said that." 'Abdullāh ibn Thābit turned to 'Umar and said: "Do you not see the expression on God's messenger's face?" 'Umar said immediately: "I believe in God as my only Lord, accept Islam as my faith and Muḥammad as God's messenger." The Prophet's face regained its normal colour and he said: "By Him who holds my soul in His hand, if Moses comes back to you tomorrow and you follow him and leave me you will go astray. You are my share of nations and I am your share of Prophets."

A *ḥadīth* reported by Jābir quotes the Prophet as saying: "Do not ask the people of the earlier revelations about anything, for they will not guide you aright when they have gone astray. You will have one of the two alternatives: either you will accept a falsehood, or you will reject a truth. Had Moses been living among you, the only course lawful to him would be to follow me." The Prophet is also quoted as saying: "Had Moses and Jesus been alive, they would have had to follow me."

This is the position of the people of earlier revelations. The Prophet makes our position abundantly clear when it comes to following their guidance in matters of faith, ideological concepts, law or way of life. However, Islam imposes no restriction whatsoever on its followers when it comes to benefiting by the advances of any group of people in any branch of science. We have only to relate these advances to our own approach to everything in the universe, knowing that God has enabled man to make use of everything on earth so as to achieve a higher and more secure standard of living. We should also be grateful to God for enabling us to make such discoveries and for facilitating our use of the resources and potentials He has placed in the universe. We express our gratitude to Him by worshipping Him alone and by making the right use of our advances.

When it comes to asking the followers of other religions about concepts of faith, the purpose of human life, its method, laws and regulations, its moral values and codes, we find the Prophet's face changing colour at the slightest indication of such. God gives the Muslim community a stern warning against being led by others in any such matter. The ultimate result of that is nothing but the total rejection of faith.

In the light of this directive from God and the guidance of His Messenger, where do we, who claim to be Muslims, stand today? I see us taking Orientalists and their disciples as our teachers when we study the Qur'ān and the *ḥadīth* of the Prophet. I also see us formulating our concepts of life and existence on the basis of what we learn from these Orientalists, as well as from Greek, Roman, European and American philosophers. We borrow our regulations and laws from these suspect sources. I also find us borrowing our manners, code of conduct, and morality from the stinking immorality into which the modern material civilisation has fallen. Yet we still claim to be Muslims! Such a claim is worse than open disbelief. For when we take such a stance, when our state of affairs is such, we testify to the failure of Islam. Such a testimony is not made even by non-Muslims.

Islam is a method with unique, distinctive characteristics in relation to its ideological philosophy, its laws regulating all spheres of life, and its moral code which governs all political, economic and social relations. It is a method designed to lead humanity as a whole. Hence, it is necessary that a certain community should implement this method in order to assume the leadership of mankind. As we stated earlier, it is contrary to the very nature of leadership that this community should receive directives from any source other than its own method of life.

It is for the good of mankind that this method was revealed by God. It is also for the good of mankind that the advocates of Islam call for the implementation of this method, now and in the future. Indeed, the urgency for its implementation today is that much greater, considering the terrible suffering of mankind under all other systems. There is simply no saviour except this Divine method which must retain all its distinctive characteristics in order for it to play its proper role and save mankind anew.

Man has made great advances in utilising the resources and potentials of the universe. His achievements in medicine and industry are miraculous when compared with his past. Fresh discoveries and triumphs still await us. But what is the effect of all this on human life? Has it given man happiness, security and peace? The answer is in the negative. What humanity has found instead is misery, worry, fear, neurological and psychiatric disease, in addition to widespread perversion and crime. Moreover, it has made no progress whatsoever in the formulation of a sound concept dealing with the purpose of human existence. When this is compared with the Islamic concept, this civilisation appears to shrink into insignificance. It seems no more than a curse which belittles man's own concept of himself and his position in the universe. It degrades him and limits his aspirations. The result is a heart consumed by a void and a soul writhing under the burden of confusion.

The simple reason is that humanity cannot find God because miserable circumstances have caused its course to deviate away from Him. Had scientific research followed the Divine method, it would have made every achievement accomplished by man a step drawing humanity nearer to God. Instead, it causes humanity to move further away from Him. Man is, therefore, deprived of the light which would have revealed for him the true purpose of his existence and which would have enabled him to work for that purpose equipped with the scientific progress God has enabled him to achieve. Furthermore, man is deprived of the method which would have established harmony between him and the universe. He is also deprived of the system which would have established a perfect equilibrium between individual and community, man's potentials and resources, rights and duties, as well as the interests and concerns of this world and the life to come.

Certain groups of people even strive to deprive man of God's method and guidance. It is they who describe man's aspiration to implement this method as "reaction". They dismiss it as a mere nostalgia for the historical past. Whether this be the result of their ignorance or their ill-will, they actually deprive humanity of the right to aspire to the only method which can lead it to perfect peace and happiness, as well as to progress and development. We, who believe in this method, know perfectly well what we call for. We see the misery of mankind and we see as well, over the horizon, the real possibility for mankind's salvation. We are also aware that unless the leadership of mankind is given over to this method, then man will sink into even further deprivation.

The first step to salvation is that this method should remain pure. Its advocates must not listen to any directive given to them by the ignorance which has spread all around them. This ensures the purity of the system until God wills it to reassume the leadership of mankind. God is too kind to man to let him fall prey to his enemies who advocate ignorant ways. This is the lesson God delivered to the first Muslim community in His revelation and which the Prophet was keen to drive home to his followers by his sound teaching.

Brotherhood After Hostility

God warns the Muslim community that it cannot hope to implement the Islamic way of life or fulfil the great trust God has placed in it, unless it acquires the two basic qualities of faith and brotherhood. It must have a faith which keeps the fear of God ever present in its mind. It must also make brotherhood in Islam a reality. Only through this brotherhood can the Muslim community acquire its strength and be able to play its most important role in human life and history, namely, the role of enjoining what is right and forbidding what is wrong. In other words, it promotes every good thing in human life and purges it from every evil.

Believers! Fear God as you rightly should, and do not allow death to overtake you before you have surrendered yourselves truly to Him. Hold fast, all of you together, to the bond with God and do not be disunited. And remember the blessings God has bestowed on you: how, when you were enemies [to one another] He united your hearts and, by His grace, you have become brothers; and how, when you were on the brink of an abyss of fire, He saved you from it. Thus God makes clear His revelations to you, so that you may be rightly guided. (Verses 102–3)

Faith and brotherhood are the two pillars upon which the structure of the Muslim community is built. If either of them collapses, the very existence of the Muslim community is undermined, and its great role comes to nothing. The first pillar is that of having faith and fear of God. It is only through such fear that man can fulfil his duties towards God because it makes him always alert. He does not lose sight of his duty for a moment of day or night.

"Believers! Fear God as you rightly should." This command is given in general terms so as to heighten its effect. It thus makes the believer keen to achieve this goal of fearing God as He should rightly be feared, according to man's understanding and ability. This is a road which attracts man more and more as he walks further and further. The nearer he draws to God through fearing Him, the higher the goal he sets for himself. He will continuously strive to achieve a greater position, so as to make his heart always alert, never asleep.

"Do not allow death to overtake you before you have surrendered yourselves truly to Him." The timing of death is beyond the reach of our knowledge. No man can be certain when death will overtake him. Hence, if anyone wants to die a Muslim, in the full sense of the word, he must surrender himself to God, right here and now. He must also abide by the requirements of this surrender at all times. The fact that Islam is mentioned after the command to have fear of God points to its wider implications: total surrender and submission to God, complete obedience and implementation of His method, and making His book the final arbiter in all affairs. This is the meaning which pervades the whole *sūrah*.

This is the first pillar upon which the structure of the Muslim community is built. Without it, no human grouping can be described as Islamic. No Divine method of life can come into operation in any community without it. In its absence, there are only ignorant methods and ignorant leadership.

The other pillar is the bond of brotherhood, based on the love of God and implementation of His method: *"Hold fast, all of you together, to the bond with God and do not be disunited. And remember the blessings God has bestowed on you: how, when you were enemies [to one another] He united your hearts and, by His grace, you have become brothers."* (Verse 103) It is a brotherhood which has its roots in the fear of God and in surrendering to Him. In other words, it is derived from the first pillar. Its cornerstone is to hold fast to the bond with God, that is, the fulfilment of His commands and the implementation of His law. It cannot have any other basis, concept, goal or bond.

"Hold fast, all of you together, to the bond with God and do not be disunited." This brotherhood which holds fast to a strong bond with God is a blessing with which God has favoured the first Muslim community. It is a blessing which God always grants to those of His servants whom He loves. He reminds the first Muslim community here of this blessing, recalling how enmity was rife among them in their pre-Islamic days. No enmity was fiercer than that which existed between the Aws and the Khazraj, the two Arab tribes in Yathrib, the city which came to be called Madinah. Alongside them lived the Jews who were always trying to perpetuate this hostility in order to weaken both tribes and destroy all ties between them. It was in such an atmosphere of hatred that the Jews worked and flourished. God, however, united the hearts of both Arab tribes with the tie of Islam. It is only through Islam that such mutually hostile hearts could be united. It was only through the bond of God, to which all can hold fast, that they could become, by God's grace, brothers. Historical grudges, vengeance killings, personal ambitions and racial ties are reduced to nothing when compared with the bond of brotherhood which unites all under the banner of God, the Almighty: *"And remember the blessings God has bestowed on you: how, when you were enemies [to one another] He united your hearts and, by His grace, you have become brothers."* (Verse 103)

He also reminds them of His grace in the form of saving them from the fire after they were about to fall in it. He saved them when He guided them to hold fast to His bond, the first pillar, and when He united their hearts so that they became brothers, the second pillar: *"When you were on the brink of an abyss of fire, He saved you from it."* (Verse 103) We note here that the Qur'ān refers to man's heart, which is the centre of his feelings and bonds. It does not say: *"He united you."* Rather, it refers to man's own deeply-seated feelings: *"He united your hearts."* Men's hearts are thus described as a solid group, united by God on the basis of His covenant. We also have here a vivid description of the Muslims' earlier situation which touches their hearts: *"...You were on the brink of an abyss of fire."* At the very moment when their fall into the abyss is expected, those hearts feel God's hand as it reaches out and saves them. They feel God's bond stretched out to them in order to protect them. We find them saved after exposure to a great danger. It is a very vivid, heart-touching scene which is raised before our eyes despite the lapse of many centuries.

In their biographies of the Prophet, Muḥammad ibn Isḥāq and others, report that this verse was revealed on the occasion of a Jewish leader from Madinah passing by a group of Muslims from both the Aws and the Khazraj. When he looked at them a sudden awareness overtook him. He realized that their past hostility had been replaced by genuine love and brotherhood. He was determined to spoil this healthy atmosphere. He sent a man with instructions to sit with those people and remind them of their past hostilities, and the fierce battles that had taken place between them, particularly the Battle of Buʿāth, in which both tribes suffered heavy casualties. The man was successful in his mission and soon tempers were boiling among that group. In their anger, some of the tribesmen repeated their old slogans. Someone called for his sword. Others repeated the same call. Someone even suggested that they should meet for battle the following day outside Madinah. When the Prophet received intelligence of what was taking place between them, he went hurriedly to them and tried hard to cool their tempers. He said to them: "Do you resort to your ignorant ways when I am living in your midst?" He recited to them the Qur'ānic verse: *"And remember the blessings God has bestowed on you: how, when you were enemies [to one another] He united your hearts and, by His grace, you have become brothers; and how, when you were on the brink of an abyss of fire, He saved you from it."* (Verse 103) They soon regained their senses and regretted what had happened. Peace prevailed anew among them and they hugged each other in genuine brotherly love. They had been rightly guided when God's revelation was made clear to them. Hence, the concluding comment in that Qur'ānic verse is an apt description of their case: *"Thus God makes clear His revelations to you, so that you may be rightly guided."*

This is just one example of Jewish efforts to sever the bond which unites those who love God and follow the Divine method and make of them a model community, providing leadership for the rest of mankind. Every time a true Muslim community comes into existence, holding fast to the bond of God and implementing His constitution, the Jews start their scheming to create division among them. When that group of early Muslims heeded what they were bid by people of earlier revelations, they were about to sink back into disbelief, about to do battle with each other. Their bond with God which unites them in a genuine brotherhood was about to be severed.

This verse has much wider significance than just this particular incident. Taken with what precedes and follows it, the verse suggests that the Jews in Madinah were engaged in a continuous effort to create division and disunity among the Muslims. Hence, the repeated Qur'ānic warnings to the Muslims not to pay heed to the people of earlier revelations and to make sure that they would not fall victim to their scheming. We detect here a feeling that the Muslim community was undergoing great troubles as a result of the plots of the Jews in Madinah. Those same tactics have been employed all the time against Muslims everywhere in the world.

The Role of the Muslim Community

The task of the Muslim community is to implement the Divine method in human society, and to help truth to triumph over falsehood, goodness over evil. This task is stated in the following verse: *"Let there become of you a nation that invites to all that is good, enjoin the doing of what is right and forbid what is wrong. Such are they who shall prosper."* (Verse 104)

It is imperative for this community to come into existence so as to invite all to that which is good, and to enjoin what is right and forbid what is wrong. The Qur'ānic statement imparts that this must be done through a real authority which can invite, enjoin and forbid. Anyone may be able to invite to what is good, but no one can enjoin and forbid unless he is equipped with real authority.

This is the proper Islamic view of the matter. It is essential that there should be an authority to undertake the task of advocating what is good and removing what is evil. The units which constitute this authority must combine together, hold fast to their bond with God, and translate their brotherhood into a reality. The prerequisites enabling this authority to implement the Divine method in life are faith and brotherhood. The Divine method cannot be put into practice without "inviting" others to every good so that people realise the true nature of this Divine method. It also requires an active authority to "enjoin" what is right and "forbid" what is wrong. Such an authority must be obeyed. God says: *"We have sent every messenger in order to be obeyed with God's leave."* (al-Nisā' 4: 64) Hence, God's method is not merely preaching and verbal explanation. This is only one part of it. The other part is an active and sustained effort to promote every right thing in human life and to reduce to a minimum every wrong. In this way, the traditions of the good Muslim community will be protected against the whims of anyone who has the power to impose his own interests on the community. It also protects these traditions against all abuse or subservience to personal desire or interest.

The task of enjoining what is right and forbidding what is wrong is not an easy one, especially when we consider that it inevitably conflicts with people's desires, interests and pride. There are in this world of ours tyrants who impose their authority by force, people who are interested only in carnal desires and who do not wish to be elevated to a nobler standard. There are also the lazy who hate to be asked to be serious, the unfair who hate justice, the deviant who do not for a moment contemplate a straightforward attitude, as well as those who think wrong of every right thing and consider every wrong thing to be right. No nation, let alone humanity as a whole, can prosper unless goodness prevails, right is upheld and wrong is thrown out. Hence, the need for an authority to promote goodness and right and to combat evil. What is more, this authority must be obeyed.

This leads us back to the point where we started: a community must be built on the two essential qualities of faith and brotherhood. It is only such a community that can undertake this difficult task, equipped with the power of faith and the seriousness it derives from fearing God as well as the strength of love and brotherhood. It is only through the fulfilment of this role that this community can prosper. Hence, God describes those who fulfil it as prosperous: *"Such are they who shall prosper."* (Verse 104)

The existence of such a community is essential for the Divine method itself. It is indeed the environment in which it can breathe and become a practical reality. It is a good, healthy environment where people cooperate to promote goodness. In such a community, right is synonymous with goodness, virtue and justice, whereas wrong means evil, vice and injustice. To do good in such a community is easier than to do evil, virtue is simpler than vice, right stronger than wrong, justice more common and beneficial than injustice. A person who wants to do good will find help while the one who wants to do evil will meet resistance. It is this fact that gives this community its greatest value. It provides an environment where goodness and right can prosper without the need for any great effort, because everything in this environment lends them support. Wrong and evil can only grow with difficulty because of the all-round resistance which neglects it.

The concept Islam formulates of life, actions, events, values and people is essentially different from all other concepts. Hence, a special environment, which is totally different from that state of ignorance which prevails in unreligious communities, is needed to enable this unique concept, with all its unique values, to flourish. This environment must be conditioned by the Islamic concept of human life and must serve it so that it may live, breathe freely and grow in it, without encountering any internal hindrances to its development. Should it encounter any obstacles, then the essential qualities of the Muslim community, to advocate all that is good and to enjoin what is right and forbid what is wrong, are certain to remove them. Should an oppressive force attempt to turn people away from God, then it will inevitably encounter those who are prepared to defend and protect the Divine method of life.

This environment is embodied in the Muslim community which is built on the twin pillars of faith and brotherhood. Its faith in God brings conformity to its concept of life, events, actions, values and people and gives it a single standard with which to evaluate everything in life. It conducts all its affairs according to the same Divine law and pledges all its loyalty to the leadership which takes upon itself the task of implementing God's method in human life. The brotherhood of faith provides this community with bonds of love and mutual care. These ties ensure the absence of selfishness in the community and help its members care for one another without pressure or ill feeling.

The first Muslim community in Madinah was built on these two pillars: faith in God based on knowing Him and recognising His attributes, fearing Him and being constantly aware of what pleases Him; and genuine, flowing love, true friendship and mutual care. The first Muslim community achieved all this in practice, an ideal normally considered closer to dreams than reality. The brotherhood established between the *Muhājirīn* (Muslims who emigrated from Makkah) and the *Anṣār* (the Muslims of Madinah) is a real story approximating absolute idealism. It is an event borrowed from the heavens, but which took place on this earth. It is on the basis of such strong faith and real brotherhood that God's method of life can be implemented in every generation.

Faces Shining with Happiness

A fresh warning to the Muslim community against falling out with one another is added here. The example of those people of earlier revelations who were entrusted with the implementation of God's method but who allowed division and conflict to creep into their ranks is given. Therefore, God deprived them of the leadership position and instead assigned that role to the Muslim community, which fosters its bond of brotherhood. Moreover, those who are not true to their task will be sternly punished on the day when faces will either shine or be blackened: *"Do not follow the example of those who became divided and fell into conflict with one another after clear proof had come to them. For these there will be grievous suffering, on the day when some faces will shine with happiness and some faces will be blackened. Those whose faces are blackened [shall be told]: 'Did you disbelieve after having embraced the faith? Taste, then, this suffering for having sunk into disbelief.' Those with shining faces shall be in God's grace; they abide there for ever."* (Verses 105–7)

A vivid scene, full of life, is drawn here in the inimitable style of the Qur'ān. The scene is one of horror, but the horror is not described in words or adjectives. It is represented in living human beings, in their faces and looks. We see bright, shining faces, full of joy and happiness, and others gloomy, dusty and blackened. Yet those people are still not left alone to suffer their fate. They have to put up with scourging comments: *"'Did you disbelieve after having embraced the faith? Taste, then, this suffering for having sunk into disbelief.'"*

The happy fortunes of the other group is also vividly described: *"Those with shining faces shall be in God's grace; they abide there for ever."* This description adds life, movement and dialogue to the scene, again in the Qur'ān's inimitable style.

The scene helps the Muslim community fully appreciate the Qur'ānic warning against division and conflict. The grace God has bestowed on it through faith and unity is also fully appreciated. The Muslim community sees with its own eyes the end of those people of earlier revelations whom it has been warned not to obey. If it follows them, it will share their doom and suffering on the day when faces will either shine or be blackened.

When the destiny of each of the two groups has been clearly stated, a comment is added which is in harmony with the broad lines of the *sūrah*. It reasserts the truth of the Prophet's message and revelation, the fact that reckoning and reward on the Day of Judgement are to be taken seriously, the fact that Divine justice in this world and in the hereafter is absolute, and the fact that all that is in heaven and on earth belong to God and to Him they shall all return: "*These are revelations of God. We recite them to you in truth. God wills no injustice to His creatures. To God belongs all that is in the heavens and all that is on earth; to Him shall all things return.*" (Verses 108–9)

All these facts, all these scenes and destinies so described are revelations given by God to His servants. They are recited to His messenger in truth. They embody the truth in the principles and values they establish. They tell only the truth about the destinies of other nations. They are revealed in truth by the One Who is able to reveal them and Who alone has the right to determine values, rewards and destinies. God does not inflict any injustice on anyone of His creatures. He is the fairest of all arbiters. He controls the heavens and the earth, and to Him belong all that is in heaven and on earth, and to Him shall they all return. By making reward fit with action God only wants to establish right, administer justice and ensure that all matters are conducted seriously as befits His majesty. Absurd is the claim of the people of earlier revelations that they will only be scourged by the fire for only a few days.

A Quality Essential to the Muslim Community

You are the best community that has ever been raised for mankind; you enjoin the doing of what is right and forbid what is wrong, and you believe in God. Had the people of earlier revelations believed, it would have been for their own good. Few of them are believers, while most of them are evildoers. (Verse 110)

This verse describes the Muslim nation so that it becomes aware of its position, value and true nature. The first part of the verse imposes a very heavy duty on the Muslim community, while at the same time honouring and elevating it to a position which cannot be given to any other community: *"You are the best community that has ever been raised for mankind; you enjoin the doing of what is right and forbid what is wrong, and you believe in God."*

We note first that the reference to the Muslim community as one which *"has been raised"* is made in the passive voice. This suggests that a highly skilful hand has neatly moulded this community and brought it forth from behind the eternal curtain which covers things known only to God. The expression adopted here indicates a subtle and gentle movement which brings forth onto the stage of existence a whole nation which has a unique role to play and a special position to occupy.

"You are the best community that has ever been raised for mankind." The Muslim nation should understand this in order to know its position and its true nature. It should know that it has been raised specially for the purpose of assuming the leadership of mankind, since it is the best nation. God wants the leadership in this planet of ours to be assumed by the forces of goodness, not the forces of evil. It follows that it should never be in the recipient position, taking what other nations have to offer. It must be the one to offer to others whatever it has of sound ideology, philosophy, morality and knowledge, and of course its perfect system. This is the duty of the Muslim nation, imposed on it by its unique position and the purpose of its very existence. It is a duty on the Muslim nation to assume the leadership of mankind at all times. By assuming it, it also takes upon itself certain responsibilities. Leadership cannot be given to any nation which claims it, unless it proves that it is the worthy leader. By its ideology and social system, the Muslim community is worthy of this position. What remains for it is to prove that in scientific advancement and in the fulfilment of man's task of building the earth, it is also an able leader. It is clear then that the system which brings this nation into existence demands much from it and gives it the incentive to excel in every field, if only it would follow this system and appreciate its requirements and duties.

The first requirement is that the Muslim nation should work hard at protecting human life from evil. It must have the power to enable it to enjoin the doing of all that is right and forbid the doing of all that is wrong. It is, after all, the best nation ever raised for mankind. This position is not given to the Muslim community as the result of any favouritism, coincidence or random selection. Far be it from God to do that. Positions and duties are not given by God to different nations on the basis of any favouritism, as the people of earlier revelations were wont to believe, describing themselves as *"God's children and beloved people."* (*al-Mā'idah* 5: 18) The criterion which makes a certain community worthy of the position of leadership is its active work for the preservation of human life from evil and the promotion of what is right, in addition to its implemention of the faith which defines what is right and what is wrong: *"You enjoin the doing of what is right and forbid what is wrong."* (Verse 110)

The position of leadership is thus earned through the active fulfilment of its tasks, heavy as they are, and through following the way defined for it, thorny as it may be. In practical terms, it means standing up against evil, promoting every good and protecting society against all elements of corruption. All these are extremely hard tasks, but they are nevertheless necessary if a good human society is to be established and protected. There is no other way to bring about the type of society which God loves.

Belief in God is also necessary so that the community has a correct standard of values and a correct definition of what is right and what is wrong. What is socially agreed by a community is not enough. For it may happen that corruption becomes so widespread that standards are no longer correct or appropriate. Hence, reference must be made to a permanent concept of good and evil, virtue and vice, right and wrong. This concept should have as its basis something other than the social norms of any particular generation.

Belief in God provides all this, since it ensures a correct concept of the universe and the relationship between the Creator and His creation. It provides the correct concept of man, the purpose of his existence and his true position in the universe. It is from this general concept that moral values and principles should be derived. The desire to earn God's pleasure and to avoid His displeasure motivates people to work for the implementation of these principles. They, in turn, are safeguarded by fear of God and by the authority of His law.

Belief in God is necessary for those who invite to all that is good, enjoin what is right and forbid what is wrong, to proceed along their appointed course and bear all its difficulties and hardships. They have to face the tyranny of evil at its fiercest, the pressures of worldly desires at their strongest, as also complacency, weakness and narrow ambition. To do this, they have to be equipped with faith. It is their only weapon. Their support comes from God. Any other aid is exhaustible, any other weapon can be overpowered and any other support is liable to collapse.

Earlier in the *sūrah*, the Muslim community is described by God as having the necessary qualities to implement His Divine method. That community, however, does not come into existence by its own volition, but only when it possesses the essential qualities which distinguish it from the rest of mankind. It either invites to all that is good, enjoins what is right and forbids what is wrong, in addition to believing in God; in this case it gives credence to its existence as a Muslim nation. Or, alternatively, it does not do any of this. In this case it is deemed not to have come into existence, and it loses its Islamic identity.

The Qur'ān stresses this in numerous places, each of which will be discussed in its appropriate context. The *Sunnah* also includes a number of such directives and commands by the Prophet, some of which may be quoted here:

Abū Sa'īd al-Khudrī reports that he heard the Prophet saying: "Let any of you who sees something wrong put it right with his own hand. If he is unable to do so, let him change it by the word of his mouth. If he cannot do even that, then let him do it within himself. This is the weakest form of faith." (Related by Muslim.)

Abū Dāwūd and Al-Tirmidhī relate on the authority of Ibn Mas'ūd that the Prophet said: "When the children of Israel began to commit sins frequently, their scholars tried to dissuade them, but they persisted. Their scholars, nevertheless, continued to attend their social gatherings, and to eat and drink with them. God left them to stray and sealed their hearts. He also cursed them in the words of David, Solomon and Jesus, son of Mary." The Prophet was saying this as he reclined, but at this point he sat up and said: "By Him who holds my soul in His hand, you must make them turn back to what is right."

Al-Tirmidhī relates on the authority of Hudhayfah that the Prophet said: "By Him who holds my soul in His hand, you will enjoin the doing of what is right and forbid what is wrong, or else, God will visit you with a punishment of His own. You will, then, pray to Him and He will not answer you."

God's Messenger says: "When a sin is committed on earth, a person who witnesses it and denounces it is the same as one who has not seen it, and the one who has been absent and approves of it is considered like one who has taken part in it." (Related by Abū Dāwūd.)

Abū Sa'īd al-Khudrī quotes the Prophet as saying:· "One of the highest forms of jihad is to confront a despotic ruler with the word of truth." (Related by Abū Dāwūd and Al-Tirmidhī.)

Jābir quotes the Prophet as saying: "The best of all martyrs is Ḥamzah and a man who stands up to a despotic ruler, enjoins him to do what is right and forbids him what is wrong, and is, therefore, killed by that ruler."

The Prophet stresses this quality of enjoining what is right and forbidding what is wrong in many other *ḥadīths*, all of which establish beyond any shadow of doubt that it is a prerequisite for the Muslim community. The *Sunnah* contains a wealth of directives which provide the best education for the Muslim community. Unfortunately, however, we tend not to give the *Sunnah* its true value.

The Fate of Deserters

> *They cannot harm you beyond causing you some trifling hurt; and if they fight against you, they will turn their backs upon you in flight. Then they will receive no help. Ignominy shall be pitched over them wherever they may be, save when they have a bond with God and a bond with men. They have incurred the wrath of God and humiliation shall overshadow them. That is because they persisted in denying God's revelations and killing the Prophets against all right. That is because they persisted in their disobedience and transgression.* (Verses 111–12)

Its unique qualities make the Muslim community the best nation ever to be raised for mankind. Having outlined these qualities of enjoining what is right and forbidding what is wrong and believing in God, the verse goes on to explain that to have faith is better for people: *"Had the people of earlier revelations believed, it would have been for their own good. Few of them are believers, while most of them are evil-doers."* (Verse 110)

This serves as an encouragement to the people of earlier revelations to accept the faith of Islam, because such acceptance works for their own good in this life and in the life to come. By accepting the faith they overcome their division over ideological concepts, which has robbed them of any chance to establish their own distinctive character. Their concepts cannot serve as the basis for a social system. Hence, their social systems have no firm foundation. This is indeed true of any social system which is not based on an ideology that provides an overall view of existence, of the purpose of human existence, as well as man's position in the universe. To believe in God works for their own good in the life to come, since it is the only means to spare them the fate of the unbelievers.

The same verse describes their attitude, giving the good ones among them due credit: *"Few of them are believers, while most of them are evildoers."* A number of the people of earlier revelations accepted Islam at the time of the Prophet and became good Muslims. Among them were 'Abdullāh ibn Sallām, Asad ibn 'Ubaid, Tha 'labah ibn Shu 'bah and Ka 'b ibn Mālik. This verse makes a general reference to them whilst a more detailed reference is given later. Most of them, however, chose the evil way of not fulfilling the covenant God made with all prophets, which stated that every one of them would believe in and support the prophet God sent after him.

They also chose evil when they refused to submit to His will that the last of His messengers would not be from among the Israelites. They rejected this messenger and declined to submit to God's law embodied in His last message, which He has made applicable to all mankind.

Since some of the Muslims at that time retained various links with the Jews in Madinah, and since the Jews still possessed military and economic power which some Muslims felt to be considerable, the Qur'ān deliberately sets out to belittle those evildoers. The Qur'ān shows their true weakness which results from their disbelief, their repeated crimes and disobedience, their division, and the consequent ignominy and humiliation imposed on them by God. It also states God's guarantee to the believers that they will be victorious over these enemies, provided that they themselves hold fast to their faith and believe in God.

> *They cannot harm you beyond causing you some trifling hurt: and if they fight against you they will turn their backs upon you in flight. Then they will receive no help.* (Verse 111)

The harm they may inflict will never be enough to trouble the Islamic message. It will never affect the basic structure of the Muslim community or wipe it out. The most they can inflict on the Muslims is the sort of trifling hurt which is bound to happen in any open conflict. It is nothing more than a superficial pain which disappears with time. When they fight against the Muslims, defeat is their ultimate outcome. They can never be triumphant over the believers. Moreover, they will have no help against, nor protection from the believers. The reason is that ignominy has been imposed on them as their fate. They are humiliated everywhere in the world. The only protection they have is that which they receive when they seek refuge with God and with the Muslims.

When they choose to come under the protection of the Muslims, their lives and their property become immune, except under the normal working of the law, and they enjoy peace and security. Since that time, the Jews have never enjoyed true security except when they have enjoyed the protection of the Muslims. Yet they themselves have shown their utmost hostility to the Muslims. *"They have incurred the wrath of God,"* as if they have returned from their journey burdened with this wrath. *"And humiliation shall overshadow them,"* remaining forever in their hearts and feelings.

All this took place after this verse was sent down. Whenever a battle flared up between the Muslims and people of earlier revelations, victory was always achieved by the Muslims, provided that they held fast to their faith and implemented God's law in their lives. Their enemies always suffered ignominy and humiliation except when they were able to establish a bond with the Muslims or when the Muslims abandoned their religion.

The Qur'ān states the reason for the fate so imposed on the Jews. It is a general reason, the effect of which may be applicable to every nation, no matter how strongly it professes to be religious. The simple reason is their disobedience and transgression: *"That is because they persisted in denying God's revelations and killing the prophets against all right. That is because they persisted in their disobedience and transgression."* (Verse 112)

Denying God's revelation, whether it is an attitude adopted outright or a refusal to implement it practically, the killing of prophets without any justification and the killing of people who enjoin fairness and justice (as mentioned in another verse of the *sūrah*), as well as disobedience and transgression, are all reasons for incurring God's wrath and bringing about defeat, ignominy and humiliation upon oneself. These reasons are still present today among the lost offspring of the Muslims who call themselves, without justification, Muslims. They present these very qualifications to their Lord and they get their fair reward: they receive all that God has imposed on the Jews of defeat, ignominy and humiliation. Some of them may well ask: why do we suffer defeat when we are Muslims? Let those who pose such a question first reflect on what the true nature of Islam is, and who are the true Muslims?

Different Ways, Different Ends

They are not all alike. Of the people of earlier revelations there are some upright people who recite the revelations of God in the depth of the night, and prostrate themselves in worship. They believe in God and the Last Day and enjoin the doing of what is right and forbid what is wrong and vie with one another in doing good works. These belong to the righteous. Whatever good they do, they shall never be denied its reward. God knows those who fear Him. As for the unbelievers, neither their riches nor their children will avail them in any way against God. It is they who are destined for the fire, where they will abide. Whatever they spend in this present life is like a biting, icy wind which smites the tilth of people who have wronged themselves, laying it to waste. It is not God Who does them wrong; they wrong themselves. (Verses 113–17)

Here the *sūrah* reassures the good minority among the people of earlier revelations who take faith seriously. They are again singled out for praise. The passage begins with a statement that the people of earlier revelations are not all alike. Some of them are true believers. Their attitude to faith and to God is described as that of true believers. This merits them the same reward which God gives to His righteous servants.

It is a bright picture of the true believers among the people who received Divine revelations in the past. Their faith is genuine, profound, and complete. They have made their stand clear. They have joined the ranks of those who surrender themselves to God and defend this faith with all the power they possess. They believe in God and the Last Day. Moreover, they fulfil the duties required of them by their faith and give practical effect to the characteristics of the community which they have joined, the best community ever raised for mankind. They desire every good thing. They enjoin the doing of what is right and forbid what is wrong. They have set themselves a goal and they compete with one another for its achievement. That goal is to do good works. Hence, they merit this testimony that is given from on high stating that they belong to the righteous. They also have the promise, which never fails, that they will not be denied their reward. The verse adds that God, Who is aware of all things and all people, knows that they belong to that special group of people who genuinely fear Him.

This picture is raised in front of the eyes of those who wish to have a similar testimony and a similar promise. They have only to follow the same line and adopt the same attitude. They will then find its light spreading over the limitless horizon of their lives.

On the other side stand the unbelievers who will not benefit by their possessions or by their children. Nothing they may spend in this life for what they may consider to be a good cause will be of any avail to them. No reward is given them for it in the hereafter because it has not originated from the straight, constant line of goodness. Every good thing must have its foundation in belief in God which combines a clear concept, a well-defined goal, and a straight uninterrupted line. If it does not, it is reduced to a passing whim or an impulsive desire. It has no clear basis and it is not related to an overall way of life.

> As for the unbelievers, neither their riches nor their children will avail them in any way against God. It is they who are destined for the fire, where they will abide. Whatever they spend in this present life is like a biting, icy wind which smites the tilth of people who have wronged themselves, laying it to waste. It is not God Who does them wrong; they wrong themselves. (Verses 116–17)

This is a moving, vivid scene, full of life, and drawn in the fine Qur'ānic style. Their riches and their children will never protect them against God. They cannot be offered in ransom so that they escape punishment. They are destined for the fire of hell which will become their permanent abode. Whatever they spend of their money, even on causes which they believe to be good, is wasted. Nothing which does not have its foundation in faith can be good. The Qur'ān does not express the ideas it wants to convey in the same way as we would. Instead, it paints a scene full of life.

When we look up, we find a field ready to yield its crops. It is described as a tilth. But suddenly the wind blows. It is a biting, icy wind. Its strong bite devastates all the tilth. The Arabic word used here sounds like a missile thrown with violence. Its onomatopoeia adds to its meaning. In a single moment, all the crops of that field are destroyed, laid to waste.

It is only a moment which changes everything. All this devastation happens before one can even draw one's breath. Nothing is left. This is the Qur'ānic way of describing what the unbelievers spend on what may seem to be good causes and what they count as their blessings of riches and children. All will be laid to waste giving them no enjoyment and no reward. *"It is not God Who does them wrong; they wrong themselves."* It is they who have abandoned the way of life which groups together every single aspect of goodness and righteousness and makes of them a straight, consistent line with a recognised motive and a clear goal. Goodness does not stem from a momentary thought, a vague desire or a sudden impulse.

It is they who have chosen to be in error and to break loose from the protection offered by their bond with God. If all their actions are wasted, including what they may spend on seemingly good causes, and if their tilth is devastated and they can benefit nothing by wealth or children, this is not an injustice inflicted on them by God. It is they who are unjust to themselves by virtue of the choice they have made.

What we have here, then, is a clear statement that no reward is given for any donation to any cause and no value is attached to any work unless it is clearly linked to the way of life based on faith, and unless it is motivated by faith. It is God Who makes this statement. It cannot be contradicted, then, by any man. No one may argue with this statement except those who argue against God's revelation.

We have examined a long passage of this *sūrah*, starting with verse 93, which aims at explaining the nature of deviation in the behaviour of the people of earlier revelations. It lays bare their twisted arguments and exposes the evil designs they forge in order to undermine the Muslim community. It also issues directives to the Muslim community to discharge its duties paying no heed to the transgressors and their deviant arguments. At the end of this passage, a warning is issued to the Muslim community against establishing an intimate relationship with its natural enemies, the unbelievers, revealing its secrets to them and trusting them with its interests. This warning is presented in the form of a detailed picture which may be seen in every age and in every community. Today, those who claim to be Muslims and to be the people of the Qur'ān have overlooked this Qur'ānic picture. This has rebounded on them; hence the evil and humiliation they suffer today.

The Sort of Friends Unbelievers Make

Believers, do not take for your intimate friends men other than your own folk. They will spare no effort to corrupt you. They love to see you in distress. Their hatred has already become apparent by [what they say with] their mouths, but what their hearts conceal is even much worse. We have made revelations plain to you, if you will only use your reason. See for yourselves how it is you who love them and they do not love you. You believe in all revelations. When they meet you they say: "We, too, are believers." But when they find themselves alone, they bite their fingertips with rage against you. Say: "Perish in your rage. God is fully aware of what is in the hearts [of people]." When good fortune comes your way, it grieves them; and if evil befalls you, they rejoice. If you persevere and fear God, their machinations cannot harm you in any way. God encompasses all that they do. (Verses 118–20)

The picture so drawn in these three verses vividly delineates, with full details, people's innermost thoughts. It records inner feelings and apparent reactions. It captures every little movement. It is a picture of a certain type of person who can be seen in every age, in every society, professing friendship with the Muslims when the Muslims are strong and victorious. Their claims, however, are belied by their every thought, every feeling and every organ. Muslims may be deceived by them, placing their trust in them when they wish nothing but trouble and confusion for the Muslims and spare no effort to inflict hardships on them. They most determinedly seek to undermine the Muslims, whenever they have a chance to do so, at any moment of day or night.

This remarkable picture drawn by the Qur'ān applies, in the first place, to those followers of earlier religions who lived close to the Muslim community in Madinah. It depicts their strong hatred of Islam and the Muslims, as well as their treachery and evil schemes against the new Muslim community. Nonetheless, some Muslims continued to think well of these enemies of God. Such Muslims were very friendly towards them and even passed them information which should have been treated as secret, belonging only to the Muslim community. They developed close friendships and intimacy with them, which meant that they grossly underestimated the consequences of their friendly gestures. The Qur'ān, therefore, issues this warning so as to open the eyes of the Muslim community to the reality of the matter and to make it aware of the machinations of its natural enemies. This warning is not limited to any particular period of history. It applies at all times. It deals with a situation which may exist at any time, as it does indeed in our present time.

The Muslims though remain heedless of their Lord's directive not to develop any intimate friendship with anyone other than their own people. All other people are inferior to the Muslims in their way of life, methods and nature. God tells the Muslims not to make any such people their advisors and confidants. Yet the Muslims do not heed this directive. They continue to refer to such people in every matter and situation and look up to them for guidance in every system, method and philosophy.

The Muslims, even nowadays, maintain their friendship with people who reject God and His Messenger. They pay little heed to God's words which apply to them in the same way as they applied to the first Muslim community: *"They love to see you in distress. Their hatred has already become apparent by [what they say with] their mouths, but what their hearts conceal is even much worse."* (Verse 118)

God also says to the Muslims: *"See for yourselves how it is you who love them and they do not love you. You believe in all revelations. When they meet you they say: 'We, too, are believers.' But when they find themselves alone, they bite their fingertips with rage against you."* (Verse 119) God also points out to the Muslim community the true feelings of such people: *"When good fortune comes your way, it grieves them; and if evil befalls you, they rejoice."* (Verse 120)

Time after time we go through bitter experiences but none of these seem to wake us up. Time after time we discover the unbelievers' evil intentions, cleverly masked, but we do not seem to learn our lesson. Yet they make many slips of the tongue which reveal their deep hatred of Islam. This which cannot be dispelled by any measure of friendliness shown to them by the Muslims or by the tolerance Muslims are taught by their faith. But we nevertheless open our hearts to them and treat them as close friends throughout life. Our courtesy, or indeed our spiritual defeat, reaches such proportions that we even avoid mentioning our faith in front of them. We refrain from taking Islam for our way of life and we distort our own history so as to avoid any mention of past conflicts between our forefathers and those enemies who work for our ruin. It is only to be expected then that we receive the punishment of those who disobey God. It is only natural that we find ourselves weak, defenceless and humiliated, suffering the distress which they love to see us in, and weakened by the corruption they spare no effort to spread among us.

God's revelations teach us, as they taught the first Muslim community, how to forestall the plots of the unbelievers, repel the harm they try to cause us and avoid the evil intentions they harbour against us and which they betray by what they say: *"If you persevere and fear God, their machinations cannot harm you in any way. God encompasses all that they do."* (Verse 120) The message is clear. We have to equip ourselves with perseverance and resolve and stand up to their might if they are powerful, and to their machinations and designs if they try to deceive us and sow division in our ranks. It is such perseverance and resolve which will set us on the road to success. The other requirement is to fear God alone and to watch Him alone. It is through this fear of God that our hearts will establish our bond with Him, seeking no other bond and making no ties with anyone except on the basis of God's Divine method. When a heart establishes its bond with God, it will look down upon every power other than His.

This, then, is the way: perseverance and fear of God, coupled with steadfastness and maintenance of the bond with God. Throughout their history, the Muslims have always been able to raise their heads high, achieve victory, repel the machinations of their enemies and achieve supremacy only when they fostered their bond with God alone and implemented His method in their lives. Conversely when the Muslims revive their bonds with their natural enemies who try in public and in private to suppress their faith, and when the Muslims listen to their advice and take friends, assistants and advisors from among them, then they always bring upon themselves defeat and subjugation. The unbelievers gain the upper hand and the Muslims are left humiliated, feeling regret when regret is of no use. History testifies to the fact that God's words remain always true and His law is always operative. Anyone who overlooks God's law, will be made to experience only humiliation and defeat.

Thus this passage ends, bringing the first section of the *sūrah* to its conclusion. The lesson has been driven home. We stand at the point which separates the Muslims from their enemies; a separation which is total, complete and final.

As we bring our own commentary on this passage to an end, we should note that Islam meets all this hostility with tolerance. It simply commands the Muslims not to take such people as their intimate friends. It does not, however, encourage a policy of measure for measure with the unbelievers. It does not require them to return the unbelievers' hate, grudges and evil schemes with similar feelings and attitudes. It seeks only to provide protection for the Muslim community. It simply warns the Muslims of the danger presented by other people.

A Muslim treats all people with the tolerance characteristic of Islam. He is motivated by his love to do good to all mankind. He tries to foil the evil schemes of others against him, but he does not scheme against anyone. He does not harbour grudges although he takes care not to fall victim to other people's grudges. Only when a Muslim faces aggression which aims to turn him away from his faith and from following and implementing the method of life God has laid down, is he required to fight back and break down all barriers which prevent people from following Divine guidance and implementing the Divine law. His fight is a struggle for the cause of God. It is not a fight in pursuit of revenge. He fights because he loves what is good for mankind, not because he nurses a grudge against those who have caused him harm. He struggles in order to remove the barriers which prevent the goodness of Islam from reaching mankind, not to win power and dominion over others. His aim is to implement the perfect system under which all mankind enjoy justice and peace. He is not after raising any national banner or building any empire.

Many a statement in the Qur'ān and the *Sunnah* confirm this fact. Furthermore, the history of the first Muslim community proves this.

This method of life is absolutely good. Only the enemies of mankind try to turn them away from it. It is those enemies who must be chased and kicked out of every position of leadership they occupy. This is the duty God imposes on the Muslim community. It once fulfilled it as it should be fulfilled. It is called upon to fulfil it all the time. Struggle under this banner and for the cause of God will continue until the Day of Judgement.

Part II

The Battle of Uḥud

6

Lessons for All Muslim Generations

Remember when you set out from your home at an early hour to assign the believers to their battle posts. God hears all and knows all. (121)

وَإِذْ غَدَوْتَ مِنْ أَهْلِكَ تُبَوِّئُ ٱلْمُؤْمِنِينَ مَقَاعِدَ لِلْقِتَالِ ۗ وَٱللَّهُ سَمِيعٌ عَلِيمٌ ۝

Two of your groups were about to lose heart, but God was their protector. In God shall the believers trust. (122)

إِذْ هَمَّت طَّآئِفَتَانِ مِنكُمْ أَن تَفْشَلَا وَٱللَّهُ وَلِيُّهُمَا ۗ وَعَلَى ٱللَّهِ فَلْيَتَوَكَّلِ ٱلْمُؤْمِنُونَ ۝

God gave you victory at Badr when you were utterly weak. Therefore fear God, that you may have cause to be grateful. (123)

وَلَقَدْ نَصَرَكُمُ ٱللَّهُ بِبَدْرٍ وَأَنتُمْ أَذِلَّةٌ ۖ فَٱتَّقُوا ٱللَّهَ لَعَلَّكُمْ تَشْكُرُونَ ۝

You said to the believers: "Is it not enough for you [to know] that your Lord should send down three thousand angels to support you? (124)

إِذْ تَقُولُ لِلْمُؤْمِنِينَ أَلَن يَكْفِيَكُمْ أَن يُمِدَّكُمْ رَبُّكُم بِثَلَٰثَةِ ءَالَٰفٍ مِّنَ ٱلْمَلَٰٓئِكَةِ مُنزَلِينَ ۝

185

"Indeed, He will, if you are patient in adversity and fear God, and if they [the non-believers] suddenly attack you, your Lord will supply you with five thousand angels swooping down." (125)

بَلَىٰٓ إِن تَصۡبِرُواْ وَتَتَّقُواْ وَيَأۡتُوكُم مِّن فَوۡرِهِمۡ هَٰذَا يُمۡدِدۡكُمۡ رَبُّكُم بِخَمۡسَةِ ءَالَٰفٍ مِّنَ ٱلۡمَلَٰٓئِكَةِ مُسَوِّمِينَ ﴿١٢٥﴾

God made this only as a happy news for you, so that your hearts might take comfort from it. Victory comes only from God, the Mighty, the Wise. (126)

وَمَا جَعَلَهُ ٱللَّهُ إِلَّا بُشۡرَىٰ لَكُمۡ وَلِتَطۡمَئِنَّ قُلُوبُكُم بِهِۦۗ وَمَا ٱلنَّصۡرُ إِلَّا مِنۡ عِندِ ٱللَّهِ ٱلۡعَزِيزِ ٱلۡحَكِيمِ ﴿١٢٦﴾

It is in order to destroy some of the non-believers, and so abase others that they lose and withdraw. (127)

لِيَقۡطَعَ طَرَفٗا مِّنَ ٱلَّذِينَ كَفَرُوٓاْ أَوۡ يَكۡبِتَهُمۡ فَيَنقَلِبُواْ خَآئِبِينَ ﴿١٢٧﴾

You have no say in the matter. [It is for Him] to accept their repentance or punish them. They are wrongdoers. (128)

لَيۡسَ لَكَ مِنَ ٱلۡأَمۡرِ شَيۡءٌ أَوۡ يَتُوبَ عَلَيۡهِمۡ أَوۡ يُعَذِّبَهُمۡ فَإِنَّهُمۡ ظَٰلِمُونَ ﴿١٢٨﴾

To Him belongs all that is in the heavens and the earth; He forgives whom He wills and punishes whom He wills. God is Forgiving and Merciful. (129)

وَلِلَّهِ مَا فِي ٱلسَّمَٰوَٰتِ وَمَا فِي ٱلۡأَرۡضِۚ يَغۡفِرُ لِمَن يَشَآءُ وَيُعَذِّبُ مَن يَشَآءُۚ وَٱللَّهُ غَفُورٞ رَّحِيمٞ ﴿١٢٩﴾

Believers, do not gorge yourselves on usury, doubling [your money] again and again. Have fear of God, so that you may prosper. (130)

يَٰٓأَيُّهَا ٱلَّذِينَ ءَامَنُواْ لَا تَأۡكُلُواْ ٱلرِّبَوٰٓاْ أَضۡعَٰفٗا مُّضَٰعَفَةٗۖ وَٱتَّقُواْ ٱللَّهَ لَعَلَّكُمۡ تُفۡلِحُونَ ﴿١٣٠﴾

Guard yourselves against the fire which has been prepared for the unbelievers; (131)

وَٱتَّقُوا۟ ٱلنَّارَ ٱلَّتِىٓ أُعِدَّتْ لِلْكَٰفِرِينَ ﴿١٣١﴾

and obey God and the messenger, that you may be graced with mercy. (132)

وَأَطِيعُوا۟ ٱللَّهَ وَٱلرَّسُولَ لَعَلَّكُمْ تُرْحَمُونَ ﴿١٣٢﴾

Hasten, all of you, to the achievement of your Lord's forgiveness, and a paradise as vast as the heavens and the earth, prepared for the God-fearing, (133)

۞ وَسَارِعُوٓا۟ إِلَىٰ مَغْفِرَةٍ مِّن رَّبِّكُمْ وَجَنَّةٍ عَرْضُهَا ٱلسَّمَٰوَٰتُ وَٱلْأَرْضُ أُعِدَّتْ لِلْمُتَّقِينَ ﴿١٣٣﴾

who spend [in His way] in time of plenty and in time of hardship, and restrain their anger, and forgive their fellow men. God loves the benevolent. (134)

ٱلَّذِينَ يُنفِقُونَ فِى ٱلسَّرَّآءِ وَٱلضَّرَّآءِ وَٱلْكَٰظِمِينَ ٱلْغَيْظَ وَٱلْعَافِينَ عَنِ ٱلنَّاسِ وَٱللَّهُ يُحِبُّ ٱلْمُحْسِنِينَ ﴿١٣٤﴾

Those who, when they commit a gross indecency or wrong themselves, remember God and pray for the forgiveness of their sins – for who but God can forgive sins? – and do not knowingly persist in doing the wrong they may have done. (135)

وَٱلَّذِينَ إِذَا فَعَلُوا۟ فَٰحِشَةً أَوْ ظَلَمُوٓا۟ أَنفُسَهُمْ ذَكَرُوا۟ ٱللَّهَ فَٱسْتَغْفَرُوا۟ لِذُنُوبِهِمْ وَمَن يَغْفِرُ ٱلذُّنُوبَ إِلَّا ٱللَّهُ وَلَمْ يُصِرُّوا۟ عَلَىٰ مَا فَعَلُوا۟ وَهُمْ يَعْلَمُونَ ﴿١٣٥﴾

These shall have the reward of forgiveness by their Lord, and gardens underneath which rivers flow, where they shall abide. Excellent is the reward for those who labour [well]. (136)

أُو۟لَٰٓئِكَ جَزَآؤُهُم مَّغْفِرَةٌ مِّن رَّبِّهِمْ وَجَنَّٰتٌ تَجْرِى مِن تَحْتِهَا ٱلْأَنْهَٰرُ خَٰلِدِينَ فِيهَا وَنِعْمَ أَجْرُ ٱلْعَٰمِلِينَ ﴿١٣٦﴾

Overview

From the battlefield of words and ideas and concepts the *sūrah* turns now to that of armed combat: the Battle of Uḥud.

Uḥud was not, however, solely an armed confrontation; it was rather a struggle within the Muslim conscience. Its scope encompassed the whole gamut of human behaviour, feelings, emotions, aspirations, instincts and limitations. The Qur'ān was there to coach the human soul in the most caring and gentle way, and in a manner that is more comprehensive and effective than any forceful confrontation.

First came the victory, and then the setback. The sweeter and greater triumph, however, was still to come. It was the triumph of enlightenment and of a clarity of understanding the facts as the Qur'ān lays them down. A triumph of having those facts established as convictions. Muslim hearts were put to the test and purified, their ranks were set apart and the whole community proceeded with clearer concepts, more definite values, and stronger feelings than before. Furthermore, the hypocrites were largely set apart. In what ensued, the characteristics of hypocrisy and sincerity, as manifested in feelings, words, behaviour and actions, became much clearer, as did the obligations of faith and the responsibilities attendant on it. The battle clearly defined the preparations required of the Muslims in knowledge, devotion, organisation, compliance and total dependence on God Almighty, every step of the way. Everything was and is up to Him alone, in times of victory as in times of defeat, in life as in death.

The unexpected defeat suffered by the Muslim community in battle, however, was immeasurably less crucial than the Qur'ānic guidelines and recommendations that followed it. The Muslims, at that time, were in desperate need of such guidance; they needed it a thousand times more than they needed a military victory or the spoils of war. The benefits of that result were even more important and enduring for later Muslim generations. In short, there was a supreme Divine purpose behind the defeat suffered by the Muslims. As far as we can ascertain from its outward natural causes, what happened conforms to the normal pattern of things. The Muslims had, in essence, the great privilege of learning from their experience, of gaining more enlightenment and maturity, and of cleansing their ranks and reorganising and coordinating their plans. The whole experience has proved immensely valuable for later Muslim generations as well.

As soon as the battle on the ground was over, the Qur'ān moved to a wider arena, the human soul and the whole life of the Muslim community. It goes on to mould the community according to God's will, knowledge and purpose. What God designed for the Muslim community was achieved and it was all for their good, despite the hardships, the travails and the trials and tribulations they experienced.

When discussing the aftermath of the Battle of Uḥud, the Qur'ān combines in a remarkable way its review of the events, portrayal of the scenes of conflict, with its pointed commentary and specific directives. These emanate from the events themselves, and they advance specific exhortations and prescriptions for purifying souls, clarifying concepts and freeing hearts and minds from the negative and dark effects of desire, greed, hatred, guilt, negligence, and coveted aspirations.

What is even more interesting is how, while reviewing a military confrontation, the *sūrah* goes on to discuss the evils of usury and the merits of consultation and collective decision-making, or *shūrā*, despite the fact that at Uḥud it led to a disappointing outcome. Furthermore, the *sūrah* deals in a vigorous and thorough style with a wide range of human behaviour.

This richness, vitality and comprehensiveness come as no surprise to those who are aware of the Divine method. In the dynamics of Islam, an armed confrontation is not merely a clash of artillery, cavalrymen and fighters, nor does it involve pure military planning alone. Rather, such a confrontation cannot be isolated from the greater struggle that takes place inside human consciousness and in the social organisation of the Muslim community. The physical battle is closely linked to the purity and dedication of the human conscience and its freedom from the shackles that darken its vision or prevent it from turning to God Almighty. Likewise, it is firmly linked to the foundations and structure on which the life of the Muslim community is organised, in accordance with God's straight and sound order. The Divine way of life is built on mutual consultation in all aspects of life, not only in matters of state and governance. It is based on a system of cooperation rather than usury, and the two can never be part of the same structure.

The Qur'ān was addressing a Muslim community in the wake of a battle which, as we have already pointed out, went far beyond a simple armed expedition. It was a battle of wider extent and implication, for individuals as well as for life as a whole. This is the reason for raising in this context subjects such as the condemnation of usury, giving charitably at times of prosperity and need, obedience to God as a condition for His mercy and generosity, the restraint of anger, kindness and the purification from sin through appealing to God for forgiveness, and repentance as a condition for gaining God's pleasure and goodwill. The *sūrah* also talks of God's mercy as reflected in the benevolence of the Prophet Muḥammad and his kindness towards others. Towards the end of the review, the *sūrah* establishes the principle of mutual consultation, or *shūrā*, as necessary even at the most difficult of times; it stresses honesty and sacrifice and warns against parsimony.

These aspects were all ingredients for raising and preparing the Muslim community for the bigger and wider battle which included armed combat but which was not restricted to it. It remains the battle for the greater prize: overcoming the powers of self-interest, desire, greed and hatred, and establishing values and healthy foundations for the total life of the community.

The object here is to highlight the integrity and the unity of the Islamic faith in dealing with the human individual and all aspects of his behaviour and activity. These should revolve around one fundamental principle: worship of, and submission to, God with sensibility and full consciousness. The *sūrah* draws one's attention to the consistency of God's method in dealing with the totality of the human being in every situation, and to the coherent and final outcome of human activity, and to the influence of every move and every action on that outcome.

The all-ranging advice given here is not altogether removed from the context of the battle. People do not triumph in war until they prevail in emotional, moral and organisational struggles. Those who retreated at Uḥud were misled by Satan as a result of some misdemeanour. We are reminded that those earlier communities whose prophets led them to victory in battles of faith only triumphed because they started their march with seeking God's forgiveness and support and by cleansing their hearts of all wrongdoing. To abandon usury and adopt an equitable financial system is an essential preparation for victory. An equitable society is more likely to prevail than an exploitative one. Suppression of one's anger and forgiving others are essential for victory, because self-control, solidarity and kindness are highly potent forces in a tolerant society.

Another fundamental tenet in this context is recognition of God's will and the attribution of all eventualities to His wish and command, a concept which this *sūrah* defines clearly and decisively. In the meantime, it confirms God's way of basing the effect of people's behaviour on the nature of their activities, whether right or wrong, compliant or rebellious. People are no more than an image of God's will and an instrument of His command which He puts to whatever purpose He chooses.

Last, but not least, the *sūrah* impresses upon the Muslims the fact that victory is not a matter for them to decide. It is up to God's will which is translated through their struggle, for which they will be rewarded. The material fruits of victory are not theirs to reap, nor is victory granted to them for their own special gratification. It is brought about for the sake of higher objectives decided by God Almighty. The same applies to defeat, which is brought about in fulfilment of God's will, pursuant to the performance of the Muslim community and whether they discharged their obligations or not. Defeat comes about to achieve certain purposes, predetermined by God and known only to Him, to test people and purify their ranks, establish facts, values and standards, and in order to reveal God's laws for all to see.

Military, political or economic predominance has no value or weight, according to Islam, unless it is based on the Divine way which requires the exercise of proper control of personal desires and greed and the upholding of the way of life chosen by God for mankind. Victory must be totally for God and His way, and every human effort must be made for the sake of God and His cause. Otherwise, it is a triumph of one godless group over another godless group, with no benefit for mankind or for human life. Real advantage is gained only when the truth, the indivisible truth, of God's way prevails. There is no other truth in this world. But for this truth to prevail it must conquer the human soul and the daily system of human life. This can only be achieved when human beings conquer their own self-interest, desires, greed and prejudice, when they break free from the chains of materialism and seek God's pleasure and put their trust fully in His hand. It happens when people do their utmost to comply with God's command in every aspect of their lives. Only then can a military, economic or political victory be considered a real one, in God's sight; otherwise it is a godless victory that carries no weight or value whatsoever.

Thus, we are able to appreciate the approach of the *sūrah* in its appraisal of the Battle of Uḥud and why it takes the wider view of the human struggle, of which the battlefield represents only one aspect.

A Brief Account of the Battle of Uḥud

Before we go into the Qur'ānic review of the Battle of Uḥud, it is fitting to give a brief account of the events of that battle, as recorded in the biographies of the Prophet, in order to gain a better understanding of the Qur'ānic appraisal of the battle and of God's approach in educating and nurturing the Muslim community through the Qur'ān.

The Muslims scored a total victory against the non-Muslim Arabs at Badr in the second year of the Islamic calendar, 623 CE. That victory had the makings of a miracle about it. The Quraysh lost its most eminent personalities and its leadership fell to Abū Sufyān, who spared no effort in launching a revenge campaign. The trade caravan carrying a substantial portion of the Quraysh's wealth, which had precipitated the Badr confrontation in the first instance, escaped the fighting and it was that wealth which the Arabs of the Quraysh used to finance the planned retaliation.

Abū Sufyān was able to recruit around three thousand fighters from among the Quraysh and their allies, the Aḥābīsh (Abyssinians), who were accompanied by some of their women so as to deter them from running away. The army left for Madinah in the ninth month, Shawwāl, of the third year of the Muslim calendar, and camped near Mount Uḥud on the outskirts of Madinah.

The Prophet Muḥammad consulted with his people over whether they should meet them outside the city or stay put inside. According to Ibn Qayyim al-Jawziyyah, in his biography of the Prophet, Muḥammad's own view was to remain in the city and fortify their defences around it; if the Arabs decided to enter, the Muslims could engage them in the streets and the women could give support from the rooftops. He was supported by 'Abdullah ibn Ubayy [the chief of the hypocrites], but a large number, mainly young men who did not attend Badr, insisted that they should go and meet the enemy outside Madinah. As this view seemed to prevail, the Prophet stood up and went to 'Ā'ishah's room, donned his fighting attire, and emerged again ready to move. By that time the people had changed their mind and decided that they should not force the Prophet to leave the city. Some of them said: "Messenger of God, if you prefer you can stay in Madinah." His reply was: "It does not befit a prophet to take off his fighting attire once he has put it on until God decides the duel between him and his enemies." That was the first lesson the Muslims were to learn: once a collective decision has been arrived at by public consultation, there is no way to go but forward. There is no room for dithering, re-consultation and indecision. Things must be allowed to take their natural course and God will decide the outcome.

Shortly prior to this, the Prophet saw in a dream that his sword was cracked, and saw cows being slaughtered, and that he had put his hand inside a strong shield. He interpreted the crack as someone from his household being hit, the cows as some of his Companions being killed and the shield as the city of Madinah. He was, therefore, aware of the outcome of the confrontation, but decided, nevertheless, to comply with the consensus arrived at with his Companions. He was also educating his followers through practical experience. Above all, he was submitting to God's will which in his heart he felt happy and contented to do.

The Prophet left the city with a thousand Muslims, leaving Ibn Umm Maktūm in charge of leading the prayer during his absence. When they were half-way between Madinah and Uḥud, 'Abdullāh ibn Ubayy, and around one-third of the Muslim contingent withdrew from the expedition, protesting that the Prophet had not respected his views, and that he listened to the boys, so to speak. 'Abdullāh ibn 'Amr ibn Ḥarām, the father of Jābir ibn 'Abdullāh, went after the retreating company, cursing, scolding, and urging them to rejoin the Muslim fighters. He called to them: "Come and fight for the cause of God or lend support." They replied: "If we knew that you would fight we would not have retreated." Eventually he gave up on them, cursed them and rejoined the Muslim army.

Some of the Anṣār, i.e. Muslims from Madinah, asked if they could seek the support of their Jewish allies, but the Prophet refused: the Jews had no part in the confrontation between Islam and the idolaters. When one puts one's trust in God and dedicates one's heart and soul to Him, victory will be granted. The Prophet asked his Companions whether anyone of them could lead them closer to the Quraysh and this some of the Anṣār did until the party came down the slope of the Valley of Uḥud with the mountain to their backs. The Prophet asked his Companions not to start the fighting until he had given the order.

The following morning, the Prophet marshalled around 700 men for battle, including 50 cavalrymen and 50 archers under the command of 'Abdullāh ibn Jubayr. The Prophet ordered Ibn Jubayr and his men to hold their positions behind the main army and not to leave them no matter what happened, even if "you see birds picking up troops" one by one. He ordered them to repel the Quraysh attackers with their arrows so that they could not attack the Muslims from the rear.

The Prophet put on two layers of body armour and handed the standard over to Muṣ'ab ibn 'Umayr. He placed Al-Zubayr ibn al-'Awwām on one flank and Al-Mundhir ibn 'Amr on the other. He surveyed the younger recruits and ordered those he thought were under age to go back. These included 'Abdullah ibn 'Amr, Usāmah ibn Zaid, Usayd ibn Ẓahīr, al-Barā' ibn 'Āzib, Zaid ibn Arqam, Zaid ibn Thābit, 'Urābah ibn Aws, and 'Amr ibn Ḥizām. Those he allowed to remain with the troops included Samurah ibn Jundub and Rāfi' ibn Khudayj who were both 15 years of age.

The Quraysh similarly mustered their troops, numbering around 3,000, and including 200 horsemen, with Khālid ibn al-Walīd in charge of the right flank and 'Ikrimah ibn Abī Jahl commanding the left one.

The Prophet gave his sword to Abū Dujānah Sammāk ibn Kharshah, a brave fighter who showed real enthusiasm for battle.

Old Loyalties Totally Disregarded

The first man to come forward from the Quraysh was Abū 'Āmir, known as "the Monk", but whom the Prophet nick-named "the Transgressor". He was a leader of the Aws tribe before Islam but he refused to accept Islam and declared open hostility towards the Prophet. He had left Madinah to join the Quraysh in Makkah with the aim of rallying them against the Muslims. He enticed the Makkans to go to war against the Muslims, promising them the support of his tribe, the Aws, whom he said would follow him as soon as they saw him. He was the first man to step into the fighting arena, introduced himself and called over to his people among the Prophet's army to come over to his side. He was rejected and cursed. Declaring that "some evil" had befallen his people, he went on to fight the Muslims with fanatical zeal.

Abū Dujānah, Ṭalḥah ibn 'Ubayd Allāh, Ḥamzah ibn 'Abd al-Muṭṭalib, 'Alī ibn Abī Ṭālib, al-Naḍīr ibn Anas, Sa'd ibn al-Rabī', to mention but a few, showed tremendous courage when the combat started.

In the early part of the day, the Muslims prevailed and 70 of the most valiant of the Quraysh fell. The bulk of the Arab troops were scattered and ran back to where the women were camped. The women lifted their dresses and themselves took flight.

As the Muslim archers saw the non-believers withdrawing, they abandoned their assigned positions which the Prophet had ordered them never to leave. They were shouting: "The booty. The booty." Their commander ordered them back, recalling the Prophet's instructions, but they took no notice. They went after the loot leaving the Uḥud positions undefended.

At that precise point, Khālid ibn al-Walīd led the Makkan cavalry in a pincer movement to occupy the Mount abandoned by the archers, so as to attack the Muslims from the rear. When the fleeing Quraysh men saw Khālid and his troops occupying the high ground, they rallied to join them.

The tables were turned. The Muslims went on the defensive and chaos broke out all over the battlefield. The surprise attack from the Quraysh had thrown the Muslims into disarray; they lost control and panicked. Many Muslims were killed in what ensued and the Makkans were even able to get very close to the Prophet himself who was being defended by a handful of followers. Although they fought back bravely, all were killed. As for the Prophet, he sustained a wound to his face, and a broken lower incisor. His helmet was shattered. A volley of stones was hurled at him by the Makkans, causing him to fall on his side into a camouflaged ditch which Abū 'Āmir "the Transgressor" had dug to entrap the Muslims. Two metal rings from his visor pierced his cheek.

Amid this confusion, someone shouted: "Muḥammad has been killed." Whatever morale the Muslims had left was shattered and they were put to flight. Overcome with despair and exhaustion, they were routed and soundly defeated.

As people moved back, some stayed behind, among them Anas ibn al-Naḍr. He saw 'Umar ibn al-Khaṭṭāb, among other Muslims from both Makkah and Madinah, looking dejected and despondent. He enquired why they were sitting there. When they replied that it was because Muḥammad had been killed, he said: "What is your life worth after him, then? Get up and die for what he died for." He turned towards the enemy camp and as he passed by Saʿd ibn Muʿādh, he said: "Saʿd, how wonderful is the scent of Paradise. I can smell it behind Mount Uḥud." He fought until he was killed, with some seventy wounds to his body. Only his sister was able to identify him, only by a mark on his finger.

The Prophet, however, was able to make his way back to the Muslims and the first person to recognise him from behind his visor was Ka'b ibn Mālik who shouted at the top of his voice: "Muslims. Hear the good news. Here is the Messenger of God." The Prophet gestured to him with his hand not to say any more, and the Muslims, Abū Bakr, 'Umar and Al-Ḥārith ibn al-Ṣimmah among them, flocked to him. He led them towards and up the mountain pass. Then they were seen by Ubayy ibn Khalaf on a horse called al-'Awd which he used to feed in Makkah, saying: "I shall ride this horse to kill Muḥammad." When the Prophet heard this he said, "It is I who will kill him, by God's will." As Ubayy charged towards the Prophet aiming to fulfil his intention, the Prophet took a lance from al-Ḥārith and threw it at Ubayy hitting him in the collar bone, whereupon he fell down like a bull. The Prophet was sure the man would never recover, as he had said, and he did indeed die on the way back to Makkah.

Soon thereafter, Abū Sufyān, the Makkan chief, called from the top of the mountain: "Is Muḥammad among you?" Muḥammad told his Companions not to answer him, and he called again: "Is Ibn Abī Quḥāfah (Abū Bakr) among you?" No one answered. He called a third time: "Is 'Umar ibn al-Khaṭṭāb among you?" Having received no answer, he turned to his own people and said: "You need no longer worry about these men." However, 'Umar could not restrain himself and called back: "You enemy of God, all the men you mentioned are still alive, and may God give you more bad news." Abū Sufyān said: "There has been mutilation among your dead. I neither ordered it nor did it cause me any anger." This was a reference to what his wife, Hind, had done to the body of Ḥamzah, the Prophet's uncle, after her slave, Waḥshī, had killed him. She cut open his abdomen, pulled out his liver, chewed it and then threw it from her mouth.

Abū Sufyān then called upon the Makkan deity, saying: "Rise and prevail, Hubal." The Prophet urged his people to answer him, but they did not know what to say, and he said: "Say, 'God is higher and more exalted.'" Abū Sufyān retorted: "We have al-'Uzzā and you do not." The Prophet said: "Say to him, 'Allah is our Lord, and you have none.'" Abū Sufyān said: "Today avenges the day of Badr, and victory in war goes by turns." 'Umar answered him, saying: "We are not equal. Our dead go to Paradise, but your dead go to Hell."

When the fighting subsided and the Makkans had departed, the Muslims were nonetheless concerned that their enemies would head for Madinah, take their women and children and loot their possessions. The Prophet, therefore, ordered 'Alī ibn Abī Ṭālib to follow them to see which direction they followed and what their intention was. He said if they dismounted the horses and rode the camels, they would be going to Makkah; otherwise they would be going to Madinah. "By God in whose hand is my life," the Prophet said, "if they go to Madinah I will go after them and fight them inside it." 'Alī, however, reported that he had seen them dismount their horses and ride their camels instead. They were moving in the direction of Makkah.

Somewhere along the way disagreement broke out among the Makkans. Some of them argued that they had achieved very little at Uḥud. The Muslim high command remained intact and they could easily regroup. Such contenders urged their people to go back to Madinah to annihilate the Muslims. This news soon reached the Prophet and he called his people to prepare to confront the enemy again, adding: "Only those who fought [on the preceding day] should join us." 'Abdullāh ibn Ubayy offered to join the expedition but the Prophet declined his offer. Many Muslims willingly and dutifully prepared themselves to go out to fight again, despite their wounds and their apprehensions. Jābir ibn 'Abdullāh requested the Prophet to make an exception in his case and allow him to join the army. He said: "Messenger of God, I love to be with you in every battle, but my father asked me to look after his daughters on the day of Uḥud, and I ask you to let me join you this time." The Prophet granted him permission and led the Muslims out in pursuit of the idolaters of the Quraysh. They went as far as Ḥamrā' al-Asad, about 15 kilometres from Madinah.

A man by the name Ma'bad ibn Abī Ma'bad al-Khuzā'ī, came to see the Prophet who asked him to catch up with Abū Sufyān's army and dissuade them from launching any attack on the Muslims. Ma'bad caught up with Abū Sufyān at al-Rawḥā. Unaware that Ma'bad had converted to Islam, Abū Sufyān asked him: "What news have you?" Ma'bad replied: "Muḥammad has come out with his Companions to pursue you with an army the like of which has not been seen before. Many of them regretted staying behind the first time round." Abū Sufyān said: "So what do you think?" Ma'bad replied: "If you were to order your troops to march now, I would imagine that by the time you have started to move, you will be seeing their horses." Abū Sufyān said: "By God, we are determined to attack them and wipe them out." Ma'bad answered: "But I advise you against it." At that point Abū Sufyān led his people back towards Makkah.

Abū Sufyān also met with some non-Muslims heading for Madinah and he offered to load their camels with raisins when they returned to Makkah, if they would: "Tell Muḥammad from me that we are set to attack and wipe him and his Companions out." When the Muslims heard the message, they said: "God is all-sufficient for us. He is the best protector." Their resolve still strong, they waited for three more days and once they were certain that the unbelievers were well on their way to Makkah, they returned to Madinah.

Glimpses of Muslim Dedication

This summary by no means covers all aspects of the battle or details all the significant events of that day. As a complement, therefore, let us review some of the more remarkable incidents of that memorable episode.

At the climax of the fighting, following the Muslim archers' desertion of their positions, the encirclement by the idolaters, the cry that "Muḥammad had been killed", and the outbreak of mayhem among the Muslims, 'Amr ibn Qamī'ah was one of the unbelievers who managed to get close to the Prophet. In that bewildering state of confusion, a lady called Nusaibah bint Ka'b al-Māziniyyah, also known as Umm 'Imārah, was staunchly covering the Prophet. She hit 'Amr ibn Qamī'ah several times with her sword, but he was well-protected by his two shields. In return, he hit Nusaibah on her shoulder with his sword, seriously wounding her.

Abū Dujānah was also shielding the Prophet. Despite the volley of arrows that were hitting his back, he never wavered, all the while leaning over the Prophet.

At one point Ṭalḥah ibn 'Ubaid Allāh rushed towards the Prophet and was the only one defending him. He took that position until he fell. Ibn Ḥibbān reports that 'Ā'ishah, the Prophet's wife, related that her father, Abū Bakr said: "When the Prophet was left on his own at Uḥud, I was the first to go to him. I found a man defending him and said, 'Let it be Ṭalḥah; let it be Ṭalḥah. 'Soon Abū 'Ubaydah ibn al-Jarrāḥ came flying like a bird towards me and we both rushed towards the Prophet to find Ṭalḥah having fallen wounded. The Prophet asked us to take care of him. The Prophet was hit by an arrow and two rings of his visor had found their way into his cheek. I went to pull one of them out when Abū 'Ubaydah pleaded with me to let him pull it out. He grabbed the ring with his teeth and began to ease it out, taking care not to hurt the Prophet. He was able to pull it out, but his own front tooth came out. Then I went to pull the other ring out of the Prophet's cheek, but Abū 'Ubaydah again pleaded with me to allow him to do it. He pulled it out carefully with his teeth and another of his front teeth fell out. The Prophet all the while urged us to go and help Ṭalḥah who had been hit in more than ten places."

'Alī ibn Abī Ṭālib was cleaning the Prophet's wound with water and Fāṭimah, his wife and one of the Prophet's daughters, was helping him. When she saw the blood oozing out of the wound, she burnt straw and put it on the wound to ensure that the bleeding stopped.

Mālik, father of Abū Sa'īd al-Khudrī, was sucking the blood out of the Prophet's wound to clean it. The Prophet urged him to spit it out, but he refused. The Prophet used to point to Mālik and say: "Whoever wants to look at a man from Paradise, let him look at this man."

Muslim reports that, at Uḥud, the Prophet was left alone with seven of his Companions from the Anṣār and two from the Quraysh. When his attackers increased their pressure on him, he called: "Who would defend me and go to Paradise?" One by one, the Anṣārī men came forward, fought the unbelievers but were themselves killed. Looking at them, the Prophet said: "We have not been fair to our Companions." Then Ṭalḥah fought hard to drive the enemy away from the Prophet, and Abū Dujānah shielded him as we have already mentioned. The Prophet was so exhausted that he was not even able to climb a rock on the mountain until Ṭalḥah squatted to allow him to step over his back. When it was time for Prayer, he led the Muslims in Prayer sitting down.

On that momentous day also, Ḥanẓalah al-Anṣārī, nick-named al-Ghasīl, attacked Abū Sufyān and managed to get a firm grip on him, Shaddād ibn al-Aswad, however, dashed forward and killed Ḥanẓalah. Now when the Muslims were called to go out and fight earlier that day, Ḥanẓalah was still in his wife's arms. He got up immediately without taking the obligatory bath. This means that he was in the state of ceremonial impurity, which required that he should take a bath or a shower. When he was killed the Prophet told his Companions that the angels were washing him. He asked them to find out from his wife why the angels should be doing this, and she explained to them what had happened.

Zaid ibn Thābit related that, at Uḥud, the Prophet dispatched him to seek Saʿd ibn al-Rabīʿ. He found him in the throes of death, with seventy wounds on his body. He said to him: "Saʿd, the Messenger of God sends his greetings and is enquiring after you." He replied: "Give God's Messenger my greetings and tell him that I can smell the scent of Paradise. Tell my people, the Anṣār, that they shall have no excuse with God if the Prophet comes to any harm and any of them is still alive." With these words his soul departed.

A Makkan Muslim passed by one from Madinah bleeding profusely. He said to him: "Do you know that Muḥammad has been killed?" The man replied: "If he has, then he has fulfilled his mission, and you should fight for your religion."

ʿAbdullāh ibn ʿAmr ibn Ḥarām said that, before Uḥud, he saw in a dream Mubashshir ibn ʿAbd al-Mundhir saying to him: "You will be visiting us within a few days." ʿAbdullāh asked him where he was, and he replied: "In Paradise, where we do as we like." ʿAbdullāh then asked: "But were you not killed at Badr?" Mubashshir replied: "Indeed, but I was brought back to life." When ʿAbdullāh related his dream to the Prophet, he said to him: "Abū Jābir, it is martyrdom."

Khaythamah, whose son was martyred at Badr, said that he had been eager to go to Badr but had missed it because his son won the draw of lots and went with the Muslim army, fighting at Badr until he fell a martyr. He said that in a dream he had had the previous night he had seen his son, looking extremely handsome, strolling around the trees and rivers of Paradise saying: "Join our company in Paradise. I have found what my Lord promised me to be true." He intimated to the Prophet his burning desire to join his son, even though he was old and frail. He asked the Prophet to pray to God to grant him martyrdom and the company of Saʿd in Paradise. The Prophet prayed for him and he died a martyr at Uḥud.

ʿAbdullāh ibn Jaḥsh was heard that day, praying: "God, I beg of You to let me meet the enemies tomorrow, and let them kill me, cut open my abdomen and cut off my nose and ears, so that when You ask me the reason, I can say, 'For Your sake.'"

ʿAmr ibn al-Jamūḥ was the father of four sons who used to go on military expeditions with the Prophet. Despite his bad limp, he wanted to join the fighting at Uḥud. His sons told him that God had granted him exemption. Hence, he did not have to go. He went to the Prophet to protest: "My sons are preventing me from going out to fight with you. By God, I pray to God that I am martyred and that, with this very limp, I would walk in Paradise." The Prophet told him that God had exempted him from fighting on account of his lameness, but he then turned to his sons and said: "Why should you not let him go out to fight? God may indeed grant him martyrdom." He fought at Uḥud and died a martyr.

In the heat of battle, Ḥudhayfah ibn al-Yamān saw some Muslim fighters going to attack his father, not knowing who he was, and thinking him to be one of the unbelievers. He called out to them that the man was his father but they did not understand what he was saying and they killed him. Ḥudhayfah asked for forgiveness for those Muslims. The Prophet offered to pay his ransom but Ḥudhayfah declined, saying that he would give it as a gift to the Muslims. In this way, the Prophet would think even more highly of Ḥudhayfah from then on.

Describing the fall of Ḥamzah, the Prophet's uncle, at Uḥud, Waḥshī, a slave belonging to Jubayr ibn Mutʿim, related that Jubayr offered him his freedom if he were to kill Ḥamzah. Being an Ethiopian, he was skilled in throwing the spear and, he said, he rarely missed. When the fighting started he went round looking for Ḥamzah until he saw him lashing out with his sword "like an angry camel", nothing barring his way. Waḥshī stalked him, hiding behind trees and rocks, so as to get as near to him as possible. Suddenly, he saw someone else aiming to strike Ḥamzah, but Ḥamzah raised his sword and struck a mighty blow, cutting his head off. Waḥshī said he raised his spear, took aim and hit Ḥamzah in the belly until it came out in between his legs. He staggered towards Waḥshī but collapsed before he could get to him. Waḥshī said that he left him to die before he went to retrieve his spear and return to camp where he sat down, "because he was the only one I wanted to kill, and I only killed him to be set free".

Hind, daughter of ʿUtbah and wife of Abū Sufyān, then went and opened Ḥamzah's abdomen, pulled out his liver and began to chew it. When she could not swallow it she spat it out.

When the fighting subsided and the Prophet saw Ḥamzah's body, he stood next to him and, deeply overcome with grief, said: "I shall suffer no greater loss than this one. I have never been so angry as I am at this moment." Then he asked whether Hind had eaten any of

Ḥamzah's liver and was told that she had not, and so he said: "God would not take any part of Ḥamzah's body to Hell."

The Prophet ordered that the martyrs of Uḥud be buried where they fell, rather than be taken back to the cemetery in Madinah. Some people had already removed their dead, but when they heard the announcement they took them back to Uḥud and buried them there. The Prophet supervised the burials, with two and three bodies interred in the same grave. He would enquire which of the dead had been more versed in the Qur'ān and he gave that person precedence. 'Abdullāh ibn 'Amr ibn Ḥarām and 'Amr ibn al-Jamūḥ were buried together as they were known to have been very close friends. The Prophet said: "Bury them together; they loved each other when they were alive."

Treatment of the Battle Events in the Qur'ān

These are some glimpses from the battlefield of a confrontation that oscillated between victory and defeat, separated only by a passing disobedience or a fleeting neglect of duty. Uḥud witnessed the highest of the high and the lowest of the low, and saw unique examples of bravery and courage as well as of hypocrisy and defeatism.

The overall picture reflects a lack of cohesion and inconsistency among the Muslims and a state of confusion and haziness in some of their minds. As was God's will, the situation led to a bitter outcome and heavy sacrifices for the Muslims. The most serious of these was the wounding of the Prophet himself, which must have been extremely painful and distressing for his companions. Thus they paid a heavy price, but they learnt a most profound lesson. God wanted to test their hearts and cleanse their ranks. He also wished to prepare their community for the greater mission of leading humankind and establishing His order on earth in its most perfect but realistic form.

Let us now see how the Qur'ān, in its unique style, tackled the situation. The Qur'ānic text does not relate the events of battle in sequence, but traces what goes on inside the hearts and minds of the participants. Events and incidents are used as material for clarification and guidance.

The aim is not to give a chronological account of what took place, but rather to identify and discern lessons, morals and values that lie beyond the events for the purpose of education and enlightenment. The Qur'ān perceives the emotions and apprehensions that outline the prevailing mood and it introduces the basic Divine laws and principles that relate to it. The events, therefore, become a basis or pivotal points for a wealth of feelings, features, conclusions and inferences around which the whole discourse revolves. The Qur'ān explores the intricacies of the human conscience and human life. This pattern is repeated again and again, eventually providing a full account of events. The narration, in fact, is no more than a vehicle, or a means, to focus the arguments and to understand clearly the effect of those events upon the human conscience. In this way, one finds no difficulty in appreciating what happened, nor experiences any confusion as to its causes or objectives.

It is also clear that the Qur'ānic discussion of the events of the day is much more comprehensive and effective than any simple account of what took place. The discussion has a formidable impact on our hearts and minds, and it is more satisfying to our human needs of learning and understanding and our sense of curiosity. It is also more valuable for the Muslim community, when it comes to facing similar situations, because it presents facts, principles and values that endure beyond the transient events themselves. It carries solid benefits that transcend considerations of time and space.

This eternal wealth of ideals and standards the Qur'ān offers to every heart that is open to faith, anywhere and at all times. Let us now look at the Qur'ānic text in more detail.

Preparation for Battle

> *Remember when you set out from your home at an early hour to assign the believers to their battle posts. God hears all and knows all. Two of your groups were about to lose heart, but God was their protector. In God shall the believers trust.* (Verses 121–2)

This is the opening scene, recalled in all its reality and vigour whilst still fresh and clear in the minds of those being so addressed. The *sūrah*, however, brings into focus other factors that were not visible at the time. First, God's presence and knowledge of all that was going on. The Qur'ān always impresses this fact upon the Muslims so as to reinforce in their hearts a clearer and deeper faith and understanding. It is the major and most fundamental facet of the Islamic system and no one can claim a full understanding of this religion without it being firmly established in both their conscience and their mind.

"Remember when you set out from your home at an early hour to assign the believers to their battle posts. God hears all and knows all. (Verse 121) This is a reference to the Prophet setting out from 'Ā'ishah's home, having donned his battle dress, consulted with his Companions and all of them having arrived at the consensus that the Muslims should go and meet the enemy outside Madinah. The Prophet went on to organise the Muslim troops, including the archers, assigning them duties and positions around the battlefield. But the *sūrah* also introduces a new fact: "God hears all and knows all." What a momentous event. God Almighty was witnessing the proceedings. How awesome! God was witnessing the consultation and was aware of what was going on inside the hearts and minds of all those present.

The other dimension, however, is that some Muslim hearts vacillated. This was a result of the treachery perpetrated by the leader of the hypocrites, 'Abdullāh ibn Ubayy ibn Salūl. Enraged by the Prophet's acceptance of the views of his Companions, in preference to his own view, 'Abdullāh ibn Ubayy broke away with one-third of the Muslim fighting force, refusing to join the expedition. Having said, as the *sūrah* puts it: *"If we know for sure that there will be fighting we will come with you,"* (Verse 167) 'Abdullāh ibn Ubayy had demonstrated that his heart did not fully accept Islam and that his self-importance was in control of him. Islam demands total dedication and does not tolerate sharing a man's heart with other beliefs.

Two of your groups were about to lose heart, but God was their protector. In God shall the believers trust." (Verse 122) According to authentic reports, the two groups were the tribes of Ḥārithah and Salamah, who were influenced by 'Abdullāh ibn Ubayy's stance. They wavered, struggled with doubt, but, as the *sūrah* affirms, God came to their rescue and gave them heart to stay and fight.

'Umar ibn al-Khaṭṭāb reported that he heard Jābir ibn 'Abdullāh say that this verse referred to his people, adding: "But I am not disconcerted about that because God says, 'God was their protector.'" (Related by Al-Bukhārī and Muslim.)

God reveals here some of people's inner thoughts and feelings, which only they and He know. It is He who steers them away from those negative feelings and gives them the courage to go ahead and fight. The Qur'ān recalls the scene, revives the emotions, and reassures the Muslims that God heard and knew all that had taken place, that He was with them all the way. It demonstrates to them that God is looking after them and helping them in their moments of weakness, so that they learn from where to seek help and support the next time they face a similar situation. It directs them to the only certain way: *"In God shall the believers trust."* In God alone, and in no one else, should the believers put their trust, for, they shall have no other resort.

Hence, in the very first two verses of this section, two major tenets of Islam are established: *"God hears all and knows all,"* and *"In God shall the believers trust."* They are presented at the correct moment and in the right context, blending perfectly together in rhythm and in nuance, at the very moment when hearts are receptive and ready to learn and understand. Here, then, we also have a good example of the way the Qur'ān deals with events while they are still live, fresh and relevant. Here, we can also see the difference between the Qur'ānic method of relating and interpreting events and other methods that do not aim to touch the human heart or direct, educate and guide human beings.

A Reminder of Past Victory

The *sūrah* takes up the discussion of the battle in which, though they were close to victory, the Muslims did not prevail. It begins with a reference to the hypocrite 'Abdullāh ibn Ubayy and his followers, who put their own selfish interests ahead of the interests of the faith. It alludes to the two Muslim groups who almost lost heart and withdrew, and cocludes with the archers' desertion of their positions, driven by greed in pursuit of booty. The exemplary conduct of some Muslims on the battlefield did not spare the Muslim camp the final and dismal outcome. This was the result of flaws in their ranks and confusion in their thinking.

Before the *sūrah* goes on to analyse and review the events of Uḥud, however, the Muslims are reminded of their victory at the Battle of Badr. This provides them with the opportunity to compare the two situations and to reflect on the root causes and results of both victory and defeat, as also on their own weaknesses and strengths. They have to realise that victory and defeat are the result of Divine providence, brought about for a specific, predetermined purpose. They have to believe that, after all, everything is in God's hands in all circumstances. The *sūrah* says in this respect:

God gave you victory at Badr when you were utterly weak. Therefore fear God, that you may have cause to be grateful. You said to the believers: "Is it not enough for you [to know] that your Lord should send down three thousand angels to support you? Indeed, He will, if you are patient in adversity and fear God, and if they [the non-believers] suddenly attack you, your Lord will supply you with five thousand angels swooping down." God made this only as a happy news for you, so that your hearts might take comfort from it. Victory comes only from God, the Mighty, the Wise. It is in order to destroy some of the non-believers, and so abase others that they lose and withdraw. You have no say in the matter. [It is for Him] to accept their repentance or punish them. They are wrongdoers. To Him belongs all that is in the heavens and the earth; He forgives whom He wills and punishes whom He wills. God is Forgiving and Merciful. (Verses 123–9)

The victory the Muslims scored at Badr had a hint of miracle about it. There were certainly no conventional reasons behind it, especially when one considers that the two sides were not equally balanced. There were around one thousand men on the side of the idolaters assembled to rescue Abū Sufyān and his caravan. They were well equipped and strongly motivated by the wish to save their wealth and defend their pride. The Muslims, on the other hand, numbered little over three hundred men who had left Madinah in pursuit of the caravan and with no intention or preparation for fighting. Furthermore, they were very poorly equipped. Back in Madinah, there were still many who had not converted to Islam, some powerful "hypocrites", and Jews awaiting the right moment to strike at the Muslims. The Muslims themselves represented a small island in a vast sea of hostility throughout Arabia. Most of them were new immigrants from Makkah, people who had hardly had time to settle down in their new environment.

The *sūrah* reminds the Muslims of all these facts and explains to them the real reason for their triumph at Badr. *"God gave you victory at Badr when you were utterly weak. Therefore fear God, that you may be grateful."* (Verse 123)

It was God Who brought them victory, and for a purpose shortly to be revealed. They had no other helper or patron, and it is He Whom they should fear and consider. He has the power and authority to grant them victory or leave them to be vanquished. Perhaps if they were to fear God they might learn to thank Him properly and appreciate the favour He bestows on them.

After this opening stroke, the *surah* goes on to recall some scenes from Badr itself. *"You said to the believers: 'Is it not enough for you [to know] that your Lord should send down three thousand angels to support you? Indeed, He will, if you are patient in adversity and fear God, and if they [the non-believers] suddenly attack you, your Lord will supply you with five thousand angels swooping down.'"* (Verses 124–5)

These were the comforting words the Prophet conveyed to the Muslims when they embarked on their expedition to intercept the caravan, not knowing they would be confronting a formidable fighting force. He conveyed to them the good news of God's support to reassure their hearts and give them strength. He also told them the condition on which that support would be given: that they should persevere and rise to the challenge of the enemy, and fear God and be mindful of Him at all times.

Indeed, He will, if you are patient in adversity and fear God, and if they [the non-believers] suddenly attack you, your Lord will supply you with five thousand angels swooping down. (Verse 125)

Then God imparts the fact that everything happens as a result of His will and wisdom. God is the power behind all events. The angels were dispatched to assist the Muslims and lend them moral as well as material support. Victory is determined by God Almighty and results from His will without intervention from anyone or any other cause or means. *"God made this only as a happy news for you, so that your hearts might take comfort from it. Victory comes only from God, the Mighty, the Wise."* (Verse 126)

The Qur'ān makes this point very strongly so as not to leave any doubt whatsoever in the minds of the Muslims. All things happen by God's absolute, unrestricted, effective and direct will. Causes and reasons cease to have any effect and become mere tools in the hands of God Who employs and operates them according to His will and command. The Qur'ān emphasises this concept in such a forceful way as to maintain that direct link between the believer and His Lord and to make the believer's heart always conscious of God's limitless, unhampered will.

With these repeated directives and exhortations, the Qur'ān emphasises this important fact in a wonderfully gentle, yet profound and enlightened manner.

The believers were made aware that God alone is the cause of everything. They realised that they were obliged to strive by all means to live up to their commitments. They understood the message and complied with the Divine instructions and thus achieved the most effective balance between the two. This was only achieved over a period of time and after numerous experiences and events, and with constant direction and education, as we see in this *sūrah*.

In this passage, the Qur'ān recalls the scenes at Badr as the Prophet promises the Muslims that God will support them with the angels if they would only fear Him, show patience and live up to the conditions of battle when they meet the idolaters. He then identifies the real power behind that action as God to Whose will everything is subjected and with Whose leave victory is achieved. He is the "Mighty" with the power to achieve victory, and He is the "Wise" Whose will decides that victory.

Then the *sūrah* explains the purpose behind that victory, pointing out that the way God deals with the unbelievers is of no concern to any human being: *"It is in order to destroy some of the non-believers, and so abase others that they lose and withdraw. You have no say in the matter. [It is for Him] to accept their repentance or punish them. They are wrongdoers."* (Verses 127–8)

Victory is granted by God for a particular purpose. Neither the Prophet nor the Muslim fighters had any say in that purpose or any personal interest in it. Furthermore, they had no part in achieving it, but were the instruments of the Divine will. They are neither the causes behind, nor the makers of victory; they have no claim to it nor can they exploit it. It is the will of God achieved through His servants, with His support for a particular purpose He has predetermined.

"It is in order to destroy some of the non-believers, or so abase others that they lose and withdraw. You have no say in the matter. [It is for Him] to accept their repentance or punish them. They are wrongdoers." God will punish the idolaters by granting the believers victory over them, or by making them fall captive in Muslim hands, or by letting them die without having the privilege of becoming believers. This would be the punishment for their disbelief, their hostility towards the Muslim community, their perpetration of corruption, and their opposition to Islam and its way of life.

That, in any case, is God's judgement, and no one can influence it, not even the Prophet Muḥammad himself. It is His sole, unshared prerogative, as the one God of all creation.

Thus the Muslims, as individuals, have no influence over this victory, its causes or results. They are, therefore, free of all the feelings of arrogance and self-delusion usually associated with military victories. They truly feel that they had no hand in their victory and that it was all up to God's Divine will and power.

The Qur'ān assigns the destiny of all people, believers or unbelievers, to God's will. The fate and future of Islam, and those who accept or reject it are determined by God. The Prophet and his followers can only fulfil their obligations and leave the outcome to God. They will receive their just reward, for their loyalty and the efforts they make in support of God's cause.

But there was another reason for stating the principle: *"You have no say in the matter."* The *sūrah* tells us that some people were wondering: *"'Have we any say in the matter?' ... 'Had we had any say in the matter, we should not have been slaughtered here.'"* (Verse 154) The object is to make it clear to the Muslims that they had nothing to do with bringing about victory or defeat. All they are required to do is obey, comply and act accordingly. The result is entirely up to God and no body else, not even the Prophet Muḥammad. It is of supreme importance that this concept is firmly and clearly established in Muslim hearts and minds.

This reminder of what happened at Badr, and the accompanying admonition, are complemented with a more universal and fundamental truth: the destiny of the whole cosmos is in the hands of God, He forgives and punishes people as He wills. *"To Him belongs all that is in the heavens and the earth; He forgives whom He wills and punishes whom He wills. God is Forgiving and Merciful."* (Verse 129)

His will and power are absolute and stem from His absolute possession and control of everything. By virtue of this universal ownership, God has the total and complete right to do as He pleases with people's lives and destinies. There is no injustice or partiality in the way He allots forgiveness and punishment. He decides with care and compassion, equitably and wisely because *"God is Forgiving and Merciful."*

The doors are wide open to God's servants to win His forgiveness and mercy. They should place their trust and confidence in Him, put their destiny in His hands, fulfil their commitments and obligations, and leave everything else to His judgement and His absolute will and power that lie behind every cause and every result.

A Comprehensive Outlook

Before the *sūrah* moves on to refer specifically to the Battle of Uḥud, we have a short passage of seven verses which speak about usury and its transactions, obeying God and His Messenger, spending money in God's cause at times of prosperity and adversity, the Islamic co-operative system as opposed to the evil usurious system, controlling one's anger, forgiving other people's mistakes, praying to God for forgiveness and turning to Him in repentance when a mistake is committed.

These directives are given immediately before the discussion of the military confrontation by way of implicit reference to a basic characteristic of the Islamic faith. Islam is a single and comprehensive system which caters for every aspect of human life and makes every human activity revolve around one essential value, namely, submission to God as represented by worshipping Him alone and dedicating everything in human life to Him. In every sphere of human life, we must first make sure of what God bids us and willingly do His bidding. The fact that these instructions are so grouped together in the *sūrah* is a clear reference to the fact that all aspects of human activity are mutually interdependent, and their interdependence has a considerable effect on the total sum of human activity.

The Islamic system deals with man as a whole entity. It organises the whole life of the Muslim community in a totally comprehensive way which it considers preferable to anything piecemeal. It is in this light that we should view this combination of preparation for a military engagement on the one hand, and the purification of souls and hearts, controlling desires and spreading love and friendliness within the community, on the other. All these aspects have mutual effects on one another. When we discuss them in detail, taking each directive individually we are bound to recognise their essential role in the life of the Muslim community and their bearing on the power and the potentials of that community on the battlefield as in all spheres of life.

Usury: The Way to Inevitable Ruin

Believers, do not gorge yourselves on usury, doubling [your money] again and again. Have fear of God, so that you may prosper. Guard yourselves against the Fire which has been prepared for the unbelievers; and obey God and the messenger, that you may be graced with mercy. (Verses 130–2)

We have discussed the subject of usury in detail in our commentary on verses 275–81 of *sūrah* 2, entitled *al-Baqarah*, or The Cow. Here we will only briefly comment on the subject of multiplication of the principal sum of a loan. Some people in our modern times want to manipulate this verse in order to make lawful what God has forbidden. They say that the prohibition is limited only to excessive usury which leads to the multiplication of the principal amount of money time after time. They further claim that rates of interest of 4, 5, 7 or 9 per cent and similar rates do not lead to any such multiplication. Hence, they argue, they are not included in the prohibition of usury.

Let us begin by stating clearly that the reference to multiples is simply a description of something that was happening in life. It is not a condition for the prohibition to operate. The Qur'ānic statement in *sūrah* 2, The Cow, makes a clear prohibition of all usury. It addresses the believers and bids them *"give up what remains outstanding of usury."* (2: 278) It applies to all that exceeds the principal amount, without qualification.

Now that we have established this principle, we have a word to say about its description. It is in fact not a description of the usurious transactions which took place in the Arabian peninsula at a particular point in history. It is a description of the horrid system of usury *per se*, regardless of the rate of interest. When a financial system is based on usury it makes the financial cycle revolve around it. We have to remember that usurious transactions are neither single, isolated transactions nor simple ones. They are both repetitive and compounded. When we add the element of time to these two aspects we find that they inevitably lead to the multiplication of the principal amount time after time.

By its very nature, the usury system leads to such multiplication. The description here is not, therefore, limited to transactions known in Arabia at the time of the revelation of this verse. It is characteristic of this system at all times.

This system inevitably leads to the corruption of the moral and psychological life of society inasmuch as it corrupts its financial and political life. It has, therefore, a definite and clear influence on the community and all its members.

As Islam began to mould the Muslim community, it was keen to ensure a pure psychological and moral life for it, as well as a sound and healthy financial and political basis. The effect of these elements on the battles fought by the Muslim community is well known. Hence, the inclusion of the prohibition of usury within the Qur'ānic commentary on the Battle of Uḥud is readily understood in the context of this complete system. This prohibition is also coupled with an order to fear God in the hope of achieving prosperity, and to guard against hell, the fire prepared for the unbelievers. This is again a most fitting comment. No one who fears God and fears the fire prepared for the unbelievers will gorge himself on usury. No one who believes in God and removes himself from the ranks of unbelievers will ever think of making profit through usury. To believe in God is not simply a word we utter; it is a conscientious following of a system which God has devised in order to be a practical translation of our faith. Believing in God is simply the introduction for this implementation and for shaping the life of the community according to Islamic directives and commands.

It is impossible in any case for faith and usury to exist side by side. Wherever usury is adopted as a system the faith of Islam, as a whole, does not exist. There can only be the fire which has been prepared for the unbelievers. Any argument against this is simply futile. The fact that these verses combine the express prohibition of usury with calling on the believers to fear God and guard against the Fire is not a mere coincidence. It is made in order to establish this fact clearly in the minds of Muslims. It is also made in the hope of achieving prosperity through abandoning usury and maintaining fear of God. For prosperity is the natural outcome of fearing God and implementing the Divine method in human life. We have already discussed the catastrophic effects of usury on human society. We have only to remind ourselves of these catastrophic effects in order to recognise the meaning of prosperity in this context, and the fact that it is made conditional on abandoning this hateful system.

The final comment here is given in these words: "...*Obey God and the messenger, that you may be graced with mercy.*" This is a general command to obey God and His Messenger which makes mercy conditional on this obedience. As it is given, however, in the form of a comment on the prohibition of usury, it acquires a special significance: God and His Messenger cannot be obeyed in any society which adopts a system of usury. No one who accepts usury in any shape or form is obedient to God and His Messenger. This comment, then, serves as further emphasis to the prohibition.

Moreover, this order is particularly relevant to the events of the battle in which the commands of the Prophet were disobeyed. It re-emphasises this obedience as the means to achieve prosperity and benefit by God's mercy.

A Reward Worth Competing For

Hasten, all of you, to the achievement of your Lord's forgiveness, and a paradise as vast as the heavens and the earth, prepared for the God-fearing, who spend [in His way] in time of plenty and in time of hardship, and restrain their anger, and forgive their fellow men. God loves the benevolent. (Verses 133–4)

The prohibition of usury is stated more comprehensively and in greater detail in the preceding *sūrah al-Baqarah,* or The Cow. In our discussion of those verses in Volume I, we noted that when the *sūrah* states the prohibition of usury, it also speaks highly of voluntary charity since the two represent opposite approaches to social relations within the economic system.

They are the most prominent characteristics of two diametrically opposed systems: the one based on usury the other on the cooperative system. Here again we find that the prohibition of usury is followed by an emphasis on the virtue of voluntary spending at times of prosperity and hardship alike.

These verses make a definitive prohibition of all usury, warn the believers against the Fire which is prepared for the unbelievers and call on them to always fear God in the hope of being granted His mercy and of achieving prosperity. This is immediately followed with an order to hasten to the achievement of God's forgiveness and admission into paradise, which is described as being as vast as the heavens and the earth. We are told that this paradise has been *"prepared for the God-fearing."*

The first quality given here of this class of people is that they *"spend [in His way] in time of plenty and in time of hardship."* They are, then, a class of people which is totally different from those who gorge themselves on usury and multiply their money by no effort of their own. Their other qualities are also defined: *"Hasten, all of you, to the achievement of your Lord's forgiveness, and a paradise as vast as the heavens and the earth, prepared for the God-fearing, who spend [in His way] in time of plenty and in time of hardship, and restrain their anger, and forgive their fellow men. God loves the benevolent. Those who, when they commit a gross indecency or wrong themselves, remember God and pray for the forgiveness of their sins – for who but God can forgive sins?"* (Verses 133–5)

The style adopted here describes the fulfilment of these duties in a physical movement representing a race towards a certain goal and for a set prize. The prize is forgiveness by God and admission to heaven. It is there to be won, and the believers are invited to make their race and vie with one another in order to win. The prize is set for those who fear God. These have certain qualities which are outlined in the next two verses: they spend their money at all times for the sole reason of earning God's pleasure. They are, then, consistent in their attitude. They follow the way which pleases God, unchanged either by prosperity or adversity. When money comes to them in plenty, they are not preoccupied with luxurious living. When they suffer hardship and adversity, their sorrow does not become their major preoccupation. They are conscious of their duty at all times and in all situations. They are free from miserliness and greed. They watch God and fear Him. Man loves money and he is always reluctant to part with his money. Nothing makes him spend his money voluntarily in all situations except a motive far stronger than that of possession and self-interest. That motive is the fear of God. It is a pleasant, profound feeling which works on man's soul so that it becomes free, unfettered by greed and personal desire.

The emphasis laid on this characteristic has particular relevance to the Battle of Uḥud. Reference to spending in the *sūrah* is made several times and in the same way as the repeated condemnation of those who refuse to come forward with their money for the cause of God.

They *"restrain their anger, and forgive their fellow men."* Fearing God also works in this respect, providing similar motives and leaving similar effects. Anger is a human reaction which is normally combined with or followed by a fit of temper. It is both natural and essential to man. However, it can only be overcome through that higher perception made possible by the positive effects of fearing God and the spiritual strength which man achieves through looking up to horizons which are far superior and more sublime than man's own needs and interests.

Restraining anger is only the first stage; it is not sufficient on its own. A person may restrain his anger but harbour a grudge. His outward fury becomes a deeply-seated, inward rancour. Needless to say, anger and fury are preferable to harbouring grudges and rancour. The Qur'ānic verse emphasises that the God-fearing do not allow their anger to become a grudge. They forgive others and do not harbour any ill feelings. When anger is deliberately restrained it becomes a burden, a fire which burns internally sending its smoke over man's conscience in order to blur his vision. Forgiveness, however, ensures a release from that burden. It gives peace of heart and conscience, as well as an easy movement in a more sublime world.

"God loves the benevolent." Those who spend their money at times of prosperity and hardship are benevolent. Similarly, those who do not hesitate to forgive others after having been angered by them are also benevolent. The Qur'ānic verse tells us that God loves all who are benevolent. Use of the term "love" here is significant. Its pleasant, friendly, bright and compassionate shades are in perfect harmony with the pleasant and honourable atmosphere of help and forgiveness.

Because God loves the benevolent and the good turns they do, those who love God also love to be benevolent. They have the best of all motives. The final comment is, then, not only an inspiring description, it is a statement of fact.

The community which enjoys God's love and, in turn, loves God and in which forgiveness replaces anger and rancour is a strong, brotherly and closely-knit community. We see here how this directive is clearly relevant to both the military battle and to the battle of life.

Man: Saint or Sinner

Those who, when they commit a gross indecency or wrong themselves, remember God and pray for the forgiveness of their sins – for who but God can forgive sins? – and do not knowingly persist in doing the wrong they may have done. These shall have the reward of forgiveness by their Lord, and gardens underneath which rivers flow, where they shall abide. Excellent is the reward for those who labour [well]. (Verses 135–6)

Another quality of the God-fearing is highlighted here. They are those who seek forgiveness whenever they slip into sin and make sure of not knowingly disobeying God's orders. How compassionate this religion is. Before He calls on people to be compassionate to one another, God, limitless is He in His glory, shows them one aspect of His own compassion of which they themselves are the recipients, so that they may learn.

In Islamic terminology, the God-fearing are among the élite of believers. God's compassion and mercy, however, include among them those who remember God after committing a gross indecency or who wrong themselves and pray to Him for forgiveness of their sins. The term "gross indecency" includes the most ghastly of all sins. This religion of ours, however, is so tolerant that it neither considers those who sink to its depth as outcasts, nor deprives them of God's mercy. They are not even given the bottom rank among the believers. Rather, they are elevated to the rank of the élite, the God-fearing, on one condition only. That condition is that they should remember God and pray to Him to forgive their sins, that they should not persist with their wrongdoing, knowing that it is sinful, and that they should not unashamedly boast about the sins they have committed. In other words, they should remain within the framework of servitude to God and ultimate submission to Him. By doing so, they remain entitled to His forgiveness, mercy and bounty.

Islam recognises man's weakness. Man may always succumb to his physical desires which may bring him down to the depths of gross indecency. His lust, ambitions or temptations may cause him to lose control and drive him to disobedience of God. Recognising this weakness in man, Islam does not adopt harsh punishments, rejecting a sinner altogether and depriving him of God's mercy when he wrongs himself by committing a gross indecency. In the Islamic view there is something important to add to his credit which is the fact that the light of faith has not been put out altogether in his soul. His heart is not totally hardened, his relationship with God is still alive and he knows that he is merely a servant who slips and makes mistakes, and that he has a Lord who forgives. This weak, sinful creature, then, remains essentially good. He clings to his bond with God and he does not sever it. He may, then, slip as many times as his weakness imposes on him. Eventually, he will get there, as long as he holds to his bond with God and keeps the light of faith within him. He must always remember God, pray to Him for forgiveness and acknowledge his submission to Him and refrain from boasting about his sins.

Never does Islam slam the door in the face of a weak sinner leaving him lost in the wilderness. Never does it let him feel permanently rejected, afraid to turn back. On the contrary, it holds for him the prospect of forgiveness. It shows him the way and holds his trembling hand, steadying him and giving him the light he needs to return to his secure refuge. It only requires one thing of him, namely, that his heart and soul are not so hardened so as to make him forget God. As long as he remembers God and keeps alive in his conscience the voice of guidance and maintains in his heart the yearning for God's grace, then light will shine again in his soul and the seed of faith will burst forth with a new plant.

When your misbehaving son who has run away knows that nothing awaits him at home except flogging, he will never return. But if he knows that there is also a tender hand which will pat his shoulder when he apologises for his misdeeds and which excuses him when he asks for pardon, he will certainly come back.

Islam knows that side by side with man's weaknesses and carnal desires there exist strength and sublime aspirations. For this reason, Islam is sympathetic to man in his moment of weakness, places him back on his way to a higher horizon, as long as he remembers God and does not knowingly persist with his wrongdoing. The Prophet says: "He who prays for forgiveness does not persist with his sin, even if he commits it 70 times a day." (Related by Abū Dāwūd and Al-Tirmidhī.) In doing so, Islam does not advocate complacency, nor does it praise the one who frequently slips or who describes sinful actions as beautiful, as those who call themselves "realists" do. It simply overlooks such errors in order to awaken both hope and a sense of shame within man. Forgiveness by God, the only One to forgive sins, does not lead to complacency; it fills the sinner with shame. Only those who persist and pay no heed remain outcasts. Thus, Islam combines its call to man to aspire to a higher horizon with its mercy and compassion, knowing man's weakness and capability. It ensures that the door of hope is always open in front of man as it motivates him to exert his utmost in his aspiration towards the sublime.

What is the reward of those God-fearing people? *"These shall have the reward of forgiveness by their Lord, and gardens underneath which rivers flow, where they shall abide. Excellent is the reward for those who labour [well]."* (Verse 136)

When people pray for forgiveness of their sins, and spend their money in times of prosperity and hardship, and when they control their anger and forgive others, they do not take a negative attitude. Indeed, they are good workers.

"Excellent is the reward for those who labour [well]." That reward is forgiveness and Paradise. The work of those people has two aspects: an internal one in their own souls and an external one in practical life. Both are fruitful.

All these characteristics of the God-fearing are relevant to the battle which the *sūrah* discusses. In the same way as the Islamic financial system based on cooperation has its effects on the life of the Muslim community and its bearing on the military battle, so these personal and communal qualities have their bearing on that to which we referred earlier. When individuals triumph over their love of money, their anger and their sin and return to God in repentance praying for His forgiveness and pleasure they only do what is necessary to triumph over their enemies on the battlefield. Their enemies only have that status because they represent niggardliness, caprice, sin and boastfulness. They do not submit themselves or their desires or their lifestyle to God and the Divine Law. It is because of this that enmity rises, battles flare up and strenuous efforts, i.e. *jihād*, are made. There is no other reason for a Muslim to stand in opposition to anyone or to fight him. He only fights for God's sake.

The link is, then, very close between these directives and the commentary on the military battle as well as certain aspects of that battle, such as the disobedience of some Muslims of an express order given by the Prophet, and which stemmed from their keenness to share in the spoils of war. Other pertinent elements include the blind attempt at self-assertion which led to the desertion by 'Abdullāh ibn Ubayy and others. Similarly the weakness of some made them forget that they must leave matters to God and caused them to ask: *"Have we any say in the matter?"*, while others said: *"Had we had any say in the matter, we should not have been slaughtered here."* (Verse 154)

7

A High Price for Heaven

Many patterns have passed away before you. Go about the earth and see what was the fate of those who described the truth as lies. (137)

قَدْ خَلَتْ مِن قَبْلِكُمْ سُنَنٌ فَسِيرُوا۟ فِى ٱلْأَرْضِ فَٱنظُرُوا۟ كَيْفَ كَانَ عَٰقِبَةُ ٱلْمُكَذِّبِينَ ﴿١٣٧﴾

This is a plain exposition for mankind, as well as a guidance and an admonition for the God-fearing. (138)

هَٰذَا بَيَانٌ لِّلنَّاسِ وَهُدًى وَمَوْعِظَةٌ لِّلْمُتَّقِينَ ﴿١٣٨﴾

Do not be faint of heart, and do not grieve; for you shall gain the upper hand if you are truly believers. (139)

وَلَا تَهِنُوا۟ وَلَا تَحْزَنُوا۟ وَأَنتُمُ ٱلْأَعْلَوْنَ إِن كُنتُم مُّؤْمِنِينَ ﴿١٣٩﴾

If misfortune befalls you, a similar misfortune has befallen other people as well. Such days [of fortune and misfortune], We deal out in turn among men. God wants to mark out those who truly believe and choose from among you such as [with their lives] bear witness to the truth. God does not love the wrongdoers. (140)

إِن يَمْسَسْكُمْ قَرْحٌ فَقَدْ مَسَّ ٱلْقَوْمَ قَرْحٌ مِّثْلُهُۥ وَتِلْكَ ٱلْأَيَّامُ نُدَاوِلُهَا بَيْنَ ٱلنَّاسِ وَلِيَعْلَمَ ٱللَّهُ ٱلَّذِينَ ءَامَنُوا۟ وَيَتَّخِذَ مِنكُمْ شُهَدَآءَ وَٱللَّهُ لَا يُحِبُّ ٱلظَّٰلِمِينَ ﴿١٤٠﴾

And God wants to test and prove the believers, and to blot out the unbelievers. (141)

وَلِيُمَحِّصَ ٱللَّهُ ٱلَّذِينَ ءَامَنُوا۟ وَيَمۡحَقَ ٱلۡكَٰفِرِينَ ۝

Do you reckon that you can enter paradise unless God has identified those among you who strive hard [in His cause], and who are patient in adversity. (142)

أَمۡ حَسِبۡتُمۡ أَن تَدۡخُلُوا۟ ٱلۡجَنَّةَ وَلَمَّا يَعۡلَمِ ٱللَّهُ ٱلَّذِينَ جَٰهَدُوا۟ مِنكُمۡ وَيَعۡلَمَ ٱلصَّٰبِرِينَ ۝

Surely, you used to wish for death before you came face to face with it. Now you have seen it with your own eyes. (143)

وَلَقَدۡ كُنتُمۡ تَمَنَّوۡنَ ٱلۡمَوۡتَ مِن قَبۡلِ أَن تَلۡقَوۡهُ فَقَدۡ رَأَيۡتُمُوهُ وَأَنتُمۡ تَنظُرُونَ ۝

Muḥammad is only a messenger: all messengers have passed away before him. If, then, he dies or is slain, will you turn about on your heels? He that turns about on his heels will not harm God in any way. God will reward those who are grateful [to Him]. (144)

وَمَا مُحَمَّدٌ إِلَّا رَسُولٌ قَدۡ خَلَتۡ مِن قَبۡلِهِ ٱلرُّسُلُ أَفَإِيْن مَّاتَ أَوۡ قُتِلَ ٱنقَلَبۡتُمۡ عَلَىٰٓ أَعۡقَٰبِكُمۡ وَمَن يَنقَلِبۡ عَلَىٰ عَقِبَيۡهِ فَلَن يَضُرَّ ٱللَّهَ شَيۡـًٔا وَسَيَجۡزِى ٱللَّهُ ٱلشَّٰكِرِينَ ۝

No one can die except by God's leave, at a term appointed. He who desires the reward of this world, We shall give him thereof; and to him who desires the reward of the life to come, We shall give thereof. We shall reward those who are grateful to Us. (145)

وَمَا كَانَ لِنَفۡسٍ أَن تَمُوتَ إِلَّا بِإِذۡنِ ٱللَّهِ كِتَٰبًا مُّؤَجَّلًا وَمَن يُرِدۡ ثَوَابَ ٱلدُّنۡيَا نُؤۡتِهِۦ مِنۡهَا وَمَن يُرِدۡ ثَوَابَ ٱلۡءَاخِرَةِ نُؤۡتِهِۦ مِنۡهَا وَسَنَجۡزِى ٱلشَّٰكِرِينَ ۝

Many a Prophet has fought with many devout men alongside him. They never lost heart on account of what they had to suffer in God's cause, and neither did they weaken nor succumb. God loves those who are patient in adversity. (146)

وَكَأَيِّن مِّن نَّبِيٍّ قَاتَلَ مَعَهُۥ رِبِّيُّونَ كَثِيرٌ فَمَا وَهَنُواْ لِمَآ أَصَابَهُمۡ فِي سَبِيلِ ٱللَّهِ وَمَا ضَعُفُواْ وَمَا ٱسۡتَكَانُواْ وَٱللَّهُ يُحِبُّ ٱلصَّـٰبِرِينَ ﴿١٤٦﴾

All that they said was this: "Our Lord! Forgive us our sins and our excesses in our affairs. Make firm our steps, and give us victory over the unbelievers." (147)

وَمَا كَانَ قَوۡلَهُمۡ إِلَّآ أَن قَالُواْ رَبَّنَا ٱغۡفِرۡ لَنَا ذُنُوبَنَا وَإِسۡرَافَنَا فِي أَمۡرِنَا وَثَبِّتۡ أَقۡدَامَنَا وَٱنصُرۡنَا عَلَى ٱلۡقَوۡمِ ٱلۡكَـٰفِرِينَ ﴿١٤٧﴾

God has granted them the reward of this life and the best reward of the life to come. God loves those who do their duty well. (148)

فَـَٔاتَىٰهُمُ ٱللَّهُ ثَوَابَ ٱلدُّنۡيَا وَحُسۡنَ ثَوَابِ ٱلۡأَخِرَةِ وَٱللَّهُ يُحِبُّ ٱلۡمُحۡسِنِينَ ﴿١٤٨﴾

Overview

This passage comments on the early events of the Battle of Uḥud up to the point at which the victory which was well within the grasp of the Muslim army turned into defeat. As the Qur'ān comments on these events, it seeks to establish certain rules and principles. The events themselves are only a means employed by the Qur'ān to drive the truth home to the Muslims. These comments begin with a reference to an ever-recurring pattern which engulfs those who reject God's message and describe it as a lie. The Muslims are told here that the Quraysh victory in this particular battle is a one-off incident delivering a particular lesson. They are called upon to demonstrate their steadfastness and to feel their superiority through faith. If they have suffered, the idolaters have also suffered in the same battle. What

221

happened to the Muslims is useful in certain ways as it helps distinguish those who are firm in their faith and select from among them martyrs who are ready to sacrifice their lives for their faith. Moreover, the Muslims are brought face to face with death, after they had wished for it. Their promises and wishes are thus put to the test. All this helps the Muslim community acquire the necessary equipment to face its enemies and to bring about the desired result of wiping out unbelievers. In both defeat and victory, the overall goal is served.

In the Battle of Uḥud, the Muslims suffered a misfortune: they were defeated and many of them were killed. Physically and mentally, they endured affliction. Seventy of the Prophet's Companions were killed. The Prophet himself was wounded as were those who defended him. All this shook the believers; they had not expected such a blow after their spectacular victory at Badr. They wondered: "How could this happen to us? How can this turn of events come about when we are Muslims?"

The Qur'ān reminds them here that there are patterns which will eventually come to pass. Muslims are not a special type of men. The laws of nature which apply to human life will continue to operate. Nothing comes about out of the blue. If they examine the laws of nature and understand what rules affect them, they will be able to learn the lessons of all events. They will realise that God's law never fails. Nothing happens in vain. They will also be able to carve out their future way in the light of what has happened in the past. They will not stand idle, relying on the fact that they are Muslims, and expect to have victory without doing what is necessary to achieve it. Foremost among these is obedience to God and to His Messenger.

Unfailing Life Patterns

Many patterns have passed away before you. Go about the earth and see what was the fate of those who described the truth as lies. This is a plain exposition for mankind, as well as a guidance and an admonition for the God-fearing. (Verses 137–8)

The patterns to which the *sūrah* refers here, and to which it draws the attention of the believers, concern the fate of those who, throughout history, denied God's message and described it as a lie, and the fact that days of fortune and misfortune alternate between people and communities. The patterns identified also test people in order to know whether they are truly believers, and patient in adversity. Another pattern of importance is the fact that victory is always granted to those who are steadfast, while the unbelievers are blotted out. As these corresponding parts are outlined, much encouragement is given to the believers to persevere and remain steadfast. They are consoled for their misfortune, which has not befallen them alone. A similar one has befallen their enemies. They should remember that they have a superior faith and aim to those of their enemies and that they enjoy Divine guidance and have a perfect constitution.

Moreover, ultimate victory will be theirs, while their opponents will be vanquished: *"Many patterns have passed away before you. Go about the earth and see what was the fate of those who described the truth as lies."* (Verse 137) The Qur'ān relates the present to the past in order to point to the future. The Arabs who were the first to be addressed by the Qur'ān had nothing in their lives, neither experience nor knowledge, prior to Islam, to enable them to have such a wide view of life and its events. Islam indeed gave them a new life and made out of them a nation to lead mankind.

The tribal system in their community could never have enabled them to appreciate the relationship between the life of the people of Arabia, or indeed human life in general, and the laws of nature which govern everything in life. The new concept, Islam, represented a great departure which could not have developed out of their tribal society or their life conditions. It was given to them by their new faith. They were elevated to this standard within a quarter of a century, while their contemporaries could not manage to reach this level for many centuries to come. They could not for many generations recognise that the laws of nature never fail. When they did, however, they overlooked the fact that God's will is free and absolute, and that to Him all matters are referred. This nation of Islam was able to recognise all this and to understand it. That enabled it to appreciate the balance between God's free will and the constant laws of nature. Thus, they conducted their lives on the basis of working within the laws of nature, reassured that God can accomplish what He wills at any time He chooses.

"Many patterns have passed away before you." These have taken place according to rules and systems which are established by God's

free will to govern life. What happened at other times will also happen in your own time, according to God's will. What was applicable to other people is applicable to you as well. *"Go about the earth"*, because the earth is a single unity and a stage on which human life is played out. Life is an open book for people of intellect to contemplate. *"Go about the earth and see what was the fate of those who described the truth as lies."* Their fate is evidenced by what they have left behind and by what we know of their history. The Qur'ān mentions some of these in different places. In some cases, it identifies people, places and times. In other instances, it makes general references which establish a general rule: what happened to those who rejected the truth and described it as a lie in past generations will happen to those who reject the truth today and tomorrow. This reassures the Muslim community in respect to what will ultimately happen, and, on the other hand, it serves as a warning against being too complacent with such people. There were important reasons for providing such reassurance and warning, as we will see in this long passage.

Having established the fact that these rules will continue to operate, the *sūrah* emphasises the need to follow Divine guidance and to learn the lessons of the past: *"This is a plain exposition for mankind, as well as a guidance and an admonition for the God-fearing."* (Verse 138) The Qur'ān makes an exposition of the truth to all mankind. It elevates people to a height which they could never attain without its guidance. But the God-fearing are the only ones who appreciate its guidance and admonition. A word of truth is not appreciated except by a believing heart which is particularly receptive to guidance. A word of plain admonition can only benefit a heart which fears God. The ability to distinguish between truth and falsehood, or between following guidance and going astray is rarely lacking among people. By nature, the truth is self-evident. What people lack is the desire to follow the truth and the ability to prefer its implementation, because these are initiated only by faith and cannot be preserved except with the fear of God. This explains the need for the repeated emphasis in the Qur'ān on the fact that the truth it tells and the guidance, light and admonition it provides are meant only for the believers and the God-fearing. It is these qualities which enable man to make use of this guidance and benefit by its light, regardless of the difficulties one may face. This is indeed the heart of the matter. There are many people who know the truth but who, nevertheless, remain immersed in falsehood either because they yield to temptation and desire or because they fear to share in the hardship which the followers of the truth may have to endure.

A Cycle of Fortune and Misfortune

Do not be faint of heart, and do not grieve; for you shall gain the upper hand if you are truly believers. If misfortune befalls you, a similar misfortune has befallen other people as well. Such days [of fortune and misfortune], We deal out in turn among men. God wants to mark out those who truly believe and choose from among you such as [with their lives] bear witness to the truth. God does not love the wrongdoers. (Verses 139–40)

Believers must not lose heart, nor should they allow grief to overtake them because of what may happen. They will gain the upper hand, because they have a superior faith. Believers prostrate themselves only to God, while others prostrate before one, or more, of His creatures. This *sūrah* makes it plain to the believers that they are indeed superior and far more exalted than other people. It tells them: You have a superior way of life, because you follow a method established by God while the methods followed by other groups have been devised by His creatures. Moreover, your role is superior, because you have been selected for a position of trust, to convey God's guidance to all mankind. Other people are unaware of this guidance, and have gone astray. Your place on earth is superior, because God has promised you to inherit the earth, while they will sink into oblivion. If you are truly believers, then you are superior. Therefore, you have to demonstrate the strength of your faith by not losing heart and you must not grieve. The rules determined by God make it possible that you may score a victory or suffer a defeat, but the ultimate end after enduring the test and striving hard for God's cause, will be in your favour.

"If misfortune befalls you, a similar misfortune has befallen other people as well." The misfortune which is said to have befallen the Muslims and the fact that a similar one befell those who rejected the truth may be a reference to the Battle of Badr, in which the idolaters suffered a heavy defeat. On the other hand, it may be a

reference to the Battle of Uḥud, in which the Muslims were initially close to victory, but were then defeated. What the Muslims suffered was fair reward for their disagreement and disobedience. Moreover, it represents an aspect of how the rules of nature established by God never fail. The disagreement among the rearguard of the Muslim army was the result of their greed. In any campaign of *jihād*, God grants victory to those who strive for His cause, looking for nothing of the petty gains of this world. Another rule of nature which is seen in full operation is the dealing out of fortune and misfortune among people according to their actions and intentions. In this way, true believers are distinguished from hypocrites. Mistakes are identified and the way ahead becomes very clear.

"If misfortune befalls you, a similar misfortune has befallen other people as well. Such days [of fortune and misfortune] We deal out in turn among men. God wants to mark out those who truly believe." (Verse 140) When hardship is followed by prosperity and the latter is followed by another hardship, people's true characters emerge. They reveal how clear their vision is, how much they panic and how patient in adversity they can be, as well as how great their trust in God is and how submissive to His will they are. Thus true believers are distinguished from those who are hypocrites. Their true hearts are apparent to all. The Muslim camp is strengthened by the fact that those who do not truly belong to it are identified and excluded.

God knows all secrets and He is aware of those who are true believers and those who are not. But the alternation of days of fortune and misfortune does not merely reveal secrets; it also translates faith into action and compels hypocrisy to express itself in practical measures. Hence, it is action that merits reward. God does not hold people to account for what He knows of their position, but He counts their actions for or against them. The cycle of hardship and prosperity is an accurate criterion. Prosperity is as good a test as hardship. Some people may withstand hardship but become complacent when they are tested with ease and prosperity. A true believer is one who remains steadfast in adversity and is not lured away by prosperity. He knows that whatever befalls him of good or evil happens only with God's permission.

In the process of moulding the first Muslim community and preparing it for the role of leadership of mankind, God has tested it with hardship after prosperity, and with a bitter defeat after a spectacular victory. Both have happened according to the laws of nature which never fail. That is because God wants the Muslim community to learn what brings it victory and what causes it defeat. Thus, it becomes more obedient to God and reliant on Him. It becomes better aware of the true nature of its Islamic constitution and way of life and what their implementation requires of it.

A Careful Selection of Martyrs

God wants to mark out those who truly believe and choose from among you such as [with their lives] bear witness to the truth. God does not love the wrongdoers. And God wants to test and prove the believers, and to blot out the unbelievers. (Verses 140–1)

The *sūrah* goes on to reveal to the Muslim community certain aspects of Divine wisdom behind which the events of the Battle of Uḥud took place, and why defeat was suffered by the Muslims after their spectacular victory at Badr. The principle of testing the believers and proving their mettle is strongly emphasised. At the same time God states that He wants to choose from among the believers people who *"with their lives bear witness to the truth."* The Arabic original states that God wants to choose from among the believers "martyrs". It should be remembered that in Arabic the word *"shahīd"* which denotes "martyr" also means "witness".[1]

The way this point is expressed in the Qurʾān is particularly remarkable: *"God wants ... to choose from among you such as [with their lives] bear witness to the truth."* God, then, takes martyrs from among those who strive for His cause. Therefore, it is neither a tragedy nor a loss that anyone is chosen to be a martyr. Indeed, it is a matter of honour because the choice is made by God and those martyrs are given, by God, a special position near Him. Moreover, they are selected to bear witness to the truth of God's message to mankind. They give their testimony in a way which cannot be contested by anyone. That testimony is to struggle to establish the truth of the Divine Message in life until they die. They testify that

---

1. For rendering the meaning of the Qurʾānic text in English, I have borrowed Muḥammad Asad's translation, which combines both meanings.

what they have received from God is the truth in which they have believed and to which they have dedicated themselves, and that human life will not be set right unless this truth is implemented. They are so certain of this that they spare no effort in fighting falsehood and establishing the truth, moulding society on the basis of its tenets. Their testimony is their struggle until death. The truthfulness of that testimony is irrefutable.

Every Muslim declares that he "bears witness that there is no deity save God and that Muḥammad is His messenger." However, he is not considered a witness unless he gives credence to his declaration that there is only one God in the universe. This means that he accepts no legislation other than that which comes from God. The most essential characteristic of Godhead is to legislate and the most essential characteristic of worship is to accept and implement God's legislation. This declaration also means that a believer does not receive God's legislation except through Muḥammad (pbuh), since he is God's Messenger. Every person who makes this declaration is required to strive hard in order to make sure that God alone is acknowledged as the only God by all mankind. The practical effect of this is to make the constitution God devised for human life, and which was conveyed to us by Muḥammad (pbuh), the established constitution throughout the world. If the attainment of that goal means that a Muslim should die, he is then a martyr, or a witness, chosen by God to make this testimony and to win this noble position.

This is the proper understanding of the remarkable Qur'ānic statement: *"God wants to ... choose from among you such as [with their lives] bear witness to the truth."* It is also the meaning of the declaration that there is no deity save God and that Muḥammad is God's Messenger. It is vastly different from the narrow meaning associated with it in the minds of many people today.

"God does not love the wrongdoers." Wrongdoing or injustice, as often mentioned in the Qur'ān, is synonymous with disbelief and polytheism, since the association of partners with God is the worst form of wrongdoing. In the Qur'ān we read: *"To ascribe partners with God is indeed to do a great wrong."* (Luqmān, 31: 13) Al-Bukhārī and Muslim relate a *ḥadīth* on the authority of 'Abdullāh ibn Mas'ūd in which he states that he asked God's Messenger: "Which is the greatest sin of all?" He answered: "To claim a partner to God when He has created you."

The *surah* has already referred to the established pattern which determines the fate of those who describe the truth as lies. Now it states that God does not love the wrongdoers. This is indeed another way of making clear the fate that awaits those who reject the truth and who are not loved by God. The statement that God does not love such people generates in the believers' hearts a feeling of hatred for wrongdoing and wrongdoers. It is also highly appropriate for it to be mentioned here in the context of striving hard for God's cause. A believer undertakes such a struggle to combat everyone and everything that God hates. It is in such a combat that martyrs sacrifice themselves and make their testimony after they have been chosen for the task by none other than God Himself.

The *surah* goes on to explain the lessons to be drawn from the events of battle and how these help in educating the Muslim community, purging it from foreign elements and preparing it for its nobler role. In this way it becomes a means which God uses to wipe out unbelievers and a manifestation of His ability to crush those who reject the truth and describe it as lies: *"And God wants to test and prove the believers, and to blot out the unbelievers."* Proving the quality of people is a harder task than drawing a distinction between them. This is something that is accomplished through working on people's hearts and souls. Its aim is to bring into the open the secret elements of which men's characters are made, in order to throw out any foreign elements. Thus, characters become purged and clear, and accept the truth without hesitation. They suffer no ambiguity or confusion.

It is often the case that man is not fully aware of himself and by what or how his character is influenced. He might not be aware of his strengths and weaknesses, of what has sunk into him and become very difficult to bring out. This process of testing and proving, which God operates through dealing out days of fortune and days of misfortune to people, enables the believers to better know themselves.

A man may think himself dedicated and free of meanness or love of material luxuries. When he is exposed to a practical test, however, and when he faces up to actual events, he may discover that he still has certain traces remaining which make it exceedingly difficult for him to withstand the sort of pressures to which he is exposed. It is far better that he becomes aware of these weaknesses in order to try again to mould his character in such a way which enables him to take in his stride any pressures the advocates of Islam may have to face and to fulfil the duties Islam imposes on its followers.

God Himself supervised the first Muslim community which He had chosen to lead mankind. He wanted them to fulfil a certain purpose on earth. Therefore, He put them to the test at Uḥud so that they could prove themselves and rise to a level which made it possible for them to accomplish what God intended for them.

"And God wants to ... blot out the unbelievers." This is again an established pattern in human life. When the voice of truth is heard loud and purged of all foreign elements, God enables it to blot out falsehood and its advocates.

Wishful Thinking in Contrast with Reality

Do you reckon that you can enter paradise unless God has identified those among you who strive hard [in His cause], and who are patient in adversity. Surely, you used to wish for death before you came face to face with it. Now you have seen it with your own eyes. (Verses 142–3)

These verses start with a rhetorical question, the purpose of which is to correct the concepts formed by Muslims on the patterns established by God for the advocacy of His faith: how victory is achieved and defeat suffered; the importance of action and what reward it merits, etc. The Qur'ān makes it clear that the road to heaven is attended by many difficulties and undesirable things. The best equipment for a believer is patience in adversity. This is totally different from hollow wishes and claims which any test may prove to be futile. *"Do you reckon that you can enter paradise unless God has identified those among you who strive hard [in His cause] and who are patient in adversity?"* (Verse 142)

The rhetoric mode is employed in this question so as to make it clear that the whole concept is wrong. It is certainly a mistake for any man to think that it is sufficient for him to only say that he has accepted Islam and be ready to die for it in order to fulfil the duties which are required of him as one of the believers. It is important to remember here that the fulfilment of such duties earns that person the greatest prize of all, namely, admission to heaven. What is needed for the fulfilment of such duties is to go through a practical test of *jihād*, to face up to difficulties and to be patient in adversity.

The phraseology of the Qur'ānic text is particularly significant: *"...unless God has identified those among you who strive hard [in His cause], and who are patient in adversity."* It is not sufficient that believers should strive hard in God's cause. They have to demonstrate their patience and fulfil the continuous and varied tasks imposed on them by their faith. Fighting on the battlefield may be one of the lightest of these tasks which demand patience and prove the strength of faith. There is, in addition, the never-ending, uphill task of maintaining the standards of behaviour commensurate with faith, developing a set of values which are not only based on the principles of faith but are also reflected in one's feelings and attitudes. There is also the need for perseverance which helps people overcome their weaknesses, whether these be within themselves or in others with whom they deal in the course of daily life. Patience and perseverance have to be demonstrated in a variety of situations, especially when to give up appears to be far more appealing. Examples of this include when falsehood appears to be victorious, and stronger than the truth; when the way ahead appears to be too long, too hard and full of difficulties; when a moment of relaxation appears to be all that one can care for after a long period of hard struggle. Fighting on the battlefield is no more than one aspect of striving for God's cause, which is the only way to heaven. Certainly, heaven is not won by wishful thinking or by paying lip-service to the requirements of faith.

"Surely, you used to wish for death before you came face to face with it. Now you have seen it with your own eyes." (Verse 143) Once more, they are put face to face with death, which they already faced on the battlefield. Since they used to wish for death, they should weigh their words against the facts they have seen with their own eyes. They are thus taught how words must reflect practical reality. In this way, they learn the value of words, wishes and pledges. What attains them heaven is the credence they give to their words and the fulfilment of their pledges. In practice, that necessitates hard striving and patience in adversity. When they demonstrate all that in practical life, all their hopes are fulfilled.

There is no doubt that God was able, from the very first moment, to grant His Prophet victory and to establish His message in practical life, without any effort made by the believers. He was indeed able to send down His angels to fight alongside the believers, or without them, and to destroy the idolaters just as He destroyed the peoples of 'Ād, Thamūd and those to whom the Prophet Lot was sent. But the question is not one of victory. The crux of the matter is the education and preparation of the Muslim community to assume the role of the leadership of mankind, after having overcome all its weaknesses and desires, and having corrected any deviation resulting from such weaknesses. To exercise mature and responsible leadership, the Muslim community should have leaders who go through stringent preparation. Among the most important qualities needed are serious morality, unshaken support for the truth, patience in adversity, awareness of the strengths and weaknesses in human nature, ability to identify the causes of temptation and deviation and how they can be successfully countered. Other prerequisites include passing the test of prosperity as well as that of hardship and the even more difficult test of hardship after prosperity.

It is through this sort of education that God prepares the Muslim community for the great and highly difficult role of leadership He has assigned to it. It is His will that man, whom He has placed in charge of building life on earth, assumes this role. The process of educating and preparing the Muslim community may take a variety of ways and means as well as incidents and events. Sometimes, the Muslim community is elated by a decisive victory and is required to control its feelings. No trace of arrogance should be apparent in its attitude. On the contrary, it must always show its humility and gratitude to God. At other times, the Muslim community may experience great hardship and defeat. In this case, it must turn to God acknowledging its weakness if it deviates from the method and way of life God has assigned to it. It must remain acutely aware of its intrinsic strength and how to tap it. When the Muslim community suffers a bitter defeat, it must continue to feel itself superior to the forces of falsehood, because it takes its stand in support of the absolute truth. It tries hard to identify its weaknesses in order to remedy its position in preparation for the next round. In either case, of victory or defeat, the Muslim community tries to enhance its strength, realising that the rules of nature set by God will continue to operate and will never fail.

All this was part of what the first Muslim community learnt from the Battle of Uḥud. The Qur'ān presents the same in the clearest of terms before the Muslim community. The lesson, however, continues to apply to every Muslim community in every generation.

Muḥammad: Man, Prophet and Messenger

Muḥammad is only a messenger: all messengers have passed away before him. If, then, he dies or is slain, will you turn about on your heels? He that turns about on his heels will not harm God in any way. God will reward those who are grateful [to Him]. (Verse 144)

This verse refers to a particular incident which took place during the Battle of Uḥud. The Prophet had stationed a detachment of soldiers on top of the mountain behind the Muslim army. They were the rearguard, equipped with bows and arrows to repel any attack launched against the Muslim army from behind. When the battle appeared to be all over, most of them left their positions, against the express orders of the Prophet. A battalion of the enemy forces were thus able to go round the mountain and attack the Muslims from the rear. The Prophet himself was injured: his front teeth were broken, and his face was bleeding.

The situation became chaotic and the Muslim army was in disarray. At this moment, someone cried out: "Muḥammad is killed!" Such a great shock was this to the Muslims, that many of them turned round to return to Madinah. They went up into the mountain, shattered, defeated, in despair. However, the Prophet himself, with a small group of his Companions, stood firm. He called to his Companions as they began to retreat. When they heard him, they began to rally. God helped them regain their moral strength and allowed them to be overtaken by a momentary slumber so as to give them strength, security and reassurance, as will be explained later.

This sequence of events is used in the Qur'ān to drive home to the Muslims certain fundamental principles about life and death and the history of Divine faith: *"Muḥammad is only a messenger: all messengers have passed away before him. If, then, he dies or is slain, will you turn about on your heels?"* Muḥammad (pbuh) is simply a messenger, having been preceded by all other messengers. He will die as other messengers have died before him. This is an elementary fact. How is it then that the Muslims show themselves to be oblivious of this fact when it stared them in the face during the battle?

Muḥammad (pbuh) is a messenger of God, entrusted with the task of conveying His message. God is Eternal and His word never dies. Believers should never turn on their heels if the messenger who has come to convey God's word to them dies or is killed. This is also an elementary fact which the Muslims, in their great confusion, overlooked.

Human beings die and perish, while the faith survives. The way of life God has designed for mankind has its own entity; it is independent of those who convey it to people, be they messengers or believers. Every Muslim loves God's Messenger (pbuh). His Companions loved him as no one had ever been loved before. They were ready to sacrifice their lives in order to spare him the slightest pain. One of his Companions, Abū Dujānah, stood as a shield to protect the Prophet, was hit by numerous arrows in the back and yet he never stirred. Only nine of his Companions were close to him when he was targeted by a determined attack by the unbelievers, and those nine defended him most courageously, until they were all killed. Many others in every generation and in all places continue to love him with all their hearts. Every Muslim who loves Muḥammad (pbuh) in such a way is required to distinguish between the Prophet as a person, and the faith he has conveyed to mankind and left intact for all people to accept and implement. It derives its continuity from God, Who never dies.

The message is much older than its advocates: *"Muḥammad is only a messenger: all messengers have passed away before him."* They all preached the same message, the roots of which go back to the beginning of history. It starts with the beginning of human life, providing mankind with guidance and peace from the very first day of its existence.

The message is also greater than its advocates and lasts longer. Many of its advocates have come and gone, while it continues to serve as guidance to succeeding generations. Its followers maintain their link with God Almighty, its originator, Who has sent messengers to convey it to mankind. He is Everlasting and believers address their prayers to Him. None of them may turn about on their heels or turn their back on God's guidance. This explains the stern warning implicit in this verse: *"If, then, he dies or is slain, will you turn about on your heels? He that turns about on his heels will not harm God in any way. God will reward those who are grateful [to Him]."* (Verse 144)

The vivid description of turning back is here to be noted: *"Will you turn about on your heels?"* The physical movement depicted here brings alive the meaning of abandoning faith as if we see it with our own eyes. The verse does not refer to the physical turning away as a result of defeat in battle. It is more concerned with the psychological turning about when a voice cried out that Muḥammad was killed. Some Muslims felt that there was no point in continuing the fight against the idolaters, since the death of Muḥammad (pbuh) signalled the end of this faith and the end of combat against idolatry. This psychological effect is delineated in terms of turning about on one's heels, which was a movement that actually took place during the battle. It is this very attitude which Al-Naḍhīr ibn Anas, a Companion of the Prophet, warned his fellow Muslims against when he saw that many of them had lain down their arms. His retort to their excuse that Muḥammad was dead, was: "What use is life to you after he has died? Get up and die for the cause God's Messenger (pbuh) has sacrificed his life for."

"He that turns about on his heels will not harm God in any way." It is indeed he who is the loser. He who deviates from the path of faith harms himself and causes God no harm. God is in no need of mankind or their worship. It is out of His grace that He has given His servants this constitution for their own good and happiness. Everyone who turns his back on it suffers from confusion and misery. Everything is thus set on the wrong footing. Life itself becomes deviant. People suffer the evil consequences of turning away from the only constitution which provides harmony in life and which achieves harmony between man, his nature and the universe around him.

"God will reward those who are grateful to Him." They know the great bounty God has given His servants by establishing for them this code of living. They show their gratitude to Him by following this code and praising Him. They reap the benefits of this way of life and achieve total happiness. This is good reward for their gratitude. But they also have an increase of happiness with the reward they receive from God in the hereafter. That is a much greater reward and, unlike everything enjoyed in this world, it is everlasting.

"God will reward those who are grateful to Him." Those who appreciate God's bounty and show their gratitude to Him by following

His guidance and by glorifying Him find happiness in their lives. Thus are they rewarded for their gratitude, and they will receive an even better reward in the life to come.

Apparently God wanted to wean the Companions of the Prophet from their over-enthusiastic attachment to him in person while he was alive among them. Their attachment should be, in the first place, with Islam itself. Their covenants should be made with God directly and they should be made to feel that they are responsible to Him directly. Thus they would feel that their responsibilities continue after the death of the Prophet. Perhaps God also wanted to prepare the Muslim community for the inevitable shock which they were bound to receive when the Prophet died. He certainly knew that his death would be a stunning blow to them. Hence, if they were made to feel that their direct relationship was with Him and His message then they would be able to overcome their shock.

When the Prophet actually died his Companions were stunned, so much so that 'Umar drew his sword and threatened anyone who claimed that Muhammad was dead. Only Abū Bakr, the best example of a true believer in God, was able to take the event in its proper perspective. He read out this verse to the Muslims and it was enough to make them realise that it was only a natural event. With this they were able to turn to God. The Qur'ān in this verse touches on man's fear of death. It dispels that fear by stating the ever-correct principle of life and death and also of what comes after life.

Death and Reward

No one can die except by God's leave, at a term appointed. He who desires the reward of this world, We shall give him thereof; and to him who desires the reward of the life to come, We shall give thereof. We shall reward those who are grateful to Us. (Verse 145)

Every human soul, then, lives up to its appointed time. No one dies before his time. Neither fear, nor the desire to live longer can postpone anyone's appointed time. Courage and adventure, on the other hand, will not shorten one's life. As this idea sinks into the minds of the believers they simply do not think of death as they go about fulfilling their responsibilities and carrying out their religious duties. This is the reason why people, throughout the ages, have seen that those who believe in God are not encumbered by their desire to prolong their time on earth or by their fear of what lies ahead. They simply rely on God as they carry out their duties with patience and reassurance.

Since everybody dies at his or her appointed time then everyone should think of the life to come and should work hard in order to achieve the greater happiness of that life: *"He who desires the reward of this world, We shall give him thereof; and to him who desires the reward of the life to come, We shall give thereof."* (Verse 145)

The gulf between the two types of life is as wide as the gulf between the concerns of those who desire the reward of either one or the other. The length of one's life on this earth is not affected by the choice one makes. So, he who makes this life his ultimate goal and seeks only its rewards leads a life which is not greatly different from the life of animals, before he dies at the appointed time. On the other hand, he who looks up to the wider horizon leads the life of a true human being whom God has ennobled, to whom He has assigned the mission of building a happy human life on earth. Such a person also dies at his appointed time.

"We shall reward those who are grateful to Us." Those who appreciate how God has ennobled man and lift themselves above the standard of animals and show their gratitude to God will certainly be richly rewarded by Him.

This is how the Qur'ān views the essence of life and death, and the end of human beings as they choose for themselves and determine their preoccupations which can be either petty like those of worms or great like those of man. In this way, the Qur'ān turns our attention from fear of death and worry about duties because we have no say with regard to our life and death. It thus enables us to concentrate on what is of much better use, namely, the life to come. Whichever choice he makes, he will receive from God the reward most appropriate for that choice.

Lessons from the History of the Prophets

God then gives the Muslims an example drawn from the history of fellow believers. The procession of faith, composed of believers, dates back to the very beginning of time. There were people who were true to their word, firm believers who fought alongside the prophets sent to them and they never weakened in times of adversity. As they stared death in the face, they demonstrated their awareness of their true position when they fought in God's cause and lived in accordance with the teachings of their faith. They said no more than a prayer to God to forgive them. They enlarged their slips in behaviour and attitude, so as to describe them as "excesses". They also prayed to God to make their steps firm and to grant them victory. This earned for them the reward of this life and that of the life to come, because they combined the right attitude in battle and the right attitude in their prayers. Thus, they have provided an example which God cites here for the Muslims.

> *Many a Prophet has fought with many devout men alongside him. They never lost heart on account of what they had to suffer in God's cause, and neither did they weaken nor succumb. God loves those who are patient in adversity. All that they said was this: "Our Lord! Forgive us our sins and our excesses in our affairs. Make firm our steps, and give us victory over the unbelievers." God has granted them the reward of this life and the best reward of the life to come. God loves those who do their duty well.* (Verses 146–8)

The Battle of Uḥud was the first major defeat suffered by the Muslims. They had earlier been granted victory at Badr when their forces were far inferior to those of their enemy. Thus, they may have felt that victory in every encounter was part of the laws of nature. The shock dealt them at Uḥud was a hard and disturbing trial. This may be the reason for the long Qur'ānic comments on this particular battle. The Muslims are encouraged at one point, and their notions are corrected at another; at times, certain principles are clearly stated, and at others, examples are cited to provide proper education for them and to correct any misconceptions they may have. They had to be well prepared for their long and arduous struggle in discharging the duties imposed on them as advocates of God's message.

The example which the *sūrah* gives here is a general one, which neither mentions any prophet by name nor specifies a particular nation or people. The outcome of this is that the Muslims feel themselves to belong to the advocates of true faith throughout history. They learn the proper manners which believers should adopt. Trials are shown to them as something to be naturally expected by the advocates of any message and any faith. Ties are established between them and the followers of earlier prophets so that they appreciate that believers in any generation are closely related to their predecessors in faith. They learn that the cause of faith is one which has been present throughout history and that they are only one battalion in a great army of the faithful: *"Many a Prophet has fought with many devout men alongside him. They never lost heart on account of what they had to suffer in God's cause, and neither did they weaken nor succumb."* (Verse 146) There were many prophets who mobilised large groups of fighters who withstood all manner of hardship and suffering. They never yielded or gave up their fight. Such determination is characteristic of believers who know that they have to fight for their faith.

"God loves those who are patient in adversity." They persevere and show no weakness. Their determination remains strong. When these are described as being loved by God, the expression has its particular effect on the present generation of believers. It helps heal their wounds and it is accepted as ample and generous compensation for every hardship.

The description so far shows only what is apparent of the attitude of those believers in situations of difficulty and trial. Now the *sūrah* goes on to describe their inner feelings. It shows them as observing all standards of propriety when they address God. The testing times, the difficulties and the dangers do not make the believers oblivious of their need to turn to God. As they do, their first request is not victory, as would have been expected, but forgiveness for their errors and excesses. Prayer for increased strength and victory over the enemy comes second: *"All that they said was this: 'Our Lord! Forgive us our sins and our excesses in our affairs. Make firm our steps, and give us victory over the unbelievers.'"* (Verse 147) They do not pray for any great bounty or reward. They have not implored God to give them the reward of either this life or the life to come. Their humility when they turn to God and address Him is too great to allow them to do this, and despite the fact that they are fighting for His cause. They pray only that He will grant them forgiveness of their sins, make firm their steps, and grant them victory over the unbelievers.

It is very important to realise here that they do not pray for victory for themselves, but rather for the defeat their opponents and the frustration of the unbelievers. This is the sort of good manners which befit believers when they address God, the Almighty.

To these very people who have asked nothing for themselves, God has given everything, out of His grace. He has given them all that is desired and coveted by those who seek the riches of this world. He has also given them everything that those who prefer the reward of the life to come yearn for: *"God has granted them the reward of this life and the best reward of the life to come."* (Verse 148) He further acknowledges that they have done well. Their good manners are combined with a very effective way of fulfilling their duty of *jihād*, exerting every effort for the cause of God. He, therefore, declares that He loves them. His love is greater than all reward and superior to all bounty: *"God loves those who do their duty well."* (Verse 148)

Within the comments given in the *sūrah* on the Battle of Uḥud, this passage establishes a number of principles which are central to the Islamic concept. It plays an important role in educating the Muslim community and provides a good example which must be understood by every generation of Muslims.

8

Forgiveness of a Disastrous Error

Believers, if you obey those who have rejected the faith, they will cause you to turn back on your heels, and you will be the losers. (149)

يَـٰٓأَيُّهَا ٱلَّذِينَ ءَامَنُوٓاْ إِن تُطِيعُواْ ٱلَّذِينَ كَفَرُواْ يَرُدُّوكُمْ عَلَىٰٓ أَعْقَـٰبِكُمْ فَتَنقَلِبُواْ خَـٰسِرِينَ ۝

Indeed, God alone is your Lord Supreme and He is the best of all who bring succour. (150)

بَلِ ٱللَّهُ مَوْلَـٰكُمْ وَهُوَ خَيْرُ ٱلنَّـٰصِرِينَ ۝

We shall strike terror in the hearts of unbelievers because they associate partners with God – [something] for which He has never granted any warrant. Their abode is the fire, and evil indeed is the dwelling place of the wrongdoers. (151)

سَنُلْقِى فِى قُلُوبِ ٱلَّذِينَ كَفَرُواْ ٱلرُّعْبَ بِمَآ أَشْرَكُواْ بِٱللَّهِ مَالَمْ يُنَزِّلْ بِهِۦ سُلْطَـٰنًا وَمَأْوَىٰهُمُ ٱلنَّارُ وَبِئْسَ مَثْوَى ٱلظَّـٰلِمِينَ ۝

God fulfilled to you His promise when, by His leave, you were about to destroy them. But then you lost heart and disagreed with

وَلَقَدْ صَدَقَكُمُ ٱللَّهُ وَعْدَهُۥٓ إِذْ تَحُسُّونَهُم بِإِذْنِهِۦ حَتَّىٰٓ إِذَا

one another concerning [the Prophet's command] and disobeyed after God had brought you within view of that for which you were longing. Some of you cared only for this world and some cared for the life to come. Then He turned you away from them so that He may put you to a test. But now He has forgiven you, for God is gracious to the believers. (152)

فَشِلْتُمْ وَتَنَـٰزَعْتُمْ فِى ٱلْأَمْرِ وَعَصَيْتُم مِّنۢ بَعْدِ مَآ أَرَىٰكُم مَّا تُحِبُّونَ ۚ مِنكُم مَّن يُرِيدُ ٱلدُّنْيَا وَمِنكُم مَّن يُرِيدُ ٱلْأَخِرَةَ ۚ ثُمَّ صَرَفَكُمْ عَنْهُمْ لِيَبْتَلِيَكُمْ ۖ وَلَقَدْ عَفَا عَنكُمْ ۗ وَٱللَّهُ ذُو فَضْلٍ عَلَى ٱلْمُؤْمِنِينَ ﴿١٥٢﴾

[Remember] when you ran away, up into the mountain, paying no heed to anyone, while the Messenger was at your rear calling out to you. Therefore, He rewarded you with sorrow after sorrow so that you may not grieve over what has escaped you, nor over what had befallen you. God is aware of all that you do. (153)

۞ إِذْ تُصْعِدُونَ وَلَا تَلْوُونَ عَلَىٰٓ أَحَدٍ وَٱلرَّسُولُ يَدْعُوكُمْ فِىٓ أُخْرَىٰكُمْ فَأَثَـٰبَكُمْ غَمًّۢا بِغَمٍّ لِّكَيْلَا تَحْزَنُوا۟ عَلَىٰ مَا فَاتَكُمْ وَلَا مَآ أَصَـٰبَكُمْ ۗ وَٱللَّهُ خَبِيرٌۢ بِمَا تَعْمَلُونَ ﴿١٥٣﴾

Then, after sorrow, He let peace fall upon you, in the shape of a slumber which overtook some of you, while others, who cared mainly for themselves, entertained wrong thoughts about God – thoughts of pagan ignorance. They ask: "Have we any say in the matter?" Say: "All power of decision rests with God." They conceal in their

ثُمَّ أَنزَلَ عَلَيْكُم مِّنۢ بَعْدِ ٱلْغَمِّ أَمَنَةً نُّعَاسًا يَغْشَىٰ طَآئِفَةً مِّنكُمْ ۖ وَطَآئِفَةٌ قَدْ أَهَمَّتْهُمْ أَنفُسُهُمْ يَظُنُّونَ بِٱللَّهِ غَيْرَ ٱلْحَقِّ ظَنَّ ٱلْجَـٰهِلِيَّةِ ۖ يَقُولُونَ هَل لَّنَا مِنَ ٱلْأَمْرِ مِن شَىْءٍ ۗ قُلْ إِنَّ ٱلْأَمْرَ كُلَّهُۥ

minds what they do not disclose to you. They say: "Had we had any say in the matter, we should not have been slaughtered here." Say: "Had you stayed in your homes, those of you who were destined to be killed would have gone to their deathbeds." For it was God's will to put to a test all that you entertain in you minds and to render pure what you may have in your hearts, God is fully aware of what is in people's bosoms. (154)

لِّلَّهِ يُخْفُونَ فِى أَنفُسِهِم مَّا لَا يُبْدُونَ لَكَ يَقُولُونَ لَوْ كَانَ لَنَا مِنَ ٱلْأَمْرِ شَىْءٌ مَّا قُتِلْنَا هَٰهُنَا قُل لَّوْ كُنتُمْ فِى بُيُوتِكُمْ لَبَرَزَ ٱلَّذِينَ كُتِبَ عَلَيْهِمُ ٱلْقَتْلُ إِلَىٰ مَضَاجِعِهِمْ وَلِيَبْتَلِىَ ٱللَّهُ مَا فِى صُدُورِكُمْ وَلِيُمَحِّصَ مَا فِى قُلُوبِكُمْ وَٱللَّهُ عَلِيمٌۢ بِذَاتِ ٱلصُّدُورِ ﴿١٥٤﴾

As for those of you who turned away on the day when the two hosts met in battle, Satan caused them to slip only in consequence of something that they themselves had done. But now God has pardoned them. Indeed, God is Much-forgiving, Forbearing. (155)

إِنَّ ٱلَّذِينَ تَوَلَّوْا۟ مِنكُمْ يَوْمَ ٱلْتَقَى ٱلْجَمْعَانِ إِنَّمَا ٱسْتَزَلَّهُمُ ٱلشَّيْطَٰنُ بِبَعْضِ مَا كَسَبُوا۟ وَلَقَدْ عَفَا ٱللَّهُ عَنْهُمْ إِنَّ ٱللَّهَ غَفُورٌ حَلِيمٌ ﴿١٥٥﴾

Believers, be not like those who disbelieve and say of their brethren, when they travel on earth or go forth to war, "Had they stayed with us they would not have died, nor would they have been killed," so that God places a source of despair in their hearts. It is God alone Who grants life and causes death. God sees all that you do. (156)

يَٰٓأَيُّهَا ٱلَّذِينَ ءَامَنُوا۟ لَا تَكُونُوا۟ كَٱلَّذِينَ كَفَرُوا۟ وَقَالُوا۟ لِإِخْوَٰنِهِمْ إِذَا ضَرَبُوا۟ فِى ٱلْأَرْضِ أَوْ كَانُوا۟ غُزًّى لَّوْ كَانُوا۟ عِندَنَا مَا مَاتُوا۟ وَمَا قُتِلُوا۟ لِيَجْعَلَ ٱللَّهُ ذَٰلِكَ حَسْرَةً فِى قُلُوبِهِمْ وَٱللَّهُ يُحْىِۦ وَيُمِيتُ وَٱللَّهُ بِمَا تَعْمَلُونَ بَصِيرٌ ﴿١٥٦﴾

If you should be slain or die in God's cause, surely forgiveness by God and His grace are better than all the riches they amass. (157)	وَلَئِن قُتِلْتُمْ فِى سَبِيلِ اللَّهِ أَوْ مُتُّمْ لَمَغْفِرَةٌ مِّنَ اللَّهِ وَرَحْمَةٌ خَيْرٌ مِّمَّا يَجْمَعُونَ ۝
If you should die or be slain, it is to God that you shall be gathered. (158)	وَلَئِن مُّتُّمْ أَوْ قُتِلْتُمْ لَإِلَى اللَّهِ تُحْشَرُونَ ۝

Obedience Bringing Utter Loss

Believers, if you obey those who have rejected the faith, they will cause you to turn back on your heels, and you will be the losers. Indeed, God alone is your Lord Supreme and He is the best of all who bring succour. (Verses 149–50)

Another passage within the context of the Qur'ān's review of the Battle of Uḥud and its events now begins. The comments it includes aim at correcting the concepts of the believers, enhancing their awareness of their situation, warning them of pitfalls which lie in their way and what the enemy may scheme against them.

The defeat of the Muslims at Uḥud provided the unbelievers, the hypocrites and the Jews in Madinah with a suitable climate to spread their hostile propaganda. Madinah was not yet a wholly Muslim city. The Muslims there were largely a foreign element, to which the spectacular victory at Badr imparted an awe-inspiring stature. When they were defeated at Uḥud, attitudes were markedly changed. The enemies of Islam found in that defeat a chance to declare their hostility and spread their poisonous rumours. They were quick to exploit the tragedy which had affected every Muslim family and to try to create confusion in the minds of Muslims.

At the outset of the Qur'ānic report of the actual events of the battle, God Himself emphatically warns the believers against obeying those who have rejected the faith. We hear Him (limitless is He in His glory) promising the believers victory over their enemy

244

coupled with striking a feeling of fear in the hearts of these enemies, and reminding them of the victory He has granted them in the first round of their war, in fulfilment of His earlier promise. They, however, had squandered that victory when they weakened, and disobeyed the express orders of God's Messenger. Now He portrays the opposite scenes of the battle when He gives reassurance to the believers after their defeat, leaving the hypocrites to their own worry and confusion. He reveals to them a part of His purpose in letting events move in the direction they did, explaining the true nature of the timing of people's deaths. He warns them at the end against the erroneous notions promoted by the unbelievers in relation to death and martyrdom. He reminds them that all people, whether they die in the normal course of events or in battle, will eventually be resurrected and return to God.

When we examine these verses carefully, we realise that they describe a vast array of scenes and emphasise at the same time a number of principles which are fundamental to Islamic philosophy, human life and universal law. The whole battle is depicted in quick, lively and penetrating sketches. They accurately describe the atmosphere, events and circumstances of the battle, along with all the feelings and attitudes displayed by the believers at that time. There is no doubt that it is beyond human expression to include all these scenes and all these principles in such a short passage and a small number of sentences, vivid as they may be. This is a point which can be better understood by those familiar with different styles and methods of expression.

> *Believers, if you obey those who have rejected the faith, they will cause you to turn back on your heels, and you will be the losers. Indeed, God alone is your Lord Supreme and He is the best of all who bring succour.* (Verses 149–50)

The unbelievers, the hypocrites and the Jews in Madinah seized the opportunity created by the defeat of the Muslims to warn them against following Muḥammad. They painted to them in dark colours the gloomy prospects of going to war and fighting the idolaters of the Quraysh and its allies. In the aftermath of defeat, the social climate provides easy opportunities to spread confusion and to weaken the trust of soldiers in their leaders. By the same token the idea of establishing a peaceful accord with the victors was painted in tempting colours. Personal grief was being exploited as part of the wicked design aiming to destroy the Muslim community and Islam altogether.

Hence, God warns the believers against giving heed to those who have rejected the faith, because that obedience will inevitably result in utter loss. Nothing good can come from it. It represents a complete about-turn from a state of disbelief. A believer either continues to fight those who cling to falsehood and reject faith, or turns on his heels – God forbid – thus becoming an unbeliever. It is not possible for a believer to take an in-between attitude, trying to maintain neutrality while at the same time hanging on to his faith. He may harbour some such thoughts in the wake of defeat and under the influence of calamity. He may even imagine that he can withdraw from battle against a mightier power, and establish peace with that enemy, and, at the same time, retain his faith. This, however, is a great delusion. In the whole question of faith, a person who does not move forward can only go backwards. If one does not fight disbelief, evil, falsehood and tyranny, one must beat retreat and turn back on one's heels to embrace all this evil. A person whose faith does not stop him from obeying unbelievers and having trust in them sacrifices, in fact, his very faith for their sake. He is spiritually defeated when he befriends the enemies of his faith and follows their directives. As he starts with defeat, he cannot escape from it at the end. He is bound to revert to rejection of the faith, although he may not imagine that such would be his end. A believer is satisfied with his faith and leadership to such an extent that he has no need to consult the enemies of his faith. If he listens to them once, he actually begins the process of turning back on his heels. This is an elementary and honest truism to which God draws the attentions of the believers: *"Believers, if you obey those who have rejected the faith they will cause you to turn back on your heels, and you will be the losers."*

What loss is greater than turning back on one's heels, after one has attained to faith? What benefits may be gained after loss of faith has taken place?

If the tendency to obey the unbelievers is motivated by hopes of protection and succour, this is also a great delusion. The Qur'ān does not discuss this delusion, but reminds the believers of where true help, protection and succour come from: *"Indeed God alone is your Lord Supreme and He is the best of all who bring succour."* It is to Him that the believers pray for support and victory. He who has God for his supporter has no need whatsoever for any of His creation. If he has the support of God, what use to him is the support of any creature?

Striking Fear in Enemies' Hearts

The *sūrah* now provides the believers with more reassurance, giving them the happy news of God's plan to strike terror into the hearts of their enemies because they associate partners with Him, against all His express orders. Indeed, God has given those alleged partners no power of any sort. Moreover, in the hereafter, the wrongdoers will receive further punishment: *"We shall strike terror in the hearts of unbelievers because they associate partners with God – something for which He has never granted any warrant. Their abode is the fire, and evil indeed is the dwelling place of the wrongdoers."* (Verse 151)

A promise from God, the Almighty, to strike terror into the hearts of the unbelievers is sufficient guarantee to bring the battle to a decisive victory for the believers who support Him, against His enemies. It is a promise which holds true in every confrontation between belief and disbelief. Every time the unbelievers come face to face with the believers, fear overcomes them, because God strikes that feeling into their hearts. What is important for this feeling to surface is that the believers themselves truly feel their faith. They must genuinely submit themselves to God alone, and have total confidence in God's help and entertain no shred of doubt that victory will be given to God's soldiers and that God will accomplish His will and that the unbelievers can never frustrate what God wants to accomplish. Sometimes, appearances may suggest the contrary, but the believers have to trust in God's promise because it will always come true, regardless of what people may see with their own eyes or judge with their own minds. The unbelievers will feel terror in their hearts, because they do not rely on any firm support. They have no power of their own, and they do not enjoy the support of any other powerful source. They have attributed to God partners

247

who have no authority or power of their own, because God has never bestowed any warrant on them.

The expression *"something for which He has never granted any warrant,"* is particularly significant. It is frequently used in the Qur'ān, sometimes to describe the partners associated with God, and at other times to describe false beliefs. It points to a basic and fundamental principle. An idea, a principle, a person or an organisation can live, survive and be effective only according to what it enjoys of real force. Such force is always commensurate with its share of the truth. This means that it is only powerful in direct proportion to its concordance with the basic principle which constitutes the foundation of the universe and with the laws God has set in operation in the universe. It is only when such harmony is achieved that God gives it effective force, which enables it to work. Otherwise, it remains shaky, false, powerless, though it may appear at times tempting and mighty.

The idolaters ascribe divinity to deities other than God. The very concept of polytheism is based on giving certain fundamental qualities to beings other than God. One of the most important of these qualities and attributes is the right to issue legislation which may affect any aspect of human life, and the right to establish values which people should implement in their community and observe in their behaviour. Also, the right to establish one's own power over others and to make other people submit to such legislation and implement such values is another aspect of practical polytheism. Offering actual worship to beings other than God is another of its aspects, which means, as we have already said, ascribing Godhead qualities to beings other than God.

How much harmony do these deities have with the truth upon which the universe has been founded? God, Who has no partners, has created the universe so that it points to its single Creator. All creation must submit to Him alone, without partners, and must receive from Him alone their laws and values and must offer worship sincerely and genuinely to Him alone. Whatever is in conflict with the general and comprehensive meaning of the concept of the oneness of God, is false and contrary to the truth inherent in the universe. Hence, it is weak, shaky, devoid of any power and authority and cannot have any genuine effect on the course of life, because it is devoid of all the elements of life and has no right to live.

As those idolaters associate with God partners for whom He has never granted any authority, they have no firm support to rely upon. They will always be weak and they will experience terror whenever they come face to face with the believers, who rely on the mighty truth.

This promise always comes true in any confrontation between truth and falsehood. Many a time, falsehood has every type of armament when it confronts the truth, which may have little or no weaponry. Nevertheless, falsehood mobilises its forces, and feels a shiver go through its constitution. It shudders at every movement and at every shout. If the truth makes a sudden attack, confusion will spread within the ranks of falsehood, even though it may have great numerical superiority. All this takes place in fulfilment of God's true promise: *"We shall strike terror in the hearts of the unbelievers because they associate partners with God [something] for which He has never granted any warrant."* All this takes place in this life. As for the hereafter, a dismal and sorrowful destiny awaits the wrongdoers: *"Their abode is the fire, and evil indeed is the dwelling place of the wrongdoers."*

At this point, the *sūrah* takes the believers back to the fulfilment of God's promise at the Battle of Uḥud in particular. Initially, the Muslims enjoyed a clear advantage which could have led to certain victory. Unbelievers lay dead left, right, and centre, until the bulk of their army turned on their heels, leaving much of their equipment and armament as spoils of war. Their banner was on the ground, and there was none to lift it until a woman managed to raise it for them. Yet at that point, the Muslims' clear victory turned into defeat because their rearguard had weakened before the temptation of sharing in the spoils. They disputed among themselves and then violated the express orders of God's Messenger, their Prophet and leader. Now the *sūrah* moves on to describe the scenes and events of the battle itself.

Victory So Near, Yet So Far

God fulfilled to you His promise when, by His leave, you were about to destroy them. But then you lost heart and disagreed with one another concerning [the Prophet's command] and disobeyed after God had brought you within view of that for which you were longing. Some of you cared only for this world and some cared for the life to come. Then He turned you away from them so that He may put you to the test. But now He has forgiven you, for God is gracious to the believers. [Remember] when you ran away, up into the mountain, paying no heed to anyone, while the Messenger was at your rear calling out to you. Therefore, He rewarded you with sorrow after sorrow so that you may not grieve over what has escaped you, nor over what had befallen you. God is aware of all that you do. (Verses 152–3)

The *sūrah* paints a full picture of the battlefield and the succession of victory and defeat. Every movement, every impression, every facial expression and every fleeting thought is recorded. The Qur'ānic description is like a film reel which shows every movement in vivid and sharp detail. This particularly applies to the image of people fleeing from the battlefield and charging up the mountain in panic, as the Prophet called out to them. Coupled with this is a picture of the thoughts, impressions and reactions people entertained. On top of it all, we have a number of directives and statements which are characteristic of the Qur'ānic style and its remarkable method of educating believers.

"God fulfilled to you His promise, when, by His leave, you were about to destroy them." This was at the beginning of the battle, when the Muslims began to steadily put an end to all resistance shown by the idolaters, and to destroy their forces. At that time, they were not distracted by the loot which loomed large. The Prophet had said to them: *"You will be victorious as long as you remain steadfast."* God has fulfilled that promise which He gave them through His Prophet.

"But then you lost heart and disagreed with one another concerning [the Prophet's command] and disobeyed after God had brought you within view of that for which you were longing. Some of you cared only for this world and some cared for the life to come." (Verse 152) This is a description of what took place among the archers. A group of them felt the temptation too strongly. They wanted their share of the booty. They argued with those who maintained that they must obey the Messenger's command literally. Their argument led to disobedience when they saw the clear indications of the victory they longed to achieve. Thus, they were split into two groups: one caring only for worldly gains, and the other looking only for God's

reward in the hereafter. Discord was sown and the believers were no longer one force, working for one goal. Dedication, which is absolutely necessary in every battle fought for the sake of faith, was tainted with greed. What is important to remember is that a battle fought for the sake of faith is unique in that it is fought both on the battlefield and in people's hearts. Victory in the former is dependent on victory in the latter. It is a battle fought for the sake of God. Therefore, God gives victory in it to those who are totally dedicated to Him.

Since they have raised the banner of God, He does not grant them victory until He has tested them and ascertained their dedication, so that there can be no false pretences. Sometimes, those who clearly raise the banner of falsehood in battle are given victory, for a purpose known to God alone. But it has to be understood that those who raise the banner of faith without demonstrating complete dedication are never granted victory by God until they have proven that they have passed the test. This is the message the Qur'ān wants to state clearly to the Muslim community, using this particular battle as their reference point. He wanted the first Muslim community to learn this as it suffered bitter defeat as a result of a confused and shaky attitude.

"Some of you cared only for this world and some cared for the life to come." Here the Qur'ān sheds light on what is deep in people's hearts. The Muslims themselves did not know that they entertained such thoughts. 'Abdullāh ibn Mas'ūd, the Prophet's Companion said: "I never thought that any of the Companions of the Prophet would care for worldly gains, until God revealed in the Qur'ān describing our situation in Uhud: *'Some of you cared only for this world and some cared for the life to come.'* " Their hearts are thus laid open before them so that they can determine the causes of their defeat.

At the same time, the Qur'ān partly reveals to the Muslims God's purpose behind letting them suffer all this pain, and behind allowing events to develop in that particular fashion: *"Then He turned you away from them so that He may put you to a test."* God's pre-destination remains operative. When people weakened, disputed and disobeyed, God turned their power away from the idolaters and let the archers abandon their positions and the fighters desert the battlefield. All this took place as a result of their own actions, but it was all predestined by God in order to test the believers with hardship, fear, defeat and loss of life. Such a trial was bound to reveal what was in their innermost hearts and to distinguish true believers from those who only pretended to be so. There is no contradiction whatsoever between allowing events to happen as a direct result of their causes and them being predetermined. The law of cause and effect remains operative but every cause is also well determined.

"But now He has forgiven you," what you have shown of weakness, dispute and disobedience as well as your running away from battle. That forgiveness is an aspect of His grace which overlooks human weakness when it is not the result of ill-will or deliberate disobedience. He has forgiven you because your errors and weakness remain within the framework of faith and submission to God. They do not come in defiance of God's orders.

"God is gracious to the believers." Part of His grace is to forgive them, as long as they follow the method He has laid down for them and they submit to His will, without claiming any of the essential qualities of Godhead for themselves. At the same time, they must not derive any of their laws, values or standards from any source other than Him. Thus, when they slipped, that error came only from weakness. When they were exposed to this trial and proved themselves, they are forgiven.

The *sūrah* then describes the scene of defeat in powerful imagery: *"[Remember] when you ran away, up into the mountain, giving no heed to anyone, while the Messenger was at your rear calling out to you."* (Verse 153) This description encapsulates their shame for what they had done and the causes which led them to do it, namely, loss of heart, dispute and disobedience. Their physical and mental attitudes are also brought alive in just a few words: they quickly ran away, climbing up into the mountain, confused, afraid, perplexed, paying heed to no one. The Prophet called on them to reassure them that he was still alive after someone had cried out otherwise. The end result is that God rewarded them for the sorrow they suffered when they fled, with a sorrow to fill their own hearts for having abandoned their beloved Prophet and letting him endure his wounds, when he remained steadfast while they turned on their heels. There is no doubt that this experience was very painful. To them, what was most difficult to bear was the sorrow and pain which the Prophet himself had endured, because it was a direct result of their actions. They were bitterly ashamed. Their sorrow is useful in the sense that it was bound to make any loss they themselves suffered seem to be of no significance, and every hardship they will be called upon to bear very easy: *"Therefore, He rewarded you with sorrow after sorrow so that you may not grieve over what has escaped you, nor over what had befallen you."* God, Who knows everything, is certainly aware of every motive behind every action: *"God is aware of all that you do."* (Verse 153)

A Trial for the Faithful

Then, after sorrow, He let peace fall upon you, in the shape of a slumber which overtook some of you, while others, who cared mainly for themselves, entertained wrong thoughts about God — thoughts of pagan ignorance. They ask: "Have we any say in the matter?" Say: "All power of decision rests with God." They conceal in their minds what they do not disclose to you. They say: "Had we had any say in the matter, we should not have been slaughtered here." Say: "Had you stayed in your homes, those of you who were destined to be killed would have gone to their deathbeds." For it was God's will to put to a test all that you entertain in your minds and to render pure what you may have in your hearts, God is fully aware of what is in people's bosoms. (Verse 154)

All the chaos, confusion and panic which the defeat spread among the Muslim soldiers was followed by a remarkable sense of peace and security among the believers who came back and rallied to the Prophet's side. They were overtaken by a gentle slumber which gave them personal reassurance. This exceptional phenomenon is described in fine and gentle words: *"Then, after sorrow, He let peace fall upon you in the shape of a slumber which overtook some of you."*

There is no doubt that this was a remarkable phenomenon, a manifestation of God's grace when it is bestowed upon His servants. When slumber overtakes people who are tired, exhausted and panicking, even for a brief moment, it brings about remarkable results. It gives them reassurance and comfort in a way which we cannot fathom and it makes of them different people altogether. I say this because I have experienced it in a situation of extreme distress. I felt God's grace in a way which no human language can describe.

Abū Ṭalḥah reports: "I lifted my head on the day of Uḥud to look around me. Everyone of them was hanging down his head because of his drowsiness." In another version, also reported by Abū Ṭalḥah: "We were overtaken by slumber in our position on the day of Uḥud. My sword kept falling from my hand and I would pick it up before it fell again and I picked it up a second time."

Of the others, the group with shaky faith, their main preoccupation was their own interest. These had not purged their minds from ignorant concepts and they had not submitted themselves totally to God. They did not experience the certitude that what had befallen them was a test which did not represent an abandonment by God of His servants, leaving them alone to face the might of His eminence. Nor was it a verdict that he had passed to allow the non-Muslims and their evil to have final victory: *"While others, who cared mainly for themselves, entertained wrong thoughts about God — thoughts of pagan ignorance. They ask: 'Have we any say in the matter?'"*

Islam teaches its followers, among other things, that they have no say whatsoever over themselves. They belong to God. When they go out on a campaign of *jihād* for His cause, they dedicate themselves to God and fight for Him, having no personal ambition whatsoever. What He has predestined for them is bound to happen and they accept it with satisfaction and total submission.

Those who care only for themselves, to the extent that they are totally preoccupied with their own interest and well-being, do not feel the true nature of faith deep at heart. The Qur'ān describes them as worried, lost and confused. They think that they have been pushed into the battle without having any say in it. Rather, they were put to a severe test and had to pay a very heavy price. They did not truly know God, and they entertained such thoughts about Him that they had carried with them from the days of their pagan, ignorant past. These false notions included the idea that they were pushed into the battle only in order to be killed, and that God did not intervene to save them from their enemies. Hence they ask: *"Have we any say in the matter?"* This statement implies objection to the battle plan. Perhaps they were of the view that the Muslims should have stayed in Madinah and never gone out to fight. Although they did not desert with 'Abdullāh ibn Ubayy and his followers, they, nevertheless, did not have the reassurance of true believers.

Before this long verse continues with its accounts of their worries and thoughts, it states the proper view with regard to what they questioned. It answers them with: *"Say: 'All power of decision rests with God.'"* Neither they, nor anyone else, has any say in the matter. Prior to this, God said to the Prophet: *"You have no say in the matter."* Islam and the fighting for its establishment and the implementation of its way of life on earth, or guiding people's hearts to accept it, are matters which belong totally to God. Human beings have nothing to do with them, except to fulfil their duties and to leave their destiny in God's hands.

The Qur'ān also reveals what they tried to conceal in their hearts: *"They conceal in their minds what they do not disclose to you."* They entertain all sorts of thoughts which imply objection and protest. Indeed their question: *"Have we any say in the matter?"* implies a protest that they have been pushed into a catastrophe which was not of their own making and that they were the victims of unsound leadership. Had they been conducting the battle, they would not have so suffered. *"They say: 'Had we had any say in the matter, we should not have been slaughtered here.'"*

This is the type of thought which those who have not dedicated themselves to their faith feel when they face defeat in battle. When they find out that the price they had to pay is much greater than they had imagined and that the effort is more painful than they had expected. When they look deep into their hearts, they do not have a clear vision and they imagine that the action taken by their leadership was responsible for their defeat, which could have been averted had they had any power of decision. With such a confused view, they cannot see that it is God Who determines events and they cannot understand God's purpose in exposing them to such a test. To them, the whole matter is nothing but utter loss.

At this point, the Qur'ān states the correct concept of life and death, and the purpose behind testing the believers: *"Say: 'Had you stayed in your homes, those of you who were destined to be killed would have gone to their deathbeds.' For it was God's will to put to the test all that you entertain in your minds and to render pure what you may have in your hearts. God is fully aware of what is in people's bosoms."* Had you stayed at home without responding to the battle cry, had you taken your own decisions concerning the battle, those of you who were destined to be killed would certainly have met their death, because death only takes place at the appointed time.

There is a bed to which every person must retire. At the appointed moment, the person concerned walks to his or her deathbed without the need for force or direction from anyone.

The remarkable Arabic expression used here speaks, literally, of "beds". The graves in which people rest, and at which all endeavours end, is only a bed to which they come with a subtle motive which they cannot fathom. That motive overtakes them and determines their fate. It is far better and more comfortable for them to submit totally to it, because it is God's predestination. He has a purpose behind it: *"It was God's will to put to the test all that you entertain in your minds and to render pure what you may have in your hearts."*

There is nothing like a trial to reveal what is in people's minds and to purge the falsehood that is in their hearts. God wants the hearts of the believers to be purged so that they entertain no false notions. All their concerns will be clear, with no trace of confusion, *"God is fully aware of what is in people's bosoms."* That which is in a person's bosom is a secret which is never allowed to see the light. However, God knows everything that people may conceal in their hearts and He wants to reveal it to all who harbour them. They themselves may not know those secrets until they are shaken by events and laid bare for them to see.

Diverging Views of Life and Death

As for those of you who turned away on the day when the two hosts met in battle, Satan caused them to slip only in consequence of something that they themselves had done. But now God has pardoned them. Indeed, God is Much-forgiving, Forbearing. Believers, be not like those who disbelieve and say of their brethren, when they travel on earth or go forth to war, "Had they stayed with us they would not have died, nor would they have been killed," so that God places a source of despair in their hearts. It is God alone Who grants life and causes death. God sees all that you do. If you should be slain or die in God's cause, surely forgiveness by God and His grace are better than all the riches they amass. If you should die or be slain, it is to God that you shall be gathered. (Verses 155–8)

God was certainly aware of what was in the hearts of those who turned away in defeat during the Battle of Uḥud. They weakened in consequence of a sin they had committed. This caused them to be shaken. Satan was able to manoeuvre them into making such a slip: *"As for those of you who turned away on the day when the two hosts met in battle, Satan caused them to slip only in consequence of something that they themselves had done."* (Verse 155) This may be a reference to the archers who could not resist the temptation of the loot being left behind by the retreating unbelievers. They also entertained the thought that God's Messenger might not give them a share of the spoils of war. That was the sin they committed, in consequence of which Satan made them slip. This verse, however, describes man after having committed a sin: his confidence weakens and his tie with God loosens. He loses balance and allows himself to fall prey to all sorts of negative thoughts. Thus, Satan whispers in his ear and leads him from one error to another, after he himself has left his safe refuge of content and reassured faith.

Earlier, the *sūrah* mentioned the case of those believers who fought with prophets in earlier times. The first thing they did before fighting was to pray for forgiveness of their sins, because that prayer brings them back to God and strengthens their ties with Him, removing any doubts and barring the way to Satan's influence over them. Satan always finds his way through man's moving away from God's care and protection.

God tells them that He bestows His grace on them and pardons them and does not allow Satan to take them far away. He reminds them of His attributes and that He is much forgiving, forbearing. He does not excommunicate sinners, nor does He visit them with swift punishment if He knows that deep at heart they look up to Him and want to maintain their bonds with Him.

The *sūrah* follows this with a statement of God's determination of life and death. It exposes the false concepts of the unbelievers and warns them against entertaining the same thoughts. It then speaks of values which encourage the believers to be ready and willing to make any sacrifices required of them.

The fact that these verses are included at this point in the *sūrah's* account of the events of the battle, makes it clear that the hypocrites who withdrew from the Muslim army before the battle and the idolaters living in Madinah who continued to maintain ties and relations with the Muslims were the ones who expressed sorrow at the loss of Muslim martyrs at Uḥud. Furthermore, they tried to make use of their deaths, in order to whip up feelings of despair among their families and to exaggerate the sense of loss which they maintained was the direct result of their going forth to fight. There is no doubt that speaking in these terms when the sense of loss among the Muslims was still acute was bound to increase confusion among the Muslims. Hence, the Qur'ān dispels all confusion and provides the right criteria and the correct concepts and values.

The unbelievers said of those who were killed in the Battle of Uḥud: *"Had they stayed with us they would not have died, nor would they have been killed."* (Verse 156) Their statement, however, shows the great gulf between the concepts of those who have faith and those deprived of it and the laws governing human life, whether pleasant or unpleasant. A believer is aware of these laws and God's will, and he accepts it with reassurance because he knows that he will only get what God has determined for him, and that what happens to him was bound to happen and what he may have missed, he could never have achieved anyway. Therefore, he neither panics in a calamity, nor is he overwhelmed with joy when good fortunes smiles on him. He does not regret not having done so and so in order to avoid something or to ensure another. Any alternatives should be considered before taking action. Once action is taken, after full consideration, and according to one's best knowledge and within the framework of what God sanctions, the believer accepts any results with satisfaction and reassurance. In other words, whatever happens must take place according to God's will. There was no way it could have been avoided, although it was he himself who provided its causes. There is a perfect equilibrium between action and acceptance of the results, between positiveness and reliance on God. A person who does not have this type of straightforward faith in God will always remain worried and hesitant, and will always say: "If only …", "Had it not been for…", "I wish that …" and "How sorrowful it is that…"

As God cultivates the Muslim community and points to the lessons they must learn from the Battle of Uḥud and what the Muslims suffered in it, He warns the believers against doing the same thing as the unbelievers. Their sorrow borders on despair every time a relative of theirs dies at work away from home or fighting for God's cause: *"Believers, be not like those who disbelieve and say of their brethren, when they travel on earth or go forth to war, 'Had they stayed with us, they would not have died, nor would they have been killed.' "* They say this because they have a false concept of what takes place in the universe and of the power behind it. They only see superficial circumstances and reasons because they have removed themselves from God.

"So that God places a source of despair in their hearts." They see their brethren travelling abroad in order to earn their living and they die, and they see them going forth to war and they are killed. They feel that in both cases, it was their setting out that had brought about their death or caused them to be killed. They experience a profound sense of sorrow that they did not prevent them from setting forth. They did not appreciate the real reason, namely, that the life span of those who die was over, their deathbeds beckoned them, and that everyone dies by God's will. Had they realised this, they would not have felt such immense sorrow. They would have accepted what God has determined. *"It is God alone Who grants life and causes death."* He grants life and takes it back at the time He has appointed, whether people are at their homes, with their families, or working to earn their living, or fighting for their faith. He rewards people according to what He knows of them: *"God sees all that you do."*

Death, whether natural or in battle, does not represent the end. Life on earth is not the best thing God bestows on people. There are other values and nobler considerations: *"If you should be slain or die in God's cause surely forgiveness by God and His grace are better than all the riches they amass. If you shall die or be slain, it is to God that you shall be gathered."* (Verse 157)

Viewed in this light, natural death or being killed fighting for God's cause, is better than life and superior to all the riches, position and authority people work for. It is superior because it ensures God's forgiveness and grace, and it is to attain these two objectives that God directs the believers. They are not supposed to work for personal glory or for material values. They are to seek what God has in store for them and to work to ensure that God bestows His grace on them.

They will all be gathered to God, whether they die in their beds at home or fending for themselves away from it, or fighting on the battlefield. That is the destiny of all people. Their death comes at the appointed time and they are gathered to God on the Day of Resurrection. They either receive God's grace or suffer His punishment. The most stupid of all is the one who deliberately chooses a miserable destiny when he knows that he will inevitably die at the appointed time.

Thus, the true concept of life and death and God's predestination becomes clear. People are reassured whatever may happen.

9

The Prophet's Message of Compassion

It is by God's grace that you deal gently with them. Had you been harsh and hard-hearted, they would surely have broken away from you. Therefore, pardon them and pray for them to be forgiven and consult with them in the conduct of public affairs. When you have resolved about a course of action, put your trust in God. God loves those who put their trust in Him. (159)

فَبِمَا رَحْمَةٍ مِّنَ ٱللَّهِ لِنتَ لَهُمْ وَلَوْ كُنتَ فَظًّا غَلِيظَ ٱلْقَلْبِ لَٱنفَضُّوا مِنْ حَوْلِكَ فَٱعْفُ عَنْهُمْ وَٱسْتَغْفِرْ لَهُمْ وَشَاوِرْهُمْ فِي ٱلْأَمْرِ فَإِذَا عَزَمْتَ فَتَوَكَّلْ عَلَى ٱللَّهِ إِنَّ ٱللَّهَ يُحِبُّ ٱلْمُتَوَكِّلِينَ ﴿١٥٩﴾

If God helps you, none can overcome you; but if He should forsake you, then who is it that can help you besides Him? It is in God that the believers should put their trust. (160)

إِن يَنصُرْكُمُ ٱللَّهُ فَلَا غَالِبَ لَكُمْ وَإِن يَخْذُلْكُمْ فَمَن ذَا ٱلَّذِى يَنصُرُكُم مِّنۢ بَعْدِهِ وَعَلَى ٱللَّهِ فَلْيَتَوَكَّلِ ٱلْمُؤْمِنُونَ ﴿١٦٠﴾

It does not behove a Prophet to act dishonestly, for he who acts dishonestly shall be faced with his dishonesty on the Day of Resurrection. Everyone will then be paid in full what he has earned, and none shall be wronged. (161)

وَمَا كَانَ لِنَبِيٍّ أَن يَغُلَّ وَمَن يَغْلُلْ يَأْتِ بِمَا غَلَّ يَوْمَ ٱلْقِيَٰمَةِ ثُمَّ تُوَفَّىٰ كُلُّ نَفْسٍ مَّا كَسَبَتْ وَهُمْ لَا يُظْلَمُونَ ﴿١٦١﴾

Can he who strives after God's pleasure be compared to one who has incurred God's wrath and whose abode is hell? How evil such a goal is. (162)

أَفَمَنِ ٱتَّبَعَ رِضْوَانَ ٱللَّهِ كَمَنْ بَآءَ بِسَخَطٍ مِّنَ ٱللَّهِ وَمَأْوَىٰهُ جَهَنَّمُ وَبِئْسَ ٱلْمَصِيرُ ۝

They have different standings in God's sight. God sees all that they do. (163)

هُمْ دَرَجَٰتٌ عِندَ ٱللَّهِ وَٱللَّهُ بَصِيرٌۢ بِمَا يَعْمَلُونَ ۝

Indeed, God bestowed a favour on the believers when He sent them a messenger from among themselves, to recite to them His revelations, and to purify them, and teach them the book and wisdom, whereas before that they were surely in plain error. (164)

لَقَدْ مَنَّ ٱللَّهُ عَلَى ٱلْمُؤْمِنِينَ إِذْ بَعَثَ فِيهِمْ رَسُولًا مِّنْ أَنفُسِهِمْ يَتْلُواْ عَلَيْهِمْ ءَايَٰتِهِۦ وَيُزَكِّيهِمْ وَيُعَلِّمُهُمُ ٱلْكِتَٰبَ وَٱلْحِكْمَةَ وَإِن كَانُواْ مِن قَبْلُ لَفِى ضَلَٰلٍ مُّبِينٍ ۝

Distinctive Marks of the Prophet's Personality

It is by God's grace that you deal gently with them. Had you been harsh and hard-hearted, they would surely have broken away from you. Therefore, pardon them and pray for them to be forgiven and consult with them in the conduct of public affairs. When you have resolved about a course of action, put your trust in God. God loves those who put their trust in Him. (Verse 159)

In the course of the *sūrah*'s commentary on the Battle of Uḥud and the attitudes of the Muslim community and other groups towards the way events developed both prior to and during that battle, a few verses are included about the noble personality of Muḥammad, God's Messenger (pbuh) and the importance of his status as a Prophet to the life of the Muslim community. This

262

demonstrates much of the grace God has bestowed on the Muslim community. While the Prophet's personality is the known theme of the following verses, certain lines also explain the Islamic method in organising the Muslim community, the basis of this organisation, as well as some basic elements of Islamic philosophy and its importance to human life generally.

We can appreciate the great aspect of Divine grace represented by the high moral standards of the Prophet and his fine manners. He had an easy, gentle, lenient and compassionate nature, which attracted people and established real bonds among them. We also find in this short passage the basic principle governing the life of the Muslim community, namely, consultative government. We have here a clear order to implement this principle of consultation. It is worthy of note that this order is given at a time when consultation appears to have led to bitter consequences. Coupled with the principle of consultative government is that of firm resolution, of implementing, without hesitation, whatever has been decided after consultation. To these two principles is added the most important value of placing our trust in God. There is a distinct conceptual, practical and organisational complementarity provided by these three principles. Moreover, the essence of God's will and predestination is explained here. All matters start with Him and return to Him. His will is supreme in conducting events and determining results. The passage also warns against treachery and greed, and distinguishes between those who follow what pleases God and those who incur His wrath. This provides a criterion with which to evaluate gains and losses. The passage concludes by emphasising the great bounty God has bestowed on this nation in the form of the message conveyed by the Prophet. Compared to this bounty, everything else appears so small and all suffering can easily be tolerated.

It is by God's grace that you deal gently with them. Had you been harsh and hard-hearted, they would surely have broken away from you. Therefore, pardon them and pray for them to be forgiven and consult with them in the conduct of public affairs. When you have resolved about a course of action, put your trust in God. God loves those who put their trust in Him.

At this point, the *sūrah* addresses the Prophet who must have felt uneasy towards his people. Initially they had been enthusiastic to meet their enemy outside Madinah. Shortly afterwards confusion crept into their ranks and one-third of the army withdrew, before the battle had even commenced. Later, they disobeyed his express order and yielded to the temptation of the loot. They weakened when they heard the rumour of his death. Defeated at heart, they turned on their heels, leaving him with a handful of his Companions and the net result was that he was wounded. He remained steadfast at their rear, calling them to persevere, while they paid no heed to anyone. The Divine address provides consolation to the Prophet and tells the Muslims of God's limitless grace, manifested in Him sending the Prophet to them. It reminds them of the fact that God has shown them great mercy in giving the Prophet a compassionate nature which makes people's hearts turn towards him.

The purpose of this address is to enhance the Prophet's compassion so that he overcomes what disappointment he may feel at their actions. For their part, they will realise how important it is to them that the Prophet is so compassionate. The Divine address tells the Prophet to pardon his Companions and to pray to God to forgive them. He is also called upon to take counsel with them on how important matters should be conducted, in the same way as he consulted them. The consequences of Uḥud must not be allowed to suspend or override the principle of consultative government which is fundamental to Islamic life.

"It is by God's grace that you deal gently with them. Had you been harsh and hard-hearted, they would surely have broken away from you." God's grace was indeed shown to the Prophet and his Companions. It is demonstrated by the fact that the Prophet himself had a compassionate nature which prompted him to take a lenient and gentle attitude towards them. Had he been hard of heart, he would not have won their hearts, nor would they have gathered around him.

People always need compassion, care, a cheerful face and patient forbearance which is not exhausted by other people's ignorance and weakness. People need someone with a large heart who gives them all he can but asks nothing of them, who shares with them their worries without burdening them with his own. They need someone who will always be caring, sympathetic, loving, content and forbearing. God's Messenger had all these characteristics and these were the distinctive aspects of his life among his Companions. He was never angry with anyone; nor was he ever impatient because of their weaknesses. Never did he take for himself anything of the enjoyments of this world; on the contrary, he gave them all that he possessed with a smile and a cheerful heart. His forbearance, compassion, care and sympathy were extended to all. Everyone who came into contact with the Prophet was full of love for him because of what he generously gave of his love.

All this was by God's grace, which He extended to the Prophet and his followers. God reminds them of this grace at this particular moment so as to build on it something which is essential to the life of the Muslim community: *"Therefore, pardon them and pray for them to be forgiven and consult with them in the conduct of public affairs."*

Consultation: The Essence of Islamic Government

We have here a distinctive order: *"Consult with them on the conduct of public affairs."* This principle, which is basic to the Islamic system of government, is established here, even when Muḥammad himself, God's Messenger, is the one who conducts public affairs. This is, then, a definitive statement which leaves the Muslim community in no doubt that consultation is central to Islamic government. Without it, no system is truly Islamic. What form this consultation takes and how the principle is implemented are matters which can be adapted to the prevailing conditions of any particular Islamic society. Any forms and mechanisms which ensure that consultation is really, not superficially, practised are acceptable to Islam.

The decisive order, *"consult with them on the conduct of public affairs"* is issued by God to the Prophet at a time when consultation appears to have produced bitter results. Appearances suggested that it was due to consultation that disunity crept in among the Muslims during the events leading to the Battle of Uḥud. By way of a reminder, one group wanted the Muslims to stay in Madinah, where they could easily repel any enemy attacks. Another group wanted to fight the unbelievers outside the city. The resulting disunity was clearly apparent when 'Abdullāh ibn Ubayy ibn Salūl withdrew with no less than one-third of the army, when the enemy was knocking at the gates of Madinah. Moreover, the plan adopted for the defence of Madinah did not appear to be the most sound from a military point of view. It was at variance with what had been learnt from past experience. The Muslims did, however adopt the opposite strategy in the following battle, staying in Madinah and digging a moat around it. Thus, they showed that they had benefited by the lessons of Uḥud.

The Prophet himself was not unaware of the serious consequences which would result from moving out. As a prophet, whose dreams always came true, he had seen in a dream that one of his own household would be killed, and that a number of his Companions would fall in battle. He also said that the dream indicated that Madinah was akin to an impregnable fortress. Under the circumstances, he was entitled to overturn the decision made on the basis of consultation. However, he preferred to go ahead with that decision because the practical establishment of the fundamental principle of consultation, and allowing the Muslim community to learn hard lessons through its implementation, was more important than avoiding temporary setbacks.

It would have been understandable if the Prophet, as the leader, had abrogated the whole principle of consultation after the battle, in view of the division and defeat it had caused. Islam was, however, cultivating a whole nation and preparing it to assume its natural role of the leadership of mankind. God knew that the best method to achieve that purpose was for the community to be educated through consultation and to be trained to take responsibility for its decisions. It was expected to err, and indeed to make serious mistakes, in order to learn how to correct its errors and to face up to their consequences. How else could it be trained to make the right decision? Losses can be borne if the net result makes the whole nation understand its responsibilities and able to shoulder them. Avoiding errors does not benefit a community, if it means that the community continues to enjoy supervision and protection. True, it could avoid material losses, but it would lose its personality and its ability to face up to all events. It would be in the same position as a child who is not trained to walk so that it may be spared the falls involved in that training, or to save the price of a pair of shoes.

It was necessary for Islam to allow the Muslim community to achieve maturity so as to prepare it for its role of leadership. There was no alternative but to allow it to practise its role, without patronage or protection, during the Prophet's lifetime and under his guidance. It may be suggested that the presence of wise leadership makes consultation superfluous and should dispense with the practical training of the Muslim community. Wise leadership should have been allowed to make its own decisions on serious matters. Such an assumption is totally false. Had it been true, the very presence of Muḥammad (pbuh), equipped with Divine revelation, would have been sufficient to deprive the Muslim community at that time of its right to consultation, especially in the light of its bitter consequences at Uḥud. Neither the presence of God's Messenger, equipped as he was with Divine revelation, nor the events and complications that took place were enough to suspend the right of the community to be consulted. God, limitless is He in His Glory, knew that consultation must be practised in the most serious of matters, regardless of the consequences, losses and sacrifices. All these were but a small price for the attainment of maturity by the Muslim community, its training in the conduct of its affairs, to bear its responsibilities and accept the consequences of its decision. Hence the Divine commandment at this particular point in the life of the young Muslim community: *"Therefore, pardon them and pray for them to be forgiven and consult with them in the conduct of public affairs."* Thus, the principle is established, despite the risks that may attend its implementation. The flimsy argument which is often raised in favour of abrogating this principle of consultation is rejected outright. The maturity of the nation cannot be achieved without putting this principle into effect. For the community to achieve its maturity is far more important and far more valuable than any loss that may be incurred in the process.

The true picture of the Islamic system does not appear complete unless we examine the rest of the verse, to discover that consultation is never allowed to lead to hesitation and delay. Nor does it replace the need to rely ultimately on God: *"When you have resolved upon a course of action, put your trust in God. God loves those who put their trust in Him."*

The role of consultation is to examine all views and select a particular course of action. When the process reaches this stage, consultation must give way to implementation with resolve and decisiveness, placing trust in God. Thus, God's will determines the outcome as He pleases.

The Prophet not only gave the Muslim community the lesson of consultation, he also gave it a second lesson as he willingly and seriously implemented the decision made and placed his trust in God. He gave his order to the Muslims to get ready to march and prepared himself to do so by putting on his body armour, even though he was aware of what awaited them all in terms of suffering and sacrifice. As will be recalled, there were those who feared that in all this they might have imposed on the Prophet a course of action of which he did not approve. Therefore, they put the matter back to him and assured him of their obedience whatever he decided. Nevertheless, even with this second opportunity, the Prophet did not reverse his decision. He wanted to teach them the whole lesson of consultation and resolve, combined with complete reliance on God and submission to His will. He wanted them to realise that there was a specific time for consultation, but once a decision was taken there could be no room for hesitation and starting the process anew. That could only perpetuate the state of indecision.

"God loves those who put their trust in Him." This is a distinctive quality of the believers. Reliance on God, putting our trust in Him and submitting to His will constitute the final line which maintains the proper balance in Islamic philosophy and Islamic life. Ultimate authority belongs to God and He does what He chooses.

This was one of the great lessons which the Battle of Uḥud taught the Muslim community. It remains a lesson to be learnt by every new generation of Muslims.

When God's Help Is Withdrawn

In order to explain what placing one's trust in God means, the *sūrah* clearly states that the power which determines victory or defeat is God's. It is from Him that support should be sought and through His help defeat is avoided. Once the believers have made their preparations and mobilised all the forces they can muster, they turn to God for help, rely fully on Him and recognise that they have no say in determining the consequences. It is God's will that determines the outcome: *"If God helps you, none can overcome you; but if He should forsake you, then who is it that can help you beside Him? It is in God that the believers should place their trust."* (Verse 160)

The Islamic concept of life demonstrates the perfect balance between asserting that God's will is absolute in shaping all events and that it comes into operation through man's own actions. The Divine law of nature establishes a cause and effect relationship in all matters, but causes do not initiate effects. The operative force is that of God, Who determines effects on the basis of causes according to His will. He then requires man to work hard, fulfil his duties, and meet his obligations. It is in relation to how far man discharges his responsibility that God determines the results. This means that results and consequences will always be dependent on God's will, for it is He alone who brings them into being whenever and however He wills. An equilibrium is thus established between the basic concept of a Muslim and his actions. He works as hard as he can and knows that the results of his actions depend on God's will. To him, there is no inevitability in the cause and effect relationship, because he does not claim that anything which God does is inevitable.

In the particular case of a military battle and its two possible results, victory or defeat, the *sūrah* refers Muslims to God's will and reminds them of His might. If God helps them, then they cannot be overcome by any force, and if His help is not forthcoming, then they will not be able to find anyone to bring them victory. This is the absolute truth: there is no ability, power or will other than those of God, Who determines all events. This basic truth, however, does not exempt Muslims from following God's method, obeying His directives and fulfilling their obligations, exerting all efforts and relying, after all that, on God alone: *"It is in God that the believers should put their trust."* (Verse 160) Thus, a Muslim does not seek anything from any source other than God. He has a direct relationship with the operative power in the universe, which means that he is in no need of help or protection from any other source. He relies totally on God to bring about events and results according to His wisdom. As for him, he accepts what God determines with total reassurance. This is a perfect bliss which no human being can experience except through Islam.

The *sūrah* refers again to the moral qualities associated with the Prophet, in order to stress the importance of honesty and to forbid deceit and cheating. It reminds people that they will have to account for their deeds and that everyone will be given his fair reward: *"It does not behove a prophet to act dishonestly, for he who acts dishonestly shall be faced with his dishonesty on the Day of Resurrection. Everyone will then be paid in full what he has earned, and none shall be wronged."* (Verse 161)

One of the reasons which tempted the archers in the Battle of Uḥud to abandon their positions on top of the hill, was that they feared that the Prophet might not give them a share of the spoils of war. Some of the hypocrites had earlier suggested that a portion of the spoils of war the Muslims collected at Badr had disappeared. They were so impudent as to even mention the Prophet by name in this connection. Here, the *sūrah* delivers a general statement which makes it clear that no prophet could ever act dishonestly. No prophet would take money, or a portion of the spoils for himself or his family, or give one section of the army more of the spoils than another, or commit any deceitful action whatsoever: *"It does not behove a prophet to act dishonestly."* This is inconceivable. Dishonesty is against the very nature of prophethood; it is repugnant to all prophets. The use of the negative here does not mean that it is not lawful for a prophet to act dishonestly, but to make it plain that it is both inconceivable and impossible that a prophet would ever do so. A prophet is by nature honest, just and well-contented. Hence, to be dishonest is to act against his own nature. It is perhaps useful to add that according to the reading of Imām Al-Ḥasan al-Baṣrī of this verse, the passive voice is used here, which means that it is totally unlawful that a prophet should be deceived, or that his followers allow themselves to hide something from him. This interpretation fits perfectly with the rest of the verse. Those who are dishonest and try to take something which belongs to the public treasury, or keep for themselves what booty they may be able to lay their hands upon, are issued with this fearful warning: *"He who acts dishonestly shall be faced with his dishonesty on the Day of Resurrection. Everyone will then be paid in full what he has earned, and none shall be wronged."*

Imām Aḥmad relates that God's Messenger appointed a man called Ibn al-Lutaibah, from the tribe of Azd, to collect *zakāt*. When he had completed his mission, he came back and said: "This belongs to you, and this has been given to me as a gift." God's Messenger said from the pulpit: "How is it that a person whom we send to complete a certain assignment says: 'This belongs to you and this I have been given as a gift?' Let him stay in his parents' home and find out whether any gift will be given to him? By Him

Who holds Muḥammad's soul in His hand, anyone of you who does this will come on the Day of Resurrection carrying that thing on his shoulders, even though it may be a camel, a cow or a lamb making its particular noise." The Prophet then lifted his hands until his armpits were visible and said: "My Lord, have I conveyed Your message?" He repeated this three times. (Related by Al-Bukhārī and Muslim.)

Abū Umayyah reports: God's Messenger mentioned dishonesty as he was addressing us. He described how serious it was, and said: "Let me not see anyone of you on the Day of Resurrection carrying on his shoulder a camel making noise, and say: 'Messenger of God, help me.' I will then say to him: 'I have no power to help you against God's judgement. I have conveyed to you God's orders.' Let me not see any one of you come on the Day of Resurrection carrying a snorting horse on his shoulders, appealing to me: 'Messenger of God, help me.' I will say to him: 'I cannot help you against God's judgement. I have conveyed to you His orders.' Let me not see anyone of you on the Day of Resurrection carrying a dumb load of gold and silver on his shoulders and appealing to me: 'Messenger of God help me.' I will say to him: 'I cannot help you against God's judgement. I have conveyed to you His orders.'" (Related by Al-Bukhārī, Muslim and Aḥmad.)

The Prophet is reported to have said: "Anyone who does an assignment for us and conceals even a needle, or anything bigger, acts dishonestly. He will be faced with his dishonesty on the Day of Judgement." A black man from the *Anṣār* (whose name is, according to Mujāhid, Saʿd ibn 'Ubādah) said: "Messenger of God, accept from me what you have assigned to me." The Prophet said: "What do you mean?" He said: "I have heard what you have just said." The Prophet said: "And I repeat it entirely: Whoever does an assignment for us, let him bring it all, big or small. Let him take what he is given and leave alone what he is not given." (Related by Muslim, Aḥmad and Abū Dawūd.)

This Qur'ānic verse, in conjunction with the Prophet's *ḥadīths*, has worked wonders in the moulding of the Muslim community, and made it unique in the value it attaches to honesty and the repugnance with which it views deceit and cheating. An ordinary Muslim may, in war, lay his hand on something valuable when no one is watching him. If he does, he should take it to his commander, entertaining no thought of keeping it for himself, so that he does not expose himself to what this Qur'ānic verse says, and so that he does not meet the Prophet on the Day of Resurrection in such a shameful condition. To a Muslim, the hereafter is a reality. He cannot see himself coming face to face with the Prophet and standing in front of God, as the Prophet has described. Hence, he knows that this will not happen. This is the secret of his scrupulous nature. The hereafter is to him part of the reality he lives, not a remote promise or threat. He entertains no doubt that everyone will be rewarded for what he does, and that everyone will be paid in full what they earn.

In his comprehensive book on history, Al-Ṭabarī reports that when the Muslims conquered Al-Madā'in and collected the spoils of war, a man came with something to give to the one in charge of those spoils. He and his assistants said: "We have never seen anyone like this man. None of our people can be compared to him." They asked him: "Have you taken any part of it for yourself?" The man answered: "By God, had it not been for my fear of God, I would not have given it to you." They asked him his name, but he said: "I am not telling you or anyone else my name in order to be praised. I praise God and I am content with His reward." When he left, they sent one of them to follow him until he arrived in his camp. He enquired about him and they learnt that he was called 'Āmir ibn 'Abd Qais.

After the Battle of Qādisiyyah, the spoils of war were sent to 'Umar in Madinah. Included in them was the crown of the Persian Emperor and his throne. They were priceless. 'Umar looked at them happily and said: "Soldiers who tender this to their ruler are certainly honest."

This is how Islam moulded the Muslim community. When we hear such stories, we may think them legends. But the fact is that there is no legend in all this; it was the plain reality.

A Great Favour Done to Believers

Within the framework of keenness to have a share in the spoils of war, which was the direct cause of the defeat at Uḥud, and dishonesty in general, the *sūrah* underlines the proper values, on which a believer's attention must be focused: *"Can he who strives after God's pleasure be compared to one who has incurred God's wrath and whose abode is hell? How evil such a goal is."* (Verse 162)

272

There is no doubt that God's pleasure is the prize to be coveted, and the winning of which determines whether one's efforts are profitable or end in utter loss. The gulf is great between the one who pursues God's pleasure until he wins it and the one who ends up incurring God's displeasure, which leads him to hell. The two have greatly different standings with God: *"They have different standings in God's sight."* (Verse 163) Each actually earns his position, which means that there is no favouritism and none is wronged: *"God sees all that they do."* (Verse 163)

This part of the *sūrah* concludes with a reference back to the personality of God's Messenger, his message, and the fact that it represents a great favour bestowed by God on the believers: *"Indeed, God bestowed a favour on the believers when He sent them a messenger from among themselves, to recite to them His revelations, and to purify them, and teach them the book and wisdom, whereas before that they were surely in plain error."* (Verse 164)

This reference to the Prophet's role in bringing the Muslim community into existence, and in moulding, educating and leading it out of a state of error to become a nation endowed with knowledge, wisdom and purity is clearly emphasised. It is typical of the Qurʾānic method of moulding the Muslim community that this reference is made in the context of defeat, pain, and loss suffered at Uḥud. All worldly gains, indeed all the riches of the world, and all the suffering and sacrifices that the Muslims may be called upon to endure seem very petty compared with the great favour God has done to mankind when He sent them His Messenger.

The practical effects of this favour, which can be seen in the life of the Muslim community, are then mentioned: *"…to recite to them His revelations, and to purify them, and to teach them the book and wisdom, whereas before that they were surely in plain error."* These effects represent a total transformation of the Muslim community. God is preparing this community to play a great role in the leadership of mankind, and this requires that a messenger be sent to them. A nation with such a mission should not be preoccupied with petty gains that it can make in a battle and should not be reluctant to make sacrifices. Great goals cannot be achieved without sacrifice.

"Indeed, God bestowed a favour on the believers when He sent them a messenger from among themselves." The fact that God

Almighty cared to send a messenger to a particular species of His creation, is a favour which can only be motivated by His limitless grace. It is a favour that cannot be returned in any way by the recipients. Who are those human beings whom God has chosen for such grace, so as to be the recipients of His revelations? Indeed, God bestows His grace on His creation even when they have not earned that grace, and can never return it.

The favour is made even greater by the fact that this messenger is *"from among themselves."* We should reflect that the Qur'ānic text did not say "a messenger from them." For him to be *"from among themselves"* is especially significant, because it identifies that the relationship between the believers and the messenger is one of human souls, not a relationship between an individual and a race. The question is not merely that the Prophet was one of them, it is far more significant than that. With faith, they establish their unique relationship with the Prophet and a great position of favour with God. That means that it is a double favour; sending the messenger, and establishing the relationship which exists between believers and the Prophet.

The first and greatest of the effects of this favour on the lives of the believers is referred to in the statement describing the Prophet's role: *"To recite to them His revelations."* When we remember that God Himself addresses man with His own words, to speak to him about His majesty, and to explain His attributes, and the nature and qualities of Godhead, we may begin to appreciate how great God's favour is. Let man reflect that God tells him about himself, an insignificant creature. He speaks to him about his life, feelings, actions and abilities in order to tell him what brings about a truly happy life and what sets him on the way to achieving the greatest of human goals, namely, admission to Paradise, which is far greater than the heavens and the earth. Such a favour can come only from God's grace, which is infinite indeed.

God the Almighty has no need for mankind, or indeed for any creature. Man, on the other hand, is poor and powerless. He needs God. But it is God Who bestows on man His favours and grace, and calls on him to adopt what brings about a total transformation in his life. Nothing that man can do is sufficient to thank God for His grace.

The Purification of a Model Community

The role of the Messenger is also *"to purify them"*. This purification touches their hearts, affects their homes, honour and worship, and characterises their lives, community and social systems. He purges them of all traces of polytheism, idol worship, and superstition and all that is associated with these, of rituals, habits and traditions which are unworthy of man. Human life is thus purged of all traces of ignorance and its effects on values, principles and social traditions.

Every type of ignorant community, including the Arabs at that time, entertained its own evil aspects. These evils were highlighted by Jaʿfar ibn Abī Ṭālib, a cousin of the Prophet, when he addressed Negus, the ruler of Abyssinia. A number of Muslims had sought refuge in Abyssinia, but the Quraysh sent a delegation which requested its ruler to extradite them. He called in the Muslim refugees to put their case. Their spokesman, Jaʿfar, made his statement in the following terms:

"We have been ignorant people who worshipped idols, ate carrion, committed all gross indecencies, severed relations with our kinsfolk, were unkind to our neighbours, and the strong among us usurped the rights of the weak. We continued in this state of affairs until God sent us a Messenger from among ourselves, who was known to us in respect of his good family position, and truthfulness, honesty and integrity. He called upon us to worship God alone, associate no partners with Him, to abandon what we and our forefathers used to worship alongside Him of stones and statues. He has commanded us to be truthful in what we say, honest, kind to our relatives and neighbours, and to refrain from sin and from killing one another. He has forbidden us every aspect of indecency, perjury, devouring what belongs to orphans, and accusing chaste women of committing adultery. He has bidden us to worship God alone, associate no partners with Him, attend to our Prayers, spend in charity [*zakāt*], and fast."

Another aspect of the evil customs that prevailed in ignorant Arabia is described by ʿĀʾishah, the Prophet's wife, as she gives this account of relations between the sexes. This report is given in Al-Bukhārī's *Ṣaḥīḥ*, the most authentic collection of the Prophet's *ḥadīths*: "There were four types of relations between men and women in the days of ignorance. One of these was the same as the marital relationships of today: a man may make a proposal of marriage to another man's daughter or some other girl in his charge. He pays her a dower and marries her. A second type was that a man said to his wife after she finishes her menstrual period: 'Go to so and so ... [he names a certain man] and get pregnant by him.' He himself stops having intercourse with her until she is manifestly pregnant by the man he named. When she becomes heavy with the child, her husband may have intercourse with her if he so desires. He resorts to this method because of his desire to have a son of superior blood. A third form is that a number of men, less than ten, shared the same woman, every one of them having intercourse with her. If she got pregnant and gave birth to a child, she sent to them asking them to come over to her a few days after delivery. None of them could absent himself from that meeting. She would say to them: 'You are aware of what has passed between us. Now that I have given birth to a child, this child is the son of ... .' She chose whoever she fancied to be the father. He could not disown that child. The fourth type was that of prostitution. Any number of men may associate with a woman who would not refuse anyone who came to her. Prostitutes used to put some sort of a flag on their doors, to indicate that they welcomed any man. If such a prostitute gave birth to a child, they collected some money for her and they called in a physiognomist to determine the father of that child. The child was then named after that man who did not decline to claim it."

This contemptible, derogatory state of affairs needs no comment. It is sufficient to imagine a man sending his wife to another man to get pregnant by him, in the same way as he sends his female camel or horse or other animal for good breeding. It is sufficient to imagine a number of men, less than ten, having intercourse with the same woman and then allowing her to choose one of them to be the father of her child. As for prostitution, it is the same everywhere. In this particular case, however, the child born to a prostitute is named after a particular adulterer. He finds no disgrace in this and does not disclaim the child. Had it not been for Islam and its purifying principles, the Arabs would have continued to live in such squalor.

All this, however, is only one aspect of the contempt which was preserved for women in the pre-Islamic days of ignorance. In his valuable work, *Islam and the World*, Abul Hasan Ali Nadwi says:

The lot of women was extremely lamentable in pre-Islamic Arabia. The right of inheritance was denied to them. Widowed and divorced women were not permitted to remarry. It was a common practice for the eldest son to take as wives his father's widows, inherited as property with the rest of the estate. Discrimination was made against them even in matters of food, men reserving certain dishes for themselves. Daughters were buried alive at birth. Pride and poverty had introduced the abominable crime of female infanticide among all the Arabian tribes. Haitham ibn ʿAdī tells us that one out of every ten men was guilty of it. Kind-hearted tribal chiefs often bought infant girls to save their lives. Ṣaʿsaʿa says that before the dawn of Islam he had rescued as many as 300 girls from that terrible fate by paying compensatory money to their fathers. Sometimes a young girl who had escaped being killed at birth or during childhood, due to her father being away from home or some other reason, would be treacherously taken to a lonely spot by her father and done to death. Several incidents of this nature were narrated from their past lives by the companions of the Prophet after they had embraced Islam.[1]

These accounts give us a glimpse of the evils from which Islam saved the Arabs and purified them.

Idolatry and Human Dignity

All systems based on ignorance of God have their evils and debased practices. Perhaps the most prominent among these in pre-Islamic Arabia was idol-worship as described by Nadwi:

The belief in an overruling Providence had grown very feeble among them (the Arabs of pre-Islamic days). It was confined to a select few, while the religion of the great mass of them was gross idolatry. The idols that had originally been introduced to serve as devotional media had become elevated to the status of divinity. Homage was still paid to one transcendent God, but only verbally; in their hearts a host of deities were enthroned, whose goodwill they sought to propitiate, and displeasure avert.

---

1. Abul Hasan Ali Nadwi, *Islam and the World*, Lucknow, 1973, pp. 30–1. (The author has referred to Shaykh Nadwi's *Mādhā Khasira al-ʿAlam bi Inḥiṭāṭ al-Muslimīn*), while the work cited by us is an abridged English translation of the above – Translators).

Each tribe, city, and locality had its own god. Al-Kalbī has stated that every household in Makkah had its own idol. When a Makkan started on a journey, his last act at home would be to invoke the blessings of the family deity, and the first thing he did on his return was to pay reverence to it.

People used to vie with one another in collecting idols and constructing temples for them. Those who could afford neither planted a slab of stone in front of the Ka'bah and performed the ritual of circumambulation around it. Such stones were called *ansāb*. In the words of Abū Rijā' al-'Uṭāridī, as reported in the *Ṣaḥīḥ* of Al-Bukhārī, "We worshipped stones. When we found a better stone than the one we had, we took it up and threw away the old one. Where no stones were available, we made a mound of sand, milked a goat over it and worshipped it." When a traveller halted at a place, he used to collect four stones, worshipped the most beautiful of them and used the other three to rest his pots on for cooking.

Angels, stars, jinns (spirits) and all the rest of the objects of veneration found in polytheistic faiths were adored as divine beings by the Arabs. The angels, they believed, were daughters of God, whom they besought to intercede with Him on their behalf, while jinns were regarded as partners of the Almighty in the practical control of the world.

Al-Kalbī says that Banū Malīḥ, a branch of the tribe of Khuzā'ah, worshipped the jinns; and Sā'id reports that the tribe of Ḥimyar worshipped the sun; the tribe of Kinānah adored the moon; the tribe of Tamīm worshipped al-Dabarān; the Lakhm and the Judhām, Ṭā'ī, Banū Qais and Banū Asad worshipped Jupiter, Canopus, the Dog Star and Mercury, respectively.[2]

A quick look at this crude, primitive form of polytheism is sufficient to give a good idea of the sort of feelings, principles and practices it generated. We can also appreciate the great transformation Islam managed to bring about in the lives of the Arabs. It purified their thoughts and their lives of those evils which gave rise to the sort of social and moral ills which prevailed in their

---

2. *Ibid.*, pp. 29–30.

society and in which they took pride. Drinking, gambling and tribal vengeance were their highest preoccupations. Countless poems boastfully described their indulgence in such practices. Shaikh Nadwi says in *Islam and the World*:

> War, in some respects, was a necessity for them, but more than that, it was a fun .... A most trivial incident could touch off a bitter inter-tribal war. The war, for instance, between the descendants of Wā'il, Bakr and Taghlib dragged on for full forty years. There were innumerable casualties in this war. An Arab chief, Muhalhil, has depicted the consequences of this war thus: "Both the tribes have been exterminated; mothers have become childless; children have become orphans; the flow of tears does not cease; the dead are not buried."[3]

The same can be said of the war known as Dāḥis and Al-Ghabrā'. What caused this war to flare up was that Dāḥis, a horse belonging to Qais ibn Zuhair, was leading in a race arranged between the horses of Qais and Ḥudhayfah ibn Badr, with bets placed on which horse will be the winner. A tribesman of Asad, on instructions from Ḥudhaifah, hit the face of the leading horse and this allowed other horses to catch up and pass him by. A killing followed and vengeance was sought. Both tribes tried to revenge the killing of their murdered children. Many were taken captive. Tribes were displaced and thousands were killed.

All this was evidence of the fact that their lives had no worthy preoccupation. They used up their energy in such trivialities. They never thought of what sort of role they should play in improving human life. They had no faith to purify them from such social evils. Without faith, people can easily sink to such debasement.

Ignorance remains the same. Every form of ignorance has its own manifestations of debasement, regardless of where and when it exists. When people live without a Divine faith or code to regulate their lives, they sink into some form of ignorance. We can easily draw parallels between the ignorance prevalent in our modern world and that which prevailed in pre-Islamic Arabia, or with other contemporary forms

---

3. *Ibid.*, pp. 31–2.

elsewhere in the world. It was only through Islam that Arabia was saved from and purified of that ignorance.

Humanity lives today in a great quagmire of vice. We have only to look at the media, the cinema, the fashion industry, beauty competitions, dancing places, public houses, and the widespread use of pornography in literature and art. Combined with the fact that its economic system is based on usury, which entails a materialism that motivates people's greed and the desire to become rich, even if they have to resort to cheating, embezzlement and other immoral methods. The moral and social fabric of society is also undermined. Doubt and cynicism have affected every individual, family, system and community. It is sufficient to cast a quick glance at all this to realise that the ignorance which prevails in our own world is leading humanity to an awful doom.

Man's humanity is wearing thin as people continue to seek animal pleasures. Indeed, animals have a standard of life which is cleaner and purer. They are governed by a serious law of nature which is applicable to them. They do not become debased as man does when he breaks loose, away from faith and its discipline, resorting to ignorance, from which God has saved him by His grace. God reminds His servants of this favour in the verse which states: *"God bestowed a favour on the believers when He sent them a messenger from among themselves to recite to them His revelations, and to purify them, and to teach them the book and wisdom..."*

Nationalism and Islamic Identity

"And to teach them the book and wisdom." Those addressed by this verse were illiterate in every sense of the word. Not only did they not read and write, but their illiteracy was intellectual as well. According to international standards of knowledge, they lagged behind in every field. Their preoccupations were not of the sort which encouraged or increased knowledge. When they received this message, they experienced a great transformation which made them pass it on to the rest of the world. It endowed them with great wisdom. They became the standard-bearers of an intellectual and social philosophy which was destined to save humanity from the depths of ignorance into which it had sunk. The same doctrine is about to play its role again, God willing, to save humanity anew

from its contemporary ignorance, an ignorance which shares with past forms the same moral and social characteristics, as it sets the same goals and objectives for human life, despite the great material advances of science and industry and the affluence such advances have brought about.

"Whereas before that they were surely in plain error." They were certainly in error with regard to concepts and beliefs, goals and objectives, habits and practices, systems and standards, as well as moral and social values. The Arabs, addressed for the first time by this verse, undoubtedly remembered what their lives were like and fully appreciated the total transformation brought about by Islam. They recognised that without Islam they would never have attained the high standards to which Islam elevated them. Such a transformation is totally unique in human history. They recognised that it was through Islam that they moved directly from the tribal stage, with all its petty concerns and narrow-mindedness, to become not merely a nation in the fullest sense of the word, but a nation to lead humanity and to set for it its ideals and systems.

They recognised that only through Islam had they acquired their national, cultural, and intellectual character. Most importantly, Islam gave them their human character, which elevated them to a position of honour through God's grace. They established their whole life on the basis of this honour and, subsequently, imparted it to the world, and taught it how to respect man and give him the position of honour God has granted him. In this they were the leaders. There was no one ahead of them, not in Arabia, not anywhere. The reference to consultative government which we discussed earlier brings out one aspect of this Divine system.

They also realised that only through Islam had they a message to present to mankind. It involved a doctrine and a system by which to mould human life. All these are basic essentials for the existence of a nation which wants to play an important role on life's stage.

The Islamic faith, its concepts of life and existence, its laws and regulation of human life, and its practical code which ensures man's happiness, were the credentials which the Arabs presented to the world and by which they earned the respect and leadership of mankind. Neither at present nor in future will they ever have any other credentials. They have no message other than Islam to give them a position in the world. The choice they have to face is either to be the standard-bearers of the message of Islam, through which they earn recognition and honour, or to abandon it and go back to their earlier position when no one recognised them. The Arabs should ask themselves what they can give to humanity when they abandon the message of Islam.

Do they offer any great achievements in literature and art? Many nations are far ahead of them in these fields, which are of secondary importance. Nations of the world will not wait for any Arab genius to make his contribution, because the need for such a contribution is not felt by anyone. Can they offer any great industrial advance to win the respect of the world and to compete in international markets? Many a nation has taken the lead over the Arabs in this respect as well. Or can they offer any social, economic, or organisational philosophy of their own? Such philosophies, with varying practical effects, are abundant in our world. What can the Arabs, then, give to mankind in order to win a leading position which commands respect and demonstrates their excellence? They can offer nothing except their great message and unique system. This is the great favour which God has bestowed on them and favoured them with as its standard-bearers. It is the message with which God saved mankind from ignorance. Today, mankind desperately needs this message to save itself from the abyss of misery and worry into which it is sinking.

This message is the identity card of the Arabs, which they presented to the world in the past, and thereby commanded its respect. They can present it anew in order to save themselves and save the world. Every great nation has a message, and the greatness of the nation is commensurate to the greatness of its message and system. The Arabs have this great message in their custody. They are its standard-bearers, while other nations are their partners in it. What devil turns them away from their great role and their infinite wealth? It is their duty to chase the devil and resist his temptation and render his actions hopeless and futile.

I O

Priorities Defined

Why, when a calamity befell you, after you had inflicted twice as much [on your enemy], did you exclaim, "How has this come about?" Say: "It has come from your own selves. Surely, God has the power over all things." (165)

That which befell you, on the day when the two hosts met in battle, happened by God's leave, so that He may mark out the true believers. (166)

And [He might] mark out the hypocrites. When these were told, "Come, fight in God's cause", or "Defend yourselves", they answered, "Had we known there would be a fight, we would certainly have followed you." On that day they were nearer unbelief than faith, uttering with their mouths something different to what was in their hearts, but God knew full well all that they tried to conceal. (167)

أَوَلَمَّآ أَصَابَتْكُم مُّصِيبَةٌ قَدْ أَصَبْتُم مِّثْلَيْهَا قُلْتُمْ أَنَّىٰ هَٰذَا قُلْ هُوَ مِنْ عِندِ أَنفُسِكُمْ إِنَّ ٱللَّهَ عَلَىٰ كُلِّ شَيْءٍ قَدِيرٌ ۝١٦٥

وَمَآ أَصَابَكُمْ يَوْمَ ٱلْتَقَى ٱلْجَمْعَانِ فَبِإِذْنِ ٱللَّهِ وَلِيَعْلَمَ ٱلْمُؤْمِنِينَ ۝١٦٦

وَلِيَعْلَمَ ٱلَّذِينَ نَافَقُواْ وَقِيلَ لَهُمْ تَعَالَوْاْ قَٰتِلُواْ فِي سَبِيلِ ٱللَّهِ أَوِ ٱدْفَعُواْ قَالُواْ لَوْ نَعْلَمُ قِتَالًا لَّٱتَّبَعْنَٰكُمْ هُمْ لِلْكُفْرِ يَوْمَئِذٍ أَقْرَبُ مِنْهُمْ لِلْإِيمَٰنِ يَقُولُونَ بِأَفْوَٰهِهِم مَّا لَيْسَ فِي قُلُوبِهِمْ وَٱللَّهُ أَعْلَمُ بِمَا يَكْتُمُونَ ۝١٦٧

283

Such were they who, having themselves stayed behind, said of their brothers: "If only they had listened to us, they would not have been slain." Say to them: "Ward off death from yourselves, then, if what you say be true." (168)

ٱلَّذِينَ قَالُوا۟ لِإِخْوَٰنِهِمْ وَقَعَدُوا۟ لَوْ أَطَاعُونَا مَا قُتِلُوا۟ۗ قُلْ فَٱدْرَءُوا۟ عَنْ أَنفُسِكُمُ ٱلْمَوْتَ إِن كُنتُمْ صَٰدِقِينَ ۝

Do not think of those who are slain in God's cause as dead. They are alive, and well provided for by their Lord. (169)

وَلَا تَحْسَبَنَّ ٱلَّذِينَ قُتِلُوا۟ فِى سَبِيلِ ٱللَّهِ أَمْوَٰتًۢاۚ بَلْ أَحْيَآءٌ عِندَ رَبِّهِمْ يُرْزَقُونَ ۝

Happy they are with what God has granted them. They rejoice that those [of their brethren] who have been left behind and have not yet joined them have nothing to fear, nor have they [cause] to grieve. (170)

فَرِحِينَ بِمَآ ءَاتَىٰهُمُ ٱللَّهُ مِن فَضْلِهِۦ وَيَسْتَبْشِرُونَ بِٱلَّذِينَ لَمْ يَلْحَقُوا۟ بِهِم مِّنْ خَلْفِهِمْ أَلَّا خَوْفٌ عَلَيْهِمْ وَلَا هُمْ يَحْزَنُونَ ۝

They rejoice in the happy news of God's blessing and bounty, and in the fact that God will not suffer the reward of the believers to be lost. (171)

۞ يَسْتَبْشِرُونَ بِنِعْمَةٍ مِّنَ ٱللَّهِ وَفَضْلٍ وَأَنَّ ٱللَّهَ لَا يُضِيعُ أَجْرَ ٱلْمُؤْمِنِينَ ۝

Those who responded to the call of God and the Messenger after misfortune had befallen them: a great reward awaits those of them who continued to do good and feared God. (172)

ٱلَّذِينَ ٱسْتَجَابُوا۟ لِلَّهِ وَٱلرَّسُولِ مِنۢ بَعْدِ مَآ أَصَابَهُمُ ٱلْقَرْحُۚ لِلَّذِينَ أَحْسَنُوا۟ مِنْهُمْ وَٱتَّقَوْا۟ أَجْرٌ عَظِيمٌ ۝

When other people warned them: "A big force has gathered against you, so fear them", that only strengthened their faith and they answered: "God is enough for us; He is the best Guardian." (173)

اَلَّذِينَ قَالَ لَهُمُ النَّاسُ إِنَّ النَّاسَ قَدْ جَمَعُوا لَكُمْ فَاخْشَوْهُمْ فَزَادَهُمْ إِيمَنَا وَقَالُوا حَسْبُنَا اللَّهُ وَنِعْمَ الْوَكِيلُ ﴿١٧٣﴾

So they earned God's grace and bounty, suffering no harm. For they had striven to please God, Whose bounty is limitless. (174)

فَانقَلَبُوا بِنِعْمَةٍ مِّنَ اللَّهِ وَفَضْلٍ لَّمْ يَمْسَسْهُمْ سُوءٌ وَاتَّبَعُوا رِضْوَنَ اللَّهِ وَاللَّهُ ذُو فَضْلٍ عَظِيمٍ ﴿١٧٤﴾

It is but Satan who prompts people to fear his allies: so, have no fear of them, but fear Me if you are truly believers. (175)

إِنَّمَا ذَٰلِكُمُ الشَّيْطَنُ يُخَوِّفُ أَوْلِيَاءَهُۥ فَلَا تَخَافُوهُمْ وَخَافُونِ إِن كُنتُم مُّؤْمِنِينَ ﴿١٧٥﴾

Be not grieved by those who hasten on to disbelief. They cannot harm God in any way. It is God's will not to assign to them any share in the [blessings of the] life to come. A great suffering awaits them. (176)

وَلَا يَحْزُنكَ الَّذِينَ يُسَرِعُونَ فِي الْكُفْرِ إِنَّهُمْ لَن يَضُرُّوا اللَّهَ شَيْئًا يُرِيدُ اللَّهُ أَلَّا يَجْعَلَ لَهُمْ حَظًّا فِي الْآخِرَةِ وَلَهُمْ عَذَابٌ عَظِيمٌ ﴿١٧٦﴾

Indeed, those who have bought disbelief at the price of faith cannot harm God in any way. A grievous suffering awaits them. (177)

إِنَّ الَّذِينَ اشْتَرَوُا الْكُفْرَ بِالْإِيمَنِ لَن يَضُرُّوا اللَّهَ شَيْئًا وَلَهُمْ عَذَابٌ أَلِيمٌ ﴿١٧٧﴾

Let not those who disbelieve imagine that Our giving them rein bodes well for their own souls. We only give them rein so that they may grow in sinfulness. A humiliating suffering awaits them. (178)

وَلَا يَحْسَبَنَّ ٱلَّذِينَ كَفَرُوٓاْ أَنَّمَا نُمْلِي لَهُمْ خَيْرٌ لِّأَنفُسِهِمْ إِنَّمَا نُمْلِي لَهُمْ لِيَزْدَادُوٓاْ إِثْمًا وَلَهُمْ عَذَابٌ مُّهِينٌ ۝

It is not God's purpose to leave the believers in your present state except to set apart the bad from the good. And it is not God's purpose to reveal to you what is kept beyond the reach of human perception. But God favours from among His messengers whomever He wills. Believe, therefore, in God and His messengers. If you believe and are God-fearing, you shall have a great reward. (179)

مَّا كَانَ ٱللَّهُ لِيَذَرَ ٱلْمُؤْمِنِينَ عَلَىٰ مَآ أَنتُمْ عَلَيْهِ حَتَّىٰ يَمِيزَ ٱلْخَبِيثَ مِنَ ٱلطَّيِّبِ وَمَا كَانَ ٱللَّهُ لِيُطْلِعَكُمْ عَلَى ٱلْغَيْبِ وَلَٰكِنَّ ٱللَّهَ يَجْتَبِى مِن رُّسُلِهِۦ مَن يَشَآءُ فَـَٔامِنُواْ بِٱللَّهِ وَرُسُلِهِۦ وَإِن تُؤْمِنُواْ وَتَتَّقُواْ فَلَكُمْ أَجْرٌ عَظِيمٌ ۝

God's Will and Man's Doing

The *surah* speaks of the Muslims' surprise at the turn of events, which betrayed their naïve concept of life. Soon, however, experience told them to look at the realities of life and how the laws of nature work. They realised that anyone who does not conform to nature and its laws should expect no preferential treatment. People must adapt themselves to the seriousness inherent in the nature of the universe, life and fate. The *surah* brings them back to reality as it explains to them that what has befallen them is the result of their own doing. But this is not all. Behind cause and effect lies God's predestination, and beyond the laws of nature lies God's free will.

The purpose of what happened is explained to them so that they learn how God directs events in the believers' favour to serve the cause which they advocate. It was an experience which made them better equipped to face what was bound to come, to put them through a serious test in order to sift their ranks and to mark out the hypocrites who were able to betray them. The whole affair, then, was part of the accomplishment of God's will. They were thus able to view the event in its totality, equipped with this Qur'ānic explanation: *"Why, when a calamity befell you, after you had inflicted twice as much [on your enemy], did you exclaim, 'How has this come about?' Say: 'It has come from your own selves. Surely, God has the power over all things.' That which befell you, on the day when the two hosts met in battle, happened by God's leave, so that He may mark out the true believers."* (Verses 165–6)

God has committed Himself to grant victory to those who support His cause and fight to defend His faith. He, however, has made the granting of victory conditional upon certain things: that the whole concept of faith be deeply entrenched in their hearts, that the practical implications of faith manifest themselves in their organisation and behaviour and that they equip themselves with all the means necessary to achieve victory and exert their maximum effort. This is the law of nature which God has set in operation and which favours no one. When the believers fall short of meeting any of these conditions, they have to accept the consequences. The fact that they are Muslims and believers does not mean that the laws of nature should be suspended or abrogated for their sake. They are Muslims because they submit themselves to God and conduct their lives according to the laws of nature God has set in operation. This means, in practice, that they achieve harmony between their nature as human beings and the laws of nature.

That they are Muslims is a fact which does not remain inconsequential. They submit themselves to God, raise His banner and determine to obey Him and conduct their lives according to His constitution. All that will eventually turn their errors and shortcomings to good effect after they bear any sacrifice or pain attendant on them. Their mistakes become lessons and experiences which have their good effect. They make their faith pure and their submission clearer. Their ranks are purged of those whose faith is suspect. They are better equipped to achieve the ultimate victory. Thus, God's mercy and care are not withheld from the Muslims. Indeed, they provide them with what they need to continue along their way, despite all the hardships they may have to face.

It is with such clarity and seriousness that the questioning and surprise of a Muslim community are answered. Both the immediate cause, the actions of the Muslim community, and the ultimate purpose, God's design, are explained. The hypocrites, on the other hand, are shown the fact that death is inevitable and cannot be avoided by staying at home at the time of battle: *"Why, when a calamity befell you after you had inflicted twice as much [on your enemy], did you exclaim: 'How has this come about?'"*

At Uḥud, the Muslims suffered a serious setback, losing 70 martyrs in addition to all the pain they experienced on that difficult day. They found the setback hard to swallow, considering that they were the believers who were fighting in defence of God's cause. Yet those very Muslims had, prior to this setback, inflicted twice as many losses on their enemy. In the Battle of Badr, they inflicted similar damage on the idolaters when they killed 70 brave warriors of the Quraysh. They achieved a similar feat at Uḥud, when they were following the express orders of the Prophet. But then they weakened before the temptation of the loot and entertained thoughts which must never be entertained by believers.

God reminds them of all this as He answers their questioning surprise. He attributes what happened to them to its immediate cause: *"It has come from your own selves."* It is you who have weakened and entered into dispute. It is you who have failed to fulfil the conditions set by God and His Messenger, and it is you who have succumbed to greed. It is you who have disobeyed God's Messenger and failed to implement his battle plan. What has happened to you, to your surprise, has come from your own souls, because the laws of nature set into operation by God have to apply to you. The laws of nature apply to all human beings, believers and unbelievers alike. Such laws are not suspended for a believer's sake. His faith is not complete unless he conducts his life according to God's laws.

"Surely, God has the power over all things." It is part of His overall power that His law should remain in operation and that matters must continue according to His will. The laws He has devised for the universe and for human life must continue as they have been set.

Nevertheless, God's will in this whole affair was accomplished for a definite purpose of His own. We must not forget that God's will lies beyond everything that takes place and every movement and action in the whole universe: *"That which befell you, on the day when the two hosts met in battle, happened by God's leave."* It has not taken place by mere coincidence or for idle play. Every movement and every action takes place according to a definite plan, with its causes and effects well reckoned. They indeed take place according to the laws of nature which must remain in operation, but in their total sum they accomplish God's purpose and complete the total design of the universe as God created it.

The Islamic view with regard to this whole issue is both comprehensive and well balanced and is not matched by any other view human beings have ever entertained.

Human life exists according to a consistent constitution and unavoidable rules, and beyond these lies God's active and free will. Yet all these are also subject to His wisdom which determines every thing that takes place. Thus the constitution governs all, and the rules apply to everything, including man. By his choice of action and what he determines, initiates and does, man makes himself subject to these rules which are bound to affect him. All this, however, takes place in accordance with God's will and fulfils His purpose. On the other hand, man's own will, thought, action and movement are part of the constitution and the rules God has set in the universe. He accomplishes with them what He wills. There is no conflict between these and the rules of nature God has set in operation. Such a conflict exists only in the minds of people who put God's will and action against those of man, weighing the one against the other.

That way of thinking is contrary to the Islamic outlook. According to Islam, man is neither equal nor an enemy to God. Indeed when God granted man his constitution, intellect, will, freedom of choice and action, He placed nothing of this in conflict with His own will or laws. Nor did He allow these to serve a purpose other than His overall purpose in the whole universe. He only made it part of His will that man should reflect and decide, take action and produce an effect, be liable to God's rules and laws and bear the full consequences of all that. These consequences may bring him pleasure or pain, comfort or trouble, happiness or misery. But behind all that stands God's free will that encompasses everything in perfect coherence.

What happened in the Battle of Uḥud provides a good example of what we have just said about the way Islam views all matters.

God has explained to the Muslims His rules and conditions which bring them victory or cause defeat. They paid no heed to those rules and, consequently, suffered pain, hardship and defeat. But the matter did not stop there. Their disobedience and their pain contributed to the fulfilment of God's purpose of testing their community so as to mark out the true believers, give them a clear outlook and help them overcome their weakness, and also identify the hypocrites.

All this will ultimately be of benefit to the Muslim community, despite the pain and suffering. It all works in accordance with God's rules and laws. That gives believers who submit themselves to God and follow the way of living He has laid down an assurance that His help and care are forthcoming. By the same token, their errors are ultimately turned to their benefit, because the suffering such errors cause them becomes a means for proving their metal and educating them.

On such solid grounds the believers stand comfortably. They are reassured, free of worry and confusion as they face God's will and interact with His laws. They feel that God determines what He wills concerning them and others. They are merely one of the tools God employs to fulfil His purpose. Whatever they do, right or wrong, and all that results from it remain in full harmony with God's will and fulfils His purpose. It will all benefit them in their life: "*That which befell you, on the day when the two hosts met in battle, happened by God's leave, so that He may mark out the true believers. And [He might] mark out the hypocrites. When these were told, 'Come, fight in God's cause', or 'Defend yourselves', they answered, 'Had we known there would be a fight, we would certainly have followed you.' On that day they were nearer unbelief than faith, uttering with their mouths something different to what was in their hearts, but God knew full well all that they tried to conceal.*" (Verses 166–7)

This verse refers to the attitude of 'Abdullāh ibn Ubayy ibn Salūl and those who joined him. They are described here as "the hypocrites". Their true feelings became clear for all to see. They were marked out by their true attitude: "*On that day they were nearer unbelief than faith.*" They lied when they protested that they only went back because they felt there would be no fight between the Muslims and the unbelievers. That was in no way their real reason. The fact is that they were "*uttering with their mouths something different to what was in their hearts.*" Their hearts were infested with hypocrisy which meant that they placed their own considerations above those of faith.

This is indeed true, because what ʿAbdullāh ibn Ubayy was thinking about that day was the fact that the Prophet did not follow his counsel, and that the arrival of the Prophet and his Companions in Madinah deprived him of the position of overall leader his people were preparing for him. Instead, the leadership belonged to faith and the messenger preaching it. These facts were indeed behind the desertion of ʿAbdullāh ibn Ubayy and his followers when the unbelievers were at the gates of Madinah. That is indeed the reason for their refusal to listen to ʿAbdullāh ibn ʿAmr ibn Ḥarām when he said to them: "*'Come, fight in God's cause', or 'Defend yourselves'.*" They said they did not think a fight would take place anyway. But the truth about them is made clear by God Himself: "*God knew full well all that they tried to conceal.*"

The *sūrah* continues to uncover the true nature of their attitude which aimed to spread a state of confusion and perplexity in the Muslim ranks: "*Such were they who, having themselves stayed behind, said of their brothers: 'If only they had listened to us, they would not have been slain.'*" (Verse 168) They did not merely stay behind when the battle was imminent, with all the confusion and turmoil that resulted from their desertion. What made things worse was that ʿAbdullāh ibn Ubayy was still thought to be an honourable man. His hypocrisy was not yet known. God had not until that point identified him as a hypocrite, which would have much detracted from his standing among his people. They continued to raise doubt, sow discord and nurture feelings of regret, particularly among the families of those who died in battle. "*Such were they who, having themselves stayed behind, said of their brothers: 'If only they had listened to us, they would not have been slain.'*"

In this way they tried to show their own desertion as both wise and beneficial, while obeying the Prophet was shown to be disadvantageous and causing harm. Furthermore, they undermined the clear Islamic concept of God's will, which makes it inevitable that every person dies at his or her appointed time, according to God's will. Hence, the Qur'ānic statement answers them with an irrefutable argument that makes clear all the issues involved: "*Say to them: 'Ward off death from yourselves, then, if what you say be true.'"* (Verse 168) Death affects everyone: the fighter in the battlefield as well as the deserter, the brave man and the coward. It can neither be prevented by taking precautions, nor delayed by cowardice or the evasion of risk. It is this fact that the Qur'ān puts to them plainly and clearly, thereby foiling all their wicked plotting, reassuring the Muslims and giving them all the comfort faith provides.

A very interesting point in the Qur'ānic review of the events of the battle is that 'Abdullāh ibn Ubayy's desertion, which occurred before the battle had even started, is commented on only at this point. Bringing it up so late in the discussion illustrates an important feature of the Qur'ānic method of educating the Muslim community. It starts with establishing the main rules which formulate the Islamic outlook, illustrating the proper feelings nurtured in a Muslim heart and explaining the criteria by which Islamic values come into play. When the Qur'ān has done that, it makes this reference to "the hypocrites", showing their action and how they subsequently behaved. By this time, we are well prepared to evaluate their action and understand how far removed it is from proper Islamic values. This is the right sequence and progress: to establish the right values and standards first, then to evaluate actions and behaviour according to them in order to arrive at the right conclusions.

There may be another purpose for delaying the reference to the desertion, namely, and that is to show that the deserters, particularly their chief, are viewed with contempt. He is not mentioned by name, so that he may sink into insignificance as "one of the hypocrites". In the scales of faith, he and his action are not worth more than this humiliating reference.

The *sūrah* then tackles another highly important matter with far-reaching effects. That is the fact that martyrs killed in the defence of God's cause are not dead; they continue to live and they receive what they need from their Lord. They continue to interact with the Muslim community and the events affecting it after they have departed. Such interaction is the most important aspect of continued life. Thus the life of the Uḥud martyrs is strongly linked to the events that followed their martyrdom before the *sūrah* describes the attitude of the true believers. These were the ones who responded to God and His Messenger after they had suffered the calamity of defeat. They immediately chased the Quraysh army so as to prevent any possible attempt by that army to attack Madinah. They paid little heed to other people's warnings that the Quraysh were marshalling large forces to attack them. They placed their trust in God and thus gave practical credence to their declaration of belief in Him: "*Do not think of those who are slain in God's cause as dead. They are alive, and well provided for by their Lord. Happy they are with what God has granted them. They rejoice that those [of their brethren] who have been left behind and have not yet joined them have nothing to fear, nor have they [cause] to grieve. They rejoice in the happy news of God's blessing and bounty, and in the fact that God will not suffer the reward of the believers to be lost.*" (Verses 169–71)

Having reassured the believers and established the true facts concerning death and the Divine will, the *sūrah* adds to the reassurance of the believers by describing the fate of the martyrs who are killed while defending God's cause. Indeed that is the true meaning of a martyr, for there is no martyrdom except that achieved through defending God's cause, and dying in the process. These martyrs are indeed alive, having all of the essential qualities of life. They "receive" their needs from their Lord, are happy with the grace God bestows on them, rejoice at the happy news of what is to befall their brethren whom they had left behind, and they witness the events of the Muslim community. Such are the qualities of the living. Why should we, then, be distressed at their departure, when they are indeed interacting with those who are alive? But they have much more than this interaction. They have all that God bestows on them of His grace. Why do believers, then, create untrue separations between a living martyr and his people whom he has left behind, between this world and the world beyond, when there should be no such separation in their thoughts as in both worlds they deal with God.

To clarify this fact is of central importance in the formulation of one's overall understanding. Indeed it initiates a Muslim's perception of the universe, what takes place in it, as well as life in its various stages. Death is not the end of all life, as other people believe. Indeed it does not even represent a barrier between what comes before it and what comes after it.

"*Do not think of those who are slain in God's cause as dead. They are alive, and well provided for by their Lord.*" This verse gives an order not to think of people killed while serving God's cause as dead, even though they have departed from this world and are no longer seen by the living. It gives also an assurance that they are very much alive, with their Lord. The verse then gives a list of the aspects of life they have. The first of these is that they are *"well provided for."*

In this life, we do not know what type of life martyrs have, except for whatever the Prophet has told us in authentic *ḥadīths*. Nevertheless, this true statement by God, Who knows all, is sufficient as a basis for us to fundamentally change our views of life and death, what separates them and what joins them together. It is enough to tell us that things need not be as they appear. Hence when we formulate our conceptions of absolute facts on the basis of their apparent features, we will not be able to arrive at a perfect understanding of such facts. It is infinitely better for us to wait for the right explanation of these facts from the One Who knows them all, God the Almighty.

Here the *sūrah* tells us about people from among us who are slain, depicting a life which is familiar to us in its visible aspects. However, because they are slain *"in God's cause"*, and because they have purged their thoughts and feelings of everything else while their souls look up to God and are sacrificed for His sake, God tells us that they are alive, not dead. He forbids us to think of them as dead, assuring us that they are with Him, well provided for, and that they receive His bounty in the same way as the living. He then tells us about other qualities of their life. Thus we learn that they are happy *"with what God has granted them."* They are certainly pleased with what is given to them by God, because they know that it is part of His grace. Hence it is, for them, an evidence of the fact that He is well pleased with them.

Moreover, they think about their brethren whom they have left behind, rejoicing at their prospects, because they know that God is pleased with those who strive to serve His cause: *"They rejoice that those [of their brethren] who have been left behind and have not yet joined them have nothing to fear, nor have they [cause] to grieve. They rejoice in the happy news of God's blessing and bounty, and in the fact that God will not suffer the reward of the believers to be lost."* That is a complete picture showing them as continuing to be concerned with their brethren, feeling happy with what they have and reassured about the prospects of their brethren. What qualities of life do they, then, miss? How are they separated from those who are left behind? Why should their departure be an occasion of sadness and grief when it is one of happiness and pleasure?

These verses provide a complete transformation of the reality of death, when it comes about in the course of dedication to God's cause, and the feelings associated with it among the fighters themselves and those who are left behind. The outlook on life gives it a far wider expanse than the present fleeting one. Indeed this wider outlook strengthened the believers in all generations. It steadied their footsteps as they sought martyrdom for God's cause. Hence, the history of Islam portrays countless examples of the type of believers ready to sacrifice their lives for their faith. Some of these examples have been given at the beginning of our commentary on the events of the Battle of Uḥud.

The Fruits of Total Dedication to Islam

Now the *sūrah* moves on to tell us about the "believers" who are concerned with the martyrs and rejoice at what is held in store for them by their Lord: *"Those who responded to the call of God and the Messenger after misfortune had befallen them: a great reward awaits those of them who continued to do good and feared God."* (Verse 172)

The Prophet called upon those who had fought in the Battle of Uḥud to turn out for battle duty with him the following day. They were wounded and exhausted; they had barely escaped death. They were still living the horrors of the battle and the humiliation of defeat. They had lost some of their finest and dearest, were weaker because of their wounds, and also less in number.

Nevertheless the Prophet called them up, and called them in person. He did not allow any new recruits to join this second expedition, which might, some would say, have reinforced the Muslim fighting force. They responded to the Prophet's call, which was, in essence, a call by God, as the verse makes absolutely clear. Their response was immediate, positive and favourable, despite their misfortune and wounds.

The fact that God's Messenger singled out those who had actually fought at Uḥud for this new call is particularly significant. Perhaps the Prophet did not wish the feelings of defeat and misfortune to

be the last that remained with the Muslims after the battle. He called
on them to chase the Quraysh in order to drive home to them that all
that had happened was merely a test and an experience which was not
the end of the matter. They remained strong while their victorious
enemies were weak. It was an experience which was certain to be
followed by victory once they had shaken off their weakness and failure,
and responded to the call issued to them by God and His messenger.

As a corollary, the Prophet may have decided that the Quraysh should
not leave the battlefield overjoyed and boastful at their victory. He,
therefore, followed the Quraysh so as to make it clear to them that
they had not caused any permanent damage to the Muslims; there still
remained enough of them to chase off the Quraysh army. Those
objectives were fulfilled, according to historical reports.

The Prophet might have also wished to make clear to the
Muslims and to all mankind the birth of a faith that meant
everything to its adherents. They had absolutely no aim or objective
in their lives other than to serve the cause of their faith. They lived
for it and they looked to nothing beyond it. They spared nothing
of themselves. They offered all as a sacrifice for their faith. This
was a new phenomenon the like of which had never been seen before.
It was necessary that all mankind realised this after the believers
themselves had realised it. Nothing could reflect the birth of this
faith better than the marching of those who responded to God's
call after misfortune had befallen them. Their march was both
spectacular and awesome. It clearly reflected the fact that they relied
totally on God. They did not care for people's scaremongering about
the size of the Quraysh host as told by the messengers sent by Abū
Sufyān, the chief of the Quraysh.

Similarly, the hypocrites depicted the Quraysh as extremely
mighty. Those believers, however, cared nothing for all this: *"Those
who responded to the call of God and the Messenger after misfortune
had befallen them: a great reward awaits those of them who continued
to do good and feared God. When other people warned them: 'A big
force has gathered against you, so fear them', that only strengthened
their faith and they answered: 'God is enough for us; He is the best
Guardian.'"* (Verses 172–3) In this way, the Muslim community
declared in the clearest of terms the birth of this faith. The wisdom
behind the Prophet's plan is now clearly apparent to us.

Nothing to Fear from Satan's Allies

The pain and the grief suffered by the Muslims at Uḥud has been recorded by the Prophet's biographers. Muḥammad ibn Isḥāq reports the following:

One of the Prophet's Companions from the *Anṣār* clan of 'Abd al-Ashhal who fought in Uḥud reports: "My brother and I were at Uḥud with God's messenger. Both of us came back wounded. When we heard the Prophet's call to us to come out and chase the enemy, I said to my brother, or perhaps he said to me: 'Can we miss an expedition led by God's messenger? By God, we have no animal to ride and both of us are wounded and can hardly move.' Nevertheless, we went out with the Prophet. My wounds were less serious than those of my brother. When he could no longer go on, I would carry him for some distance, until we reached the same destination as the rest of the Muslim soldiers."

The second report mentions that the Battle of Uḥud took place on Saturday, the middle day of the month of Shawwāl. On the following day, Sunday the 16th of Shawwāl, the call of the Prophet was made to people to go out and chase the enemy. The message was also made clear: only those who had attended the battle the day before were to come out. However, one of the Prophet's Companions called Jābir ibn 'Abdullāh ibn 'Amr, sought special permission to join the army. He said: "Messenger of God, my father ordered me to stay behind to look after my seven sisters, saying: 'My son, it does not behove you or me to leave these women without a man to look after them. Moreover, I am not one to allow you to have the privilege of fighting alongside God's Messenger and deny myself that privilege. Therefore, you stay behind and look after your sisters.' I did as he asked." The Prophet gave Jābir special permission to join him.

Such fine examples confirm the birth of this great faith in those hearts who recognise no one other than God as a guardian and whose faith is strengthened at time of hardship. When they are told that people are gathering forces against them, their answer is: *"God is enough for us; He is the best Guardian."* The practical outcome is the fulfilment of God's promise to those who rely on Him and dedicate themselves to His cause: *"...so they earned God's grace and bounty, suffering no harm. For they had striven to please God."* (Verse

174) They were saved, suffering no harm, but enjoying God's pleasure. That is indeed a manifestation of *"God's grace and bounty."* This statement emphasises the primary cause of what God may bestow. It all comes through God's grace and out of His bounty, with which He favours whomever He pleases. It is true that their attitude was uniquely splendid, but nevertheless, it is through God's grace that all bounty is bestowed.

God's bounty is certainly limitless. God records their attitude in His immortal book, with His own words echoed throughout the universe. As we contemplate this attitude and the picture so drawn, we feel that the whole community went through a fundamental change overnight. It had matured and become much more certain of its stand. Its vision was no longer blurred. No more hesitation or reluctance as those witnessed the day before. It had now acquired a seriousness which had not been experienced before. Yet the time span between these two greatly differing attitudes is only one night. The hard experience produced its results and shook the very souls of the believers. Indeed, God's bounty through this difficult test is greater than anything else.

Finally, the passage concludes with explaining the reason behind fear. It is Satan who tries to depict his allies as a source of might. The believers must be on their guard never to entertain any fear of Satan or his allies. They must fear God alone, the Almighty Who overpowers all forces: *"It is but Satan who prompts people to fear his allies: so, have no fear of them, but fear Me if you are truly believers."* (Verse 175)

It serves Satan's purpose to show his allies as powerful and mighty, able to inflict harm on, and cause benefit to others. By doing so, he has the chance to spread evil and corruption on earth. People will surrender to his allies and allow them to do whatever they want. No one will contemplate standing up to them or foiling their evil purpose. When evil appears to be too powerful and people are paralysed by fear, then Satan's allies can accomplish what he wants of them. Thus, right appears to be wrong and wrong is shown to be right. Evil and corruption become widespread while truth and justice are suppressed. The evildoers make deities of themselves to perpetuate the suppression of goodness and to protect evil. When no one is able to stand up to them, evil becomes triumphant while the truth is overshadowed and forgotten. Satan is a deceptive sorcerer who hides behind his allies while at the same time causing people to fear his allies. But God exposes him as he truly is, without cover. The believers are made aware of Satan's scheming. Thus, they can be on their guard and they have no fear of him or his allies.

Both Satan and his allies are too weak to be feared by any believer who relies on his Lord and has His support. The only power to be feared is the one which truly can cause harm and benefit. That is God's power, feared by those who believe in God. By fearing God alone they are the most powerful of all people. No other force can stand up to them. Hence, God instructs the believers in these words: *"It is but Satan who prompts people to fear his allies: so, have no fear of them, but fear Me if you are truly believers."*

How People's Actions Affect God

Be not grieved by those who hasten on to disbelief. They cannot harm God in any way. It is God's will not to assign to them any share in the [blessings of the] life to come. A great suffering awaits them. (Verse 176)

This verse addresses the Prophet in words which are meant to console him and lighten his grief when he sees people hastening to disbelief and vying with one another to embrace it, as if they were competing for a coveted prize. He is told that all such actions will harm God in no way. The question is one of temptation for them which they cannot resist. God is fully aware of what they think and do, which qualifies them to be deprived of all blessings in the hereafter. He, therefore, has left them to follow their disbelief wherever it leads them. The point is that guidance has been provided for them but they preferred disbelief and, in consequence, they were left alone to follow the way of their choosing. Indeed, they have been given plenty of time and comfort, but they have not been wise enough to understand that it will all end in their undoing. God's purpose behind all events, including the tests endured by the believers and the indulgence allowed disbelievers is then explained. Good will be distinguished from evil. People's thoughts and beliefs are known only to God, but He wanted this to be known to people in such a way that they could easily comprehend it.

This conclusion is the most suitable after the Qur'ān's detailed comments on the events of a battle in which the Muslims suffered a heavy defeat and the idolaters achieved a spectacular victory. For there will always be doubts and silent complaints whenever a battle between truth and falsehood ends up with a setback for the truth and a triumph for falsehood. Why does this happen, Lord? Why do the advocates of the truth suffer while the followers of falsehood triumph? Why is the truth not victorious in every battle it fights against falsehood? Should not the truth always achieve victory? Why is falsehood allowed to gather such strength when it only shakes people and raises doubts in their hearts?

This is indeed what happened at Uḥud when, surprised at what befell them, the Muslims exclaimed: *"How has this come about?"* (Verse 165)

At the conclusion of this long passage, the final answer is given to reassure people and remove all doubts. God's purpose and His law are explained for that particular occasion and for all time. What we are told here is that when falsehood is victorious in any confrontation with the truth then that is not the end of the matter.

Falsehood may appear to be all-conquering, but it is only temporary. No one should think that falsehood is invincible or that it can reduce the truth to a permanently weak position from which it will never recover. Nor does the apparent weakness of the truth in any particular period of time mean that God has abandoned it or that He would allow evil and falsehood to put the truth out of existence.

All this is part of a clearly defined purpose. God allows evil to go the length of its way, committing the most ghastly of crimes and sins so that it merits the worst of suffering. He also tests the truth and its advocates in order to distinguish those who remain truly steadfast and increases their reward. It all, then, ends up in a net gain for the truth and net loss for evil. Each has a double portion of what it earns.

> *Be not grieved by those who hasten on to disbelief. They cannot harm God in any way. It is God's will not to assign to them any share in the [blessings of the] life to come. A great suffering awaits them."* (Verse 176)

This is a consolation for the Prophet so that he does not grieve when he sees people driving headlong into disbelief. This portrays an actual state of affairs in which we see some people exert every effort as they go along the path of evil, disbelief and disobedience of God. They drive along as if they are chased by a fearsome enemy or as if they are promised a splendid prize.

The Prophet used to grieve when he saw such people condemning themselves to a fateful doom, driving towards hell, and he could do nothing to save them because they were determined not to listen to him. He also grieved at what befell the Muslims and his message at the hands of those hardened disbelievers. Masses of people were awaiting the final result of the battle between Islam and the Quraysh in order to choose the camp to join. When the Quraysh eventually embraced Islam, people flocked in large numbers to the religion of God. All these were considerations that affected the Prophet. Hence, the consolation from God: *"Be not grieved by those who hasten on to disbelief. They cannot harm God in any way."*

There is absolutely no doubt that such people could not cause God any harm. This is the truth which needs no explanation. But God wants to make it clear that the cause of faith is His own cause. The battle against the disbelievers is, therefore, God's own battle. The ultimate result of this cause and its battle is not the responsibility of the Prophet and, consequently, it is not the responsibility of the believers. For those who hasten on to disbelief are fighting God and they are much too weak to harm Him in any way. They can in no way harm His faith or its advocates no matter how hardened they may be in their disbelief and no matter how much harm they may cause the believers.

The question still arises: why does God allow them to achieve a victory against the believers when they are His own immediate enemies? The answer being that He has prepared something much more humiliating for them: *"It is God's will not to assign to them any share in the [blessings of the] life to come."* They utilise all the share assigned to them and they shoulder their whole burden, meriting God's punishment in full. It is towards this end that they drive headlong: *"A great suffering awaits them."* Why does God then wish them to have such a miserable end? They have earned it by choosing it themselves.

Why Disbelievers May Wield Power

Indeed, those who have bought disbelief at the price of faith cannot harm God in any way. A grievous suffering awaits them. Let not those who disbelieve imagine that Our giving them rein bodes well for their own souls. We only give them rein so that they may grow in sinfulness. A humiliating suffering awaits them. It is not God's purpose to leave the believers in your present state except to set apart the bad from the good. And it is not God's purpose to reveal to you what is kept beyond the reach of human perception. But God favours from among His messengers whomever He wills. Believe, therefore, in God and His messengers. If you believe and are God-fearing, you shall have a great reward. (Verses 177–9)

To believe in God and to follow the path of faith was available to them. The proofs and pointers which guide human beings to faith are everywhere in the universe, planted deep into human nature. The harmony and complementarity which manifest themselves in clear and unique ways, and the direct, positive response of human nature to such remarkable evidence represent a clear invitation to man to have faith. He feels that only God could have created and organised the universe. Moreover, God has sent messengers to convey to mankind His message and to call on them to believe in Him. The message meets the needs of human nature and provides a complete and harmonious way of life.

Knowing that faith is so readily available to them, they nevertheless bartered it away for disbelief. In doing so, they deserve to be abandoned by God so that they can drive headlong into disbelief, exhausting all their share of God's grace, leaving no reward for themselves in the hereafter. Immersed so totally in error and having nothing of the truth, they are too weak to cause God any harm whatsoever. Error has no justice and falsehood has no strength. Its advocates cannot harm those who respond to God's call, even though they may have forces with which they can inflict temporary harm on the believers.

"A grievous suffering awaits them." The suffering they will have to endure is incomparably more painful than what they can inflict on believers in this life. *"Let not those who disbelieve imagine that*

Our giving them rein bodes well for their own souls. We only give them rein so that they may grow in sinfulness. A humiliating suffering awaits them."

At this point the *sūrah* tackles the doubts entertained by some people and their silent remonstrations as they see the enemies of the truth and of God go about unpunished, demonstrating their power and enjoying their strength, position and wealth. What they seem to possess hardens their attitude and tempts people to side with them. Those whose faith remains weak may entertain evil thoughts so as to believe that God has acquiesced to falsehood, accepted evil and tyranny and given their advocates rein. Far be it for God to do so. They may also think that God takes a neutral position in the battle between truth and falsehood, allowing falsehood to smash the truth. They may even think that a certain brand of falsehood is right; otherwise, how is it allowed to grow and triumph? Or they may go as far as to think that it is the natural order of things in this life for falsehood to triumph over the truth. As for the transgressors who serve evil, wreak injustice and spread corruption, they continue with their erring ways and drive headlong into unbelief, imagining that they wield absolute power and that there is no force to stand up to them. All this is plainly wrong. It is an erroneous concept of how God conducts matters. God warns the disbelievers against entertaining such thoughts. If He does not visit them with immediate punishment for their disbelief and, instead, allows them a chance to enjoy themselves in this life, they should know that it is all a test which lures them away so that their attitudes harden and their errors become plainly apparent: "*Let not those who disbelieve imagine that Our giving them rein bodes well for their own souls. We only give them rein so that they may grow in sinfulness.*"

Had they deserved to be helped out of their distractions with an awakening test, God would have put them to such a trial. But He does not wish them well after they have bought disbelief at the price of faith. They no longer deserve to be awakened. Instead, *"a humiliating suffering awaits them."* Such humiliation is the exact opposite of their present position of power, prestige and affluence.

This makes it clear to us that a test in this life is a type of God's bounty which is granted to those for whom God stores up a happier future. When it comes as the result of actions made by good servants of God who strive hard in advocating His cause, it is done for a definite purpose which may not be immediately apparent. It remains part of God's grace, shown to His servants. This is sufficient to reassure the believers and to drive home some basic principles about the Islamic concept of life.

It was part of God's grace to the believers that He distinguishes them from the hypocrites who infiltrated their ranks and who had no love for Islam. He put the believers to this hard test at Uḥud as a result of certain actions of their own making, in order to set the bad apart from the good.

"It is not God's purpose to leave the believers in your present state except to set apart the bad from the good. And it is not God's purpose to reveal to you what is kept beyond the reach of human perception. But God favours from among His messengers whomever He wills. Believe, therefore, in God and His messengers. If you believe and are God-fearing, you shall have a great reward. "This is a clear Qur'ānic statement which leaves us in no doubt that it is not part of God's design or method to allow the ranks of the believers to remain loose, giving a chance to the hypocrites to join them under false pretences when they have no real faith. God has moulded this nation of Islam in order that it plays a great role in this world, implements the supreme code of living designed by God Himself. Such a great role requires dedication, purity and unity. To fulfil it the Muslims must not allow any infiltration into their ranks. For this task to be accomplished it requires, in short, that the actors be as great as the role assigned to them in this life and worthy of the position God has prepared for them in the life to come. This means that a severe test must be endured so that only the strong in faith remain within the ranks and those who are weak are moved aside. In practice, it meant that the great shake-up at Uḥud was necessary so that the believers did not remain as they were before the battle.

Nor is it God's purpose to allow human beings to know what He has chosen to remain hidden from them. They are not, by nature, ready or able to receive such a revelation because their constitution has been especially designed to fulfil a certain task in this life which does not require such knowledge. The human constitution would collapse if such a revelation was made, because it has not been made to receive of it except a portion which allows the soul to know its Creator. The least that would happen to man when he knows his eventual destiny is that he remains idle and does nothing in fulfilment of his task on earth, namely, to build human life. Alternatively, he may be worried about his destiny and this may exhaust his strength. How then does God set the bad apart from the good? How does He purge the Muslim ranks from all hypocrisy and mould the Muslim community in the proper shape to fulfil its role? The answer is given in the Qur'ānic statement: *"But God favours from among His messengers whomever He wills."* It is through His message, and through accepting it and believing in it and through the striving of the messengers and the testing of their followers that God's purpose is accomplished. This again stresses the importance of the test which distinguishes people. We now know a part of God's purpose as it manifests itself in the events of life.

Having explained this fundamental fact, an address is made to the believers to demonstrate within their world the practical effects of their faith. If they do, then a great reward awaits them: *"Believe, therefore, in God and His messengers. If you believe and are God-fearing, you shall have a great reward."* This directive, coupled with the promise of a great reward, is the best conclusion for the comments given in this *sūrah* on the Battle of Uḥud.

The Lesson in a Nutshell

The Qur'ān's analysis of the events of the Battle of Uḥud and their ramifications determine that further exploration of the facts be set forward. Only the most important and far-reaching of these facts, however, will now be pointed out.

1. The first principle relates to the nature of the Islamic system, the way of life God has chosen for mankind, and the way it works in real life. This is a basic aspect which many people overlook or fail to understand. There are those who think that since Islam is a Divine system, it ought to work in real life in a miraculous or supernatural way, with no regard for human nature, man's natural abilities or the real world in which man lives.

    However, when these people see that Islam does not work in this manner, and that it only operates within the constraints of human power and the material limits of man's existence, and that it interacts with that power and that existence, they are hit by a sudden sense of disappointment. They are surprised that Islam is affected by man's capacity and environment, and that these realities do actually influence, sometimes negatively, people's response to Islam. Their faith in the efficacy and practicality of religious faith thus becomes dented, and some may even lose all faith in religion as such.

Such misunderstandings stem from one fundamental misconception about the nature of Islam and its practical operation in human life. Islam is implemented by human efforts, within the limits of human power. It begins from where man is at a particular moment. It proceeds from his material existence and takes him all the way to the end. It goes as far as man's endeavour and capacity can take him, always mindful of his limitations and capabilities.

Islam's main characteristic, however, is that it never for one moment neglects human nature and the realities of man's physical existence, all the while allowing him to reach new heights of progress and achievement. This is unparalleled in any man-made system. It happened in the past and can always happen again if a serious attempt is made to revive Islam.

The mistake lies in misunderstanding or ignoring the nature of this religion, and in looking for supernatural miracles that distort human nature or are totally divorced from man's propensities, aptitudes, capabilities, and from his real physical existence. Is not Islam a Divine way of life? Is it not the religion chosen by the most Omnipotent power in the whole universe? Why, then, does it only operate within the bounds of human power? Why does it require human effort to succeed? Why does it, and its followers, not prevail every time? Why is it sometimes overtaken by habits, desires and material realities? Why should its opponents, who are in the wrong, prevail over its followers, who are in the right? These, as we can see, are all misleading questions that arise from a failure to understand the most basic and simplest fact about the nature of Islam and the way it works in real life.

God is, of course, capable, through Islam or otherwise, of modifying human nature, and He was able to create man with a different nature. But, He chose to create man as we know him; He chose to grant him a will and the ability to respond; He chose to make guidance dependent on effort and perception. He further ordained that human nature remains a constant and active force for all time. He intended that His way of life shall only be realised in real life through human effort and within man's power, and He planned that man's achievements correspond to the effort he makes within the constraints of real life.

No one can question God's wisdom in this whole process, because no one has the Divine qualities or knowledge to comprehend the overall system of creation or how it works. No one but God can fathom the underlying nature of every creature in this world or the purpose behind creating them in this particular way.

In this context, neither a sincere believer in God nor a hardened atheist could question God's judgement in this regard. A believer is too polite with God, whom he knows within his heart and through His attributes, to ask such an impertinent question, and he knows well that the human mind is not equipped to explore such areas of knowledge. The unbeliever would not ask simply because he does not believe in the existence of God; were he to believe, he would realise that it is a matter for God Almighty alone.

Not one of God's creation has the right to question why He created human nature as we know it? Why did He decide that human nature should be a constant and active force for all time? Why did He decide that the implementation of the Divine system could only be achieved through human effort and within the power frame of the human being?

Nevertheless, every human being has the right to understand this fact and to see how it works in real life – the right to interpret human history according to it so as to appreciate it on the one hand, and to change it on the other.

The Divine system of Islam, as taught by the Prophet Muḥammad, cannot be implemented in real life by the mere fact that it is revealed by God. Nor is it established by merely conveying it or explaining it to people. Nor is it forced on human society like any natural law governing the movement of the galaxies or the stars. The only way to set up the Islamic system is for a group of human beings to fully adopt and uphold its principles, and dedicate their life, energy and aspirations to sustain it. To persuade others of it and build their lives according to its teachings. For that group to endeavour to conquer weakness, prejudice, desire, and ignorance within themselves and within the hearts of others. To face up to those motivated by weakness, desire and ignorance in their opposition to God's system and to stem the progress of such unbelievers. For this group to go forward in their implementation of God's system, starting from where people are, and never ignoring the requirements of their real situation. This group will, at times, prevail over its own weakness as well as over others and similarly it will fail at others. Its success and failure will depend on the effort it makes and the practical means it employs, and on how successful it is in choosing the right means. But, first and foremost, success depends on its dedication to its cause and on how truly it represents its values and principles in its own behaviour, how close it is to God and how much confidence and trust it places in Him.

This is the reality of Islam and its methods. This is its true action plan and its means to achieve it. This is what God wishes to impart to the Muslim community as He takes them through the Battle of Uḥud and analyses its events.

When that community fell short in representing the true character of Islam in their conduct during the battle and failed, at certain points, to take proper measures to secure victory, when they overlooked the simple but fundamental truth and assumed that victory was guaranteed simply by virtue of their being Muslims, God left them to suffer the hurting pains of defeat. The Qur'ān draws their attention to this basic fact: *"Why, when a calamity befell you, after you had inflicted twice as much [on your enemy], did you exclaim, 'How has this come about?' Say: 'It has come from your own selves. Surely God has the power over all things.'"* (Verse 165)

The Qur'ān, however, does not leave the argument there but goes on to unveil God's purpose behind the causes and the outcome of the events. It reveals the advantages God intended by the test the Muslims had undergone.

Allowing God's system to take its course in life through human endeavour and under human influence is beneficial. It is healthy and good for human life and it polishes and refines human nature and revives it. A man's faith is only fully consummated when he is tested through direct dealings with people, teaching them, arguing with them and struggling to win them over by all means.

One has to undergo trials and tribulations and experience patience and perseverance in the face of all adversities, and learn how to tolerate defeat and how to cope with victory, which can be much harder, until one's heart is cleansed and true believers are set apart so that their community proceeds along the true path of success, trusting in God alone.

A man's faith is not complete until he experiences the hardships of expounding that faith to others, because in that process, he develops his own faith. New horizons are opened up for him that would not otherwise have opened; new facts about people and life are revealed that would not otherwise have been revealed. His feelings and outlook, his habits and practices, and his emotions and responses reach levels that would not otherwise have been attainable.

Likewise, a community has to undergo the harsh experiences of struggle until every member realises the extent of his or her own power and objectives. In this way the community understands the value and role of its constituent parts, how strong each member is and how solidly united the whole structure is.

This is what God wanted to teach the Muslim community at Uḥud and through the Qur'ānic discussion of its events. The verses come together to impress upon the Muslims the reasons for their defeat as well as the care and protection God afforded them. They emphasise the rationale behind God's will and purpose in all the events and developments that took place, and stress the underlying principle that God's natural and social laws apply equally to all human societies and individuals.

Ultimately, it is God's will and purpose that are the moving force behind all causes, events and developments. This comprehensive Islamic perspective thus underpins those momentous events and their interpretation.

2. The second principle that emerges from the Qur'ānic comments on the Muslim defeat at Uḥud shows that human nature is not perfect. It does, however, have the propensity to develop and grow to the highest standards of perfection that it is capable of reaching in this world.

In that community of Muḥammad's Companions, we have a section of humanity representing the quintessential part of the nation that God describes as *"the best nation ever brought forth for mankind."* They were the ideal human social model ever to grace the earth. But when we look at that community, what do we see? We see a group of human beings who have their weaknesses and shortcomings. The Qur'ān tells us that among them were individuals who fell for Satan's enticement, some who degenerated into dissension and disobedience, and some who were weak and faint-hearted. There were also those who ran away and cared for nothing but their own safety and self-interest.

But all were believing Muslims. However, they were at the early stages of Islam's existence, still going through their formative years. Nevertheless, they took their faith most seriously. They submitted all their affairs to God, willingly, and they accepted His religion and way of life. Hence, God did not ostracise them, but rather exonerated them and showed them mercy. He instructed His Messenger to pardon them, pray for their forgiveness and consult them on various matters, despite their unbecoming conduct and the disastrous outcome of his efforts to consult them.

Indeed, God allowed them to see for themselves the results of their own actions. He took them through that gruelling experience, but never banished them or threw them out of the Muslim community. He did not say to them: "You are not fit for this mission due to the weaknesses and shortcomings you have displayed." He acknowledged their faults and inadequacies and presented them with the opportunity to learn through experience by pointing out to them the various lessons and admonitions implicit in that experience. All this is done with a thoughtful, tolerant and caring demeanour, like that of an adult towards a child. He exposed their weakness not in order to humiliate, shame or discredit them, nor in order to overburden their souls, but rather in order to guide and inspire them. To give them greater self-confidence and self-esteem, and to teach them never to despair of reaching their goals as long as they remain loyal to God and hold fast to their strong ties with Him.

They did, in the end, prevail. The sound elements among them, who were few and far between at the beginning of the confrontation, had multiplied. The following day, they all went out with the Prophet to fight for a second time, without any apprehension, hesitation or fear of the threats people made against them. The Qur'ān spoke well of them and applauded their stance.

As the community matured, they were treated more rigorously and held answerable for their actions in a much stricter manner. This becomes quite clear if one considers the Qur'ān's treatment of the aftermath of the Tabūk expedition, in *sūrah* 9, *al-Tawbah*, or Repentance. There, a small group of Muslims who did not join the campaign are severely reprimanded. There is a remarkably different tone in the Qur'ānic approach to, and its reproach of, the Muslims at Uḥud and those at Tabūk, although they were fundamentally the same people. At Tabūk the Muslims were more mature and, therefore, more responsible. Nevertheless, they were human, with the same weaknesses, failings and imperfections. Yet they never ceased to repent and seek God's support and forgiveness.

Islam preserves and nurtures human nature. It does not change it or overburden it even when it is stretched to its limits of achievement and innovation.

This fact is of great value. It gives lasting hope to mankind that they may strive more and achieve more under Islam's unique way of life. Those early Muslims began their journey to the top from very humble beginnings. Those frail first steps were taken by a small group of Arabs whose life was, as we have seen, backward in every respect. Their example gives all humanity reason for optimism to achieve greater and further progress, no matter how low it has fallen. They did not represent an isolated case, or a miracle that can never be repeated. Their experience was a product of the Divine way of life which is accomplished through human effort and power, by human beings who are capable of achieving greater and greater things.

The Divine system starts with any society from whatever material situation it is at and takes it forwards and upwards, just as it did with that naïve and ignorant group of Arabs. Within a very short span of time, less than 25 years, that group achieved unparalleled heights of progress and civilisation.

One important requirement, however, must be fulfilled: people must fully submit to God's system; they must believe and comply with its laws and teachings; it must be the foundation of their life, the slogan of their movement, and the beacon in their journey on the long and arduous route ahead.

3. The third fact to come out of the Uḥud episode and the Qur'ān's analysis of it is the close relationship, in Islam's outlook, between the mentality of the Muslim community and the battle it fights against its enemies in every arena. The relationship between the community's beliefs, perceptions, ethics, behaviour and political, economic and social organisation, on the one hand, and its victory or defeat on the battlefield, on the other. These are crucially important factors in determining what befalls a nation and in whether or not it prevails.

The Divine way of life operates within the huge area of human psyche and human society. It is an intricate and multi-faceted arena. Plans may falter or fail when the relationship and the coordination among its constituent parts are upset or disrupted. It is after all a system which looks at life in its totality, rather than in fragments. It deals with all aspects of man and life, affecting both in a single integrated way that causes no dichotomy or fragmentation.

This is clearly illustrated in the connection the Qur'ān makes between defeat and succumbing to Satan's suggestions, as in the case of *"those of you who turned away on the day when the two hosts met in battle, Satan caused them to slip only in consequence of something that they themselves had done."* (Verse 155) Conversely, the earlier believers who fought steadfastly by their prophets' side, provided a role-model for the Muslims to emulate. They began their fighting with prayers and pleas for God's forgiveness (Verses 146–8).

When the Qur'ān addresses the believers in verses 133–5, it directs them first to cleanse their hearts of sin and to seek God's forgiveness before it urges them to stand firm and fight valiantly and bravely in the battlefield. Earlier, in verse 112, it affirms that the reasons for the humiliation and defeat of the people of earlier revelations lay in their transgressions and wickedness.

There are numerous references to wrongdoing and misconduct throughout the Qur'ān's review of the Battle of Uḥud, while the *sūrah* as a whole is filled with allusions to fear of God. This thread links the *sūrah*'s diverse themes. There is also the call to abandon usury and to obey God and His messenger. To behave with goodwill and benevolence towards others, and to control anger, all of which are qualities that purify the individual and cleanse society. The whole *sūrah* appears as one integrated effort to emphasise this major objective.

4. A fourth feature of the Islamic method of educating its followers is that it takes them through practical experiences in order to cultivate in them certain feelings, emotions and responses before giving them its judgement and interpretation of those events and experiences, as given in its review of the Battle of Uḥud. In its analysis of the events, the Qurʾān touches every possible nerve in human emotions and behaviour, correcting wrong impressions, giving reassurance and confirming certain facts. It leaves no relevant thought, sensibility or concern without highlighting it or making a direct reference to it. It unravels all aspects of human nature and human response in order to cleanse, purify, correct, clarify and refine the subjects' feelings, impressions, concepts and values. Its aim is to establish the true, sound principles of the Islamic outlook for a better and more stable life. This approach enables the Qurʾān to use every event and every experience by the Muslim community as a means for enlightenment, education and a broader understanding of things.

   Furthermore, the Qurʾān's review of the Battle of Uḥud is meticulous, incisive and comprehensive. Every scene, every move and every emotion is precisely recorded and analysed. Every corner of human feeling and behaviour is penetrated and explored; nothing is overlooked. There is precision in the analysis of the causes and the outcome of the events; there is depth in discussing the various factors involved in propelling the action; there is vitality in the descriptions and rhythms. Feelings are intertwined with imagery in a profound and dynamic way. One cannot remain impassive or detached from the scenes so described; instead one is filled with energy, enthusiasm and inspiration.

5. Another highly important principle which emerges from the Battle of Uḥud is the realistic nature of the Divine way of life. For the Divine system to be established, it has to be actually implemented in society. It is not a mere collection of abstract

principles or vague exhortations. It is a practical, tangible and realistic way of life. The best way to illustrate this fact is the Divine view of *shūrā*, or collective public consultation.

The Prophet would have been quite within his rights to spare the Muslim community the travails of their experience with consultative government; they were still a young society surrounded by enemies, both from within and from without. He could have planned and conducted the confrontation according to his own judgement, supported by the premonitions in his dream. He did not have to consult his Companions or to comply with the outcome of that consultation. Indeed, even his Companions realised that they might have forced him into a course of action he did not wish to take.

Nevertheless, the Prophet went ahead and accepted the consensus of his people. This he did, so that they would face the consequences of their judgement and learn how to take responsibility. In the Prophet's view, and according to the Islamic approach he was establishing, compliance with a collective decision takes precedence over the need to avoid losses on the battlefield or to avert the pains of the bitter experience of *shūrā*. To do that would be to deny the Muslims the benefit of their experience and deprive them of the lessons and the maturity they would gain from that experience.

The Divine instruction to pursue consultation and to comply with its outcome were received by Muḥammad after the battle as confirmation of the principle itself. This was the most effective and profound way of establishing the principle and of elaborating on the tenets of the Divine way of life.

Islam does not defer establishing a principle until the community is ready to implement it. The community needs to practise in order to learn and be prepared. To deny people the benefits of their experience of fundamental principles, such as consultative government, is more detrimental to the develop-ment of that society than any outcome that might emerge from that experience. Mistakes, no matter how great or serious, are no justification for the invalidation, withdrawal or suspension of a particular tenet or principle. This would only stunt the growth and development of the community, emasculate its expertise and threaten its whole existence.

This is the meaning conveyed by the Qur'ānic statement: *"Therefore pardon them and pray for them to be forgiven, and consult them in the conduct of public affairs."* (Verse 159)

The practicalities of this approach can also be seen very clearly in the Prophet's behaviour. He refused to take the matter for consultation a second time indicating that it would be a sign of indecisiveness to do so. It would totally undermine the very process itself. In this respect he made that historic declaration that "no prophet should lay down his battle dress until God decides the issue". Then came the Qur'ānic instruction: *"When you have resolved about a course of action, put your trust in God."* (Verse 159) Thus, the action and the instruction come together in perfect harmony.

6. Finally, we learn from the Qur'ānic review of Uḥud that God's way of life is constant and consistent in its values and standards. People may misunderstand the Divine way of life or misinterpret its principles, teachings and concepts, but none of this should in any way demean or devalue that system itself.

If people misunderstand the Divine system, they are told that they have gone wrong and if they deviate from its principles and teachings, they are depicted as mistaken or misguided. Islam does not overlook such mistakes or deviations, no matter how highly regarded the culprits are, and it does not change its nature in order to accommodate or legitimise such errors or deviations.

What we learn from this is that exonerating the individual does not justify distorting or mutilating the system. It is far more advantageous for the universal Muslim community to keep the values and principles of their way of life pure and intact and to identify and isolate those who misconstrue or misinterpret them, no matter who they are. Their mistakes and misconceptions should never be justified or lent any legitimacy by changing or modifying the values and standards of the system itself. Such course of action is far more damaging to Islam than criticising or censuring certain Muslim leaders or prominent figures. The system is greater and more lasting than any individual. The true history of Islam is not everything that Muslims have done or achieved in their life, but it is everything they have done and accomplished in total agreement with Islam and its firmly-established values and principles. The deviations and mistakes should not be attributed to Islam or associated with it, but should be credited to the individuals or societies that were responsible for them. The "history of Islam" and the "history of the Muslims" are not one and the same thing, even those who are, to all intents and purposes, Muslim. The "history of Islam" is represented by eras when Islam was truly and rightly put into practice, when its concepts and beliefs, its code of morality, and its way of life for society as a whole were truly implemented. Islam is the firm centre around which the nation's life revolves within a well-defined structure. Once people stray away from that framework or abandon the central tenets of Islam, they cease to have anything to do with Islam. In this way, Islam should not be held accountable for their behaviour nor should it be interpreted in the light of their actions. Indeed, what justification is there to continue to associate such individuals or groups with Islam, if they break away from its central beliefs and principles and refuse to comply with them in their daily lives. Muslims are only Muslims if they adopt Islam as their way of life, and not because they bear Muslim names or because they claim to be Muslim.

God intended to convey these lessons to the Muslim community by exposing their mistakes and noting their weaknesses and shortcomings. Having done that, He then absolves them and relieves them of all guilt, albeit after having taken them through a harsh and gruelling experience.

Part III

Main Issues
Re-emphasised

11

Main Issues Re-emphasised

Let not those who niggardly cling to all that God has bestowed on them of His bounty think that this is good for them. Indeed, it is bad for them. That to which they niggardly cling will hang around their necks on the Day of Resurrection. To God belongs the heritage of the heavens and the earth, and God is well aware of all that you do. (180)

وَلَا يَحْسَبَنَّ ٱلَّذِينَ يَبْخَلُونَ بِمَآ ءَاتَىٰهُمُ ٱللَّهُ مِن فَضْلِهِۦ هُوَ خَيْرًا لَّهُم بَلْ هُوَ شَرٌّ لَّهُمْ سَيُطَوَّقُونَ مَا بَخِلُوا۟ بِهِۦ يَوْمَ ٱلْقِيَٰمَةِ وَلِلَّهِ مِيرَٰثُ ٱلسَّمَٰوَٰتِ وَٱلْأَرْضِ وَٱللَّهُ بِمَا تَعْمَلُونَ خَبِيرٌ ﴿١٨٠﴾

God has certainly heard the words of those who said: "God is poor, and we are rich." We shall record what they have said, and also their slaying of prophets against all right and We shall say: "Taste now the torment of burning. (181)

لَّقَدْ سَمِعَ ٱللَّهُ قَوْلَ ٱلَّذِينَ قَالُوٓا۟ إِنَّ ٱللَّهَ فَقِيرٌ وَنَحْنُ أَغْنِيَآءُ سَنَكْتُبُ مَا قَالُوا۟ وَقَتْلَهُمُ ٱلْأَنۢبِيَآءَ بِغَيْرِ حَقٍّ وَنَقُولُ ذُوقُوا۟ عَذَابَ ٱلْحَرِيقِ ﴿١٨١﴾

"This is on account of what your own hands have wrought. Never does God do the slightest injustice to His servants." (182)

ذَٰلِكَ بِمَا قَدَّمَتْ أَيْدِيكُمْ وَأَنَّ ٱللَّهَ لَيْسَ بِظَلَّٰمٍ لِّلْعَبِيدِ ﴿١٨٢﴾

319

They declare: "God has charged us not to believe in any messenger unless he brings us an offering which the fire consumes." Say: "Messengers came to you before me with clear evidence of the truth, and with that which you describe. Why, then, did you slay them, if what you say is true?" (183)

ٱلَّذِينَ قَالُوٓاْ إِنَّ ٱللَّهَ عَهِدَ إِلَيْنَآ أَلَّا نُؤْمِنَ لِرَسُولٍ حَتَّىٰ يَأْتِيَنَا بِقُرْبَانٍ تَأْكُلُهُ ٱلنَّارُ قُلْ قَدْ جَآءَكُمْ رُسُلٌ مِّن قَبْلِي بِٱلْبَيِّنَتِ وَبِٱلَّذِي قُلْتُمْ فَلِمَ قَتَلْتُمُوهُمْ إِن كُنتُمْ صَٰدِقِينَ ﴿١٨٣﴾

Then, if they charge you with falsehood, before your time other messengers were also charged with falsehood when they came with clear evidence of the truth, and books of Divine wisdom and with the light-giving revelation. (184)

فَإِن كَذَّبُوكَ فَقَدْ كُذِّبَ رُسُلٌ مِّن قَبْلِكَ جَآءُو بِٱلْبَيِّنَتِ وَٱلزُّبُرِ وَٱلْكِتَٰبِ ٱلْمُنِيرِ ﴿١٨٤﴾

Every soul shall taste death, and you shall be paid on the Day of Resurrection only that which you have earned. He who shall be drawn away from the Fire and brought into paradise shall indeed have gained a triumph. The life of this world is nothing but an illusory enjoyment. (185)

كُلُّ نَفْسٍ ذَآئِقَةُ ٱلْمَوْتِ وَإِنَّمَا تُوَفَّوْنَ أُجُورَكُمْ يَوْمَ ٱلْقِيَٰمَةِ فَمَن زُحْزِحَ عَنِ ٱلنَّارِ وَأُدْخِلَ ٱلْجَنَّةَ فَقَدْ فَازَ وَمَا ٱلْحَيَوٰةُ ٱلدُّنْيَآ إِلَّا مَتَٰعُ ٱلْغُرُورِ ﴿١٨٥﴾

You shall most certainly be tried in your possessions and in your persons; and you shall hear much

۞ لَتُبْلَوُنَّ فِىٓ أَمْوَٰلِكُمْ وَأَنفُسِكُمْ وَلَتَسْمَعُنَّ مِنَ

hurting abuse from those who were given revelations before you and from those who set up partners with God. But if you persevere and continue to fear God – that is indeed a matter requiring strong resolve. (186)

ٱلَّذِينَ أُوتُوا۟ ٱلْكِتَٰبَ مِن قَبْلِكُمْ وَمِنَ ٱلَّذِينَ أَشْرَكُوٓا۟ أَذًى كَثِيرًا ۚ وَإِن تَصْبِرُوا۟ وَتَتَّقُوا۟ فَإِنَّ ذَٰلِكَ مِنْ عَزْمِ ٱلْأُمُورِ ۝

God has made a covenant with those who were granted revelations (when He bade them): "Make it known to mankind and do not conceal it." But they cast it behind their backs and bartered it away for a trifling price. Evil is that which they have taken in exchange for it. (187)

وَإِذْ أَخَذَ ٱللَّهُ مِيثَٰقَ ٱلَّذِينَ أُوتُوا۟ ٱلْكِتَٰبَ لَتُبَيِّنُنَّهُ لِلنَّاسِ وَلَا تَكْتُمُونَهُۥ فَنَبَذُوهُ وَرَآءَ ظُهُورِهِمْ وَٱشْتَرَوْا۟ بِهِۦ ثَمَنًا قَلِيلًا ۖ فَبِئْسَ مَا يَشْتَرُونَ ۝

Do not think that those who exult in their deeds and love to be praised for what they have not done – do not think that they will escape punishment. A grievous suffering awaits them. (188)

لَا تَحْسَبَنَّ ٱلَّذِينَ يَفْرَحُونَ بِمَآ أَتَوا۟ وَّيُحِبُّونَ أَن يُحْمَدُوا۟ بِمَا لَمْ يَفْعَلُوا۟ فَلَا تَحْسَبَنَّهُم بِمَفَازَةٍ مِّنَ ٱلْعَذَابِ ۖ وَلَهُمْ عَذَابٌ أَلِيمٌ ۝

To God belongs the dominion of the heavens and the earth; and He has power over all things. (189)

وَلِلَّهِ مُلْكُ ٱلسَّمَٰوَٰتِ وَٱلْأَرْضِ ۗ وَٱللَّهُ عَلَىٰ كُلِّ شَىْءٍ قَدِيرٌ ۝

321

Overview

The *sūrah* has now completed its coverage of the events at Uḥud, but the struggle between the Muslim community and their opponents around Madinah, the Jews in particular, was not over. The debates, the arguments, the intrigues, the rumours, the destructive propaganda, and the controversies raged on unabated. It is this unending struggle that has occupied most of the *sūrah*.

The Prophet Muḥammad had by that time, in the wake of the Battle of Badr, banished the Jewish tribe of Qaynuqā' from Madinah, in response to their seditious and subversive activities. They had reneged on agreements he made with them upon his arrival in Madinah and his establishment of a Muslim state incorporating the Arab tribes of Aws and Khazraj. The Jewish tribes of al-Naḍīr and Quraiẓah and the smaller Jewish communities in Khayber and other parts of Arabia continued to work together, forging alliances with pockets of "hypocrites" inside Madinah and with the idolaters in Makkah and around Madinah, hatching plots to subvert and destroy the young Muslim state.

Earlier in the *sūrah*, the Jews are warned against a fate similar to that of the non-Muslim Arabs, if they underestimated the Muslims' ability to retaliate. We read: *"Say to those who disbelieve: 'You shall be overcome and gathered unto Hell, an evil resting place. You have had a sign in the two armies which met in battle. One was fighting for God's cause, the other an army of unbelievers. They saw with their very eyes that the others were twice their own number. But God strengthens with His succour whom He wills. In this there is surely a lesson for all who have eyes to see."* (Verses 12–13)

When the Prophet conveyed this warning to the Jews of Madinah, in the wake of the Badr campaign, they reacted with insolence and contempt. On one occasion, a group of the Qaynuqā' Jews said to the Prophet: "Muḥammad. Do not let yourself be deluded that you were able to kill a few naïve men from Quraysh who were so inexperienced in combat. By God, if you were to fight us, you would know that *we* are the real men, the like of whom you have never encountered." They went on to perpetrate more sedition and subversion, many aspects of which are given in this *sūrah*, culminating in the revocation of their agreement with Muḥammad. Consequently, the Prophet lay siege to the Qaynuqā' forts until they yielded to his demands, and, thereafter, he banished them to a place called Adhra'āt. The two other Jewish tribes, Quraẓah and al-Naḍīr, remained in Madinah, apparently faithful to their pact, but in practice heavily engaged in clandestine activities of disinformation, rumour and intrigue. Thus, the Qurʾān records for posterity certain characteristics and patterns of behaviour that have, in many societies, come to be associated with some Jewish communities throughout history.

This section of the *sūrah* reviews some Jewish activities and claims that reflect an attitude of impertinence and disrespect, not only towards the Muslims, but towards God Almighty Himself. Not only did some of the Jews refuse to honour their financial commitments to the state, but had the impudence to say: *"God is poor, we are rich".* (Verse 181)

We can also see in this section the weak arguments advanced by the Jews of Madinah against Islam and the contrived manner in which they contradict even their own known history. They disobeyed God and broke their covenant with Him; they concealed God's revelation from other people or disregarded it altogether; they slew prophets who had come to them with clear proof from God, which they rejected.

The Qurʾān's exposure of all this shameful misbehaviour was necessary so as to explain their attitude towards the Muslims and to counteract their unholy alliance with the pagan Arabs. It was also necessary for the enlightened education and development of the Muslim community. It made them aware of their surroundings and the environment they were living and working in; they knew the obstacles and pitfalls on their path and the pain and sacrifices awaiting them. Jewish hostility towards the Muslims in Madinah was much more serious and dangerous than that of the Arabs in Makkah, and could represent the largest threat in their history.

Hence, the constant flood of directives and guidelines addressing the Muslims throughout this discussion. The *sūrah* draws their attention to values that are enduring and fundamental as well as to those that are ephemeral and short-lived. It stresses that life is finite and short; all beings eventually die and in the Hereafter there are rewards, and there are gains and losses. We read: *"He who shall be drawn away from the Fire and brought into Paradise shall indeed have gained a triumph. The life of this world is nothing but an illusory enjoyment."* (Verse 185) They are told that they will be tested regarding their lives and their wealth; they will meet with hostility and harassment from the unbelievers and the people of earlier revelations which they can only resist with perseverance, with fear of God, and in steadfast compliance of His order which will also save them from the fire.

These Divine directives continue to be as valid and as relevant for Muslims today as in the future. They are addressed to every Muslim community intending to revive and uphold Islam. God will open their eyes to the hurdles and difficulties awaiting them, as well as the suffering and sacrifices they have to endure. Ultimately, their hearts and minds should aspire to rewards God has in store for them; suffering, death, and tribulation are all quite bearable. God calls to Muslims everywhere, as He did with that first generation, that: *"Every soul shall taste death, and you shall be paid on the Day of Resurrection only that which you have earned. He who shall be drawn away from the Fire and brought into paradise shall indeed have gained a triumph. The life of this world is nothing but an illusory enjoyment. You shall most certainly be tried in your possessions and in your persons; and you shall hear much hurting abuse from those who were given revelations before you, and from those who set up partners with God. But if you persevere and continue to fear God – that is indeed a matter requiring strong resolve."* (Verse 185–6)

Today, the Qur'ān, as the book of this timeless Muslim community, remains its comprehensive constitution, its beacon and trusted guide, just as its enemies and its mission remain the same.

Impudence That Cannot Be Equalled

Let not those who niggardly cling to all that God has bestowed on them of His bounty think that this is good for them. Indeed, it is bad for them. That to which they niggardly cling will hang around their necks on the Day of Resurrection. To God belongs the heritage of the heavens and the earth, and God is well aware of all that you do. God has certainly heard the words of those who said: "God is poor, and we are rich." We shall record what they have said, and also their slaying of prophets against all right, and We shall say: "Taste now the torment of burning. This is on account of what your own hands have wrought. Never does God do the slightest injustice to His servants." (Verses 180–2)

We do not have any highly authentic report as to whom the reference is directly made in the first verse of this passage; that is, those who are warned against being miserly and the result of their miserliness on the Day of Judgement. The fact that it occurs at this particular point in the *sūrah* adds relevance to the following verses which speak of the

Jews. It is they, confound them, who said, *"God is poor and we are rich."* It is also they who claimed that God specifically charged them not to believe in any messenger unless he brought them a burnt offering.

It appears that the whole passage has been revealed when the Jews were called upon to honour their financial commitments under their treaty with the Prophet. They were also called upon to believe in the Prophet as God's Messenger and to give freely for God's cause.

The stern warning made in these verses and the exposition of the excuses given by the Jews as a justification for their refusal to believe in Muḥammad (pbuh) are revealed as a strong reply to their impudence towards God, their Lord. This is coupled with support given to the Prophet in the face of their rejection of his message. He is reminded of what the messengers before him had to face in the way of hostile reception by their peoples. These included Israelite prophets who were killed after having brought to their people clear evidence of the truthfulness of their prophethood as well as miracles. All this is well known in the history of the Children of Israel.

> *Let not those who niggardly cling to all that God has bestowed on them of His bounty think that this is good for them. Indeed, it is bad for them. That to which they niggardly cling will hang round their necks on the Day of Resurrection. To God belongs the heritage of the heavens and the earth, and God is well aware of all that you do.* (Verse 180)

This verse applies to the Jews who refuse to honour their commitments just as much as it applies to any people who refuse to come forward to support God's message with that which God has bestowed on them of His bounty. They may think that their niggardliness serves their interests by protecting their wealth, keeping it in their hands, rather than spend it for a good purpose.

The Qurʾānic statement warns them against entertaining such false delusions, making it clear that what they hoard up will be lit up as fire and hung around their necks on the Day of Judgement. It is a fearful warning, made all the more so as it reveals that they niggardly cling only to that which *"God has bestowed on them of His bounty."* They are not hoarding something they have gained of their own accord. They have come to this life penniless, with nothing they could call their own, not even their skins. It is God Who has bestowed on them of His grace and bounty. Yet, when He asks them to be charitable with what He has given them, they do not remember God's grace. Instead, they remain tight-fisted, thinking that when they hoard up their possessions, they do what is good for them, while in fact they do themselves nothing but evil. Moreover, they are bound to go away, leaving it all behind. It is God who inherits all: *"To God belongs the heritage of the heavens and the earth."* They only hoard it up for a brief period, before it all returns to God. Nothing of it remains for them except what they spend for God's sake, in the hope of earning His pleasure. It is that which He rewards them for and ensures their safety on the Day of Judgement.

This is followed by a condemnation of the Jews who thought themselves in no need of God or His reward, or even to the multiples He promises to those who spend their money for His cause. It is this which He is pleased to call a loan given to those who spend their money to serve His cause. The Jews, however, impudently say: How come that God asks us to give Him a loan of our money, and multiplies it for us over and over again, when He Himself forbids usury and the multiplication of the principal loan? This is no more than their impudent playing with words, their unashamed rudeness towards God: *"God has certainly heard the words of those who said: 'God is poor, and we are rich.' We shall record what they have said, and also their slaying of prophets against all right and We shall say: 'Taste now the torment of burning. This is on account of what your own hands have wrought. Never does God do the slightest injustice to His servants.'"*

Confusion in Jewish concepts of the true nature of God is very common in their distortion of their Scriptures. As they utter their impudent mouthful, they are clearly warned: *"We shall record what they have said,"* so that we may take them to account for it. It will neither be forgotten nor overlooked. It will be there, side by side with the record of their past misdeeds, which were perpetrated by their successive generations. They collectively share the blame for it, since they share in their practices of disobedience and sin.

"And also their slaying of prophets against all right." The history of the Children of Israel records a terrible chain of killing one prophet after another, culminating in their attempt on the life of Jesus Christ, (pbuh). They even claim that they killed him, so boasting about their ghastly crime.

"And We shall say: 'Taste now the torment of burning.'" The use of the term *"burning"* is deliberate. It adds to the horror of their torment. It makes the whole scene of suffering come to life, terrible, painful,

unabating. It is a punishment for a hideous crime, namely, killing prophets without any justification whatsoever, and for a terrible sin, when they said *"God is poor and we are rich."*

"This is on account of what your own hands have wrought." It is a fitting recompense, fair and correct. *"Never does God do the slightest injustice to His servants."* The word *"servants"* highlights their position in relation to God. They are no more than servants to Him. This makes their crime even more ghastly and their impudence even more horrid. We need only remember that it is servants of God who boast against all standards of politeness: *"God is poor, and we are rich."* In addition to their very rude attitude towards God, those Jews claimed that they would not believe in Muḥammad because God had charged them not to believe in any messenger until he brought them an offering and a miracle in the form of fire coming from the sky to consume it. Since Muḥammad did not offer such a miracle, they would remain true to their covenant with God, or so they claimed.

At this point, the Qur'ān confronts them with their own history. In the past, they killed those very prophets who came to them with the very miracles they asked of them and also gave them clear evidence of the truth.

> *They declare: "God has charged us not to believe in any messenger unless he brings us an offering which the fire consumes." Say: "Messengers came to you before me with clear evidence of the truth, and with that which you describe. Why, then, did you slay them, if what you say is true?" Then, if they charge you with falsehood, before your time other messengers were also charged with falsehood when they came with clear evidence of the truth, and books of Divine wisdom and with the light-giving revelation.* (Verses 183–4)

By so confronting them, the Qur'ān exposes their lies, deviousness and their persistence with disbelief. Also exposed are their boastful claims and the fabrications they make against God.

Thereafter, the *sūrah* addresses the Prophet with tenderness and reassurance, encouraging him to take lightly whatever they do by way of opposition to him. After all, it is the same as they did against his noble brother messengers throughout history: *"Then, if they charge you with falsehood, before your time other messengers were also charged with falsehood when they came with clear evidence of the truth, and books of Divine wisdom and with the light-giving revelation."* (Verse 184)

Muḥammad was not the first messenger to be confronted with the charge of falsehood. Many earlier messengers, especially those sent to the Children of Israel, were similarly confronted, despite what they had shown of clear evidence and miracles, as well as scrolls containing Divine commandments, described in this verse as books of Divine wisdom, and with the light-giving revelation, such as the Torah and the Gospel. It is, then, the same story with all messengers and Divine messages. It is the same way they all follow, a way of hardship and sacrifice. It is the only way.

A Drink to Be Tasted by All

Here the *sūrah* addresses the Muslim community, explaining the values it should hold dear, and for which it should make sacrifices. It also speaks of the hardships and the suffering which it is bound to encounter on the way and encourages the Muslims to remain steadfast, show strong resolve and to always maintain fear of God:

> *Every soul shall taste death, and you shall be paid on the Day of Resurrection only that which you have earned. He who shall be drawn away from the Fire and brought into paradise shall indeed have gained a triumph. The life of this world is nothing but an illusory enjoyment. You shall most certainly be tried in your possessions and in your persons; and you shall hear much hurting abuse from those who were given revelations before you and from those who set up partners with God. But if you persevere and continue to fear God – that is indeed a matter requiring strong resolve."* (Verses 185–6)

The fact that this life on earth is limited to a certain date, which will inevitably come must be well established in believers' hearts. Good people as well as bad people will certainly die. Those who fight a campaign of *jihād* and those who slacken, those who feel pride in their faith and those who are humbled by others, the brave who accept no injustice and the cowards who will do anything to remain alive, those who have great aspirations and the ones who seek only cheap enjoyment, will all die. No one will be spared: *"Every soul shall taste death."* It is a cup from which every living thing will have to drink. There is no distinction whatsoever between one soul and another when it comes to drinking this cup. What distinction there is concerns a different value: the ultimate result. *"You shall be paid on the Day of Resurrection only that which you have earned. He who shall be drawn away from the Fire and brought into paradise shall indeed have gained a triumph."* It is with regard to this value that the distinction will be made. It is this destiny which will separate one group of souls from another. The value is one worth striving for and one to be taken very seriously: *"He who shall be drawn away from the Fire and brought into paradise shall indeed have gained a triumph."* (Verse 185)

The Arabic phrase rendered in translation as *"shall be drawn away"* is much more expressive than its English equivalent. This is because its very sound adds to its meaning and connotation. It gives the listener the sense that the Fire has strong gravity, that it pulls towards it anyone who draws near or enters its orbit. Such a person, then, needs support from someone else who draws him slowly and gradually away from its overpowering gravity. He who can be forced out of its orbit and become free of its pull will enter paradise, and he will have gained a great triumph.

It is a very vivid image, its lines delineated in sharp relief. We see movement, an overpowering force and a strong resistance. The fire beckons those who yield to the overpowering temptation of sin. Is it not true that a human being needs to be gradually drawn away from temptation? This is indeed how he is drawn away from the Fire. Despite the hard work and alertness this requires, man will always be in deficit with regard to the good work he needs to do. His only hope is for God to bestow on him His grace. That is what is being "drawn away" from the fire really means. It is only through God's grace that man is spared the punishment of hell.

"The life of this world is nothing but an illusory enjoyment." There is enjoyment in this life, it is true. But it is not real enjoyment; it is deceptive indeed; an enjoyment which leads to illusions. As for the real enjoyment which gives lasting happiness and ecstasy, this can only be found in the life to come. It is the triumph gained when one is brought into Paradise. When this fact is well established in the believer's heart, when he is no longer so keen to stay alive, since every soul shall taste death anyway, and when he has recognised the illusory nature of the enjoyment of this life, God tells the believers of the trials which they shall have to endure in their possessions and persons. By then, they are well prepared for the sacrifice.

In the Face of Abuse and Hardship

You shall most certainly be tried in your possessions and in your persons; and you shall hear much hurting abuse from those who were given revelations before you and from those who set up partners with God. But if you persevere and continue to fear God – that is indeed a matter requiring strong resolve. (Verse 186)

In this verse, God tells the believers in no uncertain terms that they will have to undergo tests and trials which will affect them and their possessions. They have to persevere and remain steadfast in order to prove themselves worthy of God's trust and His great reward. It is the natural way of things when it comes to the establishment of any faith in real life that its advocates should stand a hard test. There is no escaping the fact that they will have to demonstrate their patience in adversity, their determined resistance and strong resolve as also their readiness to sacrifice whatever is required of their possessions and their persons. This is the only way to heaven which cannot be attained without sacrifice and hardship. Hell, on the other hand, is surrounded by easy pleasures and temptations. Moreover, there is no other way to mould the community which will become the standard-bearer of Islam and discharge its duties. This community must receive thorough education and cultivation in order to heighten its potentials and strengths. The only way is the practical discharge of the duties imposed by their faith and by their gaining a true and practical knowledge of life and people as they are. The trials are needed so that only the strongest in faith continue to advocate the Islamic call. It is only such people that are worthy of its advocacy since only they are fully equipped to be so entrusted. Moreover, it is through trial and perseverance that faith becomes dearer to the faithful. The more they have to endure of hardship and the more sacrifice they have to give for their faith the more valuable it becomes to them. They do not turn their backs on it afterwards, not in any circumstances.

Trials strengthen those who are tried. It is resistance which sharpens potentials and consolidates them. A new faith requires that these potentials be heightened so that it can establish its roots deep in the most fertile soil of human nature.

It is also through trials that the advocates of a faith come to know themselves as they are. They will look at themselves as they struggle and fight for their faith. They become more aware of human nature in reality and its latent potentials, and they know the true nature of societies and communities. They observe the struggle between their own principles on the one hand and desires and temptations on the other. They become aware of how Satan works on man leading him astray and causing him to err.

Moreover, it is through the trials endured by the advocates of a certain faith that its opponents come to realise that there is much good in it; its followers have stuck by it despite all the hardships they have endured for its sake. It is then that those opponents may themselves accept that faith *en masse*.

This is in the nature of faith and ideology: to withstand such trials while maintaining fear of God, so that repelling aggression by others does not turn into counter-aggression, and despair is not allowed to becloud one's vision as one goes through the hardships. But this is far from easy: *"That is indeed a matter requiring strong resolve."*

The Muslim community in Madinah was thus made aware of what awaits it of sacrifice, agony, abuse and trial in possessions and persons. These were to be inflicted by its enemies, whether these followed earlier religions or were idolaters. Despite all this, the Muslim community was determined to go along its way, without reluctance or hesitation. Members of that Muslim community in Madinah were certain that every soul will taste death, and that rewards are paid on the Day of Resurrection. They knew that true triumph is that of being drawn away from the fire and of being brought into paradise. To them, the life of this world was nothing but an illusory enjoyment. It is on such hard rocks that the Muslim community in Madinah stood and along that straight and correct way it made its strides. The same hard rocks and the same straight way are available to its advocates in every generation. The enemies of this faith remain the same. Generations follow generations and still they plot to undermine it. The Qurʾān, however, remains the same, well preserved by God.

The methods of trial may differ from time to time, but the principle remains the same: *"You shall most certainly be tried in your possessions and in your persons; and you shall hear much hurting abuse from those who were given revelations before you and from those who set up partners with God."* (Verse 186)

The *sūrah* gives many examples of the schemes adopted by people of earlier religions and the idolaters and their propaganda which aimed to cast doubt and confusion on the very fundamentals of Islam and on its followers and their leadership. These examples are always renewed and new methods and forms added to them as new means of communication become available. They are all directed against Islam and its principles of faith as well as against the Muslim community and its leadership. Hence, the same principle which God explains to the first Muslim community as He points out its way and the nature of its enemy remains always applicable.

This Qur'ānic directive remains valid for the Muslim community every time it takes upon itself to implement God's method in practical life. It reassures the Muslims that God's promise will come true. All that it has to endure of trials, abuse, false accusation and hardship becomes very pleasant, since it is no more than a confirmation that the community is going along the way God intends. It is fully certain that perseverance and maintaining its fear of God are all the equipment it needs. All enemy schemes are of little effect. Trials and abuse are of no consequence.

Seeking Praise for Nothing

The *sūrah* continues to expose the peoples of earlier revelations who have contravened their covenant with God. God took a pledge from them that when He revealed to them the Scriptures that they would always make them known to people. They, however, did not honour their pledges and concealed what had been entrusted to them of God's revelations:

> God has made a covenant with those who were granted revelations (when He bade them): "Make it known to mankind and do not conceal it." But they cast it behind their backs and bartered it away for a trifling price. Evil is that which they have taken in exchange for it. Do not think that those who exult in their deeds and love to be praised for what they have not done – do not think that they will escape punishment. A grievous suffering awaits them. To God belongs the dominion of the heavens and the earth; and He has power over all things. (Verses 187–9)

The *sūrah* relates many examples of what the people of earlier religions, particularly the Jews, were keen to do or say. Most serious among these was their concealment of the truth and their attempt to confuse that truth with falsehood. They aimed to create doubt and uncertainty in the basic concept of religion as well as in the truthfulness of the message of Islam. They tried hard to conceal the fact that Islam shared with past religions their basic principles to the extent that Islam endorsed them and they confirmed it. The Torah was in their hands telling them that the message of Muḥammad was true and that it originated from the same source.

In spite of their covenant with God to make their revelations known to mankind and never to conceal them, they have deliberately gone against their pledges. The expression given here to their attitude clearly shows their negligence and contravention of their own pledges. It is expressed in the form of an unseemly gesture: *"they cast it behind their backs."* It also reveals that they committed this dishonourable act for no more than a trivial gain: *"and bartered it away for a trifling price."*

Whatever the price, it was nothing more than a small gain by worldly standards. It could only have served the personal interests of the rabbis or the national interest of the Israelites. All this is nothing but a trifling price, even if it did amount to the ownership of all the earth for the rest of time. How trifling this price is for a covenant made with God. How little all this is in comparison with what is stored with God: *"Evil is that which they have taken in exchange for it."*

A *ḥadīth* related by Al-Bukhārī on the authority of Ibn 'Abbās states that the Prophet asked some Jews of Madinah about something. They concealed it and deliberately gave him an incorrect answer. They gave him the impression that they were right, and that they deserved to be praised for it. In fact, they rejoiced at their concealment of what he asked them about. According to this *ḥadīth*, this was the occasion for the revelation of the following verse: *"Do not think that those who exult in their deeds and love to be praised for what they have not done — do not think that they will escape punishment. A grievous suffering awaits them."* (Verse 188)

Another *ḥadīth*, also related by Al-Bukhārī, on the authority of Abū Saʿīd al-Khudrī, states that a group of hypocrites at the time of the Prophet used to stay behind when the Prophet embarked on a campaign of *Jihād*. They were very pleased for sparing themselves the trouble of accompanying the Prophet. When he returned to Madinah they gave him all sorts of excuses, swearing that what they said was true, and seeking to be praised for things they had not done. Hence, the revelation of this verse.

It is not always apparent that a certain Qur'ānic verse has been revealed on a particular occasion or to answer a specific question. It frequently happens that a certain verse is quoted to comment on a certain event because it fits the purpose; hence, some people may say that such and such verse was revealed on such and such occasion. It may also be that the verse itself includes fitting comments on a particular event, and again the same suggestion about its revelation is made. In this particular respect we are unable to say which of the two reports is more accurate. If it was the first, the *sūrah* speaks of the people of earlier revelations and their concealment of what God had entrusted to them of His revelations when He accepted their pledge that they would make them known to people. In spite of this, they concealed and lied about it persistently to such an extent that they sought praise for their fabrications.

If the second report is true, the *sūrah* includes references to the hypocrites to which this verse may be attached. It describes a type of people who may be found in every community as they were to be found at the time of the Prophet. They are those who do not have the courage of their convictions, who cannot stand in defence of what they profess to believe in. They are not prepared to fulfil the duties imposed by faith and instead they stay behind, taking no share in the struggle for faith. If those who fight and struggle for their faith suffer a defeat, these hypocrites raise their heads and boast about their wisdom and realism. If the fighters come back victorious, the hypocrites waste no time in pretending to have given them their full support, claiming that they contributed to their victory. In this way they seek praise for something which they have not done.

This is a type of people who thrive on cowardice and false pretences. Their image is drawn in a couple of touches in the Qur'ān, but the impact is very clear.

God assures His Messenger that such people cannot escape punishment. They cannot spare themselves the grievous suffering which awaits them and they may have no support in trying to evade it: "*Do not think that they will escape punishment. A grievous suffering awaits them.*" (Verse 188) They are threatened with suffering, and the threat comes from God, to Whom the heavens and the earth belong, and Who is able to do all things. How, then, can they escape it? "*To God belongs the dominion of the heavens and the earth; and He has power over all things.*" (Verse 189)

12

Issues Resolved

In the creation of the heavens and the earth, and in the succession of night and day, there are indeed signs for men endowed with insight, (190)

إِنَّ فِي خَلْقِ ٱلسَّمَٰوَٰتِ وَٱلْأَرْضِ وَٱخْتِلَٰفِ ٱلَّيْلِ وَٱلنَّهَارِ لَآيَٰتٍ لِّأُوْلِي ٱلْأَلْبَٰبِ ۝١٩٠

who remember God when they stand, sit and lie down, and reflect on the creation of the heavens and the earth: "Our Lord, You have not created all this in vain. Limitless are You in Your glory. Guard us, then, against the torment of the fire. (191)

ٱلَّذِينَ يَذْكُرُونَ ٱللَّهَ قِيَٰمًا وَقُعُودًا وَعَلَىٰ جُنُوبِهِمْ وَيَتَفَكَّرُونَ فِي خَلْقِ ٱلسَّمَٰوَٰتِ وَٱلْأَرْضِ رَبَّنَا مَا خَلَقْتَ هَٰذَا بَٰطِلًا سُبْحَٰنَكَ فَقِنَا عَذَابَ ٱلنَّارِ ۝١٩١

"Our Lord, him whom You shall commit to the fire, You will have condemned to disgrace. The evildoers shall have none to help them. (192)

رَبَّنَا إِنَّكَ مَن تُدْخِلِ ٱلنَّارَ فَقَدْ أَخْزَيْتَهُۥ وَمَا لِلظَّٰلِمِينَ مِنْ أَنصَارٍ ۝١٩٢

"Our Lord, we have heard the voice of one who calls to faith, [saying], 'Believe in your Lord,' and we have believed. Our Lord, forgive us, then, our sins and efface our bad deeds and let us die with the truly virtuous. (193)

رَبَّنَا إِنَّنَا سَمِعْنَا مُنَادِيًا يُنَادِي لِلْإِيمَٰنِ أَنْ ءَامِنُوا بِرَبِّكُمْ فَـَٔامَنَّا رَبَّنَا فَٱغْفِرْ لَنَا ذُنُوبَنَا وَكَفِّرْ عَنَّا سَيِّـَٔاتِنَا وَتَوَفَّنَا مَعَ ٱلْأَبْرَارِ ۝١٩٣

"Our Lord, grant us what You have promised us through Your messengers, and do not disgrace us on the Day of Resurrection. Surely, You never fail to fulfil Your promise." (194)

رَبَّنَا وَءَاتِنَا مَا وَعَدتَّنَا عَلَىٰ رُسُلِكَ وَلَا تُخْزِنَا يَوْمَ ٱلْقِيَٰمَةِ إِنَّكَ لَا تُخْلِفُ ٱلْمِيعَادَ ﴿١٩٤﴾

Their Lord answers them: "I will not suffer the work of any worker among you, male or female, to be lost. Each of you is an issue of the other. Therefore, those who emigrate and are driven out of their homes and suffer persecution in My cause, and fight and are slain [for it] – I shall indeed efface their bad deeds and admit them to gardens through which running waters flow, as a reward from God. With God is the best of rewards." (195)

فَٱسْتَجَابَ لَهُمْ رَبُّهُمْ أَنِّى لَآ أُضِيعُ عَمَلَ عَٰمِلٍ مِّنكُم مِّن ذَكَرٍ أَوْ أُنثَىٰ بَعْضُكُم مِّنۢ بَعْضٍ فَٱلَّذِينَ هَاجَرُواْ وَأُخْرِجُواْ مِن دِيَٰرِهِمْ وَأُوذُواْ فِى سَبِيلِى وَقَٰتَلُواْ وَقُتِلُواْ لَأُكَفِّرَنَّ عَنْهُمْ سَيِّـَٔاتِهِمْ وَلَأُدْخِلَنَّهُمْ جَنَّٰتٍ تَجْرِى مِن تَحْتِهَا ٱلْأَنْهَٰرُ ثَوَابًا مِّنْ عِندِ ٱللَّهِ وَٱللَّهُ عِندَهُۥ حُسْنُ ٱلثَّوَابِ ﴿١٩٥﴾

Let not the disbelievers' prosperity in the land deceive you. (196)

لَا يَغُرَّنَّكَ تَقَلُّبُ ٱلَّذِينَ كَفَرُواْ فِى ٱلْبِلَٰدِ ﴿١٩٦﴾

It is but a brief enjoyment. Then, Hell shall be their abode. What an evil abode. (197)

مَتَٰعٌ قَلِيلٌ ثُمَّ مَأْوَىٰهُمْ جَهَنَّمُ وَبِئْسَ ٱلْمِهَادُ ﴿١٩٧﴾

As for those who fear their Lord, theirs shall be gardens through which running waters flow, in which they shall abide, a gift of welcome from God. That which is with God is best for the truly virtuous. (198)

لَكِنِ ٱلَّذِينَ ٱتَّقَوْا رَبَّهُمْ لَهُمْ جَنَّـٰتٌ تَجْرِى مِن تَحْتِهَا ٱلْأَنْهَٰرُ خَٰلِدِينَ فِيهَا نُزُلًا مِّنْ عِندِ ٱللَّهِ وَمَا عِندَ ٱللَّهِ خَيْرٌ لِّلْأَبْرَارِ ۝

There are indeed among the people of earlier revelations some who believe in God and in what has been bestowed from on high upon you and in what has been bestowed upon them, humbling themselves before God. They do not barter away God's revelations for a trifling price. They shall have their reward with their Lord. Swift is God's reckoning. (199)

وَإِنَّ مِنْ أَهْلِ ٱلْكِتَٰبِ لَمَن يُؤْمِنُ بِٱللَّهِ وَمَا أُنزِلَ إِلَيْكُمْ وَمَا أُنزِلَ إِلَيْهِمْ خَٰشِعِينَ لِلَّهِ لَا يَشْتَرُونَ بِـَٔايَٰتِ ٱللَّهِ ثَمَنًا قَلِيلًا أُوْلَٰئِكَ لَهُمْ أَجْرُهُمْ عِندَ رَبِّهِمْ إِنَّ ٱللَّهَ سَرِيعُ ٱلْحِسَابِ ۝

Believers, be patient in adversity, and let your patience never be exhausted; be ever ready and fear God so that you may prosper. (200)

يَٰٓأَيُّهَا ٱلَّذِينَ ءَامَنُوا ٱصْبِرُوا وَصَابِرُوا وَرَابِطُوا وَٱتَّقُوا ٱللَّهَ لَعَلَّكُمْ تُفْلِحُونَ ۝

Overview

This is the closing passage of a *sūrah* rich in subject matter and imagery. It defines and establishes the fundamentals of the Islamic outlook and, through the debate with the people of earlier revelations and later on with the "hypocrites" of Madinah and the Arab unbelievers, removes all the confusion and misinterpretation all those groups tried to create. It expounds the Divine order of life, its human and financial obligations, and teaches the Muslims how to honour those obligations and how to deal with the hardships and ordeals encountered in so doing. It shows the Muslims how to dedicate themselves and their possessions to fulfilling those enormous obligations.

These concluding strains resonate perfectly with the theme and the style of the *sūrah* as a whole in content as well as context and presentation. This section presents a most profound concept: that the entire physical world is an open "book" which in itself conveys the signs and evidence of faith. It points to the hand that runs it with care and prudence, and reveals that beyond this life there is another where accountability and reward will be decided. These signs, however, are only perceived and appreciated by people *"who understand"*; those who do not go through life with their eyes and minds closed to the overwhelming marvels of this "open book".

This represents one of the most fundamental concepts of the Islamic outlook on the physical world, and the very close and harmonic relationship that exists between it and man's basic and pristine nature. This concept asserts that the physical world, in itself, is living and tangible proof of the existence of its Creator, on the one hand, as well as a manifestation of the system that underpins its existence, and the purpose, the principle and the meaning that define that existence, on the other. This concept is of the utmost importance in defining man's attitude towards the physical world and its Lord, God Almighty, and is, therefore, a central pillar of the Islamic outlook on all existence.

Then follows God's obliging response to *"those who understand,"* who turned to Him in earnest and penitent supplication while reflecting on His open book of the universe and all the signs it displays and the thoughts it evokes and inspires. This response is accompanied by a recommendation to work hard, to strive, sacrifice and persevere in fulfilling the obligations of the faith they have earned from contemplating the wonders of God's open book. The *sūrah* again underplays the effect and influence of the opponents of Islam, no matter how much material power they may possess in this world. It highlights the everlasting values of the rewards in the Hereafter to which true believers ought to aspire and hope to receive.

Further to the lengthy discussion on the people of earlier revelations and their stance towards the Muslims, the *sūrah* talks here of the believing ones among them and their just rewards.

Preserving the same context of piety, it describes them as devout people who are too polite and modest with God to demean His revelation, like some of their co-religionists, referred to earlier in the *sūrah*.

The closing verse encapsulates God's advice to the Muslims and represents what is required of them, and the obligations whose fulfilment will guarantee them success and accomplishment. *"Believers, be patient in adversity, and let your patience never be exhausted, be ever ready and fear God so that you may prosper."* (Verse 200) It is an ending that fits beautifully with the central theme of the *sūrah* and all the other subjects it deals with.

Universal Evidence of Creation

> *In the creation of the heavens and the earth, and in the succession of night and day, there are indeed signs for men endowed with insight, who remember God when they stand, sit and lie down, and reflect on the creation of the heavens and the earth: "Our Lord, You have not created all this in vain. Limitless are You in Your glory. Guard us, then, against the torment of the fire. Our Lord, him whom You shall commit to the fire, You will have condemned to disgrace. The evildoers shall have none to help them. Our Lord, we have heard the voice of one who calls to faith, [saying], 'Believe in your Lord,' and we have believed. Our Lord, forgive us, then, our sins and efface our bad deeds and let us die with the truly virtuous. Our Lord, grant us what You have promised us through Your messengers, and do not disgrace us on the Day of Resurrection. Surely, You never fail to fulfil Your promise. (Verses 190–4)*

What are these signs contained in the creation of the heavens and the earth and the succession of day and night? What is the message understood by men of wisdom when they reflect on these phenomena, as they remember God in all situations, when they stand up, sit and lie down? Furthermore, what is the relationship between their reflection on these signs and their remembrance of God in all situations? How does their reflection lead them to engage in their supplication which expresses their humility and fear of God:

"Our Lord, You have not created all this in vain. Limitless are You in Your glory. Guard us, then, against the torment of the fire."

What we find here is a vivid image of the sound and proper reception of the messages transmitted by the physical universe to a healthy mind. Proper response is made to these messages which are open to all throughout the universe, both during the day and during the night.

Telling signs appear in every new page of this open book. They awaken uncorrupted human nature to appreciate the truth which is well established both in this book of the universe and in the perfect design of its structure. They create a strong desire to respond to the Creator Who has established this truth in His creation, and couples loving Him with a feeling of fear of Him. People endowed with understanding open their minds to receive the messages God has placed in the universe. They allow no barriers to prevent them from appreciating these messages. Their hearts turn to God when they stand, sit or lie down. Hence, their faculties of understanding are sharpened and they are able to appreciate the message God has placed in the universe, its purpose and its basic nature. Thus, the laws of the universe transmit their inspiration to men's hearts.

We have only to rid ourselves of the shackles of familiarity and to open our eyes and minds to these scenes of the creation of the heavens and earth and the succession of day and night and look at them afresh, as if for the first time, so that we may be overwhelmed with awe and stand in utter wonder and amazement. When we do this, we are bound to feel that behind all this harmony and perfection there must be an organising hand, an elaborate thinking and a law that never fails. We are bound to conclude that nothing of this is deceptive, borne by coincidence or happening in vain.

Our wonder at this beautiful, awe-inspiring scene of the universe is not diminished in any way by our knowledge that the day and the night are two phenomena which result from the earth constantly revolving around the sun, or by our knowledge that the harmony apparent in the creation of the heavens and the earth relies on the law of gravity or some such force. These are mere theories which may be true and equally may be wrong. Be that as it may, they in no way diminish our appreciation of these phenomena and the precise, perfect laws which regulate and preserve them. Regardless of what human scientists may call these laws, they continue to serve as evidence of the truth and of God's power which is manifest in *"the creation of the heavens and the earth and in the succession of night and day."*

This Qur'ānic passage describes in great detail the different psychological stages which result from approaching the creation of the heavens and the earth and the succession of day and night as men endowed with understanding. At the same time, this description points out the proper approach to universal phenomena, how to respond to the universe and its nature and how to appreciate its messages and inspiration. It makes the open book of the universe a book of knowledge for the believer who maintains his relationship with God and with what God creates.

It combines man's remembrance and worship of God in all situations, when he, "stands, sits and lies down" with his reflection on the creation of the heavens and the earth and on the succession of day and night. Thus, reflection becomes intertwined with worship and an aspect of remembering God. This combination presents us with two highly important facts, namely, that reflection on God's creation is an act of worship, and the signs that God has placed in the universe do not impart their true messages except to people who always remember God and worship Him.

A Passionate Prayer by True Believers

The first fact is that reflection on God's creation and contemplation of the open book of the universe and the great wonders which God has placed in the universe constitute a definite act of worship and an essential part of remembering God. Had natural sciences which study various aspects, laws and phenomena of the universe in order to unravel their secrets and potential, been directed to remembrance of the Creator of this universe and to appreciate and acknowledge His majesty and grace, they would instantaneously have become part of worship and prayer to the Creator. Human life would have benefited a great deal by these sciences and would have turned towards God. The materialistic trend, however, severs all links between the universe and its Creator, and severs the relationship which should have always existed between natural sciences and the eternal truth of the Divine Being. Scientific research, God's great gift to man, thus becomes a curse which makes human life a continuous succession of misery, worry and spiritual emptiness which weigh very heavily on man.

The second fact is that the signs that God has placed throughout the universe do not impart their inspiring messages except to hearts and minds refined by worship and the remembrance of God. Those who remember God in all situations, when they stand, sit and lie down, and reflect on the creation of the heavens and the earth and on the succession of day and night are indeed the very people whose hearts and minds are ready to appreciate the messages imparted by these universal phenomena. They are the ones who reach beyond these messages to the Divine method which ensures salvation, goodness and prosperity. On the other hand, those who confine themselves to the study of certain aspects and appearances, and discover the secrets of some universal laws, without any attempt to know the Divine method of life inevitably destroy life and destroy themselves with the secrets they discover. They cannot escape the misery and worry which characterise their lives and they inevitably end up incurring God's wrath and deserving His punishment.

These two facts are mutually complementary, and they are presented here in this way for men of understanding at the precise moment of their reflection on universal phenomena. It is a moment which represents clarity of heart and soul, an open mind ready to receive a message and an attitude of being prepared to give the right response and abide by the implications of the truth.

It is a moment of worship, which means that it is a moment of establishing a relationship and receiving a message. It is no wonder, then, that the mere reflection on the creation of the heavens and the earth and the succession of day and night is enough to reveal the truth about them and the fact that nothing of this has been created in vain. The immediate result of this attitude is embodied in these words: *"'Our Lord, You have not created all this in vain. Limitless are You in Your glory.'"* This is immediately followed by a psychological response to the inspiration of the universe: *"Guard us, then, against the torment of the fire. Our Lord, him whom You shall commit to the fire, You will have condemned to disgrace. The evildoers shall have none to help them."*

What is the nature of the emotional relationship between recognising the truth behind the creation of the heavens and the earth and the succession of day and night and the fear of being thrown into hell? Recognition of this truth means to those endowed with understanding and insight that it is all made according to an elaborate plan and for a definite purpose, and that truth and justice will be maintained beyond man's life on this planet. This inevitably means that whatever people do will be taken into account and that rewards will be administered. This leads to the conclusion that there is another life where the truth will be established and where justice will be done.

This line of argument is both obvious and natural. Its conclusion is quickly formulated in the minds of those people of understanding. Hence, the picture of the fire is immediately visualised in their minds and the foremost thought which accompanies their recognition of the truth is to pray to God to guard them against the fire. This shows a remarkable understanding of how thoughts and feelings are aroused in the minds and the hearts of people endowed with understanding. They express their feelings in their long supplication, apprehensive, urgent, melodious, finely rhythmic: *"Our Lord, him whom You shall commit to the fire, You will have condemned to disgrace. The evildoers shall have none to help them."* This suggests that, first and foremost, they fear the disgrace which will inevitably befall those who are thrown into hell. They shiver with shame when they realise what sort of disgrace befalls such people. They stand ashamed in front of God, and they feel this shame to be more painful than the scourge of the fire. It also expresses their knowledge that there is no one to help them against God: *"The evildoers shall have none to help them."*

We move on with this humble prayer: *"Our Lord, we have heard the voice of one who calls to faith, [saying]: 'Believe in your Lord', and we have believed. Our Lord, forgive us, then, our sins and efface our bad deeds and let us die with the truly virtuous."* These hearts are open. They only need to receive the message in order to respond to it. Their sensitivity is enhanced. The first thing impressed on their minds is the fact that they commit sins and may be guilty of disobedience. Hence, they turn to their Lord, praying for His forgiveness and for their bad deeds to be effaced. They also pray to be grouped with the righteous when they die.

The message of these verses fits in with the message of the rest of the *sūrah*. The believers pray to God to forgive them their sins so that they can win their continuous battle against desire and temptation. Achieving victory in this battle is akin to victory in a military battle against the enemies of God and the enemies of faith. Thus the *sūrah* is a whole unit, each part complementing the other, and delivering a complete and harmonious message.

The last part of this prayer expresses hope, reliance on God and deriving strength from the believers' unshakable trust that He always fulfils His promises: *"Our Lord, grant us what You have promised us through Your messengers, and do not disgrace us on the Day of Resurrection. Surely, You never fail to fulfil Your promise."* They pray for the fulfilment of God's promise conveyed to them by His messengers, expressing their absolute confidence that God never fails in His promise, and their hope to be spared disgrace on the Day of Resurrection. This last expression of apprehension relates to that at the beginning of their prayer. It demonstrates their great sensitivity to this disgrace and the fact that they always remember it and mention it both at the beginning and at the end of their prayer. How sensitive and pious are these hearts and how strong their sense of shame in front of God. Taken as a whole, this prayer represents a genuine and profound response to the message which the universe and its signs and phenomena give to men whose hearts remain open and uncorrupted.

A brief word should be added here about the artistic excellence reflected in the rhyming of these verses. It is a rhythm which does not repeat the same tempo, but rather a rhythm of harmony. Most of the 200 verses of this *sūrah* maintain a rhythm which is normally associated with statement of fact. The rhythm is briefly changed in only two instances, the first occurs early in the *sūrah* and the second applies to these verses. In both instances, the verses concerned include a prayer to God. We note that the changes are made for artistic beauty, whereby the rhythm adopted gives the verses a melodious effect which suits the atmosphere of prayer.

Moreover, reflection on the creation of the heavens and the earth and the succession of day and night is particularly suitable to a long, deliberate prayer which admits elongation and musical overtone. Thus, the scene itself is maintained for a longer period so as to prolong its message and effect on people's minds and imagination.

Prayers Answered and Obligation Defined

> *Their Lord answers them: "I will not suffer the work of any worker among you, male or female, to be lost. Each of you is an issue of the other. Therefore, those who emigrate and are driven out of their homes and suffer persecution in My cause, and fight and are slain [for it] – I shall indeed efface their bad deeds and admit them to gardens through which running waters flow, as a reward from God. With God is the best of rewards. Let not the disbelievers' prosperity in the land deceive you. It is but a brief enjoyment. Then, Hell shall be their abode. What an evil abode.* (Verses 195–7)

In this passage we have God's answer to the prayer repeated at length by the believers who have come to accept the faith after their reflection on the scene of the universe. They recognise that God has not created all this in vain. They understand the message imparted by these scenes and make the appropriate response and pray to God to spare them the disgrace of being committed to hell in the Hereafter. God's answer is a detailed one, harmonious with the artistic characteristics of the Qur'ānic style which takes into account the psychological requirements of every situation. Let us consider this answer and what it tells us about the nature of the Divine method and how Islam sets about refining the characters of its followers. Those people, described in an earlier verse as *"endowed with insight"* have reflected on the creation of the heavens and the earth and on the succession of night and day and have appreciated the message of the book of the universe, responding to the truth as it is clearly explained in it. They have addressed their Lord with a long, heart-felt prayer which reflects their apprehension. Here they receive the response of their merciful Lord. Their prayers are answered as their attention is drawn to the constituent elements of the way of life God wants them to adopt and to its obligations: *"Their Lord answers them: 'I will not suffer the work of any worker among you, male or female, to be lost. Each of you is an issue of the other.'* " Here they are told that reflection, contemplation, apprehension and passionate prayer are not enough, nor is it enough to turn to God for forgiveness and for bad deeds to be effaced and salvation to be granted. These goals require positive action of a particular type that is motivated by understanding the lessons learnt through reflection on the creation of the universe.

Islam considers this an act of worship, in the same way as it considers reflection, contemplation and remembrance of God, a prayer for forgiveness and a fear of God and a hope in His bounty. Indeed, Islam views action as the practical result of such worship. It is accepted from all, male and female alike, without any discrimination on the basis of sex. All people are equal as human beings, since each one of them issues from another, and they are all judged equally.

The work required is then outlined. We can see here the obligations imposed by Islamic faith with regard to personal and financial sacrifices. We can also appreciate the nature of the Islamic method of life and in what sort of society it is to be implemented. We are made to understand further the way to establish such a society and the barriers and difficulties which work against its establishment. The need is urgent to remove such obstacles and to prepare the soil for the seed of Islam to grow and be firm, no matter how great the sacrifices: *"Therefore, those who emigrate and are driven out of their homes and suffer persecution in My cause, and fight and are slain [for it] – I shall indeed efface their bad deeds and admit them to gardens through which running waters flow, as a reward from God. With God is the best of rewards."*

This was the status of those who engaged in this prayer and who were the first generation to be addressed by the Qur'ān. They emigrated from Makkah and were driven out of their homes there because of their faith. They were persecuted for no other reason than serving God's cause. They had to fight and were killed in battle. The same applies to the advocates of this faith in every land and in every generation. Whenever the faith of Islam begins to establish itself in any environment of ignorance, in a hostile land, which could be any land, and among hostile people, any people, it then faces a bad reception because it stands up to people's illegitimate ambitions and greed. Its followers are persecuted and chased away, especially when its advocates are still few in number. This blessed plant, however, will grow in spite of persecution and hostility. It will then acquire the ability to resist persecution and defend itself against aggression. This inevitably leads to fighting in which some of its followers are killed. In return for these great efforts, bad deeds are effaced, sins are forgiven and reward, great reward, is granted.

Only in this way does the Divine system of life come to establish itself. It is a system whose implementation God has ordained must be through human effort. Effort exerted by true believers who struggle and work hard for God's cause, seeking God's pleasure.

This is the nature of this system, its constituent elements and obligations. We have also seen the course which it follows in educating its followers and refining their characters, giving them directives which ensure that they move from the stage of reflection on God's creation to the stage of positive action and are thus able to implement the system God wants man to implement.

Following this, a glance is cast on the temptation which is represented by the luxuries and comforts available in this life to the unbelievers, the disobedient and those who are hostile to the Divine faith. This only aims at making known the true weight and value of such luxuries and comforts so that they do not dazzle the eyes of their beneficiaries or the believers who suffer all the persecution of being driven out from their homes, and who have to fight and sacrifice their lives: *"Let not the disbelievers' prosperity in the land deceive you. It is but a brief enjoyment. Then, Hell shall be their abode. What an evil abode."*

Their prosperity is an aspect of affluence, wealth, position and power. It is bound to leave something in the hearts of believers as they suffer hardship, poverty, and persecution and as they have to fight in battle. All these are hardships which are very difficult to bear. Yet, the followers of falsehood enjoy themselves and are prosperous. The masses, on the other hand, are bound to feel something when they see the advocates of the truth enduring the suffering while the followers of falsehood are spared and enjoying all they want. The evildoers themselves look at the situation and become hardened in their false beliefs, erroneous ways, evil deeds and corruption.

At this point, we have this gentle touch which sets things aright: *"Let not the disbelievers' prosperity in the land deceive you. It is but a brief enjoyment. Then, Hell shall be their abode. What an evil abode."* Their enjoyment is brief. It will soon disappear. As for their final and permanent abode, it is nothing other than Hell. It is indeed an evil abode.

What Reward for a Long, Hard Struggle

In contrast to that brief enjoyment and fleeting prosperity there are for the believers eternity and blessings from God:

> *As for those who fear their Lord, theirs shall be gardens through which running waters flow, in which they shall abide, a gift of welcome from God. That which is with God is best for the truly virtuous. There are indeed among the people of earlier revelations some who believe in God and in what has been bestowed from on high upon you and in what has been bestowed upon them, humbling themselves before God. They do not barter away God's revelations for a trifling price. They shall have their reward with their Lord. Swift is God's reckoning.* (Verses 198–9)

Any comparison shall remove the slightest doubt that what is with God is infinitely better for truly righteous and virtuous people. No one will entertain any thought that what the God-fearing finally receive is much superior than what the disbelievers enjoy. Hence, anyone endowed with insight will unhesitatingly choose for himself the share chosen by the people who have been described earlier as being *"endowed with understanding."*

At this point, when the context is one of cultivating the believers' characters and establishing the essential values according to the Islamic concept of life, God does not promise the believers victory, or that they should triumph over their enemies, or that they should be established in any land. He indeed does not promise them anything in this life. He does not include in His promise here anything of what He promises them elsewhere in the Qur'ān or of what He has undertaken to provide for the believers as they engage in battle against His enemies.

Here, He promises them only one thing, namely, *"that which is with God."* For this is the basic aspect of this message, and the starting point of this faith. God wants the believers to totally disown every aim, purpose or aspiration, including their desire to see their faith triumph and the enemies of God defeated. God wants the believers to free themselves even from this desire. He wants them to leave this matter altogether to Him so that they are free from all ambitions, including those which are not personal. What is required of them is that they be ready to give and sacrifice, to fulfil their duty and perform their obligations. There is nothing for them of the comforts and enjoyments of this life. Moreover, there is no promise of victory, fulfilment of aims or gaining of power. All that is promised is in the Hereafter.

But then victory takes place and the believers are established in the land. This, however, is not part of the deal. There is nothing in the contract which stipulates any returns in this life. All that it speaks of is fulfilment of the deal made when Islam was persecuted in Makkah. The terms were very clear. God did not give the Muslims victory and the reins of power to assume the role of leadership of mankind until they had rid themselves totally of all ambitions which relate to this life and fulfilled their obligations with total dedication.

Muḥammad ibn Ka'b al-Quraẓī and others relate that when people from the two tribes of Madinah, the Aws and the Khazraj, pledged their loyalty to the Prophet and asked him to emigrate to Madinah, 'Abdullāh ibn Rawāḥah said to the Prophet: "Stipulate whatever conditions you wish to make for your Lord and for yourself." The Prophet said: "For my Lord, I stipulate that you shall worship Him alone and associate no partners with Him. For myself, I make the condition that you shall protect me as you protect yourselves and your property." They asked: "What shall we get if we fulfil our pledge?" The Prophet answered: "Paradise." They said: "It is a profitable deal. We accept no going back and we will never go back on it ourselves."

The Prophet's answer must be noted here. All he said was: "Paradise." He promised nothing more. He did not say to them that they will have victory, power, unity of the Arabian tribes, leadership, wealth, prosperity or anything else. It is true that God gave them all that and allowed them to enjoy it, but that was extra, and certainly not part of the deal.

Their attitude is also worth noting. They viewed it as a deal between a buyer and a seller. Once struck, no more bargaining could be done.

This is how God cultivated and disciplined the community in whose hands it was His will to place the control of the earth, and to whom He assigned the leadership of mankind and custody of the great faith. But He only assigned it that role after it had freed itself totally of all desires and ambitions, including those which related to its message, and the system to be implemented. Custody of this faith, the greatest treasure, could not come about until this community demonstrated that it did not care about itself and until it surrendered itself totally to God.

Just before the *sūrah* ends, a fresh reference is made to the people of earlier revelations which states that some of them have similar beliefs to those of the Muslims. These are considered to have joined the ranks of the Muslims and adopted their ways. Hence, they also deserve the same reward:

> There are indeed among the people of earlier revelations some who believe in God and in what has been bestowed from on high upon you and in what has been bestowed upon them, humbling themselves before God. They do not barter away God's revelations for a trifling price. They shall have their reward with their Lord. Swift is God's reckoning. (Verse 199)

This reference is made in order to bring to a conclusion the long account, given in the *sūrah,* of the people of earlier revelations. The *sūrah* has referred to many groups among them and to many of their attitudes. Now that the *sūrah* is speaking about true faith and how people should accept it, and portraying a scene of supplication to God and His answering of believers' prayers, it states that some of the people of earlier revelations have also followed the same path to its final end. They have believed in all God's revelations and have not sought to isolate God's messengers from Him, nor have they discriminated against any of His messengers. They believe in what was revealed to them in former times, and in what has been revealed to the Muslims. This is the distinctive characteristic of a faith which looks at all believers with loving tenderness and visualises the whole procession of the faithful as leading directly to God. It looks at the Divine system as a complete whole. The one characteristic of those believers among the people of earlier revelations which is highlighted here is humility before God and the refusal to barter away God's revelations for a trifling price. They are thus set apart from the ranks of the people of the Scriptures whose main characteristic is one of boastfulness and of being totally unashamed before God. Moreover, they fabricate lies and seek cheap worldly pleasures.

To those believers among the people of earlier revelations God promises the same reward as He gives to Muslim believers. God does not delay the reward of those who deal with Him. Far be it for Him to do so. *"Swift is God's reckoning."*

Summing Up All Obligations

> *Believers, be patient in adversity, and let your patience never be exhausted; be ever ready and fear God so that you may prosper.* (Verse 200)

The closing verse in this long *sūrah* is an address to the believers which sums up the obligations imposed on them by the constitution God has chosen for them. It is an address from on high to the believers. It calls them by their very quality which establishes their bond with the source of that address and places on them their obligations and qualifies them for the fulfilment of those obligations. It is the quality which gives them honour in this world and makes them honoured in heaven. They are called upon to show patience in adversity and to continue to do so in all situations, to be always ready for sacrifice and to maintain their fear of God.

The *sūrah* speaks repeatedly about patience in adversity and fear of God. The two qualities are mentioned on occasions separately and on others together. The *sūrah* also repeatedly calls on the believers to endure whatever hardship they have to face, to struggle and to foil the schemes of their enemies and never to listen to the defeatists or to those who sow the seeds of discord. That the concluding verse of the *sūrah* calls on the believer to be patient in adversity and to always persevere demonstrates that these are the essential ingredients of those who want to follow the path of Divine faith. It is a long and hard way, full of impediments, persecution, trials and tribulations. To follow it they must be patient.

They have to resist their own desires, ambitions, weaknesses and impetuosity. They have to persevere in the face of peoples' desires, weaknesses, ignorance, lack of understanding, perversions, selfishness, conceit, and their impatience for quick results. They have to endure the falsehood and tyranny, the power of evil and the conceit of every boastful arrogant.

They have to be patient in spite of any of their own weaknesses and in spite of the whisperings of Satan at such times when they are totally unhappy. They must persevere in spite of the fact that this can give rise to anger, exasperation, occasional lack of trust in goodness, lack of confidence in human nature, disappointment, frustration and total despair. In addition, they must also be patient and restrain themselves at the moment of victory, show humility and gratitude when adversity is replaced by prosperity, suppress every motive for revenge or for exceeding the limits of justice. They must maintain their relationship with God and submit to His will in times of happiness and in times of hardship. They surrender themselves to Him with trust and reassurance.

Words cannot express the true significance of this struggle. Only a person who has experienced such hardships can understand the full significance of such perseverance. The believers themselves knew well what this address from on high meant. They knew what sort of patience and perseverance God wanted them to show.

This verse then calls on the believers to rise to a higher standard. It is expressed in Arabic in a form of the verb "to be patient" which signifies a highly enhanced effect. This means that the believers must face up to all enemies who try hard to exhaust their patience. The believers are called upon not to allow their patience to fail them despite the prolonged struggle. They must remain more patient and stronger than their enemies, be they the inner enemies in their own souls or the external ones who are the evildoers. The case is thus described as a contest between them and their enemies,

and the believers are called upon to meet patience with stronger
fortitude, effort with even greater effort, determination with strong
resilience. When they have shown that they are stronger and more
patient than their enemies, the outcome will undoubtedly be in
their favour. If falsehood can be determined and is patient as it
goes along its own way, then the truth must be more determined
and resilient and must show greater patience as it goes along its
own way.

To be ready, in Islamic terminology, is to stay in places where
battles are expected, and in positions which are liable to attack from
the enemy. The Muslim community never used to leave its eyes
closed or to allow sleep to overtake it. Right from the moment
when it was called upon to take up the message of Islam and to
convey it to mankind, its enemies have never been allowed to rest.

Nor will they ever allow the Muslim community to rest in peace,
anywhere or at any time. Hence, it cannot overlook the need to be
ever-ready to fight and sacrifice until the end of time.

This message presents to people a practical system which
exercises control over their consciences, money, property and way
of living. It is a system which is upright, just and good. Evil,
however, does not like to see such a system being implemented.
Falsehood does not like honesty, justice or goodness. Tyranny
does not submit to justice, equality and dignity. Hence, this
message will always find enemies who uphold evil, falsehood and
tyranny. Those who exploit others and are engaged in self-
aggrandisement do not wish to relinquish their privileges. The
despots who tyrannise people do not like to stop their oppression.
The corrupt who indulge in every vice do not like to mend their
ways. They all wage a campaign of extermination against the
message of Islam. The believers must face up to all these enemies,
and must equip themselves with patience and perseverance which
can never be exhausted. They must always be on the alert for any
aggression launched against them so that the Muslim community
can never be taken unawares by its natural enemies who can be
found everywhere and in all times.

This is the nature of this message and this is the path it follows.
It does not intend any aggression, but it certainly wants to
establish its correct method and perfect system on earth. It will

always find those who hate its method and system, and who try to prevent its establishment with force, wickedness and propaganda. The advocates of Islam have no choice but to accept the challenge and to fight the battle no matter how much it costs. They must always be on their guard.

Fearing God must accompany all this, because it is a watchful guard over man's conscience. It keeps it alert and strong and restrains it from launching any aggression or indulging in any deviation. No one appreciates the need for this watchfulness except the one who suffers the difficulties of this path, the one who has to contend with contradictory feelings and reactions pulling him in opposite directions in every situation and at every moment.

This final verse sums up the message of the whole *surah*. It puts in a nutshell all the obligations Islam imposes on its followers. There is no wonder then that God attaches to it the outcome of a long struggle and makes prosperity in the Hereafter dependent on it: *"So that you may prosper."* God always tells the truth.

Index

Jordan, 84
Joseph, 96
Jubayr ibn Muṭ'im, 201
Judhām, 278
Jupiter, 278
Justinian, 26

K
Ka'bah, 116, 146, 149, 150, 151, 152, 153, 278
Ka'b ibn Mālik, 174, 195, 196
Al-Kalbī, 278
Khālid ibn al-Walīd, 194, 195
Khaybar, 138, 149, 322
Khaythamah, 200
Khazraj tribe, 5, 6, 146, 163, 164, 322, 349
Kinānah tribe, 278
Khuzā'ah, 278
Kufr, 22

L
Lakhm, 278
Lot, 232

M
Ma'bad ibn Abī Ma'bad al-Khuzā'ī, 197, 198
Al-Madā'in, 272
Madinah, 2, 3, 5, 6, 7, 8, 9, 11, 20, 21, 22, 23, 49, 64, 137, 145, 146, 147, 149, 152, 153, 156, 163, 164, 165, 167, 174, 179, 192, 193, 195, 197, 198, 200, 202, 204, 206, 233, 244, 245, 255, 258, 263, 265, 266, 272, 291, 293, 322, 323, 331, 333, 337, 349
Makkah, 2, 6, 21, 49, 64, 117, 151, 153, 168, 194, 195, 196, 197, 198, 200, 206, 278, 322, 346, 349

Mary, 25, 67, 68, 69, 73, 74, 75, 76, 77, 78, 79, 80, 82, 83, 84, 85, 88, 89, 90, 94, 98, 128, 172
Mercury, 278
Monophysites, 26
Moses, 28, 77, 89, 91, 109, 134, 146, 158, 159
Mubashshir ibn 'Abd al-Mundhir, 200
Muhājirūn, 6
Muhalhil, 279
Muhammad (peace be upon him), 5, 6, 7, 8, 13, 20, 21, 22, 23, 28, 30, 34, 35, 40, 46, 47, 49, 53, 54, 55, 65, 66, 68, 73, 75, 83, 84, 99, 100, 101, 103, 105, 114, 115, 117, 120, 121, 122, 123, 134, 138, 148, 149, 151, 152, 153, 157, 158, 159, 164, 172, 173, 174, 187, 192, 193, 194, 195, 196, 197, 198, 199, 200, 201, 202, 204, 209, 211, 212, 213, 217, 218, 220, 228, 231, 233, 234, 235, 236, 242, 245, 249, 250, 252, 253, 257, 262, 263, 264, 265, 267, 268, 269, 270, 271, 272, 273, 274, 275, 277, 280, 284, 288, 291, 292, 294, 295, 296, 297, 299, 301, 307, 310, 311, 314, 315, 322, 325, 327, 328, 333, 334, 349; Companions, 100, 149, 158, 193, 196, 197, 199, 202, 204, 222, 233, 234, 235, 236, 251, 264, 266, 277, 291, 297, 309, 314; message, 24, 28, 35, 54, 55, 66, 135, 148, 169, 325, 333; mosque, 138
Muhammad ibn Ishāq, 115, 164, 297
Muhammad ibn Ka'b al-Qurazī, 349
Muhammad 'Izzat Darwāzah, 21
Al-Mundhir ibn 'Amr, 194
Mus'ab ibn 'Umayr, 194
Muslim, Imām, 138, 151, 172, 204, 228, 271

Printed in Spain

Liberduplex Artes Gráficas

Tel.: 00 34 609 54 07 01
Fax: 00 34 937 53 09 87